Provided to

CmC Timberline

by

Regis University Libraries

in support of

Extended Campus Programs

DATE DUE

12-6-03			

D1164561

Demco, Inc. 38-293

A New Outline of

Social
Psychology

A New Outline of
Social
Psychology

Martin Gold
With Elizabeth Douvan

AMERICAN PSYCHOLOGICAL ASSOCIATION

WASHINGTON, DC

Published by
American Psychological Association
750 First Street, NE
Washington, DC 20002

Copies may be ordered from
APA Order Department
P.O. Box 92984
Washington, DC 20090-2984

In the UK and Europe, copies may be ordered from
American Psychological Association
3 Henrietta Street
Covent Garden, London
WC2E 8LU England

Typeset in Century by EPS Group Inc., Easton, MD

Cover designer: Minker Design, Bethesda, MD
Printer: Edward Brothers, Inc., Ann Arbor, MI
Technical/production editor: Ida Audeh

Library of Congress Cataloging-in-Publication Data
Gold, Martin, 1931–
   A new outline of social psychology / by Martin Gold with Elizabeth Douvan.
      p.   cm.
   Includes bibliographical references and index.
   ISBN 1-55798-408-5 (alk. paper)
   1. Social psychology.   I. Douvan, Elizabeth Ann Malcolm, 1926–   .
   II. Title.
HM251.G6655   1997
302—dc21   96-54814
                                                                      CIP

British Library Cataloguing-in-Publication Data
A CIP record is available from the British Library

Printed in the United States of America
First edition

For Sheila

Contents

Preface

Social psychology is hardly recognizable as a discipline; it wants definition and integration, and its place among the sciences is not fixed clearly. These are not new problems; they go back decades.

Practicing social psychologists must find this confusion in our field disturbing. I certainly do; it hinders my research and my teaching. Going to the social psychological literature for theoretical and empirical bases for research means rummaging through a disordered clutter: Not only are none of the boxes where they should be, there is no telling where they should be. And when I am called on to introduce undergraduates to social psychology or to explain it to graduate students who aspire to join our ranks, I am hard put to give them something definitive to read. Our texts are in some ways the same and in many ways quite different, and there is no discernible rationale for the similarities or differences.

Nevertheless, my reading of the literature in social science convinces me that there is something that can be called a social psychological analysis of a phenomenon, distinct from other kinds of psychological analyses and from other ways of doing social science. It simply has not been identified clearly. So I have felt impelled to define and order the discipline somehow and have struggled with this for several years. I like to think that I have made some progress, enough indeed to share my thinking with a wider audience than my immediate colleagues and students, some of whom have encouraged me to do so.

Of course, this is neither the final word about social psychology, nor even my final word. Nevertheless, what I present here has proved helpful enough to me and to colleagues and students that I hope it will be helpful to others as well.

I imagine myself working on a large mosaic. The organization that I have imposed on social psychology incorporates pieces of psychology, interpersonal relations, group dynamics, communications, sociology, and anthropology. I have selected the pieces with the intention of including the full range of what I call "the person and the social environment." I have tried to place these domains in relation to one another, particularly as they bear on the psychology of the person. I have tried to construct a pattern recognizable as "social psychology" and to place it among the sciences.

I refer to the pattern as a *model*. This is meant to connote both an image and a plan, a structure and a way of doing social psychology. Its primary use is to organize one's social psychological thinking. I have found the model helpful for structuring courses in social psychology so that they seem to have a beginning and an end, one topic following reasonably after another, theories more clearly juxtaposed, and seemingly disparate studies related. For example, working through the model has led me to a more heuristic conception of the field of group dynamics that might revitalize this almost abandoned line of research (see chapter 10). The model has also pointed out how such disparate approaches as psychoanalysis, social learning, and cognitive psychology are each useful in their own way to social psychology. It has helped me to understand better what the late "crisis" in social psychology was all about and what we can learn from it (see chapter 1). Some of my graduate students have found this framework useful for organizing their reviews of literature and their doctoral theses.

I have also found the model helpful as a guide for my research. It has broadened my view of the determinants of the phenomena I study and has helped me to understand better their relationships to one another. It sharpens my focus on the social psychological aspects of research problems; provides a checklist of variables that I must include; and tells me what literature—psychological, sociological, and so on—I should consult for theory, measures, and interpretations of findings.

This is the organization of the presentation: It begins with my own sense of the disciplinary problems of social psychology—framing them in terms of the field's defining mission to explain the reciprocal influence of the person and his or her social environment. Then I survey the literature of proposed conceptual strategies for relating the social and the psychological, anticipating my own resolution in the ways I discuss other strategies. The emphasis at that point in the argument is not on the substantive details of the various strategies but rather on the different strategic choices that thoughtful scholars have made. Having thus summoned the giants on whose shoulders I teeter, I then presume to offer my own integrative conceptual model. Here I risk alienating all other social psychologists by offering my own explicit definition of *social psychology*, which I discuss in some detail.

That takes us to the organization—the model—of social psychology. I present it from the inside out. That is, I first discuss the "person" from a social psychological perspective, in effect staking out where social psychology fits in the spectrum of the social sciences. Here, I lay out a sparse set of psychological concepts by which the person is characterized. Then I conduct a guided tour of the peculiarly *social* regions of the individual's environment, first proceeding level by level through the *structure* of the model, then describing the *dynamics* of the processes of social influence that flow between the person and the levels of the social environment. At each level, I pause to sample the range of influences impinging on the person there, and, to a lesser extent, to consider how the person may alter that terrain. I also dwell briefly on the relationships among the various levels of the social environment irrespective of the person's psychology, but only briefly because that takes us beyond the purview of social psychology proper.

The next chapters are intended to show how the social psychological model organizes and illuminates three specific substantive domains within the discipline: group dynamics, gender roles and identity, and Milgram's (1974) experiments on obedience.

Finally, I return to the problems of social psychology with which this treatise began, to determine whether they have been rendered more manageable.

In the course of all this, readers are warned, some familiar social psychological words are used in unfamiliar ways. Sometimes words are restored to old and (I believe) more precise meanings. At other times, one usage is drawn from a confused host of meanings and the term is stuck with it. Readers will please bear with me and lay aside for the moment all the other meanings that they have grown used to. For example, the term *interpersonal relations*, which has become a synonym for social relations generally, has been given a much more limited meaning here, for want of a better term for the kind of social relation I want to delineate. I try to alert readers to these uncommon usages wherever it seems necessary.

If the thinking of any of the social science giants has influenced this work more than the others, it is Kurt Lewin's. I never knew Lewin personally; he died suddenly at an age younger than my own at this writing. I studied and worked with many of Lewin's students, and in that sense, I feel that I am an heir to his prodigious conceptual treasure. Readers familiar with the Lewinian approach—and I fear that there are too few of them nowadays—will no doubt recognize Lewin's influence in the strategies I choose and the assumptions that I make. From time to time, I climb particularly on Lewin's shoulders when I specifically invoke a field theoretical analysis to clarify a point. Those familiar with Lewin's work also will find here a reflection of his eagerness to create a socially useful social psychology.

Acknowledgments

I am particularly indebted to certain scholars for their critical but always supportive comments on drafts of this book. First among these, and really deserving more of the share of the authorship than she is willing to claim, is Elizabeth M. Douvan. I also want to thank Sheila Feld, James S. House, Joseph E. McGrath, Sidney Perloe, François Rochat, Carol Slater, Arnold S. Tannenbaum, Harry C. Triandis, and Joseph Veroff. I am mindful too of all those colleagues, including several cohorts of graduate students in seminars with Professor Douvan and myself, whose intellectual stimulation contributed to this work in ways I appreciate but cannot specify.

The support staff at the Institute for Social Research—and especially Mary Cullen, Nancy Milner Exelby, Leslie Kucinskas, and Laura Reynolds—eased the production of the manuscript enormously. Todd K. Schackelford, an outstanding graduate student in psychology and an indefatigable bibliographer, organized the references. I also am grateful to the people at APA Books—Ida Audeh, Joy Chau, Andrea Phillippi, Peggy Schlegel, Mary Lynn Skutley, and Gary VandenBos—for their enthusiasm for this book and the help they gave me in getting it published.

Part I

Problems and Solutions

Introduction

The first two chapters explain why I have written this book (the problems that it addresses) and the kind of book it is (the nature of the solutions to the problems).

In the first chapter, I join those social psychologists who have worried about our field for about half a century. Generations of social psychologists have recognized our several critical disciplinary problems. For one, social psychology lacks useful definition, the kind of definition from which one can begin to draw theory and hypotheses, delimit the scope of journals and textbooks, organize curricula, and train professionals—in short, practice a mature discipline. The problem is obviously not that social psychology lacks theories, hypotheses, journals, textbooks, or so on, but that it is not clear in what sense they are distinctively social psychological. Implied here is the question, Why build a discipline of social psychology? Second and related to the first is the problem of the lack of integration of what is called *social psychology*, the problem of how its parts fit together. Third is the status of social psychology as science and its relationship to other sciences and disciplines. Fourth is the relationship of social psychology to the society and culture from which it draws intellectual and material support.

The first chapter ends with a proposal to solve these problems in the form of a model of social psychology. The model is an outline of a distinctive discipline that occupies a niche among the social sciences that no other discipline fills, a discipline for which "social psychology" is an appropriate name. The second chapter recalls the efforts of others to accomplish the same aim and indicates how the present proposal has built on them. It explains why I have made certain choices of definitions and strategies in building the model. The model serves as a map to the rest of this book.

1

Whatever Happened to Social Psychology?

It would be best to begin at the beginning. That, however, is precisely the problem this book addresses: how to identify a beginning in social psychology—and a middle, and an end. My aim in this book is to order the materials of social psychology so that beginning at one point rather than another makes some sense.

It is useful to distinguish among the many social psychologies and to relate them to one another. To pursue each of them effectively requires that they have well-defined concepts, theories, and methods. One kind of social psychology is exclusively psychological, or more precisely, exclusively concerned with cognitive processes. Still another social psychology is exclusively social, having to do mostly with the dynamics of small groups. A third type of social psychology (one that this book places at the core of the discipline) deals with the interaction of the social and the psychological. All of these social psychologies merit scholarly attention, and they have much to teach one another; unfortunately, they do not speak clearly to one another.

Contemporary Condition of Social Psychology

Integration

Contemporary social psychology appears to be a domain about which there are scattered isolated nodes of interests, large and small: interests in attitude formation and change, attribution of causes of behavior, self-concept, the relationship between social structure and personality development, the behavior of groups, cross-cultural variations in child-rearing practices, and so on. It is a vast domain, reaching from somewhere in psychology out into sociology and beyond. Many languages are spoken there. Indeed, there is so little overlap in the concepts used to express its interests, the methods used to pursue them, and the styles of thinking that shape them that the concepts seem hardly to belong to the same discipline. About all the social psychologies seem to have in common is that self-proclaimed social psychologists are studying them. Harold Kelley (1983) has observed:

> The topics in social psychology read more like a Sears Roebuck cata-
> logue than like a novel. They provide a listing of items of possible in-

terest to the reader rather than a story with a plot, development of characters, and so on. Our work is like that of mining engineers, who find a vein of valuable material and dig it out, and not like the work of geologists, who identify various features of the earth, describe their interrelationships, and explain their origins. (p. 8)

This condition is not new, and it has not changed. More than 30 years ago, Kenneth Ring (1967) wrote: "Social psychology today, it seems to me, is in a state of profound intellectual disarray. There is little sense of progress; instead, one has the impression of a sprawling, disjointed realm of activity where the movement is primarily outward, not upward" (p. 119). Vallacher and Nowak (1994) decried the lack of integration of social psychology; they observed that the field "suffers from an embarrassment of riches in that it is difficult to establish conceptual coherence with respect to such a diverse set of topics, findings, and ideas" (p. 290).

The research, teaching, and application of social psychology suffer from its disjointedness. Although no one can or should impose an orthodoxy on the discipline, an overall integration of the materials of social psychology would be extremely useful. In this book, I propose such an integration.

The integration focuses primarily on the interaction of the social and the psychological. It has to do with persons and their social environments. This kind of social psychology is vital to the social sciences because the nature of both individuals and the social environment depend heavily on their encounter. Although both the psychological and the social encounter environments other than each other, like the geophysical environment that affects them both, the social and the psychological have the most profound effects on one another. The defining mission of the social psychology presented here is to explain these effects. This is the niche that social psychology fills among the sciences.

Scientific Status

The belief that social psychology is a "science" has been challenged, and the challenge invoked what Elms (1975) called "a crisis of confidence" in social psychology.

> Social psychologists once knew who they were and where they were going. The field's major scientific problems were obvious, and the means to solve them were readily available. . . . During the past decade . . . many social psychologists appear to have lost not only their enthusiasm but also their sense of direction and their faith in their discipline's future . . . most seem agreed that a crisis is at a hand. (p. 967)

This crisis continues. Indeed, its scope has widened to include all of social science, if not science generally. Some discussion of it is necessary here in order to explain why social psychology is presented here as a science and just what kind of science I claim it to be.

The crisis was touched off by Kenneth Gergen's 1973 article, "Social Psychology as History," in which he asserted that social psychology cannot discover universal principles that govern individuals' relationships to their social environments. (Schlenker, 1976, and others have pointed out that Gergen is not the first to make this assertion.) The issues raised initially by Gergen were mostly methodological, and others have addressed them well (Baumgardner, 1976; Elms, 1975; Godow, 1976; Gottleib, 1977; Greenwald, 1976; Harris, 1976; Manis, 1975, 1976; Schlenker, 1974, 1976; Secord, 1976; Smith, 1976; Thorngate, 1975, 1976a; Wolff, 1977), so their arguments are not repeated here.

However, two arguments against a social psychological science have been made so persistently and forcefully that they have gained the status of a philosophical position, *social constructivism* (e.g., K. J. Gergen, 1989; K. J. Gergen & Davis, 1985; M. Gergen, 1989). They are addressed here only insofar as they make clear, by contrast, the position that I take, and I probably oversimplify them in what follows.

The fundamental assertion of social constructivism is methodological: Social psychologists cannot gain empirical knowledge of the real world because their observations are necessarily interpreted in the languages they use, and their languages inescapably distort the reality through interpretation. Because social psychological theories follow more or less on what social psychologists observe and must themselves be couched in the customary language, social psychological theories are inescapably culture bound. Indeed, theory is so culture bound, K. J. Gergen (1989) asserted, that it is in no way constrained by reality. It follows that social psychological theory cannot make any claims to expressing universal laws. Insofar as the discovery of universal laws is the goal of a science, then a scientific social psychology is inconceivable.

The other argument is a moral one, and it welcomes the status of social psychology as a conversation about people and their social environments. Social constructivism holds that our beliefs about the nature of reality—our cultures—strongly shape how we think and act, individually and collectively. That is, social psychological and other theories perform critical functions in our lives. Because our theories are unconstrained by reality, we are free to construct theories—to believe what we will—in ways that advance our welfare. Thus, social constructivism liberates us from the domination of prevailing paradigms, which constrain our imaginations and serve to sustain prevailing social hierarchies.

The model I propose for social psychology is rooted in the positive-empiricism rejected by social constructivism. This presentation assumes that it is possible to posit a theory that asserts universal laws and can be tested empirically. Whereas I acknowledge that imbeddedness in our cultures may distort our observations and limit our theoretical imaginations, it also is clear that these obstacles to accurate observation and innovative theory can be overcome. These same impediments burden the physical and natural sciences, and there is ample evidence that they have discovered laws that work—laws that, when applied appropriately, enable control over events and accurate predictions.

Four correctives enable scientists to peer above their cultures to get a better view of reality. Two of them are built into the scientific method: the intersubjective standard of objectivity requiring that more than one competent observer agree on what has been observed; and adherence to the rules of logic in stating relationships among observations. The other two correctives are social: competition among scientists for reputation and the cultural diversity of scientists' backgrounds. Taken together, these correctives have proved powerful by the pragmatic standards of control and prediction.

One might reasonably argue that, whereas the physical and natural sciences have something to show for positive-empiricism, the social sciences do not. Accurate observations of social phenomena might be beyond reach, despite the four correctives, because social phenomena are more ambiguous and more powerfully arouse distorting motivations. Hard put though one may be to point confidently to universal laws in the social sciences that have worked well enough, one should not yet jettison positive-empiricism. Indeed, one of my reasons for proposing a model of social psychology is to provide a theoretical base on which the social sciences can work with positive-empiricist methods. Social constructivists, eager to promote explorations of reality from any standpoint, may welcome this continuing effort as well (as long as it does not dominate the field).

I must at this point state an important agreement I have with social constructivists about social psychology: Like them, I do not believe that social psychology can discover universal laws. In this respect, social psychology is different from much of the rest of the social sciences, some of which can assert universals. My reasons for coming to this conclusion are not those of social constructivism; they are rooted in the conception of social psychology proposed here.

It is significant that, as far as I know, nowhere in more than 20 years of exchanges about the "crisis" in social psychology is there an explicit statement of what social psychology is. Indeed, it is clear that some of the disputants had social psychology in mind, some psychology, and still others, social science. The various authors have assumed a common image of social psychology—or something—among them, based largely, I suppose, on the literature with which each is most familiar. However, a survey of the discipline's texts and of the discussion of the crisis in social psychology indicates that the discussants undoubtedly did not share a common conception of the discipline. Consequently, they mostly argued past one another. For whether social psychology is a science, or history, or whatever —and if it is a science, as I believe it is, what kind of science it is and what its focus is—depends obviously on a definition of the discipline in terms of its central purpose, its strategies, and its substantive domain. For this reason, I should indicate what I mean by *social psychology* and assess its status as a science.

The philosophy of science is the appropriate venue for the debate about whether social psychology is a science. As I understand it, the philosophy of science aims to identify the various goals and means that define this particular epistemology and to determine the relationships among them. My view is that *science* can be taken as a relative term: To what degree a certain way of coming to know a particular reality is a science depends on where it stands on the defining dimensions of "ideal" or "pure" science. Certain disciplines may be equally "scientific" while at the same time be different *kinds* of science because of where they sit on the various dimensions. So if precision of measurement is one dimension defining science, then physics is more scientific than biology; and if another dimension is the determination of causal relations by controlled experimentation, then social psychology is more scientific than astronomy. If its potential for discovering universal laws of causality in a particular domain is another dimension of science, then social psychology is not as scientific as, say, psychology, sociology, or anthropology.

Social psychology cannot aspire to discover universal laws because of the kind of science it is. As it is defined here, *social psychology* is the study of the reciprocal influence of persons and their social environments. The kind of science that social psychology is can be clarified by comparing the present definition to other common ones in use. There is, of course, Gordon Allport's (1954) classic definition of social psychology as "an attempt to understand how the thought, feeling, and behavior of individuals are influenced by the actual, imagined, or implied presence of other human beings" (p. 5). *Social psychology* is also frequently defined as the study of social behavior. The definition of social psychology in terms of "reciprocal influence" cuts the disciplinary pie differently from the other two, being more inclusive than both. Both of the other definitions focus more narrowly on the person, whereas the first, in its incorporation of reciprocity, dwells equally on the person and the social environment. It is this inclusiveness that prevents social psychology, so defined, from asserting universal laws.

G. W. Allport's definition of the discipline excludes the study of the effect of the individual on the social environment. Surely these effects merit scientific investigation, because people do affect their environments in varying degrees, some profoundly. The kinds of questions to be asked here are, what are the characteristics of persons that account for their differential effects on the environment, what characteristics of environments make them differentially vulnerable to the effects of persons, and, perhaps most fertile, what characteristics of people make them differentially influential over environments with certain characteristics? No other scientific discipline addresses these important questions. It is social psychology's niche.

The idea of social behavior is also too limited. Presumably, it connotes behavior in the "actual, imagined, or implied presence of other human beings." This leaves a great deal of behavior to be explained, with no scientific discipline adequate to explain it. For example, consider a solitary individual raising generations of fruit flies; ordinarily his would not be thought of as "social behavior." Still, one ought to be able to explain why he was devoting himself to raising fruit flies, how he was enabled to do so, what effect his actions had on others, and why that effect waited for generations of people. Answers to these questions that do not take into account Mendel's peculiarly social environment are undoubtedly incomplete. Social psychology, as it is construed here, is uniquely fit for taking the social environment into account to explain behavior that is not obviously "social."

Because social psychology has a dual focus (i.e., on the person and on the social environment), it cannot assert universal laws. Its defining mission, to explain the reciprocal influence of psychological and social sets of realities, puts universal laws beyond its reach. Like disciplines such as political geography, neurochemistry, and sensory psychology, social psychology may be called a "boundary science," a discipline that spans two or more independent realities. Two examples clarify why such boundary sciences cannot yield universal laws.

One example is from the discussion of the "crisis" in social psychology. Schlenker (1974) took exception to K. J. Gergen's (1973) declaration that social psychology is descriptive history rather than law-seeking science:

> Gergen's reactions to the probability that some contemporary theories are transcultural and transhistorical are puzzling. For example, he dismisses such a claim for [Festinger's] theory of social comparison processes. . . . The theory hypothesizes that people have a need to evaluate beliefs and themselves accurately and that they use others for comparison purposes when nonsocial criteria are unavailable. It could be possible to further explain these particular hypotheses concerning effectance motivations present in men and lower animals . . . since to maintain effective social commerce one must accurately assess the world and one's self . . . in order to enter into social transactions. . . . However, Gergen concludes that "There is scant reason to suspect that such dispositions are genetically determined, and we can easily imagine persons, and indeed societies, for which these assumptions would not hold." . . . "Imagining" a society which does not employ social comparison processes brings back images of Anselm's ontological argument for the existence of a supreme and perfect being—if we can imagine it, it exists. I have great difficulty imagining a person (much less a whole society) who does not use other people to aid him in evaluating his beliefs and abilities when direct nonsocial evidence is unavailable. The self-concept presumably develops through such social comparison and reflected appraisals. (p. 5)

The specific argument ends in a standoff between two imaginations. Where Gergen found no encouragement in the data to presume a universal propensity for social comparison, Schlenker was persuaded that human nature makes social comparison processes universal. He was impressed by the scant repertoire of human instincts for survival. Schlenker implied that universal human reliance on learning survival behavior and human dependence for survival on other humans require social comparison "to maintain effective social commerce."

Empirical research would seem up to settling the issue: Let Gergen or someone else state the sociocultural conditions under which humans would not develop the propensity for social comparison and perform the studies of social comparison processes under these conditions, created or found. If such conditions cannot be established or if social comparisons are evident under them, then the universality of the propensity is more plausible.

However, it still would not be certain, and herein lies the problem of social psychology as a boundary science. It concerns the philosophical basis for claims of universality. The universality of scientific principles is fundamentally not amenable to empirical settlement. Universality lies only in theory. Kant made this point over two centuries ago in *Critique of Pure Reason* (1781/1965): It is inherently impossible to establish a universal principle empirically because the next observation may falsify it. Even if no research has yet identified the social and psychological conditions under which social comparison processes do not occur, some unsuspected conditions may yet occur somewhere, sometime.

Claims made for universality lie solely in theory of a particular kind, a closed theory, one that is built on primitive definitions and axioms. The universal truth of a proposition is simply asserted. That is why "two plus two *always* equals four," in theory.

The closed theories to which social psychology must attend purport to refer to real people and to real social environments. So their primitive definitions and axioms are modeled as closely as imagination and empirical evidence permit after the nature of the relevant realities. Every test of the propositions derived from these theories also tests how well their definitions and axioms model the real world. If a proposition of a closed theory is disconfirmed by data, one searches back through the derivations, to find perhaps that a premise is not realistic.

To continue with the example of social comparison processes: A reading of its original statement (Festinger, 1954) shows that the phenomenon was not derived from a set of more primitive definitions or axioms. It is itself a primitive from which propositions have been derived; no conditions are set for its presence except for the humanity of the actor. The probability of its universality is established to the degree that hypotheses derived from its assumption are confirmed under varying conditions. However, its universality remains only probable, even if more probable, by repeated inability to falsify. Absolute universality continues to reside only in the closed nature of the theory.

Putting this point generally: If social psychology is to lay claim to the universality of its principles, it must construct closed theory. This it cannot do. It shares this limitation with all of those sciences that are concerned with the boundaries between what are believed to be independent realities. The defining mission of boundary sciences is to describe the conditions under which what exists in one realm of discourse enters another realm of discourse, and in what form. Maintaining their separate realities, the distinctive mission of social psychology focuses on the multifaceted boundary between the psychological and the social and aims to understand causality at that divide.

The phenomena of the social and psychological are not defined in terms of one another to create closed theory; these separate realities are rather translated one into the other in order to explain their reciprocal effects. By *translated*, I allude to matching a word from one language with a word or phrase from another, and the implication to be drawn is that the translation is never perfect. A word in one language has a sound, appearance, root, associations, and so on that are never exactly matched by its counterpart in another language. Analogously, the conditions in one set of realities seldom replicate exactly the conditions in another.

The second example of the limits of a boundary science is prompted by a comment by social psychologist Harry Triandis (personal communication, June 24, 1996). Triandis observed that "all societies have structure, and one aspect of structure is that there are in groups and out groups." Furthermore, "It is . . . universal that people exchange more supportive, intimate behaviors with ingroup members than with outgroup members." Implicit here are assertions at single levels of analysis, which may indeed be universal, and one across a boundary that surely is not. That all societies have structure may be taken as definitional within a societal level of analysis, because it is difficult to conceive of the usefulness of the concept of *society* that has no structure. The assertion that every societal structure includes in-groups and out-groups is at that same level of analysis, where it may be axiomatic—that is, it may be a useful assumption of a relationship within societal structure from which hypotheses may be drawn—or it may be itself a hypothesis to be tested. In either case, the assertion is potentially universal because it rests within a single level of analysis. However, the assertion that people behave in different ways toward in-group and out-group members implicates two levels of analysis, and therefore its universality is questionable.

Were the assertion about people's behaviors couched in terms of how people are normatively expected to behave, it could conceivably be derived solely at the societal level of analysis, from the nature and function of ingroup/out-group differentiation. Concomitantly, were the assertion that all people tend to favor members of in-groups over members of out-groups, then this assertion could claim universality at a psychological level of analysis: if, for instance, it were rooted in a definition of *person* as someone at least minimally well socialized, and if it were then derived as a particular case of the more general that socialized people tend to act as they are supposed to. If, on the other hand, the assertion refers to individuals' behavior rather than to societal norms or psychological tendencies, then some translation is necessary and the claim to universality essentially is undermined.

People vary in their behavior toward members of socially identified in-groups and out-groups, for at least two reasons. First, individuals may not recognize the same in-group/out-group distinctions common in their society; they would behave properly if they did, but they do not. Second, they may very well recognize the prevailing distinctions, but they have reasons to ignore or defy them. Thus, Shakespeare gives us Romeo and Juliet, who are well aware of in-groups and out-groups but nevertheless exchange supportive and intimate behaviors. The social psychology of their passion requires that we translate their social environment into their psychological states and place the resultant tendencies in the gestalt of the other psychological forces acting on them at the time.

The implications of making such translations for the nature of a boundary science are raised by Miriam Lewin's contribution to the discussion of "social psychology as history." M. A. Lewin (1977) asserted that if laws are stated in conditional and genotypic terms (as her father, Kurt Lewin, said they should be), then they would not be subject to historical conditions. To be included in a complete accounting of the causal conditions of a person's thoughts, feelings, and behavior, historical conditions must be translated into psychological terms. That is, one must engage in a theoretical strategy that is quasi reductionist. Thus, aspiring to create a coherent social psychology requires making choices of theoretical strategies. Among these choices is the critical one of whether to aim for universal laws, that is, to build closed theory, or whether to eschew universality on the assumption that the psychological and the social are actually independent realities. There is considerable heuristic advantage to making the latter choice. There follows upon this choice the selection of other theoretical tools that enable the integration of the psychological and social. Succeeding chapters explore several integrative strategies and marshall their strengths for the social psychological mission.

My goal in this book is to advance the mission of social psychology not so much by presenting new theory and findings as by integrating what is already available. It ranges over that vast domain of social psychology and rearranges what is found there into a model of a community of interests. What are actually essential similarities bearing different names are brought together under common names. Important dissimilarities bearing common names are distinguished with different names. Social psychology takes some shape. What follows is a descriptive catalogue of the parts of the model.

A Model for Social Psychology

To accomplish an integration of the social and psychological, it is necessary to adopt a set of basic concepts to serve as theoretical building blocks. The field is rich with concepts from which to choose.

A useful guideline for selecting those to place at the core of social psychology is that the concepts advance integration by having their counterparts in both the psychological and social domains. In Talcott Parsons's term (1951), these concepts will be "interpenetrating." (Later, I describe them as "prismatic.") Fiske (1992) also has found the idea of interpenetration useful in constructing a "framework for a unified theory of social relations." He offered, for example, that when a form of social organization is desired by an individual, it is a *motive*; when the form is desired by more than one person, it is a *value*; when individuals are obliged to desire the form, it is a *moral standard*; when the form has a function for a collectivity, it is a *norm*; and when the value of the form is used to justify a social system, it is an *ideology*.

Parsimony is another useful guideline. The basic vocabulary of an integrative social psychology need not include many of the concepts of its constituent sciences. It is not the mission of the social psychological model that I present here to explain all psychological and all social phenomena. Its more limited aim is to describe and explain the reciprocal influence of the social and psychological, an ambitious enough mission. Too large a vocabulary can defeat the task of integration by permitting commonalities and connections to be neglected. A spare vocabulary of interpenetrating terms promotes greater coherence. It is unnecessary to make up new concepts.

A Social Psychological Vocabulary

Psychological terms. At the psychological level of analysis, the model uses only two terms to represent the person: *motive* and *resource*. These two are obviously a scant selection from the enormous vocabulary of psychology. They do, however, capture the psychological interface with the social environment. The general proposition is that the person and the social environment influence one another only insofar as the person's motives and resources are involved.

What then of those other psychological terms prominent in contemporary social psychological literature? For example, what of *attitude* and *self* and *personality*, certainly useful psychological concepts? I do not find them so useful for integrating the social and the psychological. Their usefulness is to express the purely psychological processes that are affected distally when social factors influence the person, and to express the psychological conditions that endow a person with the motives and resources with which to influence the social.

The study of attitudes remains as it has historically been, the most constant topic of social psychology. It appears most often in its literature, with whole chapters or large sections of chapters in introductory textbooks, handbooks, and annual reviews regularly and frequently devoted to it. Crano (1989) has written that "If the definitional criterion for situating a topic within the realm of social psychology does not admit studies of attitude and attitude change, then it seems apparent that it is the criterion that should be reexamined, not the place of attitude research" (p. 387). Social psychologist Dorwin Cartwright (personal communication, June 25, 1990) once told me that he tried to persuade a conference of social psychologists that "attitude" is not a useful social psychological concept, but to no avail. It is notable, however, that not all social psychology introductory textbooks, even those written from a psychological rather than a sociological perspective, include discussions of attitudes. Some textbook authors found that a presentation of social psychology could do without "attitudes." Whereas the concept of attitude may be useful for building psychological theory, I do not propose to include it among those concepts that are meant to capture the exchange at the boundary between the psychological and the social.

Discussions of *self* figure almost as frequently and as prominently as discussions of attitude in the texts of contemporary social psychology. The self is never precisely defined, but different aspects of it are taken up— the social construction of the "looking glass" self, self-justification, self-conception, and self-perception, to mention a few.

Other than attitudes and self, the concept that seems to appear most frequently is *personality*; and even then, most introductory texts do no more than mention it, without explicit definition or extended discussion. The ubiquitous concepts of attitudes, self, and personality can be derived from what I propose as more basic and integrative concepts in the social psychological model, motive and resource (see chapter 3). Thus, for the sake of parsimony, I do not include them as fundamental concepts in this model of social psychology.

The concept of *motive* occupies an important place in my own view of social psychology, but contemporary social psychology does not dwell much on motivation. Although this may be changing, the cognitive emphasis in contemporary social psychology has been on "cold" cognitions. How the social may affect the psychological by creating and altering motives has not received the attention it deserves. Largely neglected too is the general question of how motives prompt and enable individuals to influence their social environment. Nevertheless, the concept and theory of motivation is well-established within psychology. The model selects this concept from the psychological vocabulary to serve a central integrative function. How it is used to integrate the psychological person with the social is discussed in chapter 3.

The social psychological literature is also almost silent on the general subject of the resources with which individuals encounter their environment. One seldom comes across integrated discussions of the power or money individuals may command, the skills that they may possess, or the social relationships that they may call on to help them attain their goals. One finds only scattered attention to a few specific resources: leadership skills; intelligence and verbal skills; and social class, with its implications of resources.

Resources and differences among individuals' resourcefulness figure prominently in my construal of social psychology. The model incorporates the expectancy–value theory of action, which posits that any explanation of how people act must take into account both what they want to accomplish and what they have to accomplish it with. Individuals differ in crucial ways in this respect, largely because of the influence of their social environments. They encounter social forces with differential resourcefulness, and their effects on their social environment are partly a matter of their differential resourcefulness. Thus, the idea of resource gets close attention here, occupying a pivotal place at the interface of the psychological and the social.

Social terms. What are the social concepts that interpenetrate with motive and resource in a social psychological integration? Here, too, one may turn to the literature for a store of potentially useful terms but must not be seduced by the popularity of a concept.

The concept most frequently used in social psychology to refer to the social environment is *group*. Scholars who approach social psychology by way of psychology usually emphasize the influence of groups on individuals. They include in social psychology such topics as the study of conformity to group norms, personal satisfaction with groups, and the use of groups as frames of reference for assessing one's own condition.

Those who take a sociological approach to social psychology typically treat groups as entities. Taking the small group as its subject distinguishes sociological social psychology from the rest of sociology. It assumes that the small group functions differently from other, larger collectivities. I believe that sociological social psychologists arrive at this position because of the tendency in small groups toward the development of what in the proposed social psychological model is called *interpersonal relations*. These close relationships cannot be accommodated in sociological theories of social organization and demography and therefore set small groups apart.

Those who define social psychology as the study of social interaction are those most determined to carve out a separate niche for the discipline. For them, it belongs neither to psychology nor sociology but overlaps with both while possessing some features found in neither. They too tend to focus on the small group—in fact, on the dyad. This approach begins by stipulating characteristics of the interacting entities, characteristics that may be psychological, such as personality traits; or sociological, such as role requirements; or a combination of both. These characteristics are then assessed in terms peculiar to the study of interaction, such as their "balance" (Heider, 1958; Newcomb, 1961) or their joint determination of costs–benefits (Thibaut & Kelley, 1959). Consequent changes in the characteristics of the interacting entities can then be used as input to psychology (changes in the individual) or sociology (changes in the organization), but these are not the primary concern of the study of interaction. Its focus is on the social psychology of interaction itself as it strains toward balance or an optimal cost–benefit ratio. Thus, whereas the concept of *group* appears often in the social psychological literature, the gist of these discussions varies widely.

Whether and how one includes the study of groups in social psychology is a matter of some consequence. Not only are small groups influential forms of the collectivities composing the social environment, their conceptualization has implications for the treatment of the social environment generally. In the social psychological model presented here, the ubiquity and influence of the small group in the social environment is recognized, but the concept of *group* is not treated as a core concept in social psychology. Here the model departs sharply from the treatment accorded groups in contemporary social psychology, insofar as its literature concerns itself with collectivities at all. Instead, the model proposes that small groups consist of some combination of other basic social relationships;

thus, their effects and effects on them may most usefully be understood by analyses into and syntheses of these other social relationships.

For this reason, the small group occupies an important *methodological* place in social psychology. Because small groups may comprise any or all facets of the social environment, they may operationalize the social environment under close control. Thus, the small group affords social psychology the opportunity to pursue its mission of explaining the interaction of the psychological and the social with powerful experimental methods. (See chapter 10.)

The model's basic social concepts are found in theories about collectivities that may or may not be small groups. These concepts appear often in discussion of small groups because small groups may constitute one or a combination of these other collectivities. The sources for integrative terms describing the social environment are theories of social organization, culture, and interpersonal relations. This social vocabulary is spare but sufficient. The social organizational environment of individuals may be conceived as interpenetrating with psychological motives and resources by prescribing the motives and resources individuals should have in the social roles that they play. (See chapter 4.) Interpersonal relations are distinguished in the model from social organizational and other social collectivities; the term is not used here to refer to social relationships generally. In the model it is a relationship characterized by normlessness (but not anomie), affection, and trust. Mutually recognized identities are its units of analysis. Identities are conceived as a subset of individuals' motives and resources, thus linking the interpersonal social relationship with the psychology of the person. (See chapter 5.) Finally, a person's cultural environment is defined in terms of the beliefs shared by a collectivity, beliefs that are also represented at the psychological level of analysis by individuals' motives and resources. (See chapter 6.) Although these few terms constitute a seemingly limited vocabulary, they are rich in implication and provide structure for the model.

To summarize this introductory discussion so far: The defining mission of the discipline of social psychology, as taken here, is to describe and explain the interaction of the psychological and the social. A social psychology adequate to this mission must sharpen and limit its psychological vocabulary and at the same time broaden its perspective on the social environment. It should attend to a social environment that includes social organization, interpersonal relations, and culture. A lexicon that includes motives, resources, social organization and social roles, interpersonal relations and identities, and culture and beliefs is adequate to represent the structural components of an integrative social psychological model. These constitute the structure of a model of social psychology.

Process terms. By what process or processes does the social environment affect people's motives and the resources they may marshall to reach their goals? How may a person's motives and resources cause him or her markedly to affect his or her own and our social environment? Explanations of how the social and the psychological influence one another require

not only an account of the parts of each that interpenetrate the other—
structure—but also specification of the dynamic processes through which
change is effected.

Current theories, findings, and methods in social psychology already
provide a rich store of material with which to pursue answers to these
social psychological questions. Social learning theory, psychoanalytic theory, and cognitive theory each contributes distinctive insights to the model.
Each makes certain assumptions about the social relationships in which
social and psychological change occur. These assumptions are differentially represented in the model's specification of three kinds of social
relationships—social organizational, interpersonal, and cultural. Many of
the controversies about which theories are superior dissolve with the recognition that each provides valid accounts, but under different conditions.

The distinct characteristics of a social relationship permit certain influence processes to occur and disallow others. The proposed model of social psychology identifies three quite different social influence processes,
each operating between the person and one of the levels of analysis of the
person's social environment. These three processes are familiar to social
scientists. The conditions of a person's embeddedness in social organization determine that the social influence of the environment be exerted
through the process of socialization and that the person affect social organization by means of institutionalization. Interpersonal influence is exerted by mutual identification of the partners to the relationship. Culture
is transmitted to the person by persuasion, and people create culture by
invention.

The Uses of Social Psychological Theory

Neither the person nor the social environment is entirely a construction
of the other; both bring their own coherence to their encounter. Individuals
act only in the environment they know, but the environment they know is
not the only environment there is. If we as scientific observers know something independently about people's environment, we may understand better how it impresses itself on them. The better we understand this, the
greater the probability with which we can translate the social facts accurately into the psychological facts and vice versa. Then this more accurate
contemporary diagnosis of the psychological situation becomes the basis
on which closed, exclusively psychological theory explains thought, feeling,
and action. Moreover, if we compare our presumably precise understanding of the social environment with its appearance to the person, we can
make more fairly accurate probabilistic predictions about the effects of the
person's action on the social environment and its response to him or her.

The rewards of this kind of social psychologizing are both aesthetic
and practical. One can appreciate elegance in a theory, and some would
hold that a closed theory is inherently more elegant than an open one.
That is a matter of aesthetic taste. A great deal of satisfaction may be
found in a probabilistic solution to a theoretical problem, one in which the
hypothetical determinants of a phenomenon account for just about all the

variance that can be accounted for, even if the solution is not logically derived.

One can also find great satisfaction in a theory that has practical uses. Its position as a boundary science makes social psychology eminently practical. The boundaries between the psychological person and facets of the social environment are the points at which social psychology is properly focussed. Nevertheless, the social environment is treated theoretically in its own terms. This permits one to treat that social environment practically as well. Social practice occurs in the first instance in the environment, not in the mind. Social psychology ought to enable us to understand more than how individuals perceive their social environment and how they interact with their construal. It should also explain how the psyche changes because the social environment changes (and vice versa). Understanding the psychological effects of changes in the social environment is essential to a practical social psychology.

The aesthetic pleasures and practical usefulness of social psychology come from the fabric of reliable propositions we may weave about the encounters between psychological and social realities, even if those propositions are derived from strands found in separate, closed theories and are therefore probabilities. The "ifs" in the "if . . . then" propositions of this kind of social psychological theory are not assertions of truths-by-definition but rather conditional statements about the encounters between realities. This does not by any means disqualify social psychology as a science.

My strategy for defining the domain of social psychology, ordering the phenomena within it, and theorizing about their interactions is to define the psychological individual and three different facets of the social environment and to identify the processes of influence that constitute their interactions. The model conceives the psychological and the social—actually three kinds of social—as separate realities. It assumes that each of these realities can be described in terms of its own definitions and axioms. Hypothetical relationships between the psychological and the social are couched in probabilistic terms, as befits propositions relating separate realities.

I discuss strategies particularly designed to integrate the social and the psychological first because the choice of strategies already places fairly narrow limits on the concepts that are useful to a discipline and how they should be organized. For example, if one elects to use a reductionist approach to unifying a discipline, then one's central concepts are quite tightly allied and all are derived from a single discipline. If instead one turns to some sort of metalanguage like general systems theory to provide integration, then one's concepts are necessarily quite abstract and not identified with psychology, sociology, anthropology, or any other substantive discipline. Both of these strategies permit closed theories, and that in turn structures the kind of science that is practiced. After reviewing the strengths and weaknesses of these strategies, I turn to levels of analysis, which, with some elements of reductionism and metatheory, is the main integrative strategy that the model uses. This sets the stage for a more detailed outline of the structure and dynamics of social psychology.

2

Integrative Strategies

In this chapter I review three strategies that theorists have used to take psychological and social conditions jointly into account when explaining human behavior and experience. The strategies of reductionism and metalanguage are analyzed at some length here in order to bring out their strengths and weaknesses for building social psychological theory. The levels of analysis approach is discussed only briefly at this point because it is presented by using it primarily throughout the rest of this volume. Reductionism and metalanguage strategies have certain advantages that can be incorporated into a levels of analysis approach for integrating the social and the psychological. None of the three strategies alone is adequate for pursuing the mission of social psychology.

In one sense, the forthcoming discussion of integrative strategies is ancient history. It is not a report on a current, lively struggle for the soul of social psychology. Once vigorous, attempts to integrate the social and the psychological have been largely abandoned in the United States, although they still occupy some (mostly European) scholars (Himmelweit & Gaskell, 1990; Rijsman & Stroebe, 1989; Stephan, Stephan, & Pettigrew, 1991). Notwithstanding its neglect, integration remains important to contemporary social psychology. I do not expect to settle the matter here, but I hope to revive the effort.

Reductionism

Reductionism consists of explaining the events of interest to one discipline with the theoretical principles of another. Theoretical strategy sometimes works in the opposite direction: Principles concerning the larger entities cover events of the constituents (*theoretical expansionism*). For the purposes of this assessment of integrative strategies, reductionism and expansionism are equivalent. I focus on reductionism because it is used much more frequently in the domain of social psychology. Examples come easily to mind—explanations of psychological events by neurology (Hebb, 1949), of sociological events by psychology (Homans, 1961), of cultural events by psychology (Skinner, 1961). The integrative potential of reductionism is apparent. For social psychological purposes, all explanations of the nature and effects of the social environment are couched in psychological terms. The social environment is conceptualized in terms of the properties of the individuals who compose social collectivities such as groups, institutions, societies, and cultures. The principles that explain the emergence, form, and change in the collectivities—the theoretical propositions from which these are deduced—are psychological principles, so that ultimately the behavior of collectivities is explained by the same psychological laws that explain the behavior of their members.

Reductionist explanations of collective phenomena may be more complex than explanations of an individual's behavior. One has to take into account interdependence of members, differing perceptions, competing motives, and so on. Nevertheless, this complexity does not negate the reductionist position that explanations of all collective social phenomena can be constructed out of psychological theory. However many their permutations and however complicated the social interactions involved, psychological variables can (according to the reductionist view) fully account for such phenomena as group productivity: namely, the level of productivity is determined by the sum of the individual members' productivity, plus the individuals' ability and motivation to act toward one another in ways that enhance members' productivity. The level of group productivity can be determined once its members' skills and motives have been accurately assessed and accounted for.

In the reductionist view, treating collective concepts such as group structure or consensus as emergent rather than derivative does not explain anything better. The structure and processes of an organization are completely determined by psychological facts, specifically the state of mind of the individuals who compose the organization. Once we know how relevant individuals perceive the situation, what they can do, and what they want to do, we know all we need to know to predict the organizational phenomena. We need only insert the conditions of all the individuals' psyches in the psychological propositions that explain their behavior relevant to the organization; no other propositions are required.

The reductionist strategy is helpful to social psychology because it demands conceptual translation, "translation" in the sense described earlier. Reductionism emphasizes the need for some theoretical device by which psychological and social phenomena can be discussed in the same or at least commensurate terms. This strategy meets the need by reducing the social phenomena to psychological terms.

I have asserted that it is essential to theory building in social psychology that explanations of individuals' behavior and experience be stated in psychological terms, and I return to this point over and over again. At the same time, I take the position that it is necessary to explain social phenomena in social terms. Universal laws of groups, institutions, societies, and cultures cannot be derived from definitions of psychological constructs and the axioms that relate them. Any attempt to do so necessitates redefining the social fact somewhere in the process of deduction in such a way that it has no reality outside the minds of individuals. This ignores the evidence that collectivities persist with little or no change even while their members are replaced with others who are very different, and that collectivities change with no change in their individual constituents. If the mission of social psychology is to explain the reciprocal influence of individuals and their social environment, then the reality of both has to be preserved in its theory.

To clarify and substantiate my view of the limitations and usefulness of reductionism for social psychology, I discuss two quite different theoretical efforts. One is the debate over psychological reductionism between Peter Blau and George C. Homans; the other is Harold Kelley and John W. Thibaut's presentation of their theory of interpersonal relations. I discuss the former to clarify the difference between reduction and translation as a means for bridging the psychological and social levels of analysis; making a distinction between what is "given" or assumed to be a psychological constant and what is a psychological law is a key idea here. The latter discussion illustrates how identifying the social environment in an otherwise exclusively psychological theory makes the theory truly social psychological.

The Blau–Holmes Debate: Psychological Givens or Psychological Principles?

The exchange between George C. Homans (1970a, 1970b) and Peter Blau (1970) on the utility of psychological reductionism is an illuminating example of the reductionist approach in social psychology and the sociological objections to it.

Homans (1970a) began the dialogue:

> Again and again since the turn of the century scholars have been asserting that social phenomena can never be explained by the use of psychological propositions. The social whole, they say, is more than the sum of its parts; something new emerges over and above the behavior of individuals; when many individuals act, they may produce results unintended by any one of them. All the actual facts that "wholeness," "emergence," and "unintended consequences" are supposed to refer to are conceded in advance. The question is how these facts are to be explained. The usual examples of such phenomena are readily explainable by the use of psychological propositions. (p. 325)

The principles that Homans (1970a) invoked to explain these social phenomena are the law of effect and "the rationality proposition":

> Every man, in choosing between alternative actions, is likely to take that one for which, as perceived by him at the time, the value (v) of the result, multiplied by the probability (p) of getting the result, is the greater; and the larger the excess of $p \times v$ for the one action over the alternative, the more likely he is to take the former action. (p. 318)

Homans contended that only such psychological principles are ever required to explain collective phenomena and that sociological theories are needless digressions. He found sociological propositions of any validity mere restatements of psychological principles.

Peter Blau (1970) responded, "George Homans has thrown down a gauntlet that I as a sociologist feel obligated to take up" (p. 329). "The basic issue is whether it is possible to develop sociological explanations ... I shall attempt to meet Homans' challenge to illustrate that this is possible by suggesting two sociological propositions that explain some empirical relationships observed in formal organizations" (p. 332).

Drawing from his research in state employment security agencies, Blau (1970) offered these two "theoretical generalizations (premises)": (a) Increasing size of a formal organization gives rise to structural differentiation along various lines. (b) Structural differentiation in a formal organization increases the need for mechanisms of coordination (p. 333).

Blau conceded that his sociological generalizations rest on psychological assumptions. For mechanisms of coordination to be instituted, he admitted, it must be a given that the executives empowered to do so are motivated to make their organizations work and must have learned that mechanisms of coordination contribute to that end. Then it must follow that executives institute mechanisms of coordination. Blau observed that, "Here indeed we apparently have explained our sociological generalizations by one of Homans' psychological principles—the rationality principle" (p. 335).

Later in his defense against this apparent derivation of sociological propositions from psychological properties, Blau made the point about the status of psychological givens that is crucial to his argument.

> A basic assumption I make is that the behavior of organized aggregates follows its own principles, and the discovery of these explanatory principles does not require detailed knowledge of the principles that govern the behavior of sub-units. The latter principles may be taken as given in investigating the former; indeed they must be taken as given. (p. 338)

In thus characterizing the status of givens, Blau clarified one function that psychological principles play in sociological theory: They admit sociology to the empirical sciences.

Blau recognized that social organizational theory cannot be enlivened, cannot have any empirical counterpart, unless there are entities with capacities to enact social roles. Among the capacities consistent with Blau's conception of social organization are those invoked by Homans: responsiveness to rewards and punishments (obedience to the law of effect) and awareness of cause–effect relationships (rationality). (Quite different capacities of humans may be taken as givens and still be consistent with a social organizational theory, although that theory would probably be different from Blau's. A psychoanalytically based theory that takes as a given the capacity to identify with a leader comes to mind.) Reductionists like Homans claim to derive the propositions of another level from the givens at the level of reduction. Blau contended that, although an empirical sociology depends on some givens of psychology, its propositions are not derived from them.

Blau advanced his argument by invoking the danger of infinite regress. He introduced the relationship of psychology to physiology: "Whereas every single psychological proposition can ultimately be explained by the physiological processes underlying it, a theoretical system of psychological propositions cannot be built by proceeding in this fashion. Physiological processes must be taken as given in constructing a system of propositions that explain the organization of human behavior" (pp. 337–339). Homans (1970b) responded:

> I am sure Blau is wrong about one final matter. He says that "every single psychological proposition can ultimately be explained by the physiological processes underlying it" . . . The fact that human behavior would not occur without the physiological processes of the living human body does not mean that the propositions of behavioral psychology can be derived from, reduced to, the propositions of physiology. (p. 343)

Nevertheless, although he accepted the function that givens play in theorizing, Homans maintained his reductionist position. The givens, he asserted, have a dual function in the reductionist approach: They specify the linkage of the theory to the empirical world (in this case, specification of certain capable beings), and they are also the principles from which organizational principles are derived. Blau's strategy admits only of the former function of givens; the givens are not the source of derivations.

This then is one contribution of reductionism to the integration of the psychological and the social: It alerts theorists to the necessity of specifying what entities must be like at one level of analysis—what must be "given"—in order for the focal level of analysis to exist, to function in a real world. These givens are the universal structures and dynamics that are expressed by the laws of that level. Only entities endowed with certain structures that function according to certain principles can engage in social organization, culture, and interpersonal relations; conversely, only environments with certain social structures that follow certain dynamic principles allow humanity.

A distinction, not so clearly drawn by Homans and Blau, must be made to clarify a correlative strength of the reductionist strategy. Homans and Blau both invoked general propositions as grounds for their explanations. However, their "general propositions" actually include two kinds of statements. One kind of general proposition consists of an axiomatic statement of a relationship between two or more defined elements. It is the kind of general or basic proposition one finds in mathematics and which is approximated most closely in empirical sciences by contemporary physical theory. Higher level propositions of the theory are all deduced logically from this basic set of definitions and axioms. The basic propositions are not in themselves deducible from anything else because their constituents are primitives that are arbitrarily assigned properties by definition and are related by the basic propositions, called *axioms*. These basic propositions are not made up of the givens from another realm of discourse. Their components are entities at the same level of analysis as the phenomena to be explained—individuals' psychological characteristics in psychological theory, collective properties in social organizational theory, and so on.

The other kind of general proposition is an empirical generalization. This is a description of an observed regularity, of ubiquitous covariation between phenomena. General statements are arrived at by induction. Empirical generalizations are *general* propositions in the sense that they summarize many specific instances by means of more abstract terms; but the abstract terms are not *basic*, only more *general*. It is always conceivable that someone may observe other regularities that reveal an even more general case of which the original empirical generalization is itself but a specific instance. Then even more general propositions can be stated. It is not possible, however, that the first kind of general proposition, the kind that I have been calling *basic*, may someday be found, in the empirical sense, to be derivable from even more basic propositions because they exist not as concrete fact but as axioms that simply declare relationships among entities defined primitively.

This distinction between these two kinds of general propositions clarifies Homans's reductionist challenge to sociological theory. Homans meant that he had never seen a sociological proposition that was derived from definitions and axioms that refer exclusively to collective entities. All the general propositions that he had seen were empirical generalizations describing phenomena that could in turn be explained by psychological principles. Blau's defense did not convince Homans because it consisted of presenting still another set of empirical generalizations. Blau listed empirical findings, abstracted what is common among them, and stated the abstractions in terms of propositions. Blau then demonstrated that the more general propositions have the ability to generate hypotheses about relationships in addition to the ones from which they were originally induced. Homans rejoined that Blau's first proposition is clearly an empirical generalization which, Blau (1970) granted, is "not very far removed from merely summarizing the empirical statements" (pp. 333–334).

The reductionist strategy's use of the derived kind of general proposition is one of its strengths. Its propositions are rooted in but one level of analysis and may therefore belong to a body of formal closed theory, that is, theory grounded in primitive definitions and axioms. As noted earlier, closed theory has the desirable feature that it can make a philosophical claim to the universality of its propositions.

Blau's claim that satisfactory sociological theory cannot be derived from psychological propositions could be made more convincingly with a theory that is clearly grounded in collective definitions and axioms and whose propositions are logically derived from these bases. A theory of this kind that also covers certain empirical findings would have demonstrated to Homans that it is possible to formulate irreducible and useful sociological theory. Moreover, it would identify the relevance of psychological givens to theories of social phenomena.

A closed theory of social organization is conceivable. Such a theory would be grounded in definitions of collective terms such as *social roles* as requiring consensus (a collective term) about obligations and privileges of people in certain social positions. It would link these roles axiomatically to the functions they perform toward achieving organizational purposes, and it would define *social organization* in terms of interdependency of functions. It would also state axioms that assert what roles are necessary in order for functions to be performed adequately enough to achieve organizational purposes. The construction of this social organizational theory would avail itself of psychological givens, characterizations of the potential actors. The givens would not be necessary for the derivation of propositions, however, but only to accommodate the theory to its reference in the real world.

This is not the book in which such a social organizational theory is constructed. The sketchy outline I have given must suffice for the claim that such a theory is conceivable and would support Blau's argument. The main point to be made here is that closed theory is conceivable, not only at the social organizational but also at the other social (and the psychological) levels of analysis in the model presented here. (I describe efforts to create closed theories of culture in chapter 6 and of interpersonal relations in chapter 5.) These closed theories take over the task of explaining why their respective entities respond as they do when their environments have somehow changed them. The function of social psychological theory is to state what kinds of changes will probably occur to individuals and collectivities under certain psychological and social conditions. Then reductionism does its thing. The contemporary state of the level of analysis affected is assessed, and its next consequent state is derived from a closed theory at that level.

To serve its particular function, social psychological theory cannot merely posit given, constant psychological or social characteristics; it must also deal with the variable, albeit lawful, conditions of the levels of analysis in its purview. This it does by taking into account the values of the interpenetrating terms it uses in translating conditions across levels of analysis. To use Blau's propositions as an example: Given the existence of social roles at the social organizational level of analysis, and given Blau's proposition that as organizational size increases, certain coordinating roles are generated. The variable is the size of the organization. A social psychological question arises: What is the psychological effect on members if the organization's size increases? Or to put it in a way informed by Blau's proposition: What effect does the proliferation of coordinating roles in their organization have on persons? The question is prompted by a closed theory of social organization; the answer depends on a probabilistic social psychological theory that also takes into account the persons' psychological states at the time.

Social psychology can make contemporary diagnoses of situations adequate to explain the reciprocal influence of individuals and their social environment only by attending to all of its psychological and social levels of analysis. The states of the persons' psyches are contemporaneously and with various strengths under the influence of their role relationships, their interpersonal relations, and the cultures to which they subscribe. Each of these has givens and variables of its own that social psychological theory must take into account. (Indeed, many phenomena of interest to social psychology are also affected by factors neither psychological nor social—neurophysiological, geographical, and so on. Such factors are outside of social psychology's purview, however, although well-known social psychologists have studied them—e.g., Schachter, 1964, on the effects of drugs. Social psychology can take nonsocial factors into account by recognizing their influence in the individual psyche. However, it does not try to explain the processes by which the nonsocial become influential. A borderline instance of this, to be discussed later in this chapter (see p. 42, *What Is Social?*), is the way that evolved genetics may affect the way humans respond to other humans.) It is the function of social psychology to translate consequential psychological and social factors from all the levels of analysis into the terms of the level affected. Reductionist theories inform this process and carry it on to prediction and control.

Kelley and Thibaut's Theory of Social Interaction

The complementarity of social psychology's probabilistic theory and reductionism's universal theory at any level of its analysis is exemplified by the work of Harold Kelley and John W. Thibaut. In their book *Interpersonal Relations* (1978)—incidentally, an example of a different meaning of *interpersonal relations* than is used here—Kelley and Thibaut did not use reductionism in the sense that they tried to explain the phenomena at some other level of analysis with exclusively psychological principles. Their research deals with both individual and social phenomena, but they do not attempt to explain either with propositions of the other. They are reductionist only insofar as they try to explain why individuals behave as they do under the conditions created by their research, and they recognize the limitations of their theory for explaining the social phenomena that occur. The invocation of social psychological and social organizational theory becomes necessary.

Kelley and Thibaut's model of social interaction seems primarily to involve only two people. The parties to the dyad are interdependent in the sense that the acts of each determine the consequences of the acts of the other. The model is simplified by assuming that each party has only two choices of action in any specific instance. Which choice A makes sets the conditions for the outcomes of B's choices and vice versa. The conditions and outcomes are conceptualized as degrees of satisfaction or reinforcement that each may gain or does gain by his or her choice. The situation may be schematized in a 2 x 2 matrix, as shown in Figure 1. "Each of the four cells then represents the intersection or joint occurrence of one of A's behaviors and one of B's behaviors. In each of the four cells the number placed above the diagonal indicates the outcome that A receives, whereas the number below the diagonal indicates B's outcome" (Kelley & Thibaut, 1978, p. 10).

Thus, if A chooses to do a_1, B gains twice as much satisfaction by then choosing to do b_2 rather than b_1. However, that leaves A with no satisfac-

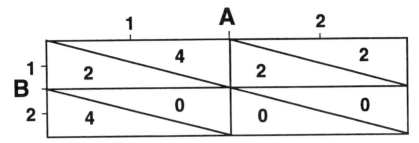

Figure 1. Choices and outcomes in a prisoners' dilemma game.

tion at all. Assuming, along with Kelley and Thibaut, that people act according to the same principles as Homans assumes, the law of effect and the principle of rationality, A recognizes that his choice did not yield the most satisfaction for him and, when the situation arises again, he chooses to do otherwise, a_2. Now if B chooses to do b_2 again, neither A nor B gain any satisfaction at all; so B chooses b_1 instead, and both A and B gain some satisfaction. As a consequence of this sort of interaction, A and B eventually negotiate an agreement to the effect that A will eschew the potential for his maximum satisfaction and always will choose to do a_2, expecting that B will then always eschew the potential for his maximum satisfaction and chose to do b_1.

From this simple model of social interaction and a sparse set of psychological assumptions, Kelley and Thibaut build an elaborate structure. By considering simultaneous and sequential choices, by varying the weights of satisfactions entered for each party in each cell, and by assuming that levels of satisfaction may change as a consequence of interaction (e.g., agreement itself may acquire some degree of satisfaction for both A and B so that over time it exceeds what were the earlier maximum satisfactions), Kelley and Thibaut show how action in a large variety of concrete social situations can be explained by their model.

In the course of developing their theory, Kelley and Thibaut (1978) encountered many of the conceptual issues that arise when one aims to construct a generalizable explanation of action. The perceptual problem is noteworthy.

> In its application to specific cases there are certain ambiguities in the delineation of the outcome matrix. One problem has to do with specifying the behavioral option for each person. This is misleadingly easy in experimental application of the matrix but often an uncertain matter for natural relationships. It seems clear that the options identified by an outsider may be quite different from those distinguished by the persons themselves. Our distinction . . . between the "objective" and "subjective" matrix recognizes this fact. The notion of the objective matrix is based on the assumption that a well-informed and thorough analysis can identify more accurately than can the participants the structure of their relationship. . . . According to this view, the objective matrix represents a causal structure which, whether recognized or not, plays a shaping role in the relationship and is therefore a reality of which it would be well for the participants to become cognizant. (p. 316)

According to the model of social psychology to be developed here, the objective matrix represents that social environment whose influence social psychology means to explain. It is not itself the proximal cause of action, but it has a probabilistic relationship to the subjective understanding of the situation on which actors base their choices. Kelley and Thibaut recognized that their theory does not adequately explain how its properties may affect its psychological translation into the subjective matrix.

The problem of how the objective social environment may affect individuals' subjective experience of it can usefully be explored by characterizing the social environment that Kelley and Thibaut create, that is, by considering Kelley and Thibaut's experimental method. What, one may ask, is the objective matrix in their studies? What is the social nature of the values in the cells such that Persons A and B get certain quantities of satisfaction depending on their joint choices? In the terms of the social psychological model, the researchers have created a social organization. They have acted as the arbiters of social norms, assigning rewards and punishments for certain acts by individuals who are playing their prescribed roles. What appears to be a simple dyad turns out to include at least one other party, the creator of the objective matrix.

Kelley and Thibaut (1978) incorporated the social environment into their model by considering the situation of a triad.

> In adding the third person to our analysis, we are not simply interested in its generalization to the triad, although that is one of our purposes. We also view the third person as epitomizing the social context in which the dyad exists. The ways in which person C can affect the A–B pair reveal how the dyad can be strengthened, changed, or disrupted by its social environment. (p. 243)

In presenting their triadic analysis, Kelley and Thibaut did not assert that the social norms that the third party, C, epitomizes are negotiated with A and B. Their theory would allow for this, and the negotiations would follow the same principles as dyadic interaction, but they would be more complex. Their discussion deals only with C's effect on the negotiations between A and B. The social environment controls their interaction but is not itself controlled.

The origin of the experimentally created formal organization requires no explanation; it suits the researchers' purposes. (Sociologists of science might be interested in explaining why Kelley and Thibaut chose to conduct this research and in the way that they did.) Kelley and Thibaut's experimental method grants participants only the power to act on values set by the researchers. Only within these normative constraints may participants decide on appropriate behavior, that is, create informal norms. The social environment the method creates is then a mixed formal and informal social organization. (See chapter 4 for a discussion of formal and informal social organization.)

To explain the forms of informal social organizations created by the research participants one needs some understanding both of the principles of social organization and of the process of socialization by which the social organizational environment exerted its influence on the subjects. Some social forces so affect negotiations between parties that an adequate explanation of how informal norms emerge from the negotiations cannot be couched solely in terms of the psychological satisfaction gained by the parties. For example, the outcomes that would give participants satisfaction would depend on whether the research task constituted a test of team work or a competitive game, each with its own norms. Furthermore, whatever the nature of the formal organization, how well it is understood by the participants and enlists their conformity depends on how well they were socialized by the researchers.

Similarly, in other situations, nonsocial factors such as physical constraints and technological advances may set conditions for the negotiation of informal norms. Trist and Bamforth (1951) analyzed how the changing natural and technological conditions of coal mining in Wales prompted renegotiation of informal norms by the miners. The thick veins of coal gave out, so it was no longer possible to work in coal-walled rooms large enough to accommodate multitasked teams. It became necessary to work in cramped tunnels along the face of narrow veins, so management formally reorganized the workers into single-tasked shifts of individual miners. Consequently, the miners needed to create among themselves an informal organization of teams, each "owning" a piece of a vein worked over the several shifts.

Reductionism's Contribution: Translation

With these discussions of Blau and Homans and Kelley and Thibaut I mean to demonstrate that reductionism cannot provide the integration of the psychological and the social that social psychology requires. Reductionism's preoccupation with one level of analysis is both a strength and a weakness. This preoccupation has the advantage of permitting the formulation of closed theory with the potential for discovering universal laws, commonly at the psychological level. However, the real forces acting in the social environment also demand attention. The mission of social psychology requires it to take several levels of analysis—psychological, social organizational, interpersonal, and cultural—jointly into account in order to explain the reciprocal influence of individuals and their social environment. Social psychology cannot accomplish this with theoretical reduction. It works instead by theoretical translation.

Translation is not derivation. This theoretical tool assumes that there is a self-contained body of useful psychology theory, but it implies that closed theories of the social environment are also useful. What effect, for example, does a certain change in the differential distribution of rewards in an organization have on the obligations and privileges of the other roles that comprise it? This is a question for organizational theory. What effect does this role change have on the behavior and experience of the individual? This is a question for social psychological theory. The answers to social psychological questions like this are statements about how collective events such as role changes will *probably* be translated into psychological determinants of behavior and experience; or how changes in the psychological characteristics of a role taker will be translated into social facts that change the organization.

Translation is not a simple matter. Its validity is facilitated when it is informed by an understanding of the several languages in which the relevant phenomena are best expressed, that is, by an understanding of the concepts and principles of the relevant levels of analysis. However, even if one were conversant in all of social science, finding just the right translations across levels is difficult.

It helps a great deal to consult a metalanguage for useful translations. The strategy of metalanguage has been proposed as a way to integrate psychological and social facts in social psychology. Like reductionism, it proves inadequate to this task when used alone, but its Esperanto-like vocabulary can guide one to optimal translations.

Metalanguage

As a theoretical strategy, metalanguage consists of abstract concepts with properties that are common to the events of interest to two or more disciplines. Because the concepts of the metalanguage are the same across all levels of analysis, translation of the conditions at one level into their influence on events at another level is greatly facilitated. Here lies the major contribution of the strategy to integrating social psychology. That it does not distinguish psychological from social phenomena or different kinds of social phenomena from one another also disqualifies metalanguage as the primary theoretical strategy for social psychology.

Two metalanguages illustrate the strategy in this section: James G. Miller's general system theory (1978) and Talcott Parsons's theory of action (1961, 1969). These two have complementary features, so together they display the theoretical potential of metalanguages. One might choose other illustrations, such as D. Katz and Kahn's open systems theory (1978) or chaos theory (Vallacher & Nowak, 1994).

The metalanguage strategy integrates disciplines in three ways. First, it is useful for what Logan, Olmstead, Rosner, Schwartz, and Stevens (1955) call *pedagogical integration*—"the development of an explicit framework in terms of which the disparate disciplines can be related one to the other" (p. 8, footnote). It can be used in this way for designing interdisciplinary science courses. A course in one of what I have termed the "boundary disciplines" can be structured for students by demonstrating how a system property like interdependence of subunits is exemplified by isomorphic relationships between the membrane of a cell that ingests matter from the environment and the endoplasmic reticulum that distributes the substance within the cell; the alveoli and the blood vessels of an organ; the digestive and vascular systems of an organism; and the sales and payroll offices of a corporation. All of these relationships theoretically obey the same basic principles that govern input and distribution in any system.

I call the second kind of integration that a metalanguage provides *methodological integration*. It is a useful tool for constructing and testing the validity of theoretical propositions because it enables scientists in one discipline to avail themselves of the theoretical and empirical advances made in another. For example, Weber's function relating the intensity of a stimulus to the response of a receptor organ has led to research on the level of cellular activity (J. G. Miller, 1978, pp. 94–95). The facilitating idea is that this propaedeutic principle can be derived wholly from the general systemic properties of cells or sense organs without involving any conditions peculiar to either. Researchers of phenomena in one system might apply principles discovered in another to explain their data or might initiate studies to test the principle under the conditions of the systems within their purview.

This kind of cross-disciplinary integration is not limited to the empirical sciences; the invention of pure mathematics (the epitome of metalanguage) can also be used by empirical sciences to generate hypotheses. To do this successfully requires that the properties assigned to the basic terms of the mathematics are also the properties of the basic concepts of the empirical science and their concrete referents. One of Kurt Lewin's aspirations was to find or create a mathematics that would serve the social sciences in this way, and he in fact bent topology to psychological purposes (Back, 1992; K. Lewin, 1936). At the time of his death, he was beginning to explore the applicability of topology to group phenomena (1947). In this tradition, Harary, Norman, and Cartwright turned to graph theory (1965).

Methodological integration is useful not only for creating propositions but for testing them as well. Scientists in one discipline may develop a new proposition but be unable to put it to empirical test: The resources required might be too great, the measuring devices may not have been perfected yet, or ethics may prohibit it. Systems theory permits the proposition to be tested in another discipline that does not face these obstacles. The objects of the other discipline can stand in for the objects of the first because they share the same systemic properties that the proposition requires. Computer systems have been used in this way to test models of human thought processes (Abelson, 1981), and experiments relating to large scale social organizations have been done on small face-to-face groups (see chapter 10). These kinds of tests are not as conclusive for the original discipline as tests made with their own concrete phenomena because unrecognized but consequential factors may actually make conditions in the two disciplines dissimilar; but confidence in the empirical validity of the proposition will have been strengthened, pending the execution of a direct test.

Raising the possibility that differences in conditions across disciplines may limit the integrative potential of a metalanguage also points to a general shortcoming charged to the metalanguage strategy. By its nature, the concepts of a metalanguage are more abstract than those of any particular discipline. The usefulness of a metalanguage lies precisely in the breadth of its applicability. This creates difficulties with operationalization—the identification of the specific phenomena in a particular discipline that match the general concepts in the metalanguage.

General Systems

One form in which metatheorists face this problem is the necessity to provide labels for their concepts: They can choose extant words from their language of common discourse or they can coin new words. J. G. Miller (1978) pointed out that "No words . . . are designed or precisely adapted to describe comparable structures and processes at all . . . levels. The accepted specialized terms at one level are not exactly appropriate to another level" (p. 4).

One of the most ambitious efforts to create a metalanguage has been J. G. Miller's *Living Systems* (1978). This theory incorporates the cell, the organ, the organism, the group, the organization, and the culture. All of these entities are conceptualized as living systems and are hypothesized to behave similarly, at least in some respects, because they are all living systems.

For example, a basic concept in the language of Miller's general system theory is *ingestor*, a word that refers to that unit in a living system that takes in materials from the environment. It is meant to cover whatever performs that function in, among others, an amoeba, kidney, mammal, bird, person, and social organization. The word *ingestor* does not point obviously to its manifestation in all of these systems, and even familiarity with its explicit definition does not clarify the matter. Part of the problem is that *ingest* has connotations that are not intended in the formal definition of *ingestor*. Miller might have avoided this problem by creating a new word, but this tactic would create its own problems of communication.

Thus, drawing on an encompassing metalanguage for propositions in a specific discipline compounds one problem of translating concepts noted earlier with still another: In addition to the choice of operations for realizing theoretical concepts, it requires the choice of theoretical concepts within the discipline that match the necessarily more abstract concepts of the metalanguage. These difficulties have discouraged widespread use of a broad metalanguage in social psychology. Its breadth renders it inadequate for solving many of the problems of social psychology because those problems are peculiarly social.

A metalanguage that covers all systems or even just all living systems may contribute to our understanding of human behavior. Ranging over its broad domain, one may gain insights from observing how humans function as systems. However, its generality, necessarily based on what humans have in common with all other living beings, limits its usefulness for social psychologists whose focus is on what is peculiarly human. J. G. Miller (1978) was cognizant of this:

> Perhaps the most profoundly significant emergent at the organism level, which is fundamental to the development of groups and higher

levels of systems, is the ability to use gamma-coded language [i.e., symbols]. It is not seen below primates. (p. 68)

Man is the only organism known certainly to process [symbols], although some other species, such as dolphins, possibly communicate at times with gamma-codes, and chimpanzees have been taught to use symbolic hand sign language and plastic chips of various shapes and colors to symbolize words. Though they cannot speak, domestic animals and primates certainly can make discriminative responses to human speech. They are probably responses to signs rather than symbols in gamma-coded speech. (p. 404)

Because of the profound discontinuity between humans and other living systems in the phylogenetic scale, a major strength of general system theory, the capability to develop propositions across a broad range of levels of analysis, is vitiated. The behavior of systems at the lower levels is dominated by the second law of thermodynamics, and a theoretical system that has accumulation, distribution, and expenditure of energy at its foundation covers that behavior quite well. Even a significant proportion of human behavior can be explained in these terms. Still, inasmuch as social psychological theory concerns events that depend on communication, principles about exhaustible energy are largely irrelevant. Social psychology is concerned with symbolic interaction.

I chose to introduce general system theory because an analysis of its strengths and weaknesses from a social psychological perspective suggests some of the characteristics of a useful metalanguage. Its major strength is to identify affinities in concepts and their concrete referents across levels of analysis. These affinities focus on the functional essentials of the phenomena in their respective systems and thereby mark the terms to be translated from one conceptual level to the other. J. G. Miller's work on "living systems" is rich in such conceptual analyses. This particular conceptualization seems too broad for social psychology, however, because it rests too heavily on assumptions of a limited quantity, energy, whereas what is essential to "social" entities is that they do commerce with a quantity that is undiminished when it is dissipated, namely, information. A metalanguage useful for social psychology is one concerned with symbols and their interrelationships, with how symbols are communicated, and with their effects on the entities on which they impinge. Thus, the span of this metalanguage is relatively narrow compared with J. G. Miller's, because it essentially covers only humans and their social environment.

An extant mathematics may be recognized as suitable for expressing propositions about humans as symbol-making and symbol-guided entities, and human interpersonal relationships, social organizations, and culture as well. Lewin's topology, Harary et al.'s graph theory (1965), and stochastic models have been used in constructing information theory. It is noteworthy that these mathematics have in common concepts that refer to points that connect between entities—boundaries, lines, paths, links—across which flows an inexhaustible supply of something. In effect, these mathematics have at their foundation the processes that J. G. Miller's general system theory locates around the concept of the *transducers*, a concept that has remained relatively undeveloped in that theory.

Extant nonmathematical models also come to mind that might inform the structure of social psychological theory. Linguistics is one, particularly that aspect of linguistics that covers grammar and syntax—the morphology of linguistics rather than the phonology—and obviously deals with information.

Social Systems

Talcott Parsons's (1961, 1969) functional theory of action systems is another particularly appropriate metalanguage that offers a set of concepts and their relationships whose dynamics are almost exclusively cybernetic. This review of the metalanguage strategy turns finally to a discussion of Parsons's theory, which in turn leads to the threshold of the strategy of levels of analysis.

Parsons's metalanguage consists of terms that refer to systemic properties, as does J. G. Miller's. Parsons's language is more useful for social psychology because it is almost exclusively social. Moreover, it includes terms that constitute the paths through which social subsystems influence one another. These terms facilitate the translation of events from one level of analysis to another. Later in this section I elaborate on Parsons's subsystems of action as levels of analysis. I also make use of his ideas about how subsystems are integrated, with a critical qualification.

A brief presentation of Parsons's systemic terms, with special attention to their appropriately limited range, is in order. Parsons's theory "analyzes any action *system* in terms of the four functional categories" (1969, p. 8). The *maintenance* function preserves the system as a system by ensuring the stability of the patterns of behavior. The *integrative* function sees to the coordination of the interdependent parts of the system. The function of *goal attainment* is responsible for progress toward the desired state of the system in a changing environment. The system is assumed to have "needs" (the quotation marks are Parsons's, intended probably to avoid the kind of confusion that arose in the Blau–Homans debate about the "needs" of a social organization), which it satisfies in interaction with its environment; the stable state of the system is need satisfaction. Finally, *adaptation* refers to the function by which the resources of the system are allocated to the other three functions, marshaled perhaps at one moment to coordinate and at another to achieve one or another goal. The hallmark of an effective adaptive system is its flexibility, enabling the system's resources to be easily shifted from the support of one function to the support of another.

It might seem from this outline of the basic functional elements of Parsons's theory of action that they could be applied to any living system. There are energid principles implied in the adaptive function that allocates apparently finite resources. In other hands, the concepts might be used widely, but Parsons's application is solely to action systems that do commerce with information and meanings. Parsons regarded an action system as cybernetic (K. Deutsch, 1963; Winer, 1955); that is, it is controlled by subsystems that are high in information and low in energy.

Parsons ordered the subsystems of action in terms of their cybernetic control over each other: the cultural system wielding the most, then the social system, followed by the personality system, and finally the behavioral organism. The importance of symbolic interaction relative to energid exchange shifts as one descends this hierarchy. The exigencies of entropy become more than negligible only at the lowest level, the level of the human as a behavioral organism. Thus Parsons's metalanguage is well suited in this respect to the requirements of a social psychology that covers only what is essentially human.

For application of these ideas, Parsons, primarily a sociologist, focussed on the social system, which he analyzed into four essential "institutions": religion, societal community, polity, and economy. These institutions are primarily responsible respectively for the systemic functions internal to the social system of maintenance, integration, goal attainment, and adaptation. At the same time, the social system as a whole functions in an environment comprised of the other subsystems of action and each of the others supports primarily a particular function of the social system: culture, through its expression of values, supports the maintenance of the recurring patterns of behavior that define the social system; personality supports goal attainment by providing the engine of individual motivations; and the human, as behavioral organism, supports adaptation by its capacity to be moved about flexibly in order to be devoted to one or another of the other functions as the changing environments demand. The social system attends to its own integration by the exercise of its norms.

The distinctions Parsons drew among these subsystems or levels are useful. Parsons's terms, like Miller's, distinguished between *culture* and *social systems* or *social organization*. Unlike Miller, Parsons did not distinguish between "organization" and "group" for good reason: Groups can be social organizations (see chapter 12). Furthermore, and also unlike J. G. Miller, Parsons provided an explicit conceptual place for the psychological person distinct from the biological organism in his specification of the "personality system." In my social psychological model, the individual and the social environment are conceptualized in terms similar to Parsons's. The equivalence of the concepts used to analyze both the internal structure of a subsystem of action and of the other subsystems that comprise its environment is extremely useful for dealing with translations among levels of analysis (the subsystems of action in Parsons's theory). Equivalent functions identify the points of tangency between levels, the points at which translation across the boundaries of the system are made. Each of the several levels of analysis is open to the influence of the others at just those points.

Parsons (1969) dealt with the problem of translating among subsystems by postulating the phenomenon of *interpenetration* and defining its function.

> In analyzing the interrelationships among the four subsystems of action . . . it is essential to keep in mind the phenomenon of *interpenetration*. Perhaps the best-known case of interpenetration is the *internalization* of social objects and cultural norms into the personality of the individual. Learned content of experience, organized and stored in the memory apparatus of the organism, is another example, as is the *institutionalization* of normative components of cultural systems as constitutive structures of social systems. We hold that the boundary between any pair of action systems involves a "zone" of structures, components or patterns which must be treated as *common* to *both* systems, not simply allocated to one system or the other. For example, it is untenable to say that norms of conduct derived from social experience, which both Freud (in the concept of the superego) and Durkheim (in the concept of collective representations) treated as parts of the personality of the individual, must be *either* that *or* part of the social system.
>
> It is by virtue of the zones of interpenetration that processes of interchange among systems can take place . . . . (p. 36)

Parsons suggested that the tangent of two levels of analysis is to be found at the point of isomorphic functions. Thus, if roles provide the normative regulation of a social system, then social systems make contact with personalities through the normative regulatory component of personalities. Because all action systems have equivalent functional elements, then it is conceptually possible to identify the points of tangency among them all. The valuable contribution of a metalanguage strategy to the integration of social psychological material is explicit in Parsons's concept of "zone of interpenetration." This is the feature of the metalanguage that facilitates translation.

Caution is needed, however, because the idea of interpenetration also presents a danger to constructing social psychological theory. The boundaries of social psychological levels of analysis are not sharply drawn by their definitions: Where is the break between social organization and culture or between interpersonal and role relations? *Interpenetration* capitalizes on the fuzziness of the boundaries, conceiving of them as having dual membership in two or more levels and serving therefore as points of translation. At the same time, this fuzziness can render as unfalsifiable propositions that are derived at a level of analysis (and therefore almost useless for constructing closed theory) by tempting one to attribute aberrant findings to the influence of "that other" level of analysis.

Another caution is needed. Because translation is never perfect, it is not strategically useful to social psychology to adopt Parsons's approach entirely. Social norms are variously perceived and only more or less accepted through the process of socialization; people are more or less persuaded of the ideas of their culture as they understand them; and people only partially and selectively identify with those with whom they share an interpersonal relation. For this reason, D. Katz and Kahn (1978) stopped short of granting that Parsons provided just the right integrative mechanism. The problem of imperfect translation is fundamental to theorizing in social psychology.

For D. Katz and Kahn, the imperfect socialization of individuals into organizational roles was the starting point for *The Social Psychology of Organizations*. They did not agree with Parsons's assertion that "it is untenable to say that norms of conduct derived from social experience . . . . must be [treated] *either* [as parts of the personality of the individual] *or* part of the social system." On the contrary, Katz and Kahn regarded that statement of the matter as the only tenable one. Nor were they persuaded of Parsons's assertion that the imperfect socialization of a person into any one role is wholly a problem of conflict among the multiple roles that individuals must play at any particular time in their lives. There are, they held, certain effects of life histories and inherent developmental properties of human personalities that prevent individuals from being shaped entirely to the contours of any role. Parsons (1969), on the other hand, made a different assumption:

> Individualistic social theory has persistently exaggerated the significance of individual "self-interest" in a psychological sense as an obstacle to the integration of social systems. The self-interpreted motives of individuals are, on the whole, effectively channeled into the functioning of social systems through a variety of memberships and loyalties to collectivities . . . . (p. 42)

Undoubtedly, the fact is that there are substantial interindividual differences in the degree of socialization into roles and substantial intraindividual differences in the degree of socialization of one person into his or her various roles. It falls to social psychology to explain these differences, and it is not useful for social psychology to make a general assumption of either perfect or imperfect socialization. Such assumptions are necessary for building closed theory in sociology. A social psychological explanation of an individual's experience and behavior insofar as they are affected by his or her social environment must somehow put social organizational variables together with psychological variables, without assuming that they are simply two sides of the same coin.

Parsons's theory of action has the several advantages of a metalanguage. It merits the attention of social psychology because it focuses on the symbolic aspect of human interaction and encompasses the social psychological levels of analysis. Its concept of "interpenetration" is a useful guide to translating among levels of analysis. Like other metalanguages, Parsons's scheme claims the potential not only for covering the phenomena at a particular level of analysis, but also for generating explanatory propositions that are common to more than one level of analysis. A sociologist, Parsons made virtuoso use of the scheme to understand what in the social psychological model is called the social organizational level of analysis. One can similarly analyze personality and cultural systems, and Parsons made some effort to do so.

This last strength of a metalanguage strategy is also its weakness. The strategy assumes identity of individuals and their social environments when it is more advantageous for social psychological theory to take into account the differences. In metalanguages, the same concepts are used to account for both psychological and social phenomena. This strategy depends too much on what the levels may have in common as systems, when what differentiates them may account for the more significant of their respective actions. Some useful analogies may be drawn between levels on the basis of their systemic similarities, and Parsons's functional analysis is as good a guide to them as any. However, it is necessary to recognize the "break" between the individual and the social environment for understanding each of them. This is particularly true of a social psychology whose mission is to explain the effects of the encounter between the social and the psychological. A useful analysis of the parties to social psychological encounters does not conceptualize them in the same terms. Each level must be described in terms grounded in the essential and distinctive properties of each. This is the basis of the strategy of levels of analysis.

Levels of Analysis: An Overview of the Model

The theoretical strategy that I use here emphasizes the distinctiveness of certain sets of phenomena within the domain of social psychology and organizes these conceptually as levels of analysis. The mission ascribed to social psychology focuses particularly on the interactions that occur at the boundaries between one of these levels—the psychological—and the others. A review of the efforts of others to integrate the social and the psychological—Yinger, Parsons, Katz and Kahn—finds that they also make some use of this strategy. It is attractive for the purpose. In this section, I want to make clear what this strategy involves and how I use it.

If one ponders for long the universe of actual events, one can certainly come to believe that everything is related somehow to everything else. The levels of analysis approach proceeds on the assumption that it is nevertheless useful for explanations to organize these interrelated phenomena into discrete sets. The distinctions one makes are not logical in a strict sense—they are not derived from any more fundamental principles. They are rather more or less informed guesses at what makes some sense out of the materials, as close observation would guide one in disentangling a snarl of strings.

The characteristic features of the level of analysis strategy are how they organize discrete sets of events and how they relate these sets of events to one another. Theory at each level is built by conceptualizing phenomena with definitions and axioms and then with other terms and propositions all derived from the set of definitions and axioms. It follows then that a level of analysis is in the first instance a conceptual creation, not a natural phenomenon. Although they may emerge inductively from observation and further observations may demonstrate the validity of a particular conceptualization, levels of analysis are not generalizations by induction. Levels are theoretical constructions.

It should be clear from previous discussion that locating various phenomena at the same level of analysis by tracing their roots to common definitions and axioms implies that the phenomena at a particular level of analysis are covered by the same closed theory. One level of analysis cannot then be reduced to or subsumed by another, nor is it conceptually related to another by propositions logically derived from the other. Whereas the events at the same level of analysis are related by definition, axiom, and logic, the relationships among events at different levels of analysis are accounted for by translation into the terms of separate closed theories. This is the theoretical function of such concepts as *ingestor* and *input transducer* in J. G. Miller's model of living systems and of interpenetrating terms such as *role–superego* in Parsons's conceptualization.

My delineation of social psychological levels of analysis makes no assumption about a hierarchy among them. In other models, levels may be conceived as nested, one level being a constituent of another, and that other level of still another (Dubin, 1969). Parsons (1951, 1969), for example, ordered levels cybernetically. In the present model, the levels are equal and independent. I do not assert, for example, that culture is regnant, that psychological individuals are ultimately creatures of their culture. Instead, I hold that an important task for the social sciences is to identify the conditions under which culture shapes individuals' behavior and experience and the conditions under which certain individuals shape their cultures. Social psychology's particular mission among the sciences is to take individuals into account both as shapers and as shaped.

Although the levels in this model are conceptually distinct, they nevertheless constitute a domain. They occupy a common domain by sharing the same set of givens, the same set of assumptions about the properties of their empirical components. Social science is a domain because all of its constituent disciplines assume a symbol-making, symbol-sharing human entity. Similarly, the physical and natural sciences are domains, each with its common givens.

This notion of a domain is helpful for identifying and understanding the nature of the boundary sciences. It makes clear in what sense, for example, geopolitics is a boundary science whereas astrophysics is not: The theories of geography and political science have different basic definitions and axioms, but they share assumptions about human needs for sustenance and human motivations for control and power; astronomy is a branch of physics, its propositions being traceable to the same basic definitions and axioms, and the compound designation *astrophysics* simply indicates the values on dimensions of gravity and mass with which the subdiscipline deals. Thus, psychophysics, physiological psychology, developmental psychology, and social psychology are all boundary sciences. Each includes two or more levels of analysis that make some common assumptions about the nature of the human organism. Because humans are the component part of the empirical phenomena with which all these sciences are concerned—the given common to them all—these disciplines belong to the same domain.

A "boundary" between levels consists of the events at one level of analysis that most probably give rise to events at the other. The events at one level are conceived as being as close to the boundary with the other as the strength of this likelihood. The organization of the social psychological model implies that the person and the specified levels of the social environment are adjacent, that is, they will in all probability affect one another. (Students of K. Lewin's field theory, 1951, will recognize this use of the term *boundary* or *foreign hull* in Lewin's conceptualization of the life space.)

The levels of analysis strategy uses some principles of the other integrative strategies that have been discussed. It is partly reductionist insofar as it recognizes that universal principles of individuals' behavior and experience must ultimately be couched exclusively in terms of psychological variables. Therefore, an adequate explanation must translate influences at other levels into psychological determinants. The strategy is not expansionist inasmuch as it recognizes the conceptual usefulness of other levels of analysis and applies the principle of translation to them as well. The strategy makes use of the metalanguage approach insofar as it searches for interpenetrating terms at the various levels of analysis in order to facilitate the work of translation. It does not follow the metalanguage approach by generating propositions common to all levels of analysis; although it may get inspiration from other levels, the approach emphasizes incorporating what is particular to each level.

The level of analysis strategy seems the most useful tool for building theory in social psychology. Whereas the strategy itself does not define the discipline of social psychology, it provides the rules for identifying its domain once the object of the discipline has been defined. The strategy does not specify levels of analysis, but it requires that levels of analysis be clearly specified and that their distinctiveness be maintained. Moreover, the strategy does not itself provide the theoretical mechanisms by which boundaries across levels of analysis are bridged, but it requires integration of that kind. It is a theoretical procedure that fits the substance and aims of social psychology as I conceive of the discipline.

The first step in using the strategy of levels of analysis is to delineate the domain of the levels to be used. For social psychology, this means to define *social* inclusively and exclusively. Next, I discuss how I deal with the fuzziness of the boundaries of the levels that I described earlier (chapter 1), with the concept of *interpenetration* and the theoretical tool of *idealization*. Finally, I review the processes posited in the model by which the levels exert influence on one another and invoke the rule of *contemporaneity* to which explanations of these processes should adhere.

What Is Social?

I defined *social psychology* as "the study of the reciprocal influence of persons and their social environments" (see p. 9). People may be said to live in three different environments: the internal, the physical, and the social.

These may not be the most useful distinctions for every purpose, but the set helps to clarify the meaning of its social member.

The most familiar of these environments is the physical, the environment of light and dark, of colors, of temperature, texture, and pressure, of sounds and smells. It is the one central to the interest of psychophysics, which is concerned with sensation.

The "internal milieu," brought to our attention by the physiologist Claude Bernard (1865/1927), comprises the state of our bodies, its temperature, chemical balances, and structural connections. It is the environment in which internal organs function. Most important to social psychology, it is the one in which the nervous system is a given and sets the conditions for the physiological bases of psychological processes. Physiological psychology studies it; the internal milieu contains its boundary conditions.

The social environment is in a theoretical sense the least familiar of the three. It has not usually been distinguished, especially from the physical. In distinguishing the "social" here, I do not claim to have found its definition explicit or even implicit in the literature. As Roger Brown (1965) wrote in the Preface to his introductory social psychology text:

> Can one abstract from the list of topics that are being successfully studied in a social psychological manner the logical chain of topics that should be studied in this manner and so identify the proper domain of social psychology and foresee its future development? I myself cannot find any single attribute or any combination of attributes that will clearly distinguish the topics of social psychology from topics that remain within general experimental psychology or sociology or anthropology or linguistics. Roughly speaking, of course, social psychology is concerned with the mental processes (or behavior) of persons insofar as these are determined by past or present interactions with other persons, but this *is* rough and it is not a definition that excludes very much. (p. xx)

Some vignettes will take us toward a definition of *social*. The first is taken from Fritz Heider's *The Psychology of Interpersonal Relations* (1958):

> When I am threatened by a danger from a nonpersonal source, all I usually need to do is change the conditions in order to escape the danger. If I am threatened by falling stones on a mountain, I can get out of the danger area and seek shelter. The stones will not change their paths in order to find me behind the shelter. If, however, a person wants to hit me with a stone and he can run faster than I can, I am exposed to the danger of being hit to a much greater degree and I have to use very different means in order not to be hit . . . . (p. 101)

To expand on Heider's example, suppose that instead of being threatened by falling stones, a woman is being stalked by a very hungry mountain lion. That lion will change his path in order to catch her. In fact, however, the lion is not after her as a human, he is after her as food. So if the woman throws him a rabbit, the stalker is likely to settle for that and let the woman escape. Imagine in contrast that the person is a soldier being stalked by an enemy; the enemy is looking for the patriotically motivated human and for anyone allied with him. The soldier cannot escape by throwing this stalker a rabbit; even throwing the enemy an ally will not distract him for long. Peculiarly human attributes are involved—social roles, allegiances, ideologies, the capacity to consider the future. Heider is clear: Something different occurs when another *person* moves about in our environment. At the least, it is the attributed presence of a motivated intelligence capable of reacting to our reaction and further capable of reacting again to our further reactions.

Another vignette demonstrates that we must be discriminating when we think of people in this way. Imagine an individual walking along a sidewalk in front of a multistoried building when an object falls out of a high window toward his or her head. That object might be a flower pot or it might be another person. To the potential victim, it makes no difference. This is the point: The personhood of the object is not a factor in the immediate situation, because the falling body cannot in this situation use his or her human mental capacities. As I shall emphasize many times, if the individual believes that the other cannot act as a person or if he or she ignores or forgets that the other can respond as a person, the other might as well be a flower pot as far as the individual is concerned. What makes situations "social" for people is their attribution of the capacities for human mental capacity to the other. If individuals do not attribute human mental capacities to the other, then their psychological responses to the situation are not explainable by social psychological principles.

Social psychology may nevertheless be interested if, despite individuals' misattribution, the other can respond as a person; that is, if the situation is to that extent objectively "social." The probability is thereby increased that people will, in the future, respond to a social situation. However, the objective human mental capacities of the other are not sufficient to make an environment "social" at the psychological level of analysis. The individual must recognize the other's humanity.

Another angle to this, from a different perspective: Some attributions of humanity are fanciful, made to creatures that do not have human mental capacities. Some people regard their pets as so nearly human that they interact with them as though they were. They are convinced, or at least act as though they were, that their cats or dogs have high-level human intelligence, make human interpretations of situations, and have human motives. For example, Friedman, Katcher, Lynch, and Thomas (1979) reported that having a pet can help patients survive a heart attack because pets provide emotional support as human companions do. It follows that all the principles of social interaction would hold as long as this attribution sticks, so that one could replicate, say, Back's experiment on personal attraction and conformity (1951) if one could enlist such a pet in the experiment. This angle brings out that essential in identifying a situation as "social" from the point of view of an individual is recognizing that the individual perceives the activity of a human psyche in it. G. E. Swanson (1965) put it this way: "Social interaction refers to situations in which people take into account each other's knowledge, intentions, preferences, hopes, beliefs, and the like. It refers, in short, to men relating to each other's minds" (p. 164).

I do not mean to limit the definition of the "social" environment to the immediate presence of humans. One of the recurring points of difference among definers of social psychology is whether the discipline is concerned only with face-to-face interaction or whether it encompasses "the imagined or implied presence of others" (G. Allport, 1954, p. 5). Even more broadly, should it include symbols in its purview? I take the widest view.

One more vignette: A small boy relieves the boredom of a rainy Saturday afternoon by exploring the bookshelf of his teenaged sister. Between the pages of her encyclopedia, he finds a brittle object, brown and silver. He is turning it over curiously, crinkling his nose as it disintegrates, bits of it falling onto the carpet. His sister discovers him and screams, "Leave that alone!" Obviously brother and sister feel differently about the object; for him it is a strange and somewhat repulsive thing, but for her, it is what's left of her first corsage. That thing resides for the most part in the boy's *physical* environment; he attends to its texture and color. For his sister, the corsage is almost entirely defined by its symbolic quality, and so it is part of her *social* environment. Of course, the faded corsage can itself make no human response to her action. However, her responses to it are heavily determined by the human responses that it symbolizes for her. So too is it with our responses to sentences, flags, crucifixes, and idols. Their symbolic character—with its implication of human mentation— makes them part of the social environment.

Thinking about the nature of the social environment in this way implies that any environment may be social to some degree. Whether individuals' behavior or experience is at any moment socially determined is a function of the degree to which they perceive the relevant environment as social, that is, carrying information that only other humans can send. Nuttin (1989) proposed that social psychological propositions be tested as to their social specificity by thought experiment: Would the proposition be invalidated a priori if it were applied to interaction with a nonhuman entity, in Nuttin's term, if the situation were "heterosocial"? To the degree that situations are "homosocial," then social psychology has a unique contribution to make in explaining the events that occur in them.

There are gray areas, areas of ambiguity in reality that do not fit so definitively into the categories of "social" or "nonsocial." How to locate, for example, an ultimate case of routinized role behavior—the vendors of tokens in a New York City subway station? They accept cash from travelers and push tokens out to them. Are they mindless? Their capacities for human response are seldom called on: to give directions, to call a policeman, to offer sympathy to someone in distress. Their task could be (and in many stations, now is) handled almost equally well by a machine. Do we call this a "social" encounter? Are the vendors part of the social environment for the people who buy their tokens? I think so, yet here we must allow for some ambiguity. I return to this issue later in the discussion of role regulated interaction and the special circumstances under which such human interaction is barely (if at all) "social."

Another ambiguous case is con-species behavior. How much of human beings' responses to other humans is shaped by instinct, triggered by the stimulus of one's own kind and having nothing to do with symbolic interaction? At the level of the phylogenetic scale where reproduction begins to be sexual, organisms exhibit unlearned responses to their own kind that they do not make to members of other species: The peahen is turned on by the unfurled tail feathers of the peacock; female dogs in heat attract males of the species; the male stickleback woos the female by getting his back up and dancing. As one follows such behavior up the phylogenetic scale, one notes that two things happen: Behavior becomes more susceptible to modification by experience, and it broadens to include more than sexual behaviors. At the human level, whatever may remain of instinctual con-species behavior is subject to substantial modification by experience.

How should social psychology take into account the influence of adaptive con-species mechanisms that evolution may have deposited in human genes? Scholars who have addressed this question generally reject the "nature versus nurture" frame for it (e.g., Buss, 1990; Tooby & Cosmides, 1992; Wilson, 1975), favoring an interactional model instead. Their models attribute a great deal of determination to the contemporaneous social environment, holding that specific mechanisms are triggered and their behavioral manifestations shaped by it. In the social psychological model proposed here, these genetic influences are treated as given characteristics of persons. What specific con-species adaptations that may have evolved —like the capacities for visual perception, emotion, and language—set the parameters within which humans interact with their social environments. Treated as givens, in the internal milieu, these genetic adaptations are taken into account by the effects they have had on the person's psyche, and the model finds these effects in the person's contemporaneous motives and resources. Through motives and resources, they interpenetrate the social environment.

Still, evolved con-species behavior at the human level occupies the "social" gray area. Social psychology might take interest in them as more than given. An "archeological social psychology" might contribute to our understanding of how these contemporaneous givens evolved as they have. After all, evolution takes place in particular ecologies, and con-species mechanisms evolved under the influence of natural selection in certain social environments. Evolutionary psychologists invoke social psychological theory when they try to account for the nature of specific mechanisms by imagining, informed by the archeological evidence, what kinds of prehistoric social environments afforded reproductive advantages to the adaptations that seem to have evolved. Insights generated by these explorations can in turn contribute to our understanding of contemporary social influence by suggesting what features of the social environment now trigger which given adaptations. Some otherwise puzzling psychological phenomena, puzzling because they seem inexplicable in terms of contemporary motives and resources, may be due to anachronistic mechanisms.

Note that I have characterized given genetic mechanisms as contemporaneous. The point is that social psychology should ordinarily treat these mechanisms as givens rather than devote itself to discovering their origins, even when their origins are partly social. This is because evolved adaptations, in their contemporaneous form, are elements of a nonsocial environment. I invoke the principle of contemporaneity here. I intend that theorizing with the proposed model adhere to the rule that only present conditions have present effects. Effects of past events cannot account for the present influence of the social and the psychological on each other. The evolution of adaptations and all past events are to be represented by their precipitates in the contemporaneous situation. Representations of the past may be precipitated at any of the social levels of analysis—as motives and resources; as social norms; as beliefs; or as identities. They may be the precipitates of social and nonsocial events—catastrophic weather, psychological trauma, or natural selection in the Pleistocene Age. In any case, by social psychological *explanation*, I mean identification of the contemporaneous social causes of social influence. I often refer to such explanations as *adequate contemporary diagnoses*.

Integrative Strategies

The rule of contemporaneity is one element of the strategy by which the model explains how the levels of analysis in the social psychological domain exert reciprocal influence. Its integrative purpose requires other strategies as well to deal with the realities of its materials.

Using Parsons's idea (1969) of "zones of interpenetration," as I have described it, is one strategy. As precisely as one tries to define them, one cannot definitively locate all social phenomena into one or the other of the four levels of analysis in the social psychological domain. The effort is persuasive that reality itself has fuzzy boundaries. The model takes this reality into account, capitalizing on it for its integrative purpose, with the idea of "interpenetration": It marks just those phenomena that have multiple conceptual existence for translating the influence of one level of analysis to another.

Reality challenges the model in another way. Theoretically, the posited levels of analysis are independent, and the distinctiveness of the several social influence processes—socialization, identification, persuasion, and so on—derive from the conceptual distinctiveness of their source and target levels of analysis. One strength claimed for the model is that it constructs its propositions about influence from the unique natures of the source and target of the influence, taken but two at a time. In reality, however, the influences of levels are interdependent in most concrete instances. The effects of the social environment on the person at a point in time do not ordinarily emanate purely from the person's interpersonal relations, social organizations, or cultures. In the real world, two or more of these processes are simultaneously active. Thus, an adequate contemporary diagnosis of the situation requires that more than one level be taken into account. The model deals with this problem with the strategy of idealization (Lopreato & Alston, 1970; Weber, 1904/1949).

Idealizing each level of analysis is to conceive of it in its pure form, an ideal type like the unattainable perfect vacuum assumed in physics. Propositions about individuals' interactions with the several social environments are constructed as if people and each of the social environments encounter only their pure forms. Concrete instances are analyzed into these dyadic components and the propositions are applied.

Idealization alone usually does not generate adequate contemporary diagnoses. The reality is mixed, and several levels of analysis are involved: Role relations intrude on interpersonal relations, social organizations have cultures, and people's motives sometimes make them imperfect role players. Therefore, synthesis must follow after idealization and analysis. I believe that we can make theoretical progress in social psychology by using idealization, but applying and testing propositions in the real world require synthesis as well.

The necessity of synthesis to generate adequate contemporary diagnoses of situations focuses social psychology on a set of theoretical problems that have not been given sufficient attention. These problems have to do with interactions among the several social influence processes. The simultaneous participation of several levels of analysis in a concrete situation implies not only that more than one influence process is operating, but also that they may be qualifying each other's effects. Social psychological theory lacks propositions about their interactions. What general statements can be made, for example, about the conditions under which friendship prevails over duty or inventions are discredited on account of their inventors?

Summary

Figure 2 provides the illustration for reviewing the model of social psychology outlined in chapter 1 and the theoretical strategies discussed in this chapter. Four levels of analysis are depicted, inclusive of what the model takes to be the domain of social psychology. Each of the levels comprises concepts related by definitions and axioms and therefore having dynamics amenable to explanation derived from closed theory.

The figure is drawn to represent that the four levels of analysis in the domain of social psychology are not hierarchical or nested; each has a boundary with the other three. That is, no assumptions are made that one or another facet of the social environment exerts regnant influence, and the influence of one level on another can be direct, without the involvement of any of the others.

The boundaries of focal interest to social psychology are the ones between the person and the three social environments. The mission of social psychology is to explain how influence is exerted across these boundaries,

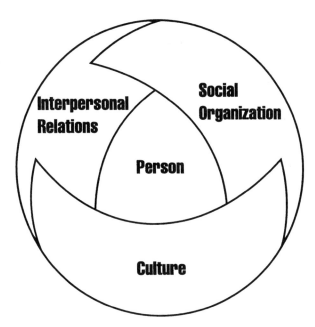

Figure 2. A model for social psychology.

that is, to state the conditions at the boundaries under which change occurs in one or the other. Social psychology is interested in the other boundaries and the dynamics across them insofar as they are the indirect paths
by which the psychological and social levels may influence one another.

The boundaries are zones of interpenetration. Certain properties of
the respective levels of analysis are located there because they have conceptual counterparts across the boundaries. Social psychological propositions assert that changes in these properties of a level of analysis are most
likely to effect change in the adjacent level.

The distinctiveness of each level of analysis generates distinctive influence processes across each boundary. Dual processes of persuasion and
invention operate at the boundary of the person and the culture. Social
organization is said to socialize the person, and the person changes social
organization through institutionalization. People engaged in an interpersonal relation identify with one another.

Social influence is exerted by and on certain properties of each level
of analysis. These properties thus serve as points of tangency with the
others, the prisms that gather the conditions at the boundary and disperse
their influence throughout their respective levels of analysis. These are
the properties in the zones of interpenetration, and, for the purposes of
social psychological theory, the model defines each level in their terms.
Thus, the psychological person is characterized as an entity having motives and resources. Interpersonal relations are composed of identities.
Social organizations are interdependent sets of roles. Cultures are systems
of shared beliefs.

The model is supposed to cover all of social psychology. It does not
cover everything in social psychological texts and journals, and it includes

some things that are not there. So actually it proposes a kind of social psychology, one defined by its specific mission. The rest of this book is intended to demonstrate that the model includes a great deal of what has been traditionally called *social psychology*, places the discipline in an otherwise unfilled niche among the sciences, and makes some integrated sense of it.

Part II

Structure

Introduction

The levels of analysis of the social psychological model are presented in this section, a chapter devoted to each—the person, social organization, interpersonal relations, and culture, in that order. Beginning with the person does not imply a hierarchy of levels, with the person either most or least in control of the social domain. Nor does it imply that the person is the one irreducible source of theoretical principles. The section begins with the psychological level in order to emphasize the focus of social psychology, on the psychological level in relation to the others.

Also for this reason, discussion of the structures of the three levels of the social environment centers about the characteristics they have that are important for their commerce with the person. Other characteristics might merit more attention in discussions of interrelationships within the social environment. Inasmuch as the model purports to encompass the whole of the social, other social sciences might find those discussions useful. They might organize the relationships of sociology, social anthropology (or "culturology"—see chapter 6), and a science of interpersonal relations to one another, as well as to psychology. Less obviously, the model can locate economics, political science, demography, and other disciplines in the social domain. Their foci being different, other disciplines' treatment of the structure would differ from this one. Certainly the dynamic processes of influence posited in the next section would have to be different from the ones the model supposes in its social psychological application.

In each of the next four chapters, I try to refine the meaning of each level of analysis, dwelling heavily for that purpose on their fuzzy boundaries, discussing what's in, what's out, and what is in and out, interpenetrating with the other levels. The interpenetrating terms constitute the levels for the purposes of this model.

In the course of describing the structural elements of the model, I often call attention to their appearance in extant social scientific, especially social psychological literature, for several reasons. First, this acknowledges that the model is built on the efforts of others; indeed, the structure of the model resembles other models proposed by researchers who have tried to integrate social psychology or the social sciences (e.g., Cushman & Craig, 1976; Doise, 1986; Parsons, 1951; Yinger, 1965). Second, it demonstrates that the model covers much more rather than less of social psychology as the discipline is commonly recognized. Third, reference to the extant literature indicates that the model can serve the purpose of organizing theoretical and empirical work in the area by bringing together heretofore isolated interests, making useful distinctions, and revealing heretofore unrecognized relationships. Fourth, and perhaps most important for progress in a science, discussion of extant social psychological theory and findings in the terms of the model points to new avenues for theory and research.

3

The Person

The person is at the core of this model of social psychology. This chapter presents how the social psychological model conceptualizes individuals so that their experience and actions can be explained insofar as they are determined by and influence the social environment. The theoretical strategy is to characterize the person in terms of constructs that serve two functions: to summarize the whole range of psychological processes that generate action and experience, bringing them thus by proxy into the zone of interpenetration with the social environment; and to facilitate translating the influence of the whole range of social influence into psychological terms and vice versa. These psychological constructs thus act in the model as prisms, collecting forces from the psychological and from the social levels and refracting them onto the others. In this chapter, these constructs are defined and their relationships to other psychological concepts and to each other are posited.

Social psychology is concerned with the person as an acting and experiencing entity. The discipline is defined by its interest in actions and experiences insofar as they are influenced by the social environment or influence the social environment. The purview of this social psychology is not limited to "social behavior." Social psychology aims to explain all action and experience insofar as they influence and are influenced by the social environment, even though the acts themselves, like raising fruit flies, may seem nonsocial.

Action and Experience

Action means purposive, goal-oriented behavior. Nonpurposive behavior does not fall within the purview of this model of social psychology because it is not under social influence. Hard-wired reflexes, for example, do not depend on contemporaneous motives and therefore are not under social control. In contrast, conditioned responses fall into the gray area of concern: When the unconditioned or conditioned stimulus is a symbol, purposes may become involved in the establishment of a response; once established, however, the response may no longer serve the person's purposes, and so it is not action. Operant responses, depending always on motives, are actions.

Irresistibly coerced behavior is not action. Consider for example the aversive therapy imposed on the protagonist of Burgess's *A Clockwork Orange* (1963). Social psychology can no more explain Alex's consequent conditioned behavior than it can explain his pain on being shocked. Social psychology should be able to explain coercive action but not the behavior of its targets, who might as well be robots undergoing repair.

Because purpose is a property of the whole person, the model attributes action to the whole person as well. Action is global behavior rather than the behavior of a single neuron, or muscle, or sense organ, or even whole arm or leg. These parts do not have goals. Action then is such behavior as running to catch a bus, speaking to convey a message, and reading for entertainment. A unit of behavior for social psychological purposes is thus delimited by the individual's purposes.

This social psychology is concerned not only with people's actions but also with their experiences of perceiving, knowing, and feeling. Here too, the organizing principle of experience is its meaning in relation to the person's purposes. The social psychological experience of "red," for example, resides not in its place on the physical spectrum but rather because it means "stop," or connotes a political position, or identifies which checkers one may move.

A brief discussion of psychosomatic symptoms helps to delineate the way the model conceptualizes the place of experience in the social psychological model. Individuals' stomach pains are meaningful experiences for them. The proximal cause, excess gastric juices burning into their abdominal wall, is not itself a part of the social environment. People's belief that that is the origin of their pain undoubtedly originates in their social environment. People may be unaware of the social origins of their pain; they may not understand that social conditions activate a chain of psychosocial events that eventuate in the excretion of excess gastric juices. They may attribute their stomach pains only to the influence of the physicochemical environment on their physiochemical, internal environment, to "something I ate." An adequate contemporary diagnosis consistent with the model would recognize the psychological aspects of the situation in terms of a person's own attributions; and that might lead to the prediction that, motivated to escape the pain and with the cultural resources at his or her command, a sufferer will take an antacid. Under the circumstances, medical technology seems to be the only social influence operative, so only it figures in a social psychological explanation. A social psychological diagnosis could proceed further, however, to develop a hypothesis that takes into account the objective social origins of the stomach pain. One might assess the probability that, antacids proving ultimately ineffective in treating an ulcer, the motive for action remains, leading perhaps to a change in the causal attribution. Under these psychological conditions, one might predict that the person will attempt a more effective psychosocial intervention. Thus, experience, as a percept, a belief, or an emotion can be a consequence of social influence.

Social psychology is interested not only in individuals' actions and experiences that are under the influence of the social environment but also in individuals' influence on the social environment, whether that was the person's purpose or not. Charles Darwin, for example, did not intend the profound social changes initiated by his discovery and announcement of natural selection as the mechanism of biological evolution, but he had that effect. When social psychology aims to explain social change insofar as it originates at the psychological level of analysis, the individual's purposes may be unintended, but that is irrelevant. This social psychology is interested in the person as shaper, even as unintentional shaper, as well as one who is shaped.

Thus, the person at the focus of social psychology is an entity capable of action and experience under the influence of and with the potential to influence the social environment. There is more to the concrete individual who is so capable and has such potential, of course, so social psychology does not encompass all of psychology. Humans are also biological organisms with reflexes and instincts that make our eyes blink and sweat pour from our brows; that enable us to read emotions in each others' faces and make us shy away from the edges of cliffs. We are subject to entropy, and our behavior is contingent to a significant degree on renewing our energy and excreting our wastes. As my colleague Carol Slater once remarked to me in this connection, "We fall off cliffs obedient to gravitation's laws." These capabilities and others are inherent in the human, but they are not at the focus of that conceptual person of concern to this social psychology.

Social psychology treats many of humankind's various properties as though they were in a black box. It does not question how individuals' psychological states are affected by their biology but is instead content to take their consequent psychological condition as a given in the condition of their motives and resources. Naturally, what is regarded as given must be plausible in light of what is known about human psychophysiology, perception, cognition, natural selection, and so on, and any inconsistency presents a critical theoretical problem; but it is not social psychology's problem. The biological human is not identified as a level of analysis in the domain of the proposed model as it is (for example) in Parsons's (1951, 1964) and in Floyd Allport's (1924) models. Rather, social psychology uses psychological concepts that incorporate biological effects on humans in order to take their psychological consequences into account in explanations of the reciprocal influence of individuals and their social environments.

Person as Life Space: Regions and Forces

This introduction to the person as the psychological level of analysis can perhaps best be organized with the metatheoretical tools of Kurt Lewin's field theory. Particularly useful is the idea of *life space* (K. Lewin, 1936), with which the conceptualization of this level of analysis is interchangeable. The exclusively psychological nature of the person is reflected first in the phenomenological character of the life space. It is phenomenological inasmuch as it comprises entities known to the person, whether consciously or unconsciously. There is a tautology here, appropriate to the conceptually primitive nature of the term: An object or event can be considered a component of a person's life space if it can be shown to have some effect on the person; and the life space comprises the totality of those objects and events that at a moment in time are having effects on the person. So when a symbol is presented tachistoscopically to people for so brief a moment that they cannot report its presence, but it nonetheless evokes a differential galvanic skin response from them, that subliminal symbol may legitimately be located in those individuals' life space. A product of people's imagination, like a hallucination, must similarly be accorded a place in their life space.

The psychological nature of the level of analysis is also reflected in the way nonpsychological factors are treated. Such factors are located in the "foreign hull," outside of the life space. For their effects to be considered, they have to be imported by translation into the field-theoretical terms of *regions* and *forces*. These translations are not necessarily isomorphic with the nature of the physical, physiological, or social factors in the foreign hull; translation is shaped also by the internal dynamics of the life space. Because social psychology aims to understand the processes by which social factors are translated, its interest in the physical and physiological factors is confined to their psychological translations, and their objective forms remain in a black box out in the foreign hull. The social environment, however, is an object for close social psychological analysis.

The purposiveness of the individual is reflected in the structure and dynamics of the life space. These consist of "goal regions," "path regions," and "forces." *Regions* represent states of being. Some of these states of being are positively or negatively valenced, that is, the person desires them or wishes to avoid them. These are called *goal regions*. For every valence associated with one of these goal regions, there is a "force" acting on the person, impelling him or her to act to remain in or to attain that state, or to escape or avoid that region. Other regions are neither attractive nor aversive in themselves but represent states of being instrumental to attaining or avoiding goal regions. These are *path regions*, means to an end. The valences and forces associated with a goal also impel a person toward the path regions leading to that goal; so path regions derive their force partly from the goals to which they are paths. Furthermore, path regions possess forces acting at their boundary, always more or less barring entrance to their path region; these forces do not act on the person unless the person is at the boundary. These forces represent the reality that paths are more or less accessible, means are more or less available to the person. The strength of the forces at the boundary of a path region are calibrated to the accessibility of the region to the person.

The location of regions and the directions of forces associated with them are thus all oriented to the person's purposes. Some examples: The certainty with which a person regards a particular state of being as a means to a goal is reflected in the distance of that path region from the goal region—the more certain, the more nearly adjacent the path region to the goal region, with the greatest certainty represented by a common path–goal boundary. Necessary means to a goal is represented by a path region that surrounds the goal region; the person does not conceive of getting there any other way. Goals believed to be mutually supportive are so positioned in the life space that their associated forces all point in the same direction; conversely, incompatible goals lie in directions opposite in the sense that forces impelling the person toward one will impel him or her away from the other.

A concrete example: A person may believe that forming a tenants' organization may enable him and other residents to gain some control over living conditions in graduate student housing. The activity of forming the organization is therefore represented as a region on a path leading from where the person is to the goal of gaining resident control. The activity is attractive, not so much in itself, but because of the goal to which it leads, and it derives as much attraction from its goal as the certainty with which the person believes it will accomplish its purpose. As a path, it is accessible to the degree that the person believes it can be done. At the same time, there is a region in the life space, to be avoided, that represents incurring the displeasure of the university's housing office; this region is so certainly associated with forming a tenants' organization that its forces invariably oppose the forces impelling the activity. Thus, the life space is organized around the person's purposes.

From time to time in the course of this book, it will be helpful to return to the concept of the life space and other features of K. Lewin's field theory. The general field-theoretical principles posited to govern regions and forces provide insights, through the theoretical strategy of a metalanguage, into the social psychology of individuals. At this point, it suffices to state that the two psychological concepts that constitute the psychological level of analysis in the social psychological model can be conceptualized in life space terms of regions and forces.

Prismatic Concepts: Motive and Resource

The two concepts of motive and resource are but a small selection from the vast vocabulary of psychology. There are large dictionaries of terms in learning theory, cognitive theory, psychoanalytic theory, and so on. The image of the prism may help to clarify use of such a sparse set of terms at the psychological level of analysis. Constructed to discipline and manage the difficult task of translating social phenomena into psychological terms and vice versa, the model makes do with as few of these terms as possible. Behind them lie all the conceptual armamentaria of psychology; the two prismatic concepts are intended to capture the psychological phenomena to which other terms refer and carry them into conceptual contact with the social environment. To use a large set of terms would make the theoretical operation both too easy and too difficult: too easy, because there would always be many terms available with which to effect a conceptual translation, relieving the theorist of the necessity for thinking very hard about how the social environment and the individual interact; too difficult because the terms would overlap and the nature of the translation would become obscure.

Motive

The need for a motivational concept in psychology is to account for main-tenance or change in the goal-orientation of action. When a person takes some action, like forming a tenants' union, and derives some satisfaction from doing so, then the law of effect would predict that the person would form still another tenants' union and another and another. People seldom act that way, however; they reach a point where what was once reinforcing no longer is so. Learning theorists say that the actor's needs are satisfied, that the person is satiated. Thus is invoked the concept of drive or motive. The social psychological model does not therefore invoke motive to account for people behaving at all; that is, the concept does not refer to an ener-gizer. It accounts rather for why individuals do or do not change their actions.

To assert that individuals act in particular ways because they have been reinforced in the past for that action implies some more or less en-during residue of the experience, a memory. Following McClelland (1951, 1965) and Atkinson and Birch (1970, 1978), the model characterizes this memory as an anticipation. The relevant residue of an experience is the individual's remembering that a certain way of acting has yielded pleasure or pain. Sufficient matching of this memory by recurring experience gives rise to an anticipation of pleasure or pain under similar conditions. This anticipation is the motive itself. In the case of anticipating pleasure, it is an approach motive; of pain, an avoidance motive. So when a person no longer anticipates pleasure or pain, the motive has dissipated. After hav-ing formed an effective union, the thought of forming still another may no longer anticipate any pleasure.

Obviously, motives in this sense are learned. They may all be rooted in unlearned needs like hunger or thirst, and the processes by which in-dividuals become motivated may involve not only learning but also per-ception, cognition, and so forth. However, it is the necessity of their being learned and the function of the social environment in the learning process that make motives of central interest to social psychology. That motives are learned is one of their crucial characteristics, because it is partly through shaping and maintaining motives that the social environment in-fluences the individual. Much of the pleasure and pain that individuals experience and learn to anticipate originate in their interaction with their social environments. The motives thereby engendered direct them toward one goal or another and cause them to persist in doing something or to stop doing it and start doing something else.

The strength of a motive is the amount of pleasure or pain anticipated in its attainment. In Lewin's field-theoretical terms, this is represented as the valence of the goal region: the greater the valence, the stronger the force impelling the person toward it. Valence is also called the *incentive value* of the goal. The term *incentive* is important here because it figures in the Incentive × Expectancy theory of action (Atkinson, 1957), to be discussed shortly.

Thus, our concern with motives focuses on the incentive values of anticipated goals and on the forces to take action which are generated by them. Motives are aroused when goals are not gained or their possession is threatened. They are aroused to the degree that their incentive value is great.

Motives are often manifested in appropriate action, but not always. Sometimes the situation does not permit relevant action. This point can be clarified with further consideration of the Incentive × Expectancy conceptualization of motivation. According to this approach, action is determined not only by the incentive value of the goal but also by the actor's estimate of the probability that a particular action will gain the incentive. *Expectancy* refers to the individual's estimate of the efficacy of action. If the chances of success are quite small, then the individual is less likely to act, however strong the incentive, as the multiplicative axiom implies. When small expectations discourage acting on a motive, then the strength of the motive may be invested in other action or found in the depth of the individual's frustration and anger. It is important to recognize that motives thus blocked nevertheless affect action and experience.

Small expectation of success is not the only factor that may inhibit goal-directed action. Other, conflicting motives may be active. Sometimes individuals find themselves in situations where they can act quite confident of their effectiveness but also feel fairly certain that their actions will have undesired consequences as well. Some other equally valenced goal may necessarily be denied. The incentive of the original goal may remain high and the expectancy of success undiminished, but people will not take apparently appropriate action. People usually feel badly in such situations, and they may take some other action, seemingly unrelated to the original goal, in order to feel better.

Resource, Including Skill

Expectancies are determined by resources. Resources in general are not identified as a property of individuals in the social psychological literature, although one instance, intelligence and its ethnic and class correlates, appears fairly frequently in the literature. Neglect of resources is unfortunate. A lot of the influence of the social environment on individuals is effected by the transmission of resources, and the influence of individuals on their social environments depends heavily on their resources.

A *resource*, defined here in terms of its function in relation to motives, is anything that an individual controls that will enable him or her to attain a goal. An individual is said to control a resource to the degree that he or she may determine its use. Resources may be material, such as money; social, such as popularity or authority; or psychological, such as knowledge or skills. Individuals may achieve resources by their own efforts, or they may be given resources. Most resources are acquired by a mixture of achievement and ascription. A college degree, for example, is an important resource in American society that is partly achieved through scholastic effort and skills and often partly attained through ascription of financial support.

Consistent with the phenomenological nature of the psychological level of analysis, resources exist at this level only in the minds of individuals. They are represented in life space terms by path regions. Their inclusion in an adequate contemporary diagnosis of the situation—in a depiction of the person's life space—depends on some demonstration that the individual is aware of them.

Consistent with the model's recognition of environments outside of individuals' ken is the idea of potential resources, resources that may enter the person's awareness. Their availability depends on individuals' awareness of them, like the discovery of a heretofore latent personal talent; or their availability may require that some action is taken to put them under the individuals' control. The social psychological processes by which potential resources become resources that a person can use are the same ones that govern the translation of other environmental conditions into psychological ones.

Whether individuals can attain their goals depends usually on the resources they can marshall toward those ends. Sometimes the necessary resources are easily come by, sometimes not; the forces at their boundaries may be weak or strong. When requisite resources are scarce, then their differential allocation among individuals is an important determinant of individual differences in goal attainment, feelings of satisfaction, and a sense of efficacy.

Sometimes, however, people are given what they want, entirely without employment of their own resources. It is noteworthy that such a situation is in some respects formally identical, in life space terms, to the coercive conditioning discussed earlier, although the emotions aroused are obviously very different. As in the case of coercion, social psychological principles cannot explain how receivers have attained their goal by considering their life space, because the receiver has not acted. A social psychological explanation in this case considers the life space of the giver, assessing that person's motives and resources.

Further discussion of resources dwells mainly on skills because their neglect in social psychology seems most unwarranted. Whereas I do not want to minimize the importance of resources ascribed through the fortunes of birth—into a particular family, a higher social class, a dominant race, a favored gender—our modern culture places an enormous value on skills. Disadvantaged status at birth can often be overcome, frequently through the acquisition and application of skills.

One way that the social environment affects individuals is by selecting out of the range of their capacities only certain ones for development as skills. There is the story of the just deceased Napoleon Bonaparte announcing before the Pearly Gates that, "The world's greatest general has arrived!" (speaking French, of course, which is an example of skill selection in itself). St. Peter replied, "The world's greatest general is already here" and pointed to a modest angel just inside the gate. "But," Napoleon protested, "that man was my tailor!" "Yes," St. Peter said, "but had he been a general . . ."

A *skill* is the ability to manipulate symbols and objects in desired ways. Included among skills are the motoric and the intellectual, carpentry and reasoning. The ego defenses identified in psychoanalytic theory—denial, projection, and so on—are also skills.

When individuals consider a course of action, their assessment of their resources determines their expectations of their efficacy. Whether these assessments are accurate or inaccurate, they are determining factors. According to the Incentive × Expectancy hypothesis, people who believe that their level of skills makes their chances of success sufficiently high will take the action they deem appropriate. The consequent experience may disconfirm their assessment, they may reassess their resources, and they may consequently change their view of the odds of success and quit trying. On the other hand, and for various defensive reasons, failure may cause individuals to deny the reality: They may insist that their skills are adequate but that a temporary condition prevented success, and so they try again.

To illustrate how social psychology can make use of the concept of resource: It is with the concept of skills as resources that social psychology takes into account individuals' cognitive development as Piaget (1928) conceptualized it. There seems to be a fixed sequence to the acquisition of capacities to deal cognitively with concrete realities and with symbols that cannot be altered readily by experience; still, there is evidence that experience with the social environment can affect the pace of cognitive development and the level of development ultimately attained. For example, exposure to the typical curriculum of an industrialized society's school system tends to accelerate and make more likely the achievement of concrete operations as late as adolescence (Douglas & Wong, 1977; Heron & Simonsson, 1969), and certain kinds of interaction with a mentor can hasten someone's grasp of formal operations (Danner & Day, 1977). The inherent sequential aspects of cognitive development are not of immediate interest to social psychology; its focus is on the consequent cognitive skills, insofar as they are shaped by social experience and are capacities that empower the individual to influence the social environment. The limits and opportunities presented by the sequential character of cognitive development are taken as givens and are included in an adequate contemporary diagnosis of the situation as characteristics of the resource. The developmental factor is represented in the life space as a force more or less resistant at a point in time to the person's progress toward acquiring cognitive skills.

Detection of children's mastery of a certain level of cognitive skill through testing is not sufficient to assume that, psychologically, the children possess it. Absent evidence that children are aware of their level of skill, such as their confident attempt of a cognitive task, the skill is not a resource that figures in the children's action. It is not part of their life space and cannot explain anything the children do. Propositions such as action being a function of Incentive × Expectancy do not apply. The children's skill may nevertheless help to explain the effect they have on their social environment as their teachers take it into account in placing the children in appropriate classes. In this case, the effect is functionally equivalent to a person's actions having an unintended social consequence. Whereas the skill does not help to determine the children's action, it figures in explaining what happens at the environmental levels.

Cognitive skill affects experience as well as action. For example, children's inability to solve a problem when they want to makes them feel frustrated. Solving the problem with the necessary skill can be a source of pleasure and high self-regard. In general, field theory regards emotional experience as a function of the pattern of forces in the life space. Frustration, anger, love, sorrow, and so on are aroused by people's location in relation to their goals and the means to reach them.

Resources are of course means by which individuals purposefully influence their environments, and social psychology is especially interested in individuals' influence on their social environments. Almost all individuals are part of the social environment of other individuals and may influence others through their direct and indirect interactions with them. The social significance of cognitive resources, for example, is apparent in Kohlberg's work (1981, 1984) on the relationship of cognitive skills to individuals' resolutions of moral dilemmas and in Adelson and his associates' findings (Adelson, Green, & O'Neil, 1969; Gallatin & Adelson, 1971) about how children and adolescents think about law and social policy. In both of these lines of research, it has been found that more skilled individuals consider more facets of the situation, recognize more complex relationships among factors, and entertain more conditional solutions to social problems. These capabilities enable their owners to deal with social problems differently than those without such skills. In general, how much influence one exert depends on the resources one has. Some few individuals wield broad influence over their social environments because their abilities have helped them to achieve powerful positions. Even fewer individuals make enduring changes in the social environment because of the timely interaction of their skills with social conditions ripe for lasting change.

Thus, according to the present model, social psychology accounts for the individual in his or her reciprocal relationship with the social environment with the terms *motive* and *resource*. Together they depict an individual who sets goals and strives to achieve them with the material, cognitive, and other resources at his or her command. The person's emotions emerge from the pattern of the person's motives and resources. Both psychological properties must be taken into account in an adequate contemporary diagnosis that is intended to explain the individual's action and experience.

Accounting for the Rest of Psychology: Three Examples

A myriad of psychological processes operate in the formation and maintenance of motives and resources. The model assumes that all of psychology lies behind these two prismatic concepts. Only these two are used, however, to effect the translation between social and psychological phenomena. I admit that I have sometimes found that it takes some conceptual scurrying to make translations into just these two concepts. However, the relationships of motives and resources to three psychological concepts commonly used by contemporary social psychologists are reasonably obvious.

Attitude

Attitudes are commonly defined as individuals' evaluations of objects. It is understood that these "objects" are psychological representations of objects in the environment and may include processes as well as things. Evaluations are ordinarily arrayed on a scale from positive to negative. Attitude has been deemed an important concept in social psychology (G. W. Allport, 1954; Crano, 1989), although the relationship of attitudes to behavior is highly variable, depending on situational and other personal conditions (Kraus, 1995).

Their explanatory power improves when attitudes are cast as actions tied to specific contemporaneous goals. Ajzen and Fishbein (Ajzen, 1987; Kraus, 1995) have developed a model of attitudes that links them thus to a person's intentions. When one takes into account whether people look favorably or unfavorably on doing something specific with or about the object of an attitude, then the attitude's predictiveness is markedly increased. That is, the person's attitude toward the action understandably predicts whether the person takes it. Apparently, attitudes unconnected to any contemporaneous purpose are potentialities so vulnerable to qualification by the situation at the moment when they become salient that they themselves account for little.

In terms of the model, attitudes as evaluations of objects constitute latent resources. Holding an attitude is a state of being, a region in a person's life space, but, as is the character of resources, the region has no intrinsic valence. Thus, until the motives to which they are salient become aroused, attitudes have no directive force. When relevant motives are aroused, then related attitude objects are charged. More precisely, what to do with or about the object (i.e., an intention) forms, and its goal endows it with some valence as a path. At the same time, the path is also subject to augmenting or opposing valences of other contemporaneous goals to which people may believe it related, thus perhaps blocking or otherwise qualifying the action the person takes. Moreover, at salient moments, actors in the person's social environment may be prompted to exert more active influence, injecting still other forces into the person's life space. Whereas the simple attitude had no context, the intention is located in a pattern of forces that the person can assess in deciding what to do.

The model recognizes that the social environment often plays a central role in creating and maintaining attitudes as resources. Beliefs about the nature of attitude objects and how they may serve or oppose the person's purposes often originate in the person's social environment, the more so when the person has little direct experience with the object. The social environment also charges up attitudes by arousing the motives to which they are related. When the action taken has some significant effect on the person's social environment, the person's attitudes, originating to some degree in the social environment and translated into an active resource, help to explain the person's influence.

Personality

The idea of "personality" has been regarded as so important to social psychology that several journals are dedicated to reporting studies in both fields. Nevertheless, as far as I know the reason for its special significance has not been made clear. The model offers a reason.

Assume that *personality* means the organization of enduring characteristics of a person. *Enduring* is the operative word here. Included among the characteristics of people are their motives and resources. According to the proposed model of social psychology, an explanation of the reciprocal influence of people and their social environment requires that people's contemporaneous motives and resources be taken into account. Accurate assessments of people's personality thus identify motives and resources that they bring to the contemporaneous situation. Furthermore, their stable character implies that these motives are most heavily valenced, along with their related resources. The idea of *personality* is therefore extremely useful to social psychology for making the adequate contemporary diagnoses that explain people's actions and experiences either as influenced by or as influencing the social environment.

A controversy once raged in psychology about whether the concept of personality represented anything in the real world (e.g., Bem & Allen, 1974; Block, 1977; Mischel, 1968). Do people have enduring psychological characteristics? Do they consistently bring certain motives and resources to their encounters with the social environment? Or are people's behavior and experience wholly subject to contemporaneous forces impinging on them from their several environments, including the social? This controversy has now abated, as many of these do, with the contestants agreeing that "it depends." The model suggests how social psychology might contribute to discovering on what personality depends.

A heuristic approach to this issue starts with the assumption that people differ with respect to whether they have personalities. Personality may be taken to be a variable. Some people may have more stable characteristics than others, characteristics whose influence is evidenced across time and across many very different situations; and some people may have less. Under this assumption, the fundamental problem in the study of personality is to identify the conditions under which characteristics become stable. The major questions this approach raises for social psychology are, What if any of these stabilizing conditions are social? and What effect does the enduringness of a person's motives and resources have on the person's social influence? I return to these questions when I discuss the idea of identity in the chapter on interpersonal relations (chapter 5).

Self

Elsewhere, I have expressed my unease when contemplating the idea of "self": "Thinking about the *self* makes me feel queasy. It is like standing between two facing mirrors, my reflection reflected, and reflected again, in infinite regress. Who is thinking about the self? Myself? Who just thought about who is thinking about the self? Who . . . . ? And so on . . . " (Gold, 1994, p. 89). However ambiguous the concept, "self" is ubiquitous in contemporary social psychological theory and research, so the adequacy of the model's coverage of the discipline is tested by whether it accommodates the idea.

It seems to me one can make social psychological sense out of "self" by emphasizing its agentic character. In the article that I just quoted, I defined *self* as "that which responds exclusively to one's will" (p. 90). This relates "self" to the psychological concepts of the model by implying that one's self is the organization of a subset of one's resources. Resources are, by definition, whatever enables persons to attain their goals. A subset of resources are those exclusively under the control of the person who possesses them. Not all resources are: For example, most of us fully control our leg muscles, but people suffering from multiple sclerosis cannot reliably will them to move; and one may hold one's own bank account or it may be held jointly with another.

Surely not all exclusively controlled resources define the self. Only some form the core of one's self-definition, and the idea of the self as agent suggests which resources those are: those associated with the person's most heavily valenced goals. That is, people's conceptions of who they are may consist of those characteristics that enable them to fulfill their most eager purposes. We feel we are what empowers us to do what we most want to do.

The idea of the self as agent sharpens the meanings of *self-concept* and *self-esteem*. *Self-concept* takes on the meaning of one's description of one's own resources, particularly with respect to their efficacy and their locus of control. This then suggests that a poor self-concept is more precisely a "diminished self-concept," one poor in needed resources under one's exclusive control. *Self-esteem* is the global assessment one makes of the degree to which one controls important resources.

Common observation challenges the idea of the self as synonymous with one's resources in at least two instances, but these challenges can at least be reasonably engaged. One is that people frequently present themselves in terms of their goals rather than their resources. They feel that they are their values. In these instances, their self-defining goals may take on the cast of resources, means to ends such as social approval or to define their role in social interaction. The other instance is that people often describe themselves as members of a category, such as "male" or "lower class," which on first thought are not resources. However, both descriptions may actually refer to resources exclusively under the persons' control. Being male may mean taking for granted the privileges that define male as a social role, as, for example, control over the household bank account. Describing oneself as "lower class" may be an acknowledgment of a diminished self.

This discussion of three psychological terms frequently used in social psychology is meant to illustrate the prismatic function that the concepts of *motive* and *resource* perform in the social psychological model. They are related by psychological theory to all the other psychological concepts with which social psychology needs to deal. *Motive* and *resource* are intended to account for the psychological givens and variations as they enter the person's encounter with the social environment.

Beyond the Person

Outside of the individual's life space are objects or events that at any moment may or may not have psychological significance. They are treated as the foreign hull or boundary condition. Those that most probably have psychological import are conceived to be closest to the boundary of the individual's psyche. One function of social psychology is to identify and to order (in terms of the probability of their effects) the objects and events in the social environment that cross the boundary, there affecting the individual's behavior and experience. Furthermore, the model set forth here requires that the crossing of the social psychological boundary be conceptualized on its psychological side solely in terms of the effects on the individual's motives and resources and their interrelationships.

The processes by which social factors become psychological factors and vice versa depend on the nature of the social environment as well as the psychological individual. The social comprises three environments, and their boundaries with the individual are crossed by different means, different processes of social influence. The nature of each of the three social environments is described in the next three chapters, followed by a discussion of the processes of social influence.

4

Social Organization

The first paragraph of chapter 1 announces that my purpose is "to order the materials of social psychology so that beginning at one point rather than another makes some sense." I should now confess that the decision to discuss social organization first among the social environments is theoretically arbitrary. Placing it first does not imply that social organization is more basic or more pervasive in its influence on the individual than the other environments. That may or may not be so, depending on conditions.

I take up social organization next for a didactic rather than a theoretical reason. Subsequent discussion of the interpersonal and cultural levels of the social environment profits from comparisons with the social organizational level. For one thing, the way social organization is conceived within the model is probably more familiar to most readers than the ways interpersonal relations and culture are conceptualized. As used here, it follows the current mainstream of social organizational theory quite closely, whereas there is currently no discernible mainstream to the study of interpersonal relations or culture. The concrete phenomena of interpersonal relations and culture are familiar enough, but this approach to them from a social psychological perspective is likely to be unfamiliar and so better follows the more familiar. Second, I hope the juxtaposition of the familiar central structural concept in social organizational theory, social role, with the main concepts of the other social levels clarifies the discussions of the others.

The main theme of this chapter is that not only is social organization a phenomenon amenable and worthy of scientific study in its own right, but it also is an essential component of the social environment with which social psychology must be concerned. The chapter begins by marshalling the support of the preeminent source of the idea of social organization, Emile Durkheim, recalling his justification for carving out a science of sociology. Then I contrast the sociological and social psychological uses of the idea of social organization with a comparison of the disciplines' markedly different psychological givens. Next, the nature of social organization is described in a way that hews closely to the sociological assumption of individual conformity but is nevertheless useful to social psychology; the emphasis here is on how objective roles and their organization differ along dimensions that affect their influence on persons. The discussion shifts its base at this point toward the social psychological assumption of individual differences by contrasting formal and informal social organization and invoking the idea of personal role definition. Finally, the importance of this level of analysis to social psychology is underscored with examples of its ubiquity in social psychological research, including a characterization of many social psychological experiments as social organizations.

Durkheim: The Reality of the Social Order

The utility of social organization as an explanatory construct was asserted by Emile Durkheim in the 19th century (1894/1950; 1897/1951). I cannot do more in the compass of this work than to acknowledge my debt to Durkheim and to recall three of his basic contributions that are particularly relevant to social psychology. First, Durkheim advanced a social psychological proposition, namely, that the moral order of collectivities exerts enormous influence over individuals. What individuals want, what they believe is true and good, and their capacities for action, Durkheim argued, are consequences of experiences with or interpreted by the social order. It has the power to shape individual beliefs and values. "Sentiments created and developed in the group have a greater energy than purely individual sentiments" (1924/1972, p. 228). The effects of the social order on the person are considered later, in our discussion of the dynamics of social psychology. Second, Durkheim made the distinction between the collective term *norm* and its psychological counterpart *social representation*, thus pointing out the need for mechanisms of translation from the sociological to the psychological. Third, Durkheim conceived of the social order not as relations among individuals but rather as an impersonal, consensual force. Sometimes its moral legitimacy is ascribed to a god or gods, sometimes to custom, sometimes to social contract, but always it is actually a product of collective life.

   Of immediate concern in this chapter is Durkheim's sociological proposition, his insistence on regarding the social order as a reality in nature whose existence and forms demand explanation as much as the acceleration of a falling object or an act of suicide. "[Society] is not a mere sum of individuals," Durkheim wrote (1901/1982, p. 129). Rather, the systems formed by human association are entities governed by their own principles. Of course, nothing collective can be produced if individual mentality does not participate, but this necessary condition is insufficient by itself. Mental process must be combined in a certain way.

> Social life results from this combination and is, consequently, explained by it. Individual minds, forming groups by mingling and fusing, give birth to a being, psychological if you will, but constituting a psychic individuality of a new sort. It is, then, in the nature of this collective individuality, not in that of the associated units, that we must seek the immediate and determining causes of the facts appearing therein. (1901/1982, p. 129).

   In terms of theoretical strategies, Durkheim asserted the possibility of closed theory at the social organizational level of analysis. The moral or social order can in theory be modeled by a system of definitions and axioms, leading logically to principles about interrelationships among the parts of the social order that are mirrored in the empirical world. From this perspective, individuals are regarded for most purposes as constants, with given properties that permit the social order to exist and function.

The Psychological Given

Faced with the fact of individual differences, social organizational theory and concrete social organizations incorporate mechanisms of social control whose object is to eliminate the differences by obtaining conformity. As "the father of scientific management," F. W. Taylor advised, "Under scientific management initiative . . . control is obtained with absolute uniformity. This is the job of management to establish rules, laws, formulas, to define the tasks to be performed and the means to be used in doing the work" (quoted in Czander, 1993, p. 107). Closed theory necessarily assumes what practice seldom achieves. It deals with ideal types. Thus, the social organizational component of the social environment theoretically excludes the psychological.

Social organizational theory takes as a given that humans can be induced to act as we are supposed to: that we can become aware of the social norms governing our actions and experience; that we have the capacity to obey the norms that apply to us; and that we are motivated to do so. Furthermore, inasmuch as the social order governs people, whatever behavioral consistency individuals may show over time resides not in their psychology but rather in the sameness of the norms that apply from one instance to another. In this way, social organizational theory uses the construct of *role* as psychological theory invokes the construct of *personality*, to account for the consistency of behavior and experience.

Social psychological theory, on the other hand, does not take conformity as a constant but as a variable to be explained. It assumes that individual psychological differences interact with variation in the social order to generate varied effects. To facilitate explanation, I integrate organizational and psychological theory with the help of metatheoretical strategy. As Krebs and Miller (1985) have noted, "There is a certain parallel between the construct of norm and the construct of trait. Both constructs may be used to describe patterns of behavior and both tend to be invoked to explain the regularities they describe" (p. 30). That the concepts of norm and personality serve the same function at their respective levels of analysis locates them in the zone of interpenetration between the two levels.

The Nature of Social Organization

Social organization is defined here as a system of social roles. *Role* is defined by social norms.

Norm and other basic concepts at the social organizational level of analysis were presented previously, in the discussion of the Homans–Blau debate on psychological reductionism. To recapitulate briefly: A role consists of a set of obligations and privileges that apply to incumbents of social positions. The obligations and privileges are the social norms. They are characterized by moral imperatives. The *obligations* are acts that individuals in a position must perform, and the *privileges* are acts that the incumbent is permitted to perform. Obligations and privileges are not confined to acts, however; they often include the motives and resources that underlie action. So it is not enough for clergy to worship God; they should feel worshipful as well or else they are considered hypocritical, and they must know how to perform the rituals of worship.

Obligations are imposed and privileges granted by social consensus. A norm is social because it is shared by two or more individuals in the sense that the individuals agree and know that they agree that someone—anyone—in a particular social position ought to act in and feel a certain way. None of the parties to the agreement need be incumbents of the role; their agreement brings the role into existence even though it may be unoccupied. Therefore, two people can create a social organization, and if they are incumbents of the roles they have agreed on, the two realize the social organization.

An important distinction should be noted: Not all social values are social norms, pertaining to particular roles. Norms vary in their generality. Some transcend roles, applying to broad categories of people, perhaps to everyone. The Ten Commandments are of this kind. To the degree that they have broad application, "shalls" and "shall nots" are called *values* in this model and are considered the stuff of culture. The norms that are the stuff of social roles apply more specifically, to people who occupy the relevant social positions. When Schwartz (1994) defines *values* as "desirable transituational goals" (p. 21), the model takes *transituational* to mean transcending specific roles and social organizations. Surely, there is here too a fuzzy boundary; thus, the close affinity of the concepts of norm and value identify the pair as a locus of interpenetration of the social organizational and cultural levels of analysis.

A relationship ideally typifies a social organization when all the behaviors and feelings of the parties are regulated by social norms. Recall here the theoretical strategy of idealization: It defines a condition in its purest form even though that condition may rarely if ever occur in nature. Pure role relationships, ones that have no interpersonal or cultural elements, may indeed be rare even while the idea of such relationships is theoretically useful. In the ideal typical role relationship, action and experience are attributed to the role. Personal commitment to roles varies, but that is another matter. Individuals are constants at the social organization level of analysis, all having merely the same requisite properties to enact the roles. Social organizations may be characterized by their affective prescriptions. Bureaucracies, for example, are affectively neutral (Parsons, 1951). ("Now, don't take this personally, I'm only doing my job.") This is not to minimize the potential of prescribed affect; for on such grounds people die out of loyalty, or kill. It is only to say that the affect goes with the role, not with the person.

To characterize a role relationship as normatively regulated places it in sharp contrast to the interpersonal relation defined earlier and to be discussed more fully later. Recall that the ideal typical interpersonal relation is normless. The affect that flows between the parties to the relationship are not prescribed but emerge from the encounter of their identities. Of course, the roles the parties occupy may affect their interpersonal relation, just as their individuality does, and their culture. However, the parties to an ideal interpersonal relation are not socially constrained, and the parties to an ideal role relationship are, completely. Thus, social organization and interpersonal relations lie on a bipolar dimension (Tajfel, 1974). In reality, social relationships are rarely found at either pole.

Some familiar role relationships come quite close to the ideal typical, however. Vendors of subway tokens were mentioned earlier. The encounters of bank tellers with customers are almost never anything but role regulated, including a prescription for pleasantness. The nature of their tasks does not require that tellers take individual differences into account, neither their own nor their customers'. Indeed, because they are dealing with money, about which there are very strict norms, tellers must ignore individual differences. Their actions in the encounter are for the most part so routinized, and therefore so predictable, that they can and have been programmed for automatic teller machines. Then the encounter ceases to be social, which reveals that some ideal typical role relationships may be just barely social—may come close to ignoring the peculiarly human capacities of the parties—when the roles hardly require what only humans can do.

These are the roles that have been called dehumanizing because their incumbents and their counterparts recognize that there is nothing particularly human in their enactment. One of the consequences of progress in technology is that such roles may disappear, their functions being taken over by computers and computer-directed robots. It was the insight of Kapek, who invented the term *robot* for his play "R.U.R." (1923), that if tasks require human levels of skills, then the entities designed with these skills might also develop other human attributes as well. This idea is personified by HAL, the space ship's computer in the Kubrick and Clarke film "2001: A Space Odyssey" (1968) and by the "replicants" in the film "The Blade Runner" (Fancher & Peoples, 1982).

As humans enact roles, even a highly regulated role relationship may depart further and further from the ideal type. It may become more interpersonal. This happens sometimes when one or another of the role takers does not have the skills necessary to enact the role. For example, when a small child nervously approaches the bank teller's window to make a Christmas Club deposit, the normal teller–customer role relationship may break down noticeably, and not just on account of an infusion of another, adult–child role relationship. The teller anticipates that the routine may not hold and becomes alert to idiosyncracy. In the process, the teller starts to play it by ear instead of by the book, the teller's behavior takes on some personal style, and personal affect creeps in.

Dimensions of Objective Roles

Structural

What is it about social roles that influence and are influenced by individuals? In our social psychological model, objective social organizations—sets of interdependent, consensual roles—occupy a boundary position relative to the individual's phenomenal world. Those organizations closest to the person—most likely to become part of the person's life space—are the ones in which the person is expected to participate as a role taker. Others' roles and other organizations affect the individual indirectly, perhaps without his or her awareness of them, as some obscure roles deep in the structures of large corporations may affect us all. It is one function of social psychology to understand what features of roles determine the likelihood of their psychological translation, the form they take as personal role definitions (Yinger, 1965), how they affect the individual, and how individuals may affect them. This task requires that variable dimensions of roles be specified.

It is worthwhile to distinguish two kinds of dimensions of roles, the structural and the substantive, because the two function differently in social psychological theory about the reciprocal effects of roles and persons. The structural dimensions of roles are more determinative of how influential the roles are; and to the degree the roles are influential, their substantive dimensions describe the consequent location in their life space of individuals' motives and resources. Furthermore, formal theory can be built only with respect to the structural dimensions; assertions about the substance of roles can be descriptive only. Social psychological propositions about social organization are thus of the form: To the degree that a role is so structured, it influences the person's motives−resources to conform to its norms.

Jackson (1960) has offered a useful list of structural dimensions of roles that informs this discussion.

Consensus. A critical dimension of a role is the *consensus* with which it is defined. Inasmuch as roles are, by definition, shared understandings, then consensus about the obligations and privileges constituting the role has a minimal limiting condition beyond which the role does not exist. Within the limits, those who occupy the roles in an organization empowered to define other roles may more or less agree about the nature of a role. To the degree that they agree, then the role probably is clear to its incumbents; that is, their personal role definitions probably correspond to the consensus held by the role senders. Another limiting condition is when one person, "The Boss," perhaps the only other person in the social organization, has the authority to define the role.

Sanction potential. The clarity advanced by the consensus regarding a role does not itself ensure conformity. The effectiveness of socialization depends also on a role's *sanction potential*. This refers to the likelihood and strength of the positive sanctions (incentives) and negative sanctions (punishments) that may legitimately be applied to role incumbents. A role in the military is rather strong on this dimension: Certain derelictions of duty are punishable by imprisonment or even death by firing squad. In contrast, their inadequate performance in the classroom threatens university professors hardly at all. The dimension of consensus enters here as well (as it does for all dimensions of a role); for the sanction potential of a role is probably as clear to role takers as there is agreement, among those who should know, about how likely and strong the sanctions could be. The probabilistic nature of a social psychological proposition is nicely illustrated here; for the effectiveness of a sanction to induce conformity depends also on the motives and resources of the person to whom it may be applied—who may feel, "Who cares?" Still, at the organizational level of analysis, one may formulate universal propositions that take into account the degree of sanction potential of organizational roles.

Rigidity–flexibility. One may also develop organizational propositions about the rigidity–flexibility dimension of roles. A role is said to be rigid to the degree that its norms specify exactly the actions and experiences required of its incumbents, leaving little if any room for individuals to inject their personal styles into their role enactment or for the situation to qualify role prescriptions. In this sense, roles on factory assembly lines and in the performance of the Japanese tea ceremony are rigid, whereas roles as salespersons, craftsmen, and hosts are flexible. Because more rigid roles are inherently less adaptable to persons or situations, it follows that the organization cannot depend on the motives of role takers, whose variation is given in the psychology of role incumbents, to obtain conformity. Therefore, rigid roles have more sanction potential to assure the necessary motivation. A related proposition concerns organizational selection and retention of personnel: To the degree that its roles are rigid, an organization attracts, selects, and retains personnel whose motives and resources prompt them to enjoy such structures. That is, authoritarians may select themselves into rigid roles and perform them happily "by the book."

Scope. The organizational and psychological effects of roles and individuals' effects on roles depends also on the dimension of their *scope*, the range of actions and feelings over which the role has authority. A role with the broadest scope can regulate all the actions and feelings of individuals, around the clock, every day. This dimension describes the precedence of one role over other roles, individual propensities, interpersonal relations, and cultural values.

One common role with broad scope in contemporary Western society is parenthood. Among other obligations, being a parent entails broadly modeling one's society's norms and teaching one's culture's values to one's children. This obligation reaches into all domains of the lives of parents. The scope of the role sometimes becomes so impossible for parents to deal with that they turn from modeling to instructing, "Do as I say, not as I do!"

Among occupations, professions tend to have broader scope than others, especially callings that have particularly moral functions, such as clergy and teacher. Like parents, clergy and teachers are supposed to be role models beyond their own roles because they are required to demonstrate dedication to overarching cultural values that in turn imply norms specific to many social positions.

This dimension of scope is particularly useful for understanding the idea of "total institutions" (Etzioni, 1961). In his review of literature on the subject, McEwen (1980) observed that Goffman meant to define an ideal typical social organization whose central feature is "a breakdown of the barriers ordinarily separating . . . three spheres of life . . . sleep, play, and work" (Goffman, 1961, p. 5). The examples that Goffman gave were 24-hour facilities like hospitals and prisons, where at least one constituent role—patient, inmate—engages in all three activities. Although such places are informative illustrations of the concept because their encompassing nature is "built right into the physical plant" (p. XIII), genotypic to these as total is that "all aspects of life are conducted . . . under the same single authority" (p. 6). Trahair (1975) focussed on this feature of total institutions:

> In most institutions, persons are involved on a segmental or partial basis, i.e. the organization requires only part of a person and persons do not commit themselves to organizations completely . . . But for persons who are assigned to the position of inmate in a total institution, the degree of partial inclusion is zero, i.e. the person has no other position in society. (pp. 35–36)

Coser (1974) referred to these social organizations as "greedy institutions" (pp. 4–8).

An institution is a social organization, and it is total to the degree of the scope of its role demands. Contrary to most usage after Goffman— usage probably impressed by the most dramatic of Goffman's illustrations—this approach requires neither fixed residence nor even coercion. Goffman's conceptualization admits of voluntary as well as involuntary commitment to the role, including people who are "assigned" (Trahair's interpretation) or "fully committed" (Coser's interpretation). Thus, monks of a religious order are "inmates" of a total institution, and this is true whether they are permanently cloistered or sent to travel throughout the world. Furthermore, this view of total institutions implies that a social organization may be more total to some constituent roles than to others; obviously a prison is more institutionally total to prisoners than to guards.

Elkins (1976) made good use of this way of conceptualizing total institutions in his essay on the differences between social organizations of slavery in the United States and in the West Indies. In the U.S., slave was the preeminent if not the sole role of role incumbents. In the West Indies, the Roman Catholic Church was powerful enough to claim some independent authority over those who were in slavery and to protect them in their roles as "children of God" and sometimes as "congregants." In the West Indies, therefore, people in slavery were not "under the same single authority" (Goffman, 1961, p. 6). The scope of the slave role was limited by the obligations and privileges of other roles. Inasmuch as the religious role was also broad in its scope, it substantially compromised the role of slave. Elkins asserted that West Indian slaves' personalities and culture developed quite differently from American slaves' because of this difference in the scopes of their roles.

The totality of a role's scope may not be a property of the objective role but rather only of the personal role definition. This personal construal is not a social organizational fact but a psychological one; it involves social psychological translation. People may perceive the scope of a role mistakenly, or they may make a total commitment to a role that they correctly perceive to have more limited scope. Consensual or only personal, totality should be similarly influential. The influence of a self-imposed scope would however be qualified by at least two differences from consensually total roles: First, the personal commitment would enhance the role's capacity to overcome reactance and to effect more than superficial compliance; and second, the element of deviance implied in a self-imposed total commitment might ultimately weaken it.

When people occupy roles in a malintegrated social organization, they are likely to become tense. The relevant dimension of roles is their coherence. *Coherence* refers to the compatibility among a role's demands. In some social organizations, the privileges accorded its roles are not adequate for the fulfillment of their obligations, nor are other roles designated to provide the necessary help. For example, organizational policy urges scoutmasters to permit boys, within limits, to determine their troop's program democratically, but this norm often conflicts with the directive that scoutmasters ensure that boys devote a substantial part of their scouting to work on merit badges. With some imagination, scoutmasters can integrate merit badge work into activities that boys select. Otherwise, scoutmasters find themselves subject to opposing motivational forces, a tension-producing situation.

Formal–informal. The dimension of *formality* of roles is an important dimension in the model because its polar minimum, informality, describes a condition in which the person and the social organization become closely integrated. The distinction commonly made between formal and informal roles does not seem useful. This distinction refers to whether the norms are codified, that is, put into writing (Sarbin & Allen, 1968). Formal norms are codified and, the reasoning goes, because they are, they are more widely known and achieve a greater consensus. There is no evidence, however, that written prescriptions achieve a wider consensus. Studies of work groups, like W. F. Whyte's electrical circuit wirers (1961), demonstrate that unwritten rules often achieve more consensus among the people who enact the roles: Wirers were able to set and enforce rates of production effectively without any written agreement, whereas the written contract was often violated. Codification might plausibly be held to stabilize norms, making them harder to change. There may be a tendency in that direction, but it is not the basis for a strong distinction. Numerous instances of written rules rewritten before the ink is dry and of unwritten laws that endure for generations contradict the association between codification and stability. In many cases, codification confirms long-standing unwritten agreements. It seems that codification is a negligible factor in the structure of social organization and in their effect on individuals.

More insightful is the observation of Blau and Scott (1962) that in most of the role relationships referred to as informal, the norms have been negotiated by the parties. In his review of social organizational theory from a social interactionist perspective, Maines (1977) also wrote of a "negotiated order." Roles that have been negotiated by the parties may or may not be written down, they may endure or they may be only temporary. Participation of role incumbents in defining the relationship is the essential characteristic of informality. It follows from this that when the particular incumbents terminate an informal relationship, the roles disappear.

Informal role relationships may fit the ideal type as nearly as formal ones do. They may be as completely governed by social norms, as the ideal is; at the same time, because their norms are negotiated by the parties occupying the roles, they may take into account the personal characteristics of the participants. Therein lies an inherent tendency toward informality of all formal organization. Inasmuch as individuals come to formal roles with their idiosyncratic patterns of motives and resources, they tend to negotiate personally suitable ways of enacting their roles. The opportunity to do so, which varies with the flexibility of the roles, is one kind of incentive to perform the role well; for it permits satisfaction of personal motives that may not otherwise be possible.

Although roles often become less regulated by the process of informalization, they remain roles nevertheless. Informal roles, once negotiated, may be as restrictive and compelling as those of any formal role, admitting of little spontaneity. Moreover, informal roles may be renegotiated, but they must nevertheless be reckoned with when an individual's personal styles or mood change in ways incompatible with prior agreements. Renegotiation is typically made more problematic when the original negotiation was not explicit but rather took place as a relatively lengthy process of mutual, unverbalized agreements.

The negotiations that generate informal roles are not always accommodations to the psyches of the parties to them. Sometimes they accommodate the organization's task. Formal roles may have become incoherent, perhaps because the technology or some other feature of the environment has changed. Perhaps the formal roles were ill-suited to the task from the very beginning. To the degree that they are dedicated to the organization's goals, role occupants may then avoid tension by negotiating more functional informal roles. In such instances, it is likely that the informal roles eventually become formalized. Norms negotiated originally by participants may then be imposed without negotiation on new occupants of the role, assuming that the norms are still advantageous for doing the work. They may or may not be codified in the process; "unwritten laws" may be established.

So far, this discussion of the formal–informal distinction has used examples found within formal organizations, organized as functional amendments to formal roles. However, one can conceive of instances in which informal social organizations exist apart from any formal organization. They may originate as interpersonal relations. For just as there is a tendency toward informalization in formal organizations, so is there also in interpersonal relations. After all, there must be a limit to the amount of idiosyncracy and spontaneity permitted; otherwise it becomes impossible to coordinate social interaction. So partners to an interpersonal relationship typically negotiate norms mainly to serve the maintenance of their relationship but also perhaps to enable them to work together on tasks of common interest. It is likely that their negotiations in effect transform expectations about one another in the predictive sense of the word into expectations in the moral sense.

This way of thinking about the informality of norms illuminates the subtle shift that occurs in ongoing groups from one kind of expectation to another. *Expectation* may mean either "prediction" or "obligation." (Which of the two is often conveyed by inflection, heavier stress being put on expectation as *obligation*.) For example, children occupy certain niches in their informal play groups, as leaders, clowns, and so forth. What begins as their regular "role" in the sense of function becomes "role" in the sense of moral obligation. So youngsters who clown around by predilection may be cast into that informal role after a while, altercast by their playmates and criticized by them when they neglect their antic duties. That is, the partners' stable personal characteristics, their ways of behaving and feeling, become normative.

This conceptualization of the formal–informal dimension of roles also sheds light on the nature of another of Cooley's "primary groups," the family. Blau and Scott (1962, pp. 6–7) and Maines (1977) asserted that because American families are not part of a larger, formal organization, as for example, informal work groups are, they should not be considered informal social organizations. In contrast, if the negotiated characteristic of the norms is the sole criterion for differentiating informal from formal organizations, families are included among the informal. That is how the model characterizes families in modern society.

Indeed, many of the collectivities that Cooley (1909) called *primary groups* are thus understood to be informal social organizations. Some of their norms are not negotiable. In families, law and custom have defined certain duties and privileges of spouses, parents, and children. Even in children's play groups, some adult-mandated rules are applied for playing together and specific rules about games, which children inherit from previous generations. More compelling than these formal norms, however, are the norms that the parties negotiate among themselves. Families develop divisions of labor, ways of sharing property, unspoken agreements about how individuals ought to be treated, and so on.

More than anything else, most primary groups are informal social organizations. Cooley's observation that they are the primary contexts for socialization is correct. Thus, conceptualizing them as social organizations makes it possible to apply theory and research on the reciprocal influence of social organization and the individual applicable to primary groups as well.

It seems useful to build theory about informal roles from the conceptualization that they are negotiated by their incumbents. Explanations of concrete informal organizational phenomena would necessarily begin with the specification, "To the degree that the norms are negotiable, then . . . ." One advantage of this approach is that it offers an obvious way to understand at least two of the phenomena of informal social organizations that make them especially interesting. One is the conflict characteristic in informal relations between treating people as persons and as role occupants. The other phenomenon is that they humanize the formal organizations in which they occur, shaping roles to the contours of their incumbents. This makes informal organization especially welcome to subordinate members and anathema to the interests of order and formal authority.

Substantive

The substantive dimensions of roles may be conceptualized in many ways. Only some of those that seem most useful for social psychology are taken up here. Because one aim of social psychology is to link social organization with individuals, substantive dimensions of roles that are compatible with or even identical to psychological dimensions of motives and resources recommend themselves. Such terms are more easily translatable across levels of analysis. (For theorizing at the social organizational level itself, other substantive dimensions are more useful. For example, Bales and Slater's, 1955, explanation of the development of decision-making groups involved conceptualizing roles in Parsons's terms of their functions for group maintenance — "expressive – integrative" — and task accomplishment — "instrumental – adaptive.")

Psychosexual. Substantive dimensions of roles that bridge social organization to individual psychology include the psychoanalytic psychosexual terms used by Bordin, Nachman, and Segal (1963). Norms are characterized in terms usually used to describe personalities, as Bordin et al. did in describing the role of social case worker as masochistic and dentist as sadistic. Obviously role descriptions are not typically cast in quite these terms. Social work educators do not explicitly socialize their students to be masochistic, but they may well impress on students the importance of empathy with clients. From a psychoanalytic perspective, empathy partakes of identification, and encouraging identification with suffering clients is in effect to prescribe a norm of masochism. A useful description of roles is not necessarily in the terms used by role senders. Often the terms are selected from the researcher's favorite personality theory.

Psychosocial. One may also borrow Erikson's psychosocial modalities (1950) to describe roles. With these terms one can describe, for example, the shift in the nature of studenthood from elementary to secondary education in contemporary America. In elementary school, a greater emphasis is placed on aural and visual incorporation and autonomous control than there will be later. Young students are expected to absorb information passively, often learning by rote, as with the alphabet, the names of things, and the multiplication tables. They are also expected to acquire the capacity for delay of gratification and muscular control as they learn to take turns, go to the toilet and eat according to schedule, and to sit in one place for longer and longer periods. Moving on to a secondary school brings older students into a role that puts greater emphasis on intrusiveness and initiative. They are expected to seek out knowledge, specifically by manipulating substances in laboratories or searching through books. The role of elementary student demands a greater level of interpersonal trust in relation to teachers and greater concentration on autonomy. Secondary school studenthood, on the other hand, tolerates lower levels of trust, encourages more susceptibility to peer control, and at the same time stresses the more mature capacities for taking initiative and working industriously.

Needs. In a similar fashion, Veroff and Feld have adopted Murray's terms to describe facets of personality to describe the major roles of adult Americans. In *Marriage and Work in America* (1970), they analyzed occupations and familial roles in terms of three of Murray's "needs"—for achievement, power, and affiliation. The purpose was to explain why individuals were differentially satisfied with their lives. Veroff and Feld's guiding hypothesis was that satisfaction is a function of the compatibility between the demands of major social roles and the stable personal characteristics of the individuals who play them. Ordering individual and the social organizational properties on the same dimensions facilitates such social psychological translation.

Which structural and substantive dimensions one uses to describe roles depends on one's purposes. Those who aim to understand social organization in its own right typically invoke terms that have to do only with the structure and function of social organization. (This is not always the case, as evidenced by the Tavistock school of industrial organization that psychoanalyzes organizations to explain them. See, e.g., Trist, 1981.) Explorations into the relationship between culture and social organization invoke still another set of categories that seems suitable to that purpose, for example, describing roles as *sacred* and *profane* (Sorokin, 1957). Systems theorists, who intend to generate identical propositions at several levels of analysis, use functional concepts at high levels of abstraction, like *transducer* (J. G. Miller, 1978), which signifies the function of transmitting substance or information across a system's boundary, as a research librarian should do for the staff of a magazine. Later, when considering how social organizational phenomena affect the psychology of individuals and vice versa, some additional dimensions appropriate for social psychology are offered.

Social Organization in Contemporary Social Psychological Theory and Method

Although the concepts of norms, roles, and social organization are seldom explicit in mainstream contemporary social psychology, the ideas are inevitably omnipresent. Their implicit manifestations in several popular concerns of contemporary social psychology demonstrate the necessity of this level of analysis.

Situation as Social Organization

Social psychology has been preoccupied with the "situation" (Nisbett & Ross, 1980). Grounding an understanding of an individual's action and experience in an adequate contemporary diagnosis makes this preoccupation appropriate. The here-and-now as understood by the person is determinative. As long as consideration of the situation is limited to the psychological level of analysis, however, social psychological work is not being done. Close attention must be paid to the current state of the social environment to explain how it strikes the person.

One does not have to peer very closely to find social organization in the situation. In their introduction to a collection of articles in *Personality at the Crossroads* (1977), Magnusson and Endler described the situational component of the Person × Situation interaction thus:

> The situation as a whole forms a contextual framework for the individual. Examples of total situations would include church services, job situations, baseball games, club meetings, etc. *Each situation has certain implicit rules*, and the individual's interpretation of the rules determines his or her behavioral strategy. In some situations the options are very few, because the situational rules have a very strong effect on the person's behavior . . . In other situations, . . . there are more degrees of freedom. (pp. 15–16; emphasis added)

The rules to which Magnusson and Endler referred are, of course, social norms. "Implicit rules" suggests that they have in mind uncodified social relationships, although there is nothing in their discussion that rules out explicit laws, manuals of organizational regulations, books of etiquette, and so on.

Recall too that social norms were said earlier to govern what Kelley and Thibaut (1978) called *interpersonal relations* (see pp. 3–28). The researchers predetermined the amounts of benefits that players might get, depending on the choices each player made, and they set the rules by which the players might interact. Thus, Kelley and Thibaut created social organizations around the prisoners' dilemma game to test hypotheses about individuals' behavior in social organizations generally.

Implicit invocation of social norms is common in social psychological conceptualizations of the environment. They are intrinsic to Kurt Lewin's (1951) first systematic theoretical foray into the social environment. His analysis of the processes by which organ meats reach American dining tables is a description of the social organization of the meat business. The "channels" through which Lewin traced meat from pastures and paddocks to dining tables are constructed of the social roles of ranchers, meat packers, distributors, butchers, and consumers; there are no people as such manning these channels.

Following close on to Lewin are Barker and Wright's descriptions of "settings" in their psychological ecology (1949), which are also almost entirely social organizational. Similarly, Abelson's "scripts" (1981) were written mostly according to individuals' expectations of what would transpire on the basis of their understanding of how people *ought* to act in the situation.

Social Organization of Social Psychological Experiments

The bulk of experimental social psychology can usefully be considered as accounts of how people act and feel when they are assigned certain explicit roles that are variations on the more general and implicit role of "Subjects in an experiment" (see also, Alexander & Knight, 1971; Ickes, 1983; Touhey, 1974).

My own awareness of the importance of social norms in social psychological experimentation developed very early in my training as a social psychologist, in my personal introduction to the role of Subject. Typically, I was conscripted into the Subject role as a student in the introductory course in psychology. It turned out that five of my classmates and I were part of a "run" in an early replication and extension of the Bavelas–Leavitt studies of communication structures (Bavelas, 1950; Leavitt, 1951). The experimenter was an undergraduate psychology major doing his senior thesis. He was neither very competent nor, it seemed, very interested. He mumbled and bumbled his way through the inductions and instructions, made several false starts, and generally gave us the impression that none of this mattered very much to him or should to us—except in one respect: He told us that if our team accomplished our assigned tasks faster than the other teams, we would win a keg of beer. This induction to conform took, and we became eager to play.

It happened that our team was being run in the Bavelas–Leavitt wheel structure, which meant that there was a central position, a hub through which all our communications were supposed to flow. Unfortunately, the fellow who fell at random into the hub position was dense and could not seem to grasp the nature of the tasks to be done. His handling of the team's messages was terribly inefficient, and his own messages were uninformative. It soon became apparent that, at this rate, our team was not going to win the keg.

This realization, combined with the inept experimenter's loss of authority, prompted our team to violate our instructions, first surreptitiously, then openly: We passed our messages around the hub, took to flying them as paper airplanes over the plywood partitions that separated our positions, and wound up shouting information to one another. That is, we violated the norms that were supposed to govern our behavior as Subjects in the experiment, specifically those norms that constructed the channels of communication in the wheel structure. Our run disintegrated, and the experimenter dismissed us in anger. (When in the next semester I took a course in social psychology and learned how frequently deception was practiced in social psychological experiments, I wondered whether the senior's incompetence and indifference had been merely a put-on, and whether the dense human had been the experimenter's confederate. I learned however that the experimenter was merely hapless.)

In that same social psychology course I read about the Bavelas–Leavitt experiments. Nowhere in the discussion of the method or the interpretation of the results was the concept of social norms invoked, although it was a prominent concept elsewhere in course materials (we used the new Newcomb text, 1950). I remember being struck at the time with how social psychological experimentation was a kind of role playing. My unusual experience with the procedure impressed on me how much this method depended on everyone subscribing to social norms that were usually taken for granted but were not taken explicitly into account.

Thus, one reason for social psychology to pay close attention to the social organizational level of analysis is that much of its work is done there even though the social psychological experiment is not commonly thought of in that way. Much of the experimental in social psychology varies the social norms that govern the participants' relationships with their environment. Even the research findings on the effects of physical environments are often strongly determined by social norms. There are, for example, demonstrable differences in the acceptability to individuals of certain levels of crowding, depending on whether the others are strangers, acquaintances, or friends (Sundstrom & Altman, 1976). Similarly, individuals' comfort with eye contact varies, depending on their accustomed norms.

Implications for Generalizability

Disparaging social psychological laboratory experiments because their findings have little if any generalizability seems misguided. Their findings are as generalizable as those observed under any other essentially genotypically similar conditions. The trick is to recognize what is genotypic. The structure and substance of the roles involve important considerations. For example, the roles imposed on participants vary in their scope. Experimental findings reveal that when scope is narrow, limited perhaps to a peculiar experimental task, then the influence of the role tends to be limited, having little if any affective charge and hardly detectable beyond the immediate situation. When the scope is wide, as it was in Rokeach's (1968) experiment, influence is more enduring and transituational. Recognizing that an experiment has a social organization prompts one to suppose that its findings are generalizable to other social organizational situations similar in structure and substance, concentration camps and prisons perhaps.

"Laboratory" and "Field"

Looking at social psychological experiments this way appropriately erases the usual distinction made between the laboratory and field experimentation. The usual criterion is where the experiment is done, the laboratory being a space especially set aside for that purpose, the field being a space where other activities are also going on. This is not a genotypic criterion. A more useful distinction has to do with the rigor of control the researcher exercises over the variables: the more rigorous the control, the more "experimental" the method. (Of course, the more experimental the method, the more certain the attributions of causality.) Rigorous control may be harder to obtain in the field, because other things are happening there, but it is demonstrably possible. Again, Rokeach's (1968) study of values, conducted over the course of 6 months in dormitory rooms and through the ordinary mail, demonstrates that rigorous experiments can be done out in the "field."

Psychological Effects of Roles

From the perspective of the social psychological experiment as a social organization, it is noteworthy that experiments are frequently successful in producing meaningful, even predicted, findings. Their success has implications for two fundamental issues in sociology and psychology. One has to do with the assumption underlying the relevance of social organizational principles to individual behavior, namely that the objective role itself is determinative. One need not deny that individuals' subjective understandings of their role's prescriptions are the proximal determinant of how individuals act; one need only assert that for practical purposes, under most conditions, with specifiable exceptions, individuals' interpretations of their roles correspond to the distal determinant, the objective role. The other assumption is that most people most of the time conform to their role prescriptions, not only as they understand them but also, if the first assumption is true, as others understand them. Social psychological experiments support the validity of these assumptions, insofar as the general role of Subject carries well-understood, albeit implicit, norms, and the experimental instructions constitute explicit normative prescriptions. Milgram's (1974) study—and Haney, Banks, and Zimbardo's simulation of the prison experience (1973) is also especially apposite here—demonstrates that roles in experiments can shape behavior even when the behavior touches on central social values.

A theoretical explanation of how social roles are implicated in the reciprocal influence of individuals and their social environment is presented at a later point, in the section on social psychological dynamics. What follows is a sample of the psychological effects of role taking (to distinguish it from the treatment modality of role playing). These are meant to illustrate the ubiquity and variety of social organizational influences.

Many social psychological experiments that vary the role of Subjects merely secure participants' transitory behavioral conformity. The motives and resources that participants bring with them to the laboratory usually remain substantially unaffected by experimental manipulations. The conformity of most of Milgram's (1974) participants contradicted heavily valenced motives and seriously violated the values that underlay those motives, but it did not change them. In postexperimental interviews and debriefing sessions, people struggled to justify their behavior somehow in terms of their motives, often weighing their obligation to fulfill their implicit contract with the researcher against wanting to satisfy their need to abide by humane standards.

Under other experimental conditions, changes in motives and resources endure, as Rokeach (1968) demonstrated. In the course of a survey on the values of college students, some randomly chosen respondents were told that their values differed substantially from those of their fellow students. Specifically, they were told that they placed equality much lower in their scale of values than others did. In social organizational terms, the survey interviewer thus communicated a social norm about the appropriate motivation of students at that university. Six months later respondents received mailed solicitations for contributions to the National Association for the Advancement of Colored People. Rokeach found that significantly more contributions were mailed in from those who had learned earlier that they were not in conformity with the norms of their student role, compared with those who had placed a similar lower value on equality but were not told what the norm was. This more enduring effect was perhaps produced by role-sending engaging participants in their role as students, a role that mattered to them more than being a participant in an experiment did. Perhaps subtlety of the influence enhanced its effectiveness because it avoided the participants' reactance (Brehm, 1966). For whatever reasons, conveying the norms of a role to an incumbent can engage an incumbent's eagerness to conform to the role and thereby change his or her perceptions of what motives he or she should have.

In the social organization of a social psychological experiment, as in other situations, roles can exert effective influence indirectly. Their obligations may place role takers in situations that generate psychological change that is not itself required by the role's norms. The changes that were effected by Zajonc and Rajecki's variations of the role of the Subject in their experiment (1969) were not prescribed. It is because of the subtlety of the participants' experience in the role and the complete absence of any normative pressure for the change that the Zajonc and Rajecki study is instructive here. Although their experiment seems to bear no similarity to Rokeach's on values, it set up some identical conditions from the social organizational perspective.

Zajonc and Rajecki's participants merely had to perform a series of simple learning tasks. It was critical, although participants were unaware of this, that their role required them to move from one experimental room to another in a carefully manipulated order. Movement from room to room was the controlled variable, and the tasks themselves were irrelevant; for their carefully prescribed travels brought participants into varying face-to-face contact with the other participants in their experimental trial.

Zajonc and Rajecki were studying the effect of mere exposure on attitudes toward objects. They found that participants rated as more attractive those whom they had encountered more frequently in the hallways between laboratory rooms. One conclusion to draw from this study is that the experiences that individuals have while enacting a role affect them in ways that may have nothing directly to do with role prescriptions.

Finally, Lieberman's (1956) study of changes in the attitudes of workers as they moved in and out of roles in a factory nicely illustrated several of the uses of the social organizational level of analysis for social psychological theory and method. Lieberman's was initiated as a "field" experiment that took advantage of events that would have occurred even if there had been no study. Lieberman measured the attitudes of factory workers toward management and their union, anticipating that some of the workers would later be promoted to foremen and others would be elected as shop stewards in the union organization. After some workers' roles changed in these two ways, Lieberman remeasured the workers' attitudes and found, as he had predicted, that the new foremen had, on the average, become more pro-management and less pro-union and the new shop stewards more pro-union and less pro-management. This was true even though the attitudes of the workers in the two groups had been about the same when measured initially.

Did role change cause attitude change? It is plausible that becoming foremen or shop stewards was the cause of workers' attitude change. Taking these roles placed workers in new configurations of forces that might very well have changed their motivations and resources in such ways that their attitudes changed. Although plausible, this attribution of causality was by no means certain. Initial similarity in attitudes did not altogether rule out the possibility that the workers had entered their new roles with attitudes already pro-management or pro-union. Their attitudes may have changed during the months between initial measurement and their promotion or election. Or they may have been differentially selected for their new roles because of some unmeasured predispositions favorable to management or the union. At this point, something happened out in the field to improve the rigor of the experiment: The company was forced by an economic recession to cut back on production and lay off workers, with some of the foremen and some of the shop stewards becoming workers again. The effect of role occupancy could now be more certainly ascertained by observing whether this second shift in roles was also followed by a shift in attitudes. So Lieberman measured workers' attitudes a third time and found that they indeed had shifted again, toward what they had been initially. As roles changed, attitudes changed.

Lieberman did not create the social organization whose effects he studied. The experimental conditions were intrinsic to the ongoing lives of the role takers. The relevant roles thus had a great deal of scope for their incumbents, touching substantially on their lives inside and outside the factory, affecting virtually all of their other social relations. The roles' potential for sanctions was also great, manifested in wages, power, privileges, and prestige. The roles might similarly be located on the dimensions of coherence, rigidity, and formality in order to account for their apparent psychological effects.

Lieberman did not ask his respondents to describe the roles of foreman and shop steward. He assumed that they shared with him and with each other an understanding of the norms defining these roles, particularly the attitudes expected of their incumbents. That is, this study, like the bulk of social psychological studies, assumed the power of objective roles to shape the behavior and experience of individuals. Had he obtained personal role definitions, Lieberman would probably have been able to account for even more of the variance in attitude change than he did, would perhaps have been able to explain why the attitudes of some workers-cum-foremen or -shop stewards did not change as predicted.

A methodological lesson of Lieberman's study lies in the researcher's alertness to how concrete circumstances could improve the rigor of his research design. Experiments are where one finds them: in factories, in college dormitories, in institutions for delinquents, and on sidewalks. Rigorous studies of the interaction between individuals and social organizations can be done in any of these places if one recognizes what is social organizational in what goes on there, controlling and varying these factors appropriately to the inquiry. Again, the rigor and informativeness of experiments are increased if researchers recognize their social organizational character.

Lieberman did not analyze in any detail the social psychological processes that caused the changes he observed. He attributed attitude changes to role changes without describing how the boundary between social fact and psychological fact was crossed. Nor did Lieberman specify the psychological and social conditions that made that crossing happen. These are a matter of social psychological dynamics, specifically of the process of socialization, which are discussed in some detail later.

Here I anticipate that discussion by pointing to some of the plausible forces. Obviously there are the valences of being foreman or shop steward—the higher wages, the privileges, and so on that have already been mentioned. To the degree that holding the "correct" attitudes is a necessary path to getting and keeping those attractive roles, those attitudes also share compelling valences. However, one should not overlook more subtle sources of influence flowing from the role changes, for example, the increased exposures to different people and cultures attendant on occupying the different roles. That is, foremen conversed more often with higher levels of management than they did as workers, and perhaps they were required to attend meetings and training sessions at which facts and values about the company and the union were presented by congenial people; similarly, shop stewards communicated more with earnest union people and became more immersed in the union culture. In these ways, involving other levels of analysis, role change may indirectly effect psychological change.

Summary

The phenomena of social organization should be restored to a central place in social psychological theory. As facts, they have been important to social psychology all along, but as concepts they have been only implicit in theorizing and in method. As long as the concepts remain only implicit, social psychology cannot develop adequate theory to deal with the way social organizations affect and are affected by individuals. Nor can it make optimal use of experiments.

Social organization is a boundary condition of the psychological world in which individuals act. That is, it has an objective reality independent of the consciousness of any one person. How this reality is translated into the psychological terms that constitute the determinants of action and experience or is itself transformed by the acts of individuals are among the defining questions of social psychology.

These translations cannot be accomplished with closed theory. Merging phenomena at more than one level of analysis is a matter of probabilities. However, closed theory at the psychological and social organizational levels of analysis are useful guides to the interpenetrating terms of open social psychological theory. In chapter 3, I proposed that, on the psychological side, concepts of motives and resources suffice to capture the reciprocal influence of individuals and the social environment. This chapter has proposed that the concept of social role lies at the point of interpenetration between the psychological individual and the social organizational sector of the social environment. Roles may vary along certain structural and substantive dimensions that determine the probable strength and nature of their influence on individuals' motives and resources, and how amenable they probably are to the influence of individuals.

Many kinds of social relationships fit the definition of social organization as a system of role relationships. "Social organization" by no means describes only corporations, agencies, and institutions. Inasmuch as normative regulation pervades social life, almost all social relationships are to some degree social organizational, including families, children's play groups, friendships, psychological experiments, and so on. Many of these are informal social organizations, whose roles are negotiated by their incumbents, but they are social organizations nevertheless, with more or less compelling norms.

At the same time, few relationships are ideal typical social organizations. Interpersonal and cultural facets of the social environment are usually operating as well. Nevertheless, an understanding of the effects of and on concrete relationships in social organizational terms requires first an analysis that identifies the degree and nature of role regulation involved, followed by a synthesis with the other social relationships that takes into account how they combine and conflict in the concrete case. This approach from the social organizational level suggests that intimacy must be a recurring, not a constant, feature of a relationship. It subscribes to Buber's (1957) insight that such relationships are ephemeral, interpersonal moments in an ongoing relationship. For the most part, the relationship is rather of partners to a negotiated, informal social organization. In these negotiations the partners' personalities are kept very much in mind, and the more interpersonal their relation is, the more ready they are to renegotiate. Obviously, these informal relationships may stand outside any formal organization.

I have identified *socialization* as the process by which the effects of social organization are translated into psychological terms and *institutionalization* as the process by which individuals influence social organizations, but so far these processes have only been mentioned. They are described more fully later, in the section on the dynamics of social psychology (chapter 7). Before that, the social environments of interpersonal and cultural relationships must be defined and placed in this social psychological model.

5

Interpersonal Relations

The term *interpersonal relations* refers here to a very special kind of social relationship. The elements of *interpersonal* denote so nicely what I have in mind that I have expropriated the term from its more general usage. Elsewhere, it usually refers to any relationship among people. Here, *interpersonal relation* is a kind of social relationship that is far from general, at least in its ideal typical state. Indeed, social philosopher Martin Buber (1957) held that the "I–Thou" relationship (by which he seems to have meant something very much like an interpersonal relation) is rare and ephemeral.

Even though it is seldom if ever found in its pure state, some degree of interpersonal relation frequently functions along with the social organizational and cultural environments, and evidence indicates that it does not take a great deal of "interpersonalism" to affect the dynamics of concrete relationships substantially. Because interpersonal relations have important and distinctive effects on individuals, and because they also set critical conditions for individuals' influencing the social environment, social psychology requires a separate level of analysis for them.

The idea of interpersonal relations in the sense that it is meant here can already be found in the literature of social psychology—indeed, in the social sciences generally—as well as in philosophy and other humanities. Social scientists are familiar with it, but in many guises. One can find the germ of the idea of interpersonal relations in the writings of Georg Simmel, who attended much more than Emile Durkheim did to social relationships that are not governed by the moral order. Most familiar to social psychologists is Simmel's observations on the differences in the decision processes of dyads and larger groups (1950b). Here, Simmel did not invoke roles or legitimate authority for explanation but rather considered simply the participants themselves. This is an essential feature of theory about interpersonal relations, as they are conceived here. In his article "The Sociology of Sociability" (1910/1949), Simmel called attention to the playfulness of certain relationships that he called "sociable," pointing out that such relationships had no purpose outside of themselves: "sociability in its pure form has no ulterior end, no content, and no result outside itself, it is oriented completely about personalities" (1908/1950b, p. 126). Elsewhere, Simmel took up other social phenomena whose distinctiveness derives from their *not* being obligatory, like giving unexpected gifts and pledging faithfulness (1908/1950a). Philosopher Michael Oakeshot also noted the playful and end-in-themselves character of friendship: "Friends are not concerned with what can be made of one another, but only with the enjoyment of one another; and the condition of enjoyment is a ready acceptance of what is and the absence of any desire to change or improve" (quoted in A. Sullivan, 1991, p. 42).

Other 19th- and early 20th-century social theorists took note of the kind of relationships that occupied much of Simmel's attentions. Among the sociologists, Cooley (Cooley, Angell, & Carr, 1933) identified "the primary group"; Tonnies (1887/1957) alluded to interpersonal relations in his distinction between community (*Gemeinschaft*) and society (*Gesellschaft*); and Schmalenbach (1977) wrote about communion (*Bund*). Psychology's interest is more recent, in its investigations of bases of attraction to small groups (Cartwright & Zander, 1968) and of the emotional and behavioral effects of friendship (Douvan, 1974; Duck, 1979, 1983; Jourard, 1971; Rubin, 1973). Among psychotherapists, Rogers (1961), Carkhuff (1969), and Rollo May (1967) have emphasized the interpersonal element of the therapeutic relationship, de-emphasizing the roles of patient and therapist and asserting that the interaction of personalities is the instrument for change. Students of communication have studied how substance and style in the exchange of personal information figure in the development and maintenance of interpersonal relations (e.g., Cushman & Craig, 1976; Nicotera & Associates, 1993; P. H. Wright, 1978).

I continue this discussion of interpersonal relations by defining the relationship in terms almost impossible to satisfy except by idealization. Then their reality is asserted by pointing to traces of interpersonal relations in the familiar collectivities of primary groups, particularly nuclear families and friendships. The idea of an interpersonal relation is further delineated by positing its unit of analysis, a mutually recognized identity. Social psychological use of the idea is illustrated in a discussion of group cohesiveness, and examples from mass media and psychotherapy illustrate its practical uses. Rounding out the chapter is a discussion of how variations among interpersonal relations and the character of potential partners affect whether an interpersonal relation develops in the persons' encounter, what configuration it may assume, and what effects it may have on the partners.

The Nature of Interpersonal Relations

Recall the previous description of a bipolar dimension with the ideal typical role relationship at one end and the ideal typical interpersonal relation at the other. Two defining features of an interpersonal relation are in sharp contrast to those of a role relationship: Interpersonal relations are free of norms, and the partners trust[1] one another. Third, interpersonal

---

[1]In an earlier presentation of our thinking about interpersonal relations, Douvan (1974) included loyalty as the sole norm governing interpersonal relations. At the time, that conceptual strategy seemed the most useful way of taking into account the concern that the partners had for one another. Since then, as a consequence of seminars on this model of social psychology, I have come to believe that it is conceptually neater to put this property of interpersonal relations in the cognitive term of *trust* rather than the normative term of

relations, like some role relationships, are charged with a high level of mutual positive affect. In contrast to role relationships, however, this affect is not prescribed; it emerges from the interaction of the partners.

To say that the relationship is without norms is not to say that it is without expectations. The partners come to expect certain things of each other, but only in the sense that they can predict the behavior of the other. They do not impose normative expectations on each other. The critical expectation in an interpersonal relation is the conviction that the partner can be trusted with one's welfare. Partners to the relationship in its ideal typical form share the belief that they regard each other's well-being as indistinguishable from their own. Therefore, to care for the other is to care for oneself as well. Subsequent discussion of the dynamics of influence in interpersonal relations proposes that their influence over participants derives from the partners' identification with one another. It should become clear later how this kind of influence flows from the essential trusting nature of the relationship.

An important implication of characterizing the interpersonal relation as trusting is that when the one becomes convinced that the other has acted contrary to one's welfare, one hesitates to believe that one has been betrayed. At the first sign that the other may be acting to one's detriment, one tries to interpret the other's action in ways more compatible with one's beliefs about the relationship: The other acted in error, but with good intentions; the other was, at worst, thoughtless, and will make amends when he or she realizes what he or she has done; the other acted out of desperation, is now feeling as badly as oneself, and should be forgiven (Holmes & Rempel, 1989; Murray & Holmes, 1994). Ultimately, if it becomes undeniable that the other did not, does not, and will not believe that one's own welfare is also his or her own, one feels not so much victimized as sadly mistaken. Trust in an interpersonal relation is not a command and a duty but a guiding faith.

The issue of trust in friendship was captured by E. M. Forster (1939) when he said that if faced with a choice between loyalty to a friend and loyalty to his nation-state, he would hope to have the courage to commit treason. This statement clarifies the importance of trust in any interpersonal relation, and it also clarifies by allusion another aspect of the relationship, namely, that one would suspend judgment of a friend if he or she were to violate even those norms that society imposes on all individuals in the form of law. When a friend breaks a law, one seeks to understand the act or one interprets the behavior to bring it into conformity with some higher law or moral principle. Ideally, one is slow to damn the acts of a friend.

The absence of normative regulation in an interpersonal relation has implications for one's reactions to the other's unexpected behavior. When the other acts in an unexpected (in the sense of unpredicted) way that

---

loyalty. In this way, the relationship is defined as truly normless, and it becomes possible to derive its dynamic of identification. (I believe that Aisha Ray, then a graduate student in social psychology, was the first to articulate the idea of trust in this connection.)

does not violate one's trust, one is likely to be surprised and delighted. Unexpected behavior reveals a new facet of the other, allows one to view him or her with a fresh vision or perspective. One is enlarged and charmed. In contrast, when unexpected behavior occurs in a role relationship, one is probably neither enlarged nor charmed but rather annoyed, at least. Breaking a pattern that is normatively prescribed is a distraction from the business at hand. The relationship is not supposed to be spontaneous or playful. The overture to interpersonalism is often unwelcome.

Primary Groups

Some further attention to the primary group helps to explicate an interpersonal relation. I observed in the previous chapter that what Cooley usually had in mind matched what in the model is identified as an informal role relationship. Nevertheless, one of Cooley's (Cooley, Angell, & Carr, 1933) several definitions of the *primary group* includes elements of what here is called an interpersonal relation.

> A primary group may be defined as a group of from two to possibly fifty or sixty people—i.e., a small number—who are in relatively lasting face-to-face association for no single purpose, but merely as persons rather than as specialized functionaries, agents or employees of any organization. Type examples of the primary group are the family, or household group, the old-fashioned neighborhood, and the spontaneous play-group of children.
>
> The chief characteristics of a primary group are:
>
> 1. Face-to-face association
> 2. The unspecialized character of that association
> 3. Relative permanence
> 4. The small number of persons involved
> 5. The relative intimacy among the participants. (p. 55)

Some of these "chief characteristics of a primary group" come quite close to the present conception of interpersonal relations. Most are face-to-face, although not all. Lee (1964) has pointed out that here Cooley was recognizing the dependency of intimacy on face-to-face contact and that certain corollary examples are exceptional, such as Elizabeth Barrett and Robert Browning, who became ardent friends by mail (Cary 1899; Kinter, 1969). Furthermore, relative permanence is characteristic of many interpersonal relations (although Buber, 1957, believed that the "I–Thou" relationship is highly ephemeral). It might be supposed that by "the unspecialized character of that association," Cooley meant that the primary group is not a role relationship. He described members of a primary group relating to one another "merely as persons rather than as specialized functionaries, agents or employees of any organization" (p. 55).

In several respects, however, Cooley's description of a primary group does not fit the interpersonal relation. Cooley imagined the primary group as consisting of as many as 50 or 60 persons, but that number seems too large for an interpersonal relation, which is most often dyadic, although larger groups are acceptable by definition. More important, Cooley allowed that the primary group can be normatively regulated. When he discussed the elements of the unity—the "we feeling"—of the primary group, Cooley named loyalty as among its most salient characteristics. Loyalty, insofar as it is a moral obligation, is not a characteristic of the normless interpersonal relation.

(Cooley apparently invoked loyalty to help account for the vital socializing function that primary groups perform. The influence of interpersonal relations derives from its own properties. Considering that normative regulation is not only consistent with his concept of the primary group but is deemed by him essential to a major function of such groups, then it is understandable that Cooley should find the foremost example of the primary group in the family, which is not taken here to be an interpersonal relation. Cooley pointed to the normative element of families as the condition for their humanizing influence on their members.)

The difficulty in knowing which of the various characteristics of the primary group Cooley meant to be *defining* prompted Bates and Babchuk (1961) to perform a conceptual analysis. Bates and Babchuk concluded that it is useful to distinguish between social psychological and sociological definitions of *primary group*. They hold that the former is more critical for identifying those relationships responsible for the socializing effects that Cooley had invented the term to explain, whereas the latter identifies the conditions conducive for the formation of primary groups.

Bates and Babchuk's "social psychological" definition of *primary group* conforms closely to the present definition of *interpersonal relation*. Bates and Babchuk included the absence of role regulation as a defining component of a social psychological primary group. One of the authors' contributions was to draw the connection between the primary group and the expressive-task dimension that others have found useful for describing small groups (cf. Bales & Slater, 1955; Jennings, 1947). In the course of doing so, Bates and Babchuk noted that when "members do not impose any instrumental condition for continuation of the group, there is no question of insistence upon an equivalence of exchange in rights and obligations. Such high value is placed on the association that expressions suggesting a contractual relationship are eschewed" (p. 184). Bates and Babchuk also placed mutual positive affect at the core of the definition.

However, their second defining attribute, that "members are predisposed to enter into a wide range of activities," may be characteristic of interpersonal relations, but it is not taken here as defining. As Bates and Babchuk noted, people who like one another will, of course, tend to engage in a lot of mutual activities if they can.

Bates and Babchuk clearly have found the interpersonal relation in certain aspects of Cooley's "primary group." Having thus defined the social psychological primary group, Bates and Babchuk then are led, as I have been, to question whether "the family, or household group, the old-fashioned neighborhood, and the spontaneous play-group of children"

(Cooley et al., 1933, p. 55) are apt examples. That these groups are important socializing agents neither I nor Bates and Babchuk deny. The question, however, is whether such relationships exert social influence by the same processes as other relationships—compare the example of the adult friendship—that are actually, in Cooley's words, more "unspecialized" and "intimate." The different processes by which interpersonal and role relations are hypothesized to influence individuals are discussed later.

Friendship and Family

A comparison of friendship and family as relationships further delineates the interpersonal relation. Rarely do even very close friendships realize the ideal interpersonal relation, but they typically come closer than familial relationships do. Friends are chosen and friendships are maintained only because they are satisfying in themselves. Blood relationships are ascribed and inescapable, and so are spousal relationships in some societies. Moreover, even when spouses are largely freely chosen, social norms regulate their relationship.

Normative expectations are not part of the mechanisms of friendship. One does not expect a distant friend to call or write every week—as one might expect one's distant sons and daughters or brothers and sisters or parents to. Friends are permitted to act as they find comfortable. To press normative expectations ("Why don't you call more often?") is to imply that a friend's style is somehow unacceptable. One might rather look for a new friend, someone whose behavior more fully satisfies one's needs.

Familial relationships are less infused by interpersonalism simply because they are more heavily governed by normative regulations, many codified into law. Spouses have widely recognized rights and obligations vis-à-vis one another, and their marriage bond imposes legal obligations on others. That they share a household tends to impose routinized divisions of labor and informal roles. The family becomes even less interpersonal when it includes children. Parents must support their dependent children; the law requires it and imposes penalties for noncompliance. For their part, children owe their parents fealty, respect, and obedience. If child or parent do not meet these role obligations, the law can step in, declare the child incorrigible or the parent neglectful.

Although family relationships sometimes partake of the interpersonal, they are typically not as strongly or completely interpersonal as intimate adult friendships are. Familial roles are clearly more flexible than most others in our society. Some of the norms governing familial relationships are formal, even codified, but many of its roles are at least partly negotiated among family members; that is, the family is largely an informal social organization. Their negotiations take into account the particularities of the members. At some point, this particularism may amount to the virtual suspension of norms and approach interpersonalism. Spouses then may be close friends, and children sometimes show a glimmer of appreciation of what their parents are as well as for what their parents can do for them.

The parent–child relationship is less interpersonal than an adult friendship also for developmental reasons. The interpersonal relation requires mutual recognition of the partners' identities. It is hardly conceivable then that children can be friends with their parents because children's dependency impels them to ignore so much of the parents' own needs. At the same time, the fluidity of children's psychic organization prevents them from establishing an identity, and it is difficult for the parents to commit themselves to affirming a still developing identity wholeheartedly because they are obliged to try to constrain their children's identity within the parameters of their society and culture. Thus, the establishment of interpersonal relations with parents must wait, if it occurs at all, until children grow into late adolescence and may have achieved what they and their parents recognize as their identity.

Laying out the nature of the interpersonal relation and, for clarification, considering how primary groups, including the family and particularly parent–child relationships, are typically not very interpersonal has brought this discussion to the concept of *identity*, the unit of analysis at this level.

Identity in the Interpersonal Relation

The model's conceptualization of the interpersonal relation converges on Erik Erikson's (1963a) hypothesis about how the development of the capacity for intimacy (a requisite resource for participating in the relationship) depends on the development of a person's identity. It is necessary to dwell for a bit on the nature of an identity in order to clarify what I, and, I think Erikson, mean by it. The term is widely used nowadays both in the social scientific and popular cultures, indeed used in so many ways that it has well nigh lost any useful communicative function.

"Identity" is frequently used synonymously with "self-concept," as the answer to the question, "Who am I?" Erikson (1968) rejected this usage:

> I must register a certain impatience with the faddish equation, never suggested by me, of the term identity with the question "Who am I"— the pertinent question, if it can be put into the first person at all, would be, "What do I want to make of myself, and what do I have to work with?" (p. 314)

Rather, *identity* denotes a particular quality of the self-concept, its continuity. This continuity is of two kinds, which Erikson sometimes distinguished with the terms *role identity* and *ego identity*. Both kinds refer to a person's sense of sameness in different situations. *Role identity* is the sense that one carries a core of enduring motives and resources into whatever roles one takes. *Ego identity* is the sense that one's contemporary motives and resources have their origins in one's life history and help shape what one becomes in the future; it is the sense that the course of one's life is not arbitrary, however obscure. In the terms of the model, *identity* is people's construal of their personality.

The distinction between *identity* and *personality* resides in two related elements of persons' construal. One is the importance with which people endow their enduring characteristics: the more heavily valenced these are, the more they constitute persons' identity. The other is the degree to which people are aware of their enduring characteristics: the more aware people are of them, the more they constitute their identity. Personality, in contrast, consists of all the person's enduring characteristics regardless of their importance or their availability to consciousness. Whereas elements of an identity may be unconscious, they are not deeply repressed. Repressed elements are felt to be alien to oneself. They may very well be active constituents of a personality, but they are not components of one's identity.

Perhaps an example of the absence of an identity will clarify matters. Erikson phrased the potential outcomes of an individual's working through the developmental task of formulating an identity as a polarity, as he has phrased the outcomes of all eight of the developmental tasks with which he finds us confronted over our lifetimes. At first the bipolar terms were "ego identity vs. role diffusion" (1950, p. 227); more recently, he used the terms "ego identity vs. role confusion" (1963a, p. 261). The confusion lies in the person's inability to find any trace of his or her own motives and resources common to role demands. Moreover, one despairs of ever achieving one. A moving example of fundamental identity confusion appears in J. D. Salinger's novel, *Catcher in the Rye* (1951). Holden Caulfield is a 16-year-old who has already given up the search for his identity because he denies a basic premise on which a positive identity can be founded, that one can distinguish between one's real commitments and mere conformity. The revealing episode occurs when Holden slips one night into his family's elegant apartment on Manhattan's Upper West Side in order to gather up some of his things in preparation for running away. He cannot face his parents because he has for the third time just been flunked out of a boarding school. However, he quietly awakens his younger sister, Phoebe, of whom he is very fond, to say goodbye. Phoebe quickly realizes that Holden is in trouble and senses that the trouble is more profound than merely having been flunked out of still another school. Phoebe asks Holden: "Name something you'd like to be. Like a scientist. Or a lawyer or something". But Holden cannot:

> "I couldn't be a scientist. I'm no good in science."
> "Well, a lawyer—like Daddy and all."
> "Lawyers are all right, I guess—but it doesn't appeal to me," I said. "I mean they're alright if they go around saving innocent guys' lives all the time, and like that, but you don't do that kind of stuff if you're a lawyer. All you do is make a lot of dough and play golf and play bridge and buy cars and drink Martinis and look like a hot-shot. And besides. Even if you did go around saving guys' lives and all, how would you know if you did it because you really wanted to save guys' lives, or because what you really wanted to do was be a terrific lawyer, with everybody slapping you on the back and congratulating you in court when the goddamn trial was over, the reporters and everybody, the way

it is in the dirty movies? How would you know you weren't being a phony? The trouble is, you wouldn't." (pp. 223–224)

To oversimplify for present purposes a very complicated and critical process, people construct their identities in essentially two ways. One is by choosing one or a few of the roles that they play to rule their actions and feelings; those norms govern in all situations. Thus, "the family comes first," or one is dedicated to one's profession, or one would rather risk divorce than miss a night out bowling. The other way is by subscribing to a transcending ideology, a set of values that govern across situations; one's life is guided by a small set of principles that cover what one should do under any circumstances: communalism or individualism, humans-in- or over-nature, order or freedom, this religion or that. These two modes of identity formulation are not mutually exclusive; they converge in roles that have the broadest scope, like parenthood or a profession. Still, the distinction is helpful for understanding the formulation of an identity, for it indicates that an identity may be drawn from social organization, through role reification, and from culture, through ideological commitment.

It follows from the norm-free and trusting character of an interpersonal relation that the partners should relate to one another as mutually recognized identities. Trust cannot be reliable when the other is neither socially constrained nor personally committed. Nor, for reasons to be given in the later discussion of the dynamics of interpersonal relations, can one trust oneself to enter an interpersonal relation bare of an identity. The danger of a loss of self is too great. Herein lay the bases for Erikson's developmental hypothesis that individuals acquire the capacity for intimacy only in the course of or after establishing a firm sense of identity. In the model, the environment of interpersonal relations interpenetrates the person at the tangency of the person's motives and resources, specifically, those motives and resources that the partners recognize as the most stable and most important in themselves and in the other.

Group Cohesiveness

Another perspective on interpersonal relations can be gained from the standpoint of the study of group dynamics. There, interpersonal relations are found in the dyadic relationships of members of larger groups. These relationships are important in groups because they help to determine other properties of groups, including the social psychological phenomenon of group influence on its members. A key concept is group cohesiveness, which refers to forces that attract people to groups.

Hagstrom and Selvin (1965) have noted that various indices of cohesiveness—"the degree to which members choose friends from within the group, verbal experiences of satisfaction with the group, participation in group activities, willingness to remain in the group when alternatives exist, and consensus of values relevant to the group's activities" (pp. 32–33)—are not consistently correlated with one another. This raises the question of whether they are indicators of the same concept. Hagstrom and Selvin's survey of college women demonstrates that distinguishing interpersonal relations as a basis for group cohesiveness is useful for understanding individual members' behavior. Individuals' participation in group activities was shown to be a joint function of the basis for the groups' cohesiveness and the number of "best friends" individuals found in the group: In groups attractive to their members mainly on account of the groups' collective goals and activities, a member's participation was unrelated to the number of best friends participating; but, in groups whose cohesion was based on attraction to other specific members, a member's participation depended on a best friend joining the activities. Furthermore, when attraction to the group was low but attraction to specific members was high, friends tended not to participate in the group's activities as much as members who had friends outside the group. Thus, interpersonal relations—termed *sociometric cohesion* by Hagstrom and Selvin—reduced some members' participation, which is an example of the lack of consistently positive correlations among measures of cohesiveness that piqued the researchers' interest in the first place.

Hagstrom and Selvin pointed out that this phenomenon led Festinger, Schachter, and Back (1950) to "correct" an index of group cohesiveness by subtracting the factor of subgroup ("clique") formation so sociometric cohesiveness would relate more consistently to indices like members' participation. However, Hagstrom and Selvin took exception to this strategy on conceptual grounds, asserting that it is more useful to recognize different bases of cohesiveness in the process of constructing theory.

The work of Hagstrom and Selvin and others (e.g., Lott & Lott, 1965) provided an important principle to guide future research in what has been generally identified in social psychology as the field of group dynamics. In terms of the model, small groups, including dyads, can be interpersonal relations, social organizations, repositories of culture, or some mixture of these. (How the model conceptualizes collective behavior is still another matter, which is discussed later.) The group functions quite differently depending on its balance of interpersonal, social organizational, and cultural properties. More important to social psychology, the process by which the individual members and the group influence each other differs.

Thus far, research in group dynamics has not made much of the distinction between these three analytic types of groups. It has not been necessary to do so because research designs have usually insured that the groups observed are social organizations by composing them of strangers who are carefully instructed about the roles they are to follow in the course of the experiment. Individuals are also conscious of their roles as participants and often as students. So norms operate in the experimental situation, and most of the group dynamics research concerns the behavior of role systems—social organizations—and the systems' effects on the role incumbents.

Interpersonal relations have not received much attention in group dynamics. This is not because social psychologists are not aware of their important influence on individuals but rather because of the methodological difficulties of studying them experimentally. Interpersonal relations are not easily created, but methods have been devised to create relatively more or less interpersonal relations by standard experimental manipulations. Most frequently, participants are told that some psychological tests that they have taken make it clear that they and their experimental partner, whom they have never met before, will "get along very well together" and that the other member of their pair will like them; or, conversely, that they will probably not get along very well (e.g., Back, 1951, and many others after Back). However, interpersonal forces created in such ways are normally weak relative to the norms that the participants bring with them to the experiment prescribing how strangers, however compatible or cordial, should treat one another and how participants in experiments should behave. It is testimony to the power of interpersonal forces that these weak manipulations have detectable effects on individuals, which they consistently do. Still, the study of interpersonal relations in their stronger forms, the forms found often in human social life, has been largely neglected.

The field of group dynamics would find fresh impetus if it turned to exploring the distinctive effects of groups as interpersonal relations, as distinct from social organizations and cultures. (See chapter 12.) There are already instances of such research (e.g., Brenner, 1977; Dion & Dion, 1979; Latané & Rodin, 1969; and see chapter 12 on Stanley Milgram's study). They demonstrate that when individuals have experiences while they are embedded in interpersonal relations, they act differently than when they have the same experiences in other social environments.

Mass Media

Another example, this one of only seeming interpersonal relations, rounds out what *interpersonal relation* means. There is a form of this relationship that exists at the psychological level of analysis and is not part of the social environment. It is a kind of pseudo-interpersonalism that sometimes develops between an expressive charismatic leader and his or her followers or audience. This is reflected in the intense, affective, personal but nonmutual response of members of the public to the leader. People feel that they know the leader, that he or she is in many ways like them, understands them, is their friend. Yet they have never met him or her personally, and certainly the relationship is not mutual. Many intellectuals responded to John Kennedy as a congenial and understanding friend.

President Franklin D. Roosevelt was a master at creating this kind of response. When life in the United States became difficult, complicated, and potentially overwhelming to the average citizen, Roosevelt would speak on the radio, in one of his "fireside chats," to reassure his audience and to lead them to a clearer understanding or sympathy with national policy. The "chats" invoked the imagery of intimacy: the hearth, allusions to a pet (Faro, a Scottish terrier), the tone of Roosevelt's delivery. These had the effect of creating an aura of friendship. People found it reassuring to know that "their friend the President was confident" and that he "came into their homes" to explain to them the reasons for his confidence. As a child during this period, I remember vividly the emotional response my parents and I had to "our friend in the White House."

Variations in Interpersonal Relations

Interpersonal relations are not all the same. Even those that are ideally interpersonal—highly affective, completely nonnormative, with trusting partners—can still differ from one another. These differences are important not only for social psychology but for a discipline of interpersonal relations as well. That is, variations make for differences in the quality and quantity of the influence they have on the individuals involved, and they also demand explanation at their own level of analysis.

A discipline of interpersonal relations began to take shape only in the late 1970s. By the 1980s it was possible to put together anthologies of articles on "close relationships" (Derlega, 1984; Kelley et al., 1983) and friendship (Derlega & Winstead, 1986; Gottman & Parker, 1986). With few exceptions, this material is social psychological in the sense that it aims to explain the effects of the relationship on individuals. This work is not for the most part on interpersonality in the sense that it addresses stability and change in such relationships in terms of the dynamics of the relationships themselves.

What should the concepts of a discipline of interpersonal relations be? Its constants are its defining characteristics, that is, that the partners feel strongly positive toward one another (with perhaps some ambivalence), they do not hold one another to social norms, and they trust one another. The dimensions along which interpersonal relations may vary must be compatible with these givens. Furthermore, the dimensions must be ones along which the relationships, the collective entities, vary, not the individuals.

It is desirable for social psychological purposes that these collective dimensions be translatable into the sparse terms by which individuals are conceptualized, their motives and resources. In this way, the social psychological effects of variation in the relations can be traced across the boundaries. What follows then is a discussion of only that limited part of the interpersonal level of analysis that can be expressed in terms of motives and resources, or terms closely related to these. For broader purposes of a discipline of interpersonal relations, other terms may prove more useful.

Distribution of Power

One kind of variation among interpersonal relations is especially relevant to our forthcoming discussion of how individuals influence and are influenced by their participation in this social environment. Interpersonal relations may differ in the relative influence of the participants over one another. At first it may seem that a positive, nonnormative relationship is necessarily egalitarian, and there is a sense in which that is so. In the terms of French and Raven's categories of the bases of social power (1959), neither person has legitimate power. Because there is no role regulation in the ideal typical interpersonal relation, there is no normative legitimacy by which one partner can claim ascendance over the other. They are peers in the strict sense of that term. Nevertheless, interpersonal relations vary in the degree to which one partner dominates the other. What are the conditions within the relationship that account for this?

The primary source of influence in an interpersonal relation is naturally *referent power*, which is derived from the high level of affection that the partners have for one another, their eagerness to please one another, and, most important, their mutual identification. The process of identification in the influence of the interpersonal relation is discussed in chapter 8. Now I point out only that in the ideal typical interpersonal relation, this identification is mutual and cannot account for the differential influence of the partners. Given the nature of the relationship, the employment of coercive power by either partner is disallowed. Trust would quickly erode and with it the relationship.

There remains among French and Raven's categories the *expert* base of power, the recognition by the partners that one is more skilled and knowledgeable than the other in matters relevant to their joint or personal goals. In the terms of the model, one is more resourceful than the other. Unhampered by the constraints of role regulation and mutually committed to each other's and their common welfare, partners to an interpersonal relation defer to one another when differential levels of resources are relevant and apparent. When the differential is general—if one partner is more expert in a wide variety of matters touching on their lives—then that partner's dominance characterizes the relationship. This would not be on account of some norm of equity; even that norm is inconceivable in the ideal typical case. The differential influence becomes established because it is functional to the relationship.

This functional explanation of hierarchy in interpersonal relations is neither teleological nor reductionist. It implies a characterization of the interpersonal level of analysis that includes forces impelling the collective toward its goals. The goals of the relation consist of the inclusive set of the partners' goals insofar as they are known to both partners. It follows from this that the collective organizes its resources to facilitate accomplishing its goals, given the shared awareness of resources by the partners. It should be noted that conceptualizing the goals and means of interpersonal relations in terms of motives and resources provides the theoretical points of interpenetration at the social psychological boundary between the individual and interpersonal levels of analysis.

Absorption of Partners

Interpersonal relations may also vary in the degree to which they so absorb the partners' lives that all of their personal motives and resources are invested in the relationship and are responsive to its viscissitudes. The work of Newcomb (1953, 1961) on the acquaintance process provides an example, and the theoretical basis of that work posits a dynamic principle at the interpersonal level.

In their study *The Acquaintance Process* (1961), Newcomb and his colleagues observed two successive groups of male transfer students to the University of Michigan living together in an off-campus house over the course of an academic year. Their relationships generally conformed to Newcomb's description of the acquaintance process: The students got to know one another and to form attitudes toward one another. Whether they came to like one another or not depended in part on whether they shared similar attitudes toward other objects. Once their feelings about one another crystallized and their attitudes toward objects become known between them, then the attitudes of pairs who liked one another tended toward similarity.

The finding to note here is that the absorption of friends in their relationship varied from one equally strong friendship to another. Between some ultimately close friends, the similarity of their attitudes was general; they agreed on almost everything, from very specific tastes to broad philosophies of life. Among others, the similarity of their attitudes was restricted to only a few but apparently quite important objects, and they agreed to disagree about the rest. For example, one pair of students came to the university with very dissimilar attitudes and backgrounds. Yet their attraction to each other became and remained high. Newcomb noted:

> neither of them succeeded, in their interviews, in pointing to any special basis for this relationship. The first of them put it this way: "It's hard to explain. We never had much in common, but we got along extremely well; I've *always* got along *really* well with every roommate I ever had; we disagreed about many things, but never got mad about it. (p. 219)

Accounting for the differences among interpersonal relations in the absorption of partners requires understanding the dynamics of these relationships within their own level of analysis. Newcomb's hypothesis of *balance* is such a dynamic, although he did not use it to explain differential absorption.

Newcomb's hypothesis posits the condition that two individuals, A and B, either like or dislike one another. No assumption is made that any social norms regulate the partners' relationship. The underlying theory reasons only from their personal attraction. When that attraction is positive, then in effect, the theory posits a relationship resembling the interpersonal, and it is implied in Newcomb's theory that the purer the interpersonality, the more likely it is that the hypothesized events will occur. Thus, the hypothetical principle of balance is attributed to the interpersonal level of analysis.

The balance hypothesis states that if both partners have attitudes toward one another and toward a common object, X, then only certain patterns of attitudes in the A to B re X system occur: If A and B like each other, and one of them likes X, then the other will like X; and if A and B like one another and one of them dislikes X, then the other will dislike X. In other words, the more the relationship between A and B is interpersonal, the more similar their attitudes toward some objects will be. It is important to recognize that this hypothesis pertains to collective, not individual phenomena: It reasons from the nature of a mutual relationship between individuals to dependent *patterns* of the attitudes of both. Although balance has also been attributed to the psychological level of analysis—"if A likes B and believes that B likes X, then A will tend to like X"—Newcomb's hypothesis pertains to a social level, not the psychological.

The hypothesis as propounded is not restricted to the interpersonal case. It is also supposed to cover instances in which A and B dislike one another, and it predicts that their attitudes are dissimilar under these conditions. The hypothesis in the negative case has not been confirmed, however, whereas the hypothesis in the positive case has been consistently confirmed (Aronson & Cope, 1968; Backman & Secord, 1959; Curtis & Miller, 1986). Thus, it is reasonable at this time to regard balance as a principle that operates only under the condition of an interpersonal relation.

The balance principle can account for the finding that equally interpersonal relations differed in their absorption of partners' attitudes. The conditions for the principle to operate selectively to encompass more or less of the partners' attitudes may be cast in collective terms at the interpersonal level, terms that refer to patterns of partners' motives and resources: To the degree that partners share motives to maintain the relation (i.e., agree that they want to continue to like each other), they also share motives for whose satisfaction only one of them is a resource. That is, balance eventuates in the absorption into an interpersonal relation those motives about which the partners are interdependent. Thus, if A and B have an interpersonal relation and if A somehow requires B in order to accomplish a particular goal, then A and B come to share the relevant goal. The goal is absorbed in the relationship. The consequence of this is commonly observed, even cross-culturally—friends help each other (Nicotera & Associates, 1993).

It is noteworthy that only a few of the attitudes of the participants in Newcomb's study were actually absorbed in their relationships. Contrary to the original predictions, partners' political and social attitudes, for example, usually proved to be irrelevant. The only kind of attitude that varied consistently with interpersonal relations were attitudes whose objects were other residents. That is, A's and B's attitude toward housemate X tended to be similar when A and B liked one another. The explanation implied by the logic of interpersonal relations is that partners were consistent resources only for satisfying partners' wanting to interact with other residents. This seems quite plausible: If A wanted to include X in whatever he and partner B were doing together, then B's agreement was at least desirable if not necessary; on the other hand, A might very well have been able to pursue his political and social goals without involving B.

In terms of the strategy of levels of analysis, the principle of balance is an axiom of a closed theory at the interpersonal level. It asserts that a certain relationship holds among primitive concepts under certain conditions of the primitives. Given the conditions of shared motives to maintain a highly affective bond, and in the absence of any normative constraints (i.e., given an interpersonal relation), the joint patterns of the partners' other motives and resources eventuate in still other specifiable patterns of motives, such as the degree of their absorption.

Similarity and Complementarity

As used by Newcomb, the balance principle at the interpersonal level of analysis accounts for similar attitudes. Similarity is not its only logical derivation, however, nor is it limited to attitudes. Put in terms of motives and resources, the principle can account for another kind of variation among interpersonal relations: The motives and resources of the partners may vary in their mix of similarity or complementarity.

Winch (1958) recognized the importance of similar attitudes for the formation of interpersonal relations. "It seems almost self-evident that similarity of interests and attitudes would provide spouses with more gratification than would differences. Hence it would seem that mate-selection should follow a principle of homogeny with respect to interests and attitudes" (p. 10). Winch pointed out that similarity of attitudes helps to explain why mate selection tends to be endogamus to racial, religious, ethnic, and status categories even in the pluralistic American society. In addition, these categories tend to be geographically segregated: People work, recreate, worship, and live in places such that individuals in the same categories are more likely to meet and get to know one another. Propinquity and attitudinal similarity set some limits on the pool from which people select mates.

Winch's research on mate selection revealed the function that complementary motives also serve in the formation and nature of interpersonal relations. Winch asserted that, although circumscribed within limits, "It seems almost as self-evident . . . that complementariness of motivation (e.g., dominance in one and submissiveness in the other spouse, nurturance in one and receptivity in the other) would maximize gratification at the motivational level and hence that at the level of such needs mate selection should follow a principle of complementariness" (p. 10).

Winch did not limit his thinking about complementary motives to the phenomenon of mate selection, nor did he assert that mate selection follows that principle under all conditions. His familiarity with cultural differences in the way people are espoused and with the differences in the bases for sociometric choices in small groups suggested to him the essential conditions under which complementarity of needs is determinative: On the one hand, societies must permit love matches rather than require arranged marriages; on the other, groups must be ends in themselves rather than devoted to the accomplishment of certain tasks. Thus, Winch arrived at the condition of the interpersonal relation for the maximum effect of motive complementarity on the formation and stability of a dyad.

> This reasoning leads us to conclude that complementary needs should be important in the formation of dyads (including the marriage couple) and in other small groups of more than two persons to the degree that (a) there is a lack of clarity of roles in the group, (b) there is a lack of definiteness in the criteria for competence for performing roles, (c) there is an absence of strong sanctions or rewards contingent on the quality of the group's performance of a task, and hence (d) there is a disposition for members of the group to regard each other in terms of personality rather than of role. (p. 308)

Thus, equally ideal interpersonal relations may vary as to the patterns of the motives of their participants, being more or less similar or complementary. These variations may be substantive or structural. Winch presented two structural variations. Type I complementarity is that pattern in which the partners have the same goal, but the strength of the incentives differ. In one example, one partner is strongly motivated to dominate the other, whereas the other has little need to do that. The implication is that the latter does not mind if the former is dominating. Type II complementarity means that the partners have equally strong but different motives, and their motives are mutually gratifiable. For example, one partner is strongly motivated to dominate, and the other ardently wishes to be submissive. In Type II cases, one partner eagerly serves as a resource for the other.

Interpersonal relations may differ in their mix of Type I and Type II complementarities. They may also differ, of course, in the substance of the motives absorbed in the relationship. Variations along such lines are not merely interesting features of interpersonal relations; they may be important for determining the nature and direction of the social influence that the relationship has on the participants and that they have on the relationship.

A theory that posits similar and complementary needs as bases for the formation and stability of interpersonal relations fits well with the nonnormative character of those relations. For if the partners are each directed internally to provide what the other desires, then expectation, in the moral sense, is not required. Each partner comes to expect, in a *predictive* sense, that the other will satisfy the needs of both of them concomitantly.

Winch noted (1958) that American middle-class marriages seem to have a life cycle that can be understood in terms of interpersonal and role relations. These marriages usually begin as predominantly interpersonal relations but also with some normative regulation that flows both from the tasks that are indigenous to an American family and from the informal and formal (legal) norms that govern it. With the birth of offspring, the forces toward role regulation increase significantly and the needs of the spouses must be subordinated to the task of socializing the children and managing the re-organized family. Now the limits to the interpersonality of a married couple that I mentioned earlier become quite obvious. "It seems reasonable," Winch wrote, "that the pressure of these responsibilities would give greater emphasis to *role*. Then twenty to thirty years later the pressure is off. The children leave home, and the mates turn back to each other . . . the third state, then represents a renewed emphasis on *personality*" (p. 309).

It is helpful here to point in the direction that later discussion of interpersonal dynamics take. The model posits that the process of reciprocal influence between an interpersonal relation and the individual is *identification* of each partner with the other. Relevant here is the proposition that identification occurs to a significant degree *unconsciously*. The process includes a fantasy that one is actually the other, and in this respect it tends to be unbounded, rather unselective as to the motive patterns of the other. Clearly, Type II complementarity of motives inhibits such identification; for if one eagerly wishes to dominate, for example, then one cannot comfortably identify with another who wishes just as eagerly to submit. This presents either a theoretical challenge for the proposition that identification is the process of interpersonal influence or an intrinsic problem for the maintenance of interpersonal relations.

Candor

An interpersonal relationship is candid to the degree that its agenda is open to whatever is on the mind of the partners. One might suppose that partners in a trusting relationship are completely open and honest with one another, so that there would be no variation in the degree of candor. However, trust in an interpersonal relation has centrally to do with caring for each other's welfare, and this may under certain conditions require withholding truth or even dishonesty. The psychological analogue to interpersonal candor is unconsciousness. If *unconsciousness* means that individuals cannot express something in words, then its analogue at the interpersonal level is that the partners cannot converse about something. This does not mean necessarily that either of the partners is unconscious of the unspoken substance; rather, it means that the topic is not on their agenda. It may be irrelevant to their relationship, not having been absorbed, or it may be painful to one or both of them. In any case, the partners judge that the matter's absence from the agenda does more good than harm to the relationship.

Where an interpersonal relation is located on this dimension has implications for both its behavior as a collectivity and for its influence on its members. The proliferation of research on self-disclosure is a measure of the importance of this dimension (cf. Collins & Miller, 1995; Dindia & Allen, 1992).

Exclusiveness

Swanson (1965) asserted that all interpersonal relations must deal with the early and continuing problem of *exclusiveness*. This refers to the insulation of the relationship from outside influence, particularly the norms of its social organizational environment. Inasmuch as the interpersonal relation is itself unregulated by social norms, it permits what is regarded from the organizational perspective as deviant and perhaps dangerous. The insularity of the relationship may therefore be of some consequence. A more mature relationship has achieved consensus on its degree of exclusiveness.

A closed theory of interpersonal relations might account for variations in the development of a consensus about exclusiveness by considering how interdependent its partners are in satisfying their deviant motivations. Greater interdependence favors more candor in order to settle the problem and generates forces resistant to societal influence, that is, greater exclusiveness. In the absence of such interdependence, the relationship may tend to be less exclusive and in any case can tolerate less consensus on the issue.

Development

Swanson's (1965) focus on exclusiveness is part of his more general hypothesis about the development of interpersonal relations. A developmental approach is one that posits an invariant sequence of changes common to all normal instances of an entity; the entity is conceptually endowed with inherent patterns of change or growth. Swanson derived the developmental course that an interpersonal relation takes from three intertwined problems inherent to the relation that must be addressed: exclusiveness, absorption, and the distribution of power. Each of these are problems because they each harbor some contradiction to the constants required of the relationship, contradictions emerging either from the level of analysis itself or from the psychological, social, or cultural sectors of its environment.

Although events at other levels of analyses undoubtedly affect variation in the ways these problems arise and are dealt with, Swanson held that an adequate contemporary diagnosis of change can be stated solely in terms of concepts indigenous to the interpersonal level of analysis. Thus, it is expected that a viable interpersonal relation over time achieves greater consensus about absorption, exclusiveness, and its divisions of power and labor. Its stage of development is a dimension of maturity along which interpersonal relations can be ordered.

This discussion of dimensions along which interpersonal relations may vary illustrates that the interpersonal relation is no stranger to social psychological theory. Many social psychological theories suggest ways in which interpersonal relations may be considered in their own right, at their own level of analysis. They imply ways that the relation itself can vary, ways that can be translated into the terms of motives and resources; and they suggest dynamic principles, such as balance and development, that operate at the interpersonal level to shape the patterns.

Psychological Conditions

Although the strategy of levels of analysis assumes that closed theory can be built at any level, it also recognizes the openness of a level to the influences of other levels. Indeed, when it is used, as it is here, to advance a boundary discipline, the influences of the other levels are of central interest. Interpersonal relations are located in the social psychological model in the midst of psychological, social organizational, and cultural environments. Conditions in all those environments are hypothesized to determine whether interpersonal relations form and what form they take, and how interpersonal relations may influence them. The social psychological aims of this work focus it on the psychological environment of interpersonal relations.

Individuals vary in their participation in any of the three social environments delineated here. One implication of this general proposition is that, within limits, individuals may be active choosers as well as sharers and shapers of their social environments. Not only do they choose their friends, but they also choose whether or not to have friends; not only do they opt to take some roles rather than others and shape the roles they play, but they choose how much role taking they do; not only do they subscribe to only certain beliefs and values, but they also decide how completely they subscribe to any culture. Accrued personal experience makes a difference in individuals' choices in this regard, and in this sense, individuals are not necessarily members of every social environment that presses for their participation.

Individuals' participation in interpersonal relations is not imperative, but their participation in social organization and culture is. It seems weird even to imagine that some individuals opt not to participate much in any social organization or to reject much of the culture available to them. The idea is indeed weird; it is the very definition of *weird*, that is, of deviancy, or of pathology. What is meant by *deviancy* is that individuals violate social roles and defect from the local consensus about truth and virtue. Of course, roles vary in the degree to which they compel certain actions and the motives and resources implied by those actions; and cultures are equivocal. However, every social organization and culture has limits beyond which deviance is unacceptable. Individuals who exclude themselves from the local consensus are playing at these limits or beyond. This is not the case for interpersonal relations.

There is greater tolerance for friendlessness. Individuals may not participate in anything approaching an interpersonal relation and still not be thought sick or deviant, although in some times and places they may be regarded as pitiful and maladjusted. Cultures vary with regard to beliefs about friendship. American culture values it. We worry about children and adolescents who cannot or will not make friends and about loveless adults. To like others is considered almost as important as to be liked, and social isolation is bad. In other cultures, interpersonalism is not so highly valued. Margaret Mead (1928/1933) described relationships among the early 20th century Samoans as shallow, and she reported that their culture disparaged heavy interpersonal emotional investments. Authoritarian cultures of the right and left put loyalty to the state ahead of friendship. In a bureaucracy, the values of rationality and achievement come before intimacy. When friendships are not deemed important, people are free to opt out of them without sanction, as they may not opt out of the social organizational or cultural environments.

Therefore, the psychological environment is relatively more determinative of individual differences in participation in interpersonal relations. Interpersonal relations are not believed to be so essential to the adequate socialization and acculturation of the person. Where there are not strong sociocultural forces for or against participation in interpersonal relations, then individual differences weigh heavily.

The psychological conditions for individuals' participation in interpersonal relations can be characterized in terms of the concepts at the individual level of analysis. Relative proneness to interpersonality or intimacy has to do with individuals' motivation to commit themselves to affective, socially unregulated, and trusting relationships; and with the resources that allow them to engage in such relationships. People vary with respect to the degree that they desire friendships, that is, with respect to the pleasure they anticipate will flow from loosening or dissolving the boundaries of their selves in relation to specific others and with respect to the danger they fear in the intimate merging of self with another. Furthermore, people come to the opportunities for friendship with different capacities to embrace them.

> Friendships do not just happen; they have to be made—made to start, made to work, made to develop, kept in good working order, and preserved from going sour. To do all this we need to be active and skillful . . . To develop a close friendship with someone who used to be a stranger we have to assess the other person accurately, adopt appropriate styles of communication and bodily posture, and find out how to satisfy mutual personality needs; we have to learn how to adjust our behavior to the other person and to select and reveal the right sorts of information and opinions in an inviting, encouraging way in the appropriate style and circumstance; we have to build up trust, to make suitable demands and build up commitment; and we have to perform. . . other more difficult skills . . . (Duck, 1983, p. 10)

Theory and data about motivation to participate in interpersonal relations may be found in relation to the need to affiliate (e.g., Schachter, 1959; Shipley & Veroff, 1952) and about what makes some people more attractive than others. Individual propensities to become friends have received a great deal of attention from students of personality, foremost among these Erik Erikson and Harry Stack Sullivan.

Erikson (1968) proposed that the development of the capacity for intimacy reaches its critical point during late adolescence and early adulthood. Its establishment depends on the adequate resolution of previous crises in the life cycle, particularly the earliest crisis of trusting and the adolescent crisis of identity formation. Interpersonal trust, according to Erikson, is a central component of individuals' more general optimism about encounters with the world, cultivated out of infantile experiences with mutual regulation of their needs and impulses with the attentions of caregivers. Infants instinctively experience panic when their survival seems to be threatened by pain, hunger, and thirst; conversely, when their security is assured, they experience a sense of well-being. When well-being consistently flows from the timely and appropriate ministrations of caregivers, the infant learns to trust associations with others, that is, to regard them generally as a source of satisfaction. Whereas the effects of infantile experiences are not irreversible, the centrality of the issue of survival through dependency is so great at infancy that early experiences strongly affect the enduring orientation to trust or to mistrust others. Obviously a tendency to be trustful of others is implicated in an individual's propensity to enter into interpersonal relations.

Because an adequate sense of identity is requisite to the capacity for intimacy, interpersonal fusion is an important consideration here. The prototype of interpersonal fusion—though it is not by any means its only realization, as Erikson pointed out—is sexual intercourse. There is always in the sexual encounter the potential for both exhilaration and danger in the dissolution of the boundary of the self. Whether this potential is a threat or promise depends on the confidence of the individual's sense of identity. When one is sure of the basic continuity of one's being, then fusion with another in the sexual act is anticipated as a temporary and liberating experience. Having a firm sense of identity means that one has organized an image of oneself, recognizes its origins in what one was, and (most important in this context) is confident that that image has a future. Under these circumstances, one can abandon oneself in a sexual encounter with the assurance that one will find oneself again. But

> where an assured sense of identity is missing even friendships and affairs become desperate attempts at delineating the fuzzy outlines of identity ... During lovemaking or in sexual fantasies, a loosening of sexual identity threatens: it even becomes unclear whether sexual excitement is experienced by the individual or by his partner ... the ego thus loses its flexible capacity for abandoning itself to sexual and affectual sensations, in a fusion with another individual who is both partner to the sensations and guarantor of one's continuing identity: fusion with another becomes identity loss. (Erikson, 1959, p. 125)

An interpersonal relation can threaten insecure ego identity whether or not the relationship includes sexual intimacy. This is so, despite the element of identity affirmation inherent in interpersonal relations. Interpersonal relations also elicit self-abandonment from time to time, as when one is ready to cast aside one's comfort or one's principles in the service of a friend; or when one identifies so strongly with the other that the boundary of the self dissolves. Unless one were confident of recovering oneself, and even more, that the other can be trusted to assist in the recovery, one could not comfortably enter into an interpersonal relation.

Harry Stack Sullivan (1953) speculated that the need for intimacy is the last of the major developments toward a mature personality. For Sullivan, intimacy meant "collaboration with at least one other, preferably more others; and in this collaboration there is a very striking feature of a very lively sensitivity to the needs of the other and the interpersonal security or absence of anxiety in the other" (p. 310). *Collaboration* connoted for Sullivan a fusion of personalities, "a matter of *we*" (p. 246). Sullivan's conception of interpersonal intimacy is independent of sexuality, from what he called the "lust dynamism."

> And so I trust that you will finally and forever grasp that interpersonal intimacy can really consist of a great many things without genital contact; that intimacy in this sense means, just as it always has meant, closeness, without specifying that which is close other than the persons. Intimacy is that type of situation involving two people which permits validation of all components of personal worth. Validation of personal worth requires a type of relationship which I call collaboration, by which I mean clearly formulated adjustments of one's behavior to the expressed needs of the other person in the pursuit of increasingly identical—that is, more and more nearly mutual—satisfactions, and in the maintenance of increasingly similar security operations. (p. 246)

Like Erikson, Sullivan hypothesized that the emergence of the need and the capacity for intimacy was a developmental phenomenon, depending on the consequences of earlier experiences. Unlike Erikson, Sullivan traced the taproots of intimacy to preadolescence rather than to infancy and adolescence.

> Just as the juvenile era was marked by a significant change—the development of the need for compeers, for playmates rather like oneself —the beginning of preadolescence is equally spectacularly marked, in my model of development, by the appearance of a new type of interest in another person. These changes are the result of maturation and development, or experience. This new interest in the preadolescent era is not as general as the use of language toward others was in childhood, or the need of similar people as playmates was in the juvenile era. Instead, it is a specific new type of interest in a *particular* member of the same sex who becomes a chum or close friend. This change represents the beginning of something very like full-blown, psychiatrically defined *love*. In other words, the other fellow takes on a perfectly novel relationship with the person concerned: he becomes of practically equal

importance in all fields of value . . . thus the developmental epoch of preadolescence is marked by the coming of the integrating tendencies which, when they are completely developed, we call love, or, to say it in another way, by the manifestation of the need for interpersonal intimacy. (pp. 245–246)

Even though he was not so committed to the idea of a critical period as Erikson and other psychoanalytic theorists, Sullivan maintained that the absence of same sex friendships during preadolescence was likely to warp the developing personality. Whereas such a warp might be corrected by timely experience or by skilled and deliberate intervention, failure to develop a capacity for intimacy beginning in preadolescence and culminating in late adolescence had pervasive consequences. For example, Sullivan asserted that all social relationships with other men, the quite impersonal as well as the more personal, were uneasy ones for men who had not experienced preadolescent chumship. Furthermore, lacking the capacity for intimacy, people are especially prone to profound loneliness, a feeling even more painful, Sullivan believed, than fear and anxiety.

Maas (1968) looked into the files of the Berkeley Guidance Study to investigate whether preadolescent chumship is actually a precursor of the adult capacity for intimacy. Judges identified 24 middle-aged men and women whose materials gave evidence of their interpersonal warmth and 20 who were clearly quite aloof. Data had been collected on the peer relationships of all 44 of these individuals when they were 8 through 12 years old. Maas found that about equal proportions of the warm and aloof adults had experienced close relationships with peers during their preadolescence. These relationships endured for a year or more and included a mutual concern for the others' needs and interests. Whereas the experience of close preadolescent friendships did not distinguish the warm from the aloof adults, the inclusion in these friendships of opposite sex peers and somewhat older peers did: The greater capacity for intimacy at adulthood was preceded by close heterosexual and cross-age friendships. Maas found some gender differences as well: Fewer warm than aloof adult men had broken off with their close friends during their preadolescent years; more warm than aloof adult women had been members of friendship groups, whereas the aloof women more often maintained dyadic relationships. Maas's study suggested that the level of intimacy in friendships that Sullivan attributed to preadolescents may indeed be reached by a substantial proportion of individuals, but that having a preadolescent chum is not a precondition for the development of the capacity for adult intimacy. However, the extension of friendship against prevailing norms for preadolescents—to members of the opposite sex and to older peers— seems to characterize more intimate adults.

An Interpersonal Discipline

Thus, interpersonal relations are implicit throughout much of social psychological theory and research. These are relationships between people who like each other a great deal and whose behavior toward one another is governed not by social obligation but by the motives and resources of each taking into account those of the other. Such relationships are found in some but not all of what have been called primary groups. They lie at the heart of mature friendships.

No demarcated science of interpersonal relations exists. One can identify a formal domain for each of the other levels of analysis in the social psychological scheme, but interpersonal relations has no recognized place among the disciplines. Nevertheless, one can find pertinent theory and research scattered throughout the social sciences. There is a basis for an interpersonal discipline.

Most attention has been focused on how interpersonal relations form —the characteristics of people who chose one another, the circumstances under which they meet, become acquainted, become friends—and dissolve. Most of the theory is open, relating events at other levels of analysis to interpersonal events. At the individual level, for example, is found the capacity for intimacy; at the social organizational level, social status; at the cultural level, the value of friendship. Such variables set the conditions more or less conducive to interpersonal relations generally or between certain individuals.

Social science has little to say about variations in the nature of interpersonal relations and their internal dynamics, that is, closed theory is lacking. Balance theory has some of this character when it is applied to events between people rather than to what goes on in one person's mind. Newcomb's version of balance theory simply assumes that each partner's perceptions of the other's attitudes tends to be accurate, and the theory then generates hypotheses not only about the formation and dissolution of bonds of attractions but also about interpersonal patterns of attitudes. Although it is conceptually too sparse in its present state to account for more than a few variations in patterns, balance theory has some promise.

During the course of this discussion of the interpersonal relation, it has been noted that sometimes social norms develop in the process of solving relational problems. It has been stated, for example, that partners "agree" and that they "come to expect." This implies that there is a strain toward role relationships in any interpersonal relation. This indeed seems to be the case (just as under some conditions, such as its longevity and frequent face-to-face interaction, there are strains toward interpersonal relations in a role relationship). Interpersonal relations need not become social organizations however, or at least not to a high degree. Agreements may be made and yet remain always open to change. Expectations may be entirely predictive rather than normative. The title of Swanson's (1965) chapter, "The Routinization of Love," expresses this idea nicely: Recurrent patterns of action can develop outside of normative constraints. Whereas they may become expectable, especially when there is work to be done or a compelling social organization to accommodate, the routines of interpersonal relations may remain simply a joint function of the psyches of the partners. In this respect they stand conceptually on the interpersonal side of informal social organization.

It is useful for social psychological theory and research to recognize interpersonal relations and to take them into account. They are found in their ideal form rarely if at all, but at least some small degrees of inter-personality often infuse situations and have important effects. When one tries to understand why individuals act as they do and the effects of their action—whether this involves conformity to group norms, attitude change, mate selection, a sense of personal well-being, the revolutionary impact of a single personality, or a host of other phenomena—the explanatory potential of interpersonal relations should be considered. An adequate contemporary diagnosis of the situation that leads to or flows from action does not nearly so often require an account of interpersonal dynamics as it does of social organization and culture, but such an account sometimes substantially increases the adequacy of an explanation. So, in the initial analysis of a theoretical or concrete problem, one is advised to determine to what degree the individuals involved have affective bonds, are disposed to suspend the common rules of role regulation in their interaction, and trust each other. If these conditions pertain, then they should be synthesized with psychological, social, and cultural conditions to formulate an adequate diagnosis.

In introducing the interpersonal component of this social psychological model, I recognize that I have tended to make the "ideal" seem so in a moral or beneficial rather than simply in a theoretically strategic sense. I hope that this affinity of mine does not distract readers from the theoretical position.

6 _____

Culture

Anatol Rapoport (1976) wrote, "The world of symbols is itself a part of our environment. We live in an ocean of words, concepts, slogans, ideas, beliefs, loyalties, and enmities as literally as we live in an atmosphere" (p. 236). Rapoport was calling attention to an important component of the social environment. A concept of culture is necessary in the theoretical model of the social psychological domain because it captures a social source and a social effect of psychological phenomena that otherwise are not accounted for. Culture is not a person with whom one may share an interpersonal relation and with whom one identifies (but culture may figure in whether one has any interpersonal relations and with whom). Nor is culture composed of social organizations to which one becomes socialized (although culture has a great deal to do with what roles are available or mandatory). Culture is also the chief vehicle by which some rare individuals profoundly alter the environments in which they and others live.

I begin this discussion of the cultural level of analysis by asserting its reality because its reality is difficult for many to accept. I then define *culture* and elaborate on the definition by relating familiar terms to it— ideology, technology, subculture, contraculture. Culture is then located as a level of analysis, first among its social environments and then, in order to serve its special translating function for the model, in relation to the material environment beyond the model. Cultural variation, a consequence and cause of environmental variation, is described next in a discussion of structural and substantive dimensions along which cultures may differ. Finally, the main points of the chapter are reviewed as they appear in a striking illustration drawn from the literature of cultural anthropology, an account of a people confronting a powerful, alien technology.

The Nature of Culture

Shared Beliefs

Individuals are born among people who share beliefs about the world into which they have been born and values that impose a moral order on that world. These beliefs have already had their effects on the very circumstances of the individuals' birth—in what place, by what means, in whose company, and with what hospitality their nativity is greeted. Most of those beliefs existed long before they were born, indeed long before the birth of any of those present, and the beliefs persist after they are all gone. The point is, it is not completely accurate to say that the beliefs reside *in* people. In the sense that is important here, beliefs also reside *among* people. In the words of Liang, Moreland, and Argote (1995), it resides in "transactive memory." There, culture is *sui generis.*

The scientific potentiality of a concept of *culture* as a system of shared beliefs has had several champions. A "science of ideas" was proposed as early as 1801 (Destutt de Tracy, 1801). According to Kroeber and Kluckhohn's review of the scientific history of the term (1952/1963), "culture" as ideas or beliefs was introduced to American sociocultural literature by Lester Ward in 1903 with this metaphor: "A culture is a social structure, a social organism, if anyone prefers, and ideas are its germs" (Ward, 1919, p. 235). Parsons identified a separate level of "belief systems" in his general theory of action (cf. Parsons, 1951; Parsons & Platt, 1973), Geertz (1973) has written of a "system of symbols," and Sorokin (1947/1962) distinguished an "ideological culture" that is the progenitor of "material" and "behavioral" culture.

I was first impressed with the usefulness of the concept by my late University of Michigan colleague Leslie A. White (1969). White was an articulate and persuasive proponent of culture as a distinctive level of analysis. After spending the earlier part of his career in field studies of Native Americans, White became increasingly preoccupied with the promulgation and defense of a "new science of culturology and with training cohorts of students in its principles" (1969, p. x). He marshaled to this effort a keen understanding of science generally, a broad familiarity with both its social and natural branches, and a colorful and provocative style.

Defining *culture* as shared beliefs leaves out some things that other writers have used the term to encompass. Sorokin (1962/1947) included both "material" and "behavioral" components, and together with ideas, they cover the usage pretty well. Material culture consists of human artifacts, both tools and what tools produce. These materials have traditionally occupied the attention of social anthropologists, who often have no other way of retrieving the culture of an ancient people except by what they have left behind by way of pots, shelters, tombs, and axes. The behavioral component of culture consists of what a collectivity of people do, habitually and similarly.

(It seems that the importance given to this behavioral component was a consequence of cross-cultural diffusion between social anthropologists and philosophical positivism, especially as that philosophy was manifested in behavioristic psychology. So Linton included in his definition of culture, along with ideas, "conditioned emotional responses, and patterns of habitual behavior which the members of that society have acquired through instructions or imitation and which they share to a greater or less degree" [1936, p. 288]. Perhaps it was not only the successes and popularity of behaviorism and positivism that prompted this behavioral approach to culture. The conceptualization also directed investigators' attention to evidence other than the verbal statements of informants, on which field methods of the time heavily relied. It grew out of a recognition of what C. Kluckhohn [Kroeber & Kluckhohn, 1963] labeled *implicit culture,* beliefs that informants could not or would not articulate but which had to be postulated to account for recurring behaviors by many of the people in frequent interactions with one another. The behavior itself was the only empirical evidence for the implicit culture.)

From the perspective of the social psychological model's definition of culture, materials and behaviors are important evidence for culture, but they are not culture itself. Materials and behaviors express and reflect beliefs, but they are obviously not the beliefs. A stone carving of a fish may be an artifact of a culture, a gesture expressing a belief; but in different contexts, it represents different beliefs. To Native Americans fishing in the Klamath River, the sign was a way of wishing for a plentiful salmon run; for the early Christians, it was a badge of membership. Social psychology attends to the meaning of the fish, not to the carving. (The material carving itself may be of interest as a clue to the technological knowledge of the carver.) Similarly, an adult's putting his thumb in his mouth is interpreted as immature by Americans and derisive by Italians; the meaning, not the location of the thumb, is pertinent. In a consideration of culture, one is interested in the acts and products of people only insofar as these reveal the beliefs to which the people collectively subscribe. The conceptualization of culture as consisting of shared beliefs captures its essence as it concerns social psychology.

The "shared beliefs" of culture are of two kinds: beliefs *about* and beliefs *in*, facts and faith, technology and ideology. Geertz (1973), drawing in turn on Craik (1952), has expressed the distinction quite well:

> cultural patterns are "models" . . . sets of symbols whose relations to one another "model" relations among entities, processes or what-have-you in physical, organic, social, or psychological systems by "paralleling," "imitating," or "simulating" them. The term "model" has, however, two senses—an "of" sense and a "for" sense—and though these are but aspects of the same basic concept they are very much worth distinguishing for analytic purposes. In the first, what is stressed is the manipulation of symbol structures so as to bring them more or less closely, into parallel with the pre-established non-symbolic system, as when we grasp how dams work by developing a theory of hydraulics or constructing a flow chart. The theory or chart models physical relationships in such a way—that is, by expressing their structure in synoptic form—as to render them apprehensible; it is a model *of* "reality." In the second, what is stressed is the manipulation of the nonsymbolic system in terms of the relationships expressed in the symbolic, as when we construct a dam according to the specifications implied in a hydraulic theory or the conclusions drawn from the flow chart. Here, the theory is a model under whose guidance physical relationships are organized: it is a model *for* "reality." For psychological and social systems, and for cultural models that we would not ordinarily refer to as "theories," but rather as "doctrines," "melodies," or "rites," the case is in no way different. Unlike genes, and other nonsymbolic information sources, which are only models *for* not models *of*, culture patterns have an intrinsic double aspect: they give meaning that is in objective con-

ceptual form, to social and psychological reality both by shaping themselves to it and by shaping it to themselves. (p. 93)

Those beliefs that make up the technological component of culture are what Geertz referred to as "models of"; they assert the existence of specified objects or events or the relationships, causal and otherwise, among them. The ideological component of culture consists of "models for," the values that state the desirable rather than the actual.

Technology and ideology cannot always be sharply distinguished. It is sometimes hard to tell whether an assertion about human nature, for example, is a fact or a wish, a description of what is true or of what could or should be true. Nevertheless, the two components are often, as Geertz has written, "very much worth distinguishing for analytic purposes," for their reciprocal relationships with individuals and with the other two levels of the social environment seem to be somewhat different. I suggest later that individuals' acceptance of what they perceive to be facts or perceive to be values depends on somewhat different conditions.

One of the reasons ideology and technology are sometimes indistinguishable is that values are often implied in what seem to be merely assertions of facts. When LeVine described culture as, among other things, a "body of rules concerning the ways in which individuals . . . *should* . . . think about themselves and their environments" (1973, p. 4; emphasis added), he touched on the question of sanity. Individuals simply must subscribe to much of the consensual reality to avoid being outcast. Believing in the ghostly manifestations of the departed and taking their advice could get one into a lot of trouble in some times and in some places; and so could not believing this in others. In this way, technology, like ideology, has an imperative obligation about it. A lot of facts must be taken for granted; they are considered inarguable.

The other defining characteristic of culture is that the ideological and technological beliefs of which it consists are shared. This attribute imbues the concept with the extra-individual (Leslie White, 1973: "extrasomatic"), the environmental status that it occupies in the model. A person cannot have his or her own culture. People are carriers of beliefs that are derived directly or indirectly from their cultural environment, but in their minds these ideas are motives, resources, and so on. Culture is a boundary condition to the psychological level of analysis.

As few as two people may share a culture; it does not seem useful to require that there be more. Allowing this minimal collectivity permits one to conceive of the culture of a small group. Whereas there are few cases in which two people share beliefs that are much different from the beliefs of a larger number, there are cases of "folie a deux" in which an elaborate structure of strange beliefs is mutually agreed on by only a pair of people. Those beliefs constitute their culture, and it affects their action and experience as though it were more widely shared.

Shared means more than similar belief. It includes as well mutual awareness of the consensus. It is conceivable, in these terms, for individuals to have the same beliefs but not share a culture. Hence, having the technology of fire does not put two peoples in the same culture–group. The technology of fire was discovered independently by peoples who had no communication and therefore a similar but not a common culture. Only if members of each culture know that the others also have the technique do they share the technology.

It is apparent that collectivities can share their cultures in different degrees. Two sets of beliefs may include some of the same elements, whereas each has other elements as well, and one set may completely encompass another and have additional elements as well. Our language to describe this situation is unfortunately misleading. We speak of "cultures" and "subcultures," almost inevitably implying a degree of consensus that does not really exist and a superordinate–subordinate relationship that sometimes denigrates certain sets of beliefs. Subculture here simply means a relatively small set of differentiated beliefs that are included in a larger set.

Subcultures and Contracultures

One may speak, for example, of the subculture of a science, that system of shared beliefs that defines a particular scientific discipline. People who share what Kuhn (1970) called the "paradigm" of a science are subscribing to "the entire constellation of beliefs, values, techniques and so on shared by the members of a given community" (p. 175). Presumably, practitioners of that discipline also subscribe to the more general culture of science, which is itself a subculture to an even more general culture. (If Kuhn's "paradigm of a science" is such a cultural concept, then Kuhn's approach to the study of the history of science is essentially anthropological or culturological. The course of a science could be considered a kind of culture change, susceptible to explanation by the same general principles that explain the course of any culture.)

Yinger's (1965) definition of a contraculture illustrates concept building at the cultural level of analysis. A *contraculture* is "a series of inverse or countervalues (opposed to those of the surrounding society) in the face of serious frustration or conflict" (p. 231). Reference to "inverse or countervalues" defines contraculture strictly in terms of relational properties of ideas themselves. "Contraculture" identifies an attribute of value conflict. It does not simply mean that two beliefs or belief systems are contradictory. It means that at least one of the sets of beliefs includes a rejection of the other. In Yinger's application, the delinquent contraculture is a system of beliefs that includes rejection of conventional values. It follows from this definition that whenever a significant change occurs in conventional values, the delinquent contraculture will change to contradict it, regardless of the specific content of the new convention. So, for example, if the use of marijuana becomes acceptable to the conventional culture, it diminishes in value in the delinquent contraculture.

A culture is not in the first instance identified with any collectivity. A culture is not necessarily coterminus with a society, and members of a society may subscribe to different, contradictory, or contracultures. That interdependent social organizations may subscribe to countervalues has consequences which Abraham Lincoln warned of at the brink of the American Civil War: "A house divided against itself cannot stand." However, the consequences may be felt more severely at the social organizational level than at the cultural. Belief systems may not be much affected merely by encountering contradiction. The social organization of the American South—its economy, its politics, its class structure—were profoundly altered by the Civil War. At the same time, Southern White culture did not change as rapidly or as much. Cultures may tolerate contradiction better than social organizations do because interdependency has different meanings at the two levels and represents conditions with different implications. This is one reason why it seems useful to maintain a notion of culture that is independent of its social or physical location. Social and physical location is important only insofar as it affects the capacity for people to communicate to effect the emergence and change in a culture.

To summarize this conceptualization of culture: A culture exists to the degree that two or more people are convinced of the same beliefs and are aware of their common conviction. The units of analysis of culture are ideas—facts, which are its technology, and values, its ideology; and the status of some ideas as facts or values is ambiguous. The terms with which cultures are described and explained are properties of ideas themselves, not of the collectivities that share them.

Culture is certainly the most disembodied level in the social psychological model. Interpersonal relations include personal identities as their elements, and social organization consists of roles that persons occupy. The ideas that constitute culture, however, have a more abstract character. People do not occupy beliefs; rather, they are occupied by them. More precisely, the ideas of culture are among persons, outside of each.

Of course, the empirical possibility of culture and the forms it takes depend partly on its environments. One of these is the psychological and involves the givens of human minds in communication. An adequate explanation for the existence of culture as defined here must be compatible with the nature of human beings and their interaction. Thus, cultures develop when symboling beings discover through communication that they have common problems and through continuing communication formulate ideological and technological solutions to those problems. Nevertheless, as White (1973) repeatedly insisted, the nature of human beings, being fairly constant over historical time and geographical space, cannot explain cultural *variation*. Differences in cultures from time to time and place to place are not generally the consequences of changes in human minds but are more often among the causes of psychological differences.

Culture has a dynamic of its own. The rules of the levels of analysis strategy require that, for the purpose of formulating universal explanatory laws, culture must be considered a closed system. An adequate explanation for the state of culture must be stated in terms of the immediate prior state of that culture. All of those influences in the environments of a culture on culture must be translated into properties of the ideas of the culture.

Environments of Culture

Social Organization

Ward's metaphorical description of culture (first published in 1903; see Ward, 1919) has two implications regarding the relationship between what the model terms *social organization* and *culture*. It demonstrates that the cultural level of analysis is not always sharply distinguished from the social organizational and also that there is some at least vague recognition that culture and social organization interpenetrate. On the one hand, the inclusion of nonnormative technological beliefs in culture most definitively distinguishes the cultural from the social organizational level of analysis. Assertions of fact cannot be subsumed in roles. On the other hand, the ideological or values component of a culture can also be distinguished from social norms by the breadth of their application, but not so clearly as the technology component.

The ideology of a culture consists of those values that are meant to be applied universally, irrespective of roles. Duveen and Lloyd (1990) made this distinction when they conceived of values as exerting *imperative* obligations and norms as exerting *contractual* obligations. Whereas values oblige everyone, norms oblige only those who enter certain roles and by doing so contract to obey their norms. (*Contract* is not the appropriate word in those cases of role casting, when individuals are assigned roles whether or not they want to play them.) "Culture" asserts fundamental values, the ones that imply "*Everyone* should . . . ." Gaskell and Fraser (1990) distinguished similarly between "strong" and "weak" definitions of "widespread beliefs," that is, of widely shared ideas: A strong definition is one that is normative for a role; a weak one forms the basis for individuals' judgments of value. Schwartz (1994) defined *values* as "desirable transituational goals, varying in importance, that serve as guiding principles in the life of a person or other social entity" (p. 21), where *transituational* means "across roles."

Surely there are sometimes exemptions from "universal" values, but their universality can nevertheless be detected when their excused violations are occasions for rituals of forgiveness and reaffirmation. For example, the value placed on human life in many cultures forbids deliberate homicide; but certain role takers—soldiers, police, doctors, executioners—are specifically excused under certain conditions, in the name of patriotism, another life, or justice. That the norm is supposed nevertheless to be generally inviolable is revealed in the narrow and explicit statements of mitigating circumstances and the tight control exercised over exempted occasions. Here, as in all cases, the fundamental values that are the ideological component of culture shape the norms that are specific to roles.

Of course, breadth of application is a matter of degree, and the distinction between what belongs to the cultural and what to the social organizational level of analysis is not always clear. This is not a theoretical weakness. To the contrary, that the conceptualizations of values and norms sometimes make them indistinguishable in abstract and concrete instances nominates them as points of tangency between the cultural and social organizational levels of analysis.

There are problems for whose solutions the merger of "sociocultural" is useful, and there are problems for which "socioculture" hinders adequate explanation. Anthropologist Kroeber and sociologist Parsons (1958) collaborated in making this point:

> Separating cultural from societal aspects is not a classifying of concrete and empirically discrete sets of phenomena. They are distinct systems in that they abstract or select two analytically distinct sets of components from the same concrete phenomena. Statements made about relationships within a cultural pattern are thus of a different order from those within a system of societal relationships. Neither can be directly reduced to terms of the other; that is to say, the order of relationship within one is independent from that in the other. Careful attention to this independence greatly increases the power of analytical precision. . . . We suggest that it is useful to define the concept *culture* (as) transmitted and created content and patterns of values, ideas, and other symbolically meaningful systems . . . . On the other hand, we suggest that the term *society*—or more generally, *social system*—be used to designate the specifically relational system of interaction among individuals and collectivities. To speak of a "member of a culture" should be understood as an ellipsis meaning a "member of the society of culture X." (pp. 582–583)

Individuals

Having earlier asserted the independence of cultural from psychological theory, I elaborate now on the ways the psychological givens condition the general nature of culture. (Reserved for the next section, on the dynamics of social psychology, is the discussion of how individual differences affect and are affected by the cultural environment.) Humankind is an environment—a boundary condition of a culture. No adequate closed theory of culture can be constructed that does not take human nature into account, for there would be no one to think the ideas of culture.

At the same time, were it not for shared beliefs, humans could not coordinate their activities and would not survive. Our joint survival requires coordination of our behavior, which depends on our communicating and agreeing. Like theories of other social phenomena, cultural theories begin with the essential social character of human beings, often epitomized in the helplessness of the human infant. To paraphrase the song (Merrill, 1964), people who need people are the *onliest* people in the world. Thus, there are both cultural prerequisites to humanity and human prerequisites to culture.

Some theorists have begun their search for the causes of cultural variation explicitly in apparently universal properties of human nature. LeVine (1973) suggested that a comparative study of cultures should be based on what humans everywhere have in common. Among these, LeVine cited physical manifestations of affective reactions, like weeping, blushing, nausea, sexual arousal, anxiety; the diurnal cycle of waking, eating, activity, and resting; and the life cycle from birth to death. Cultural variation, LeVine proposed, can most usefully be described as different values affecting the way these universals are managed from group to group. So human constants would provide the framework for the analysis of cultural variation.

Nevertheless, LeVine did not argue that human variation can account for the differences in the way these universals are managed. Forces that generate variability are to be found mainly in the other environments of culture, physical and social organizational. These are the conditions to which cultures adapt in order to perform their functions for human survival. These environments throw down series of challenges (Toynbee, 1934) and create crises (Sorokin, 1947/1962); and cultures change to meet them. Certain modal differences among human collectivities might present them with different challenges and thus lead to different cultures. Were there a distinctive race of humans—all of them sightless, for example—then they would presumably create a distinctive culture. This idea is the premise for a lot of science fiction. It is also the basis for distinctive subcultures of the physically challenged. It appears however that genetic variation in ways critical to culture are similarly distributed around the planet and cannot account for differences among cultures.

Are psychological factors to be entirely discounted in the explanation of cultural variation? Whereas White and others answer emphatically, "Yes!!," Geertz (1973) reserved a place for the psyche. Crises arise, he asserted, not only when biological man is threatened but also when the psyche itself is challenged. Geertz quoted Langer (1960): "[Man] can adapt himself somehow to anything his imagination can cope with; but he cannot deal with chaos" (p. 287). Events must be interpretable; it is a human need. Piaget (1928) said as much when he assumed that humans somehow try to restore a cognitive equilibrium. A baffling event is to the human mind as a grain of sand to the oyster; a more or less perfect pearl of wisdom develops to contain it. Then a solitary thinker may offer an explanation, so he or she communicates and exhorts; and culture may change. In this view, psychological factors matter a great deal in the process of cultural variation because they give force to certain events in other environments.

Most contemporary social anthropologists discount psychological variation in accounting for cultural variation. Specifically, genius, the greatest challenge to this view, is granted negligible influence. Sorokin (1947/1962), however, accorded it a place among the "chief facilitating factors of the discovery, creation, and invention of the new major ideological systems."

> One is not obliged to subscribe to the claims of extreme hereditarians and racialists to perceive that a favorable heredity is a prerequisite

condition. Otherwise, no amount of training can make one a Mozart or Beethoven in music, a Homer, Dante, or Shakespeare in literature, an Isaac Newton or Galileo in science, a Plato or Kant in philosophy, a Buddha or Saint Paul in religion, and Edison or Bell in technology, a Carnegie or Ford in economic organization. . . . Precisely what this "fortunate heredity" is we do not know, but whatever it is, it is an indispensable factor. (p. 541)

Others point out that important technological and ideological innovations are in the *Zeitgeist* rather than in individuals, and they often cite Ogburn's (1950) list of 148 independent and almost simultaneous discoveries and inventions as evidence.

My own position is that the disciplines of culturology and social psychology should collaborate in the investigation of the conditions under which variation in the psychological environment of culture generates variations in culture itself. When does an individual's unique understanding achieve a wide consensus? In what roles do individuals exert the most influence on culture? Are innovative individuals able to make more impression on their cultures if they have supportive interpersonal relations? In what variations are cultures most receptive to an individual's new ideas? What are the facilitating relationships between the properties of the individual's insights and the extant beliefs? The science of culture must use the strategy of translation to bring the forces in culture's psychological environment into the closed theoretical system of its own level of analysis. Theory construction and its empirical test profit from the collaboration of social psychologists and culturologists.

Interpersonal Relations

The wholehearted acceptance of the other that characterizes interpersonal relations may be a critical factor for individual contributions to cultural change. Erikson (1963b) provided a theoretical handle for grasping this connection in his concept of "negative identity." Recall (see chapter 5) that identity refers to a person's sense of continuity over his or her life history and of sameness while filling multiple roles. A negative identity is one that is recognized by those who matter, but they disapprove.

Its "negativity" unfortunately has induced many into assuming mistakenly that such an identity is a developmental flaw, dysfunctional for individuals and their society. A common example given of a negative identity is the juvenile delinquent. On the other hand, Erikson himself has documented negative identities that were neither personally nor socially dysfunctional, in the psychobiographies of Martin Luther (1958) and Mohandas K. Gandhi (1969). In both cases, almost all of those who mattered disapproved vigorously of what these two stood for. Both prevailed, however, and made the negative positive.

Implicating the interpersonal environment with culture is the hypothesis that engagement in an interpersonal relation facilitates the contribution of a negative identity to cultural change. That is, whereas those who matter may strongly oppose the identity, some*one* who matters provides critical emotional support. A problem for the psychobiographer of culture shapers is to identify who that someone was in the life of the subject. Generalizing from this hypothesis, one may say that the more that persons who share a culture are engaged in interpersonal relations, the more susceptible the culture is to change originating at the individual level of analysis.

Natural Ecology

As the schematic diagram of the social psychological model (see chapter 2, Figure 2) indicates, the cultural level borders on the other three levels of analysis in the social psychological domain—psychological, interpersonal, and social organizational. The diagram does not indicate, however, that the cultural level has still another environment, the physical, which includes natural resources, climate, topology, and so on. That the natural environment forms the boundary at the nonsocial side of culture is worth noting here because this spatial conception implies a particular function that culture fills for the social psychological domain. Parsons (1969) pointed out that culture is the vehicle that transports the physical environment to the social environment: "Technological organization . . . should be regarded as a boundary structure between the society as a system and the organic-physical environment" (p. 17).

The concepts of culture are prisms through which the natural environment affects the individual both directly and through other levels of the social environment. At the same time that the physical world impinges directly on individuals, it also filters through their culture. Tuan (1977) has alluded to this dual physical and symbolic character of the natural environment in his distinction between *space* and *place*, the former a physical and the latter, a cultural entity. "Enclosed and humanized space is place. Compared to space, place is a calm center of established values" (p. 54).

Porter (1978) called attention to the relationship between the culture and the physical environment with the concept of the "perceived environment":

> A perception of environment approach in research has been independently invented thousands of times by scholars confronted by the logic of necessity and their own incompetence. I invented it myself in East Africa when attempting to understand the environments of Sebei, Pokot, Kamba, and Heke . . . Of what relevance were the categories of the [U.S. Soil Conservation Series] Seventh Approximation to the way the Sebei farmer used the soils found on the slopes and at the base of Mount Elgon? None. Sebei use of soils was guided by Sebei understanding of soils. If I hoped to understand Sebei agricultural practice and soil assessment and management, it made much greater sense to attempt it using Sebei terminology, criteria, and taxonomy. (p. 26)

For another example, environmental psychologists have found that crowding has psychological effects (Rodin, 1976; Rodin, Solomon, & Metcalf, 1978). The density of humans in the individual's immediate space is a physical fact of the order of heat and pressure and presumably operates according to the same principles. At the same time, crowding and other physical phenomena have symbolic meanings as well, and these meanings are encoded at the cultural level. They may be translated into beliefs of an ideological or technological nature. Crowded conditions may indeed have a physical impact on people, but the ultimate psychological effect of being crowded depends as well on the situation in which it occurs. A crowd may intrude on an individual or it may join him or her; which of the two it is makes a significant psychological difference. The density of population is a physical fact that may be translated into a component of a culture's technology, and there it interacts with other facts, like the knowledge of ways of obtaining food and of disposing of human waste, and with values, like collectivism or individualism. Out of this interplay of ideas emerges a shared orientation to crowds, which is a boundary condition for a crowded individual.

Cultural Dynamics

Thus, cultures are affected by the environments, social and nonsocial, in which they are rooted. These environments impinge on the beliefs of which cultures consist, challenging or buttressing them, perhaps to alter them and their organization. So, if cultures are to be considered closed analytic systems about which universal laws can be formulated, some of these laws must be laws of change.

Sorokin (1957) maintained that cultural systems change, not only as a consequence of changes external to them, but sometimes also wholly in response to internal processes. This potential for "imminent change," as he called it, is inherent in any system: "any system not only bears in itself the seeds of its change, but generates the change incessantly, with every act, every reaction, every activity it discharges" (p. 645). The degree to which change in a culture is imminent rather than reactive to its environment depends on the integration and scope of the culture; the more tightly organized is the structure of beliefs and the wider the relevance of the totality of beliefs, the more its future state is determined by its own present condition. The culture's environments may accelerate or retard its development, and they may make their mark on some of the more peripheral of the culture's beliefs, but they cannot "change fundamentally the imminent potentialities of the system and its normal destiny in the sense of making the life career of an unfolding acorn that of a cow" (p. 645). Sorokin thus proposed that there are dynamic tendencies to cultural systems, an idea that could account for change within a closed theory of culture without requiring translation of extra-system events. Sorokin did not describe principles that govern change, however.

Campbell (1975) suggested a functional law of dynamic selection, drawing an analogy between cultural evolution and biological evolution.

He posited that cultures survive over generations when they naturally select and retain beliefs that eventuate in practices that effectively compete for the allegiance of subscribers. This is not a reductionist approach; it does not depend simply on individuals choosing to believe what works for them as individuals. Beliefs and their consequent practices may be more or less functional for the social organizations of the culture groups and for their interpersonal relations. Cultural evolution, as Campbell conceived of it, is an emergent at that level of analysis that takes into account its several environments and accommodates to their influence.

To put the idea of cultural dynamics in terms of the model, an idea is more "reproductively fit" if it is more persuasive. The persuasiveness of an idea inheres in its compatibility with other ideas in the extant culture and also in its relationships to other levels of analysis: Is the idea likely to persuade those who occupy influential roles in the social organizations of potential believers? If the idea is generally antagonistic to the prevailing culture, does it nevertheless convince partners in mutually supportive interpersonal relations? Drawing on the psychological level of analysis, is the idea persuasive to anyone with the personal resources to persuade others? Conceiving of cultural dynamics in terms of persuasion anticipates the discussion in chapter 9.

Dimensions of Culture

When cultures change, along what dimensions should these changes be described? If cultures differ, along what dimensions do they differ? To incorporate the cultural level in the social psychological enterprise, it is necessary to identify its useful dimensions. The principles of its internal dynamics, those by which culture acts as a closed system, or the probabilistic principles about the reciprocal effects at the psychocultural boundary, should be stated in relative terms: "The more . . . the more; the less . . . the less." This review of some of the dimensions that have been proposed for the description and comparative analysis of cultures begins with some structural dimensions because these may have greater social psychological utility than substantive dimensions do.

Structural Dimensions

Breadth. Cultures may have more or less breadth. That is, their constituent assertions may include many or few phenomena. This is the dimension alluded to earlier in making a distinction between *culture* and *subculture*. The latter is a more circumscribed set of assertions than the former but may be "subordinate" to it because it includes in its beliefs one or more that are shared with the latter. For example, the legal subculture of Western culture is a relatively circumscribed set of ideas, almost wholly normative, that justifies itself by its claims of consistency with the values and facts of the wider culture. The rule by which the legal status of a person's sanity is established has its explicit basis in a system of facts and values that includes much more than the principles of the legal system. By definition, then, subcultures have less breadth than the larger cultures of which they are a part.

One culture is broader than another if its technology covers a wider set of phenomena. The electron microscope on the one hand and the radio telescope on the other have widened the horizons of our culture to realities that were unknown to our ancestors and even the previous generation. Consequently our modern system of beliefs includes assertions about the existence of and relationships among phenomena that the culture of our forebears could not have identified. It should be clear that the relative accuracy of assertions of two cultures is irrelevant to their relative breadth. Presumably the microscope and telescope have made modern beliefs more accurate; but in any event, modern culture is broader because it makes assertions about more objects and events.

Integration. The hypothetical one-belief culture is the limiting case of the dimension of integration. With at least two ideas in the set, integration, in any meaningful sense, becomes possible. Cultures may vary in their degree of integration, the implication being that a culture is still a culture even if its ideas are not integrated. According to LeVine (1984), however, they tend toward integration: "No ethnographer . . . has failed to find increasing connectedness and coherence in customs—particularly in their ideational dimension—as he or she becomes better acquainted with their meanings . . . The shreds and patches concept of culture has simply not survived the test of intensive field investigation . . . " (p. 72). Sorokin allowed that there is variation in the integration of cultures. Cultures may consist of ideas that have not only positive implications for one another, but neutral and even negative implications as well. Sorokin called ideas integrated if their implications are positive—if one assertion is true, the other must be also true; if the truth of one carries no implication of the truth of the other, the ideas are *neutral*; and if they cannot both be true, then they are *contradictory*. These terms describe not categories but a dimension of the structural relationships among ideas; for ideas may probably or partially imply the truth or falsity of one another. Sorokin labeled beliefs having neutral relationships as *congeries* of ideas. Sorokin (1947/1962) observed that "there are very few, if any, vast systems of meanings, values, and norms which are absolutely free from some inner contradiction or tension and from unrelated congeries in their propositions" (p. 316).

Sorokin recognized two criteria for consistency: logic and aesthetics. Logic and aesthetics are themselves cultural phenomena, ideas that are not universally recognized, much less accepted, by all human collectivities. These criteria are themselves ideas developed in modern culture and applied by Sorokin to cultures to which they may be foreign. It may prove more useful to measure the integration of a culture in its own terms, that is, according to its own criteria for ideational consistency. However, the integrated state of a set of beliefs is an identifiable and potentially important dimension of the set, whether it ultimately proves to be based on universal or culturally specific standards.

The state of a culture's integration is not always obvious. For example, some may, from their own cultural standpoint, argue with Sorokin's (1947/ 1962) example of a congery: "A Romantic poem, Republican political ideology, Baptist system of beliefs, Culbertson's bridge playing, give us in their totality an unintegrated conglomeration of unrelated, meaningful systems" (p. 316). There may be subtextual constancies among the values and realities on which these apparently unrelated beliefs systems are based, depending on the criteria for consistency one applies.

Complexity. Another potentially important dimension of culture is complexity, which refers to the conditionality of the assertions. There are simple facts and complex facts: "everything that goes up must come down" is a simple assertion of fact, referring to everything without any conditions. Nowadays that statement is untenable in our culture; for clearly not everything that goes "up" must come "down." The ultimate upward or downward course of an object is now asserted conditionally, depending on the size and density of the object, the speed of its motion, and its location relative to other objects of specified mass and speed, not to mention the reference point for "up" and "down." There are similarly simple and complex values. "Never tell a lie" is a simple normative assertion—"never." If the value of a lie is conditioned both on its consequences for the well-being of individuals and the integrity of social communication, however, assertions about when lying is impermissible become quite complex. Simple cultures are characterized by their simple truths; in the extreme, they consist of nothing but "basic" facts and "fundamental" values. In complex cultures, on the other hand, assertions almost never say "never."

Development. Some scholars of culture ascribe to the entity the property of sequential change, or development. This dimension is closely tied to the dimension of complexity inasmuch as development is often asserted to proceed toward greater complexity.

Various bases have been suggested for the sequential order of development. White's (1969) sequence is based on the efficiency of the use of energy. Other bases assume a kind of "ratchet effect" to technology, that is, that useful knowledge is cumulative. Still other developmental sequences find their inspiration in a hierarchy of human needs like that posited by Rollo May (1975), and they propose that cultures develop from the satisfaction of the most basic of human needs (e.g., survival) to the fulfillment of higher needs (e.g., creativity).

Whatever the supposed nature of the sequence, cultures may be said to vary in the degree of their development.

Stability and pace of change. Whether cultural change is developmental or not, cultures may vary in the pace at which their constituent ideas are modified or replaced. The pace of cultural change seems generally to be uneven, cycling from rapid to slow. This pattern gives change a

stagelike rather than a phaselike character and allows for certain demarcated slopes and plateaus to be named (Medieval, Renaissance, etc.).

M. Mead (1970) has noted the way different paces of change select the
carriers of culture among the living generations that share it. Postfigur-
ative cultures are those that are in a plateau of slow change, and the older
generation passes the belief system on to the younger. In prefigurative
stages of rapid change, the younger generation imparts the new ideas to
the older. At points of transition between slow and rapid paces of change,
cultures are cofigurative, when both older and younger generations have
something to teach the other.

Hierarchy. A culture may be said to be hierarchical to the degree that
a subset of its beliefs validates the rest. Modern Westerners are perhaps
more used to thinking about this dimension in terms of ideology rather
than technology because our own culture has regnant values. The Ten
Commandments, the Golden Rule, and the Bill of Rights express them.
The truth of other assertions of value is assessed by the criterion of their
compatibility with the dominant, basic, or fundamental values.

Still, it should be recognized that cultures may also have dominant
facts as well as dominant values. Marx's assertion about the inevitable
course of social history is such a reigning assertion of fact in the culture
of communism; indeed that culture regards values as "mere ideology" without effect. Darwinian (1859/1958) principles of evolution govern the acceptability of other facts in contemporary life sciences. Here again one
comes upon Kuhn's (1970) notion of a "paradigm" of a science; it refers to
the dominant assertions of the science, along with its accepted methods
and so on. When a technology turns on a few assertions of the existence
of entities or their causal relations, it is hierarchical.

Substantive Dimensions

The idea of a hierarchical dimension to culture is implied in many substantive descriptions of cultures, because they refer to dominant beliefs.
It was noted earlier that some theorists have sought comparative dimensions of culture in the constants of the human givens, for example, in
human needs. Psychoanalytic developmental theory has been one source
of such substantive dimensions. Cultures have been characterized as oral,
anal, and so on, by analogy with personal characterology. Just as he has
elaborated on psychoanalytic characterology, so Erikson also reformulated
its cultural application. Erikson (1943) described the culture of the Yurok
Indians in terms of the psychological modalities of oral incorporation and
anal retention, linking the Yurok belief system to the people's dependence
on the salmon runs in the Klamath River. Hamilton's comparison of classic
Greek with pharonic Egyptian culture (1949) is also in terms of the human
life cycle inasmuch as she describes the former as a *life* and the latter as
a *death* culture.

Triandis and others have offered as central the dimension of traditional—modern, another combination of technological and ideological components:

> modern man is apparently open to new experiences, relatively independent of parental authority, and concerned with time and planning and willing to defer gratification; he feels that man can be the master over nature and that he controls the reinforcements he receives from his environment; he believes in determinism and science, has a wide, cosmopolitan perspective, and uses broad ingroups; he competes with standards of excellence and is optimistic about controlling his environment. Traditional man has narrow ingroups, looks at the world with suspicion, believes that good is limited, and that one obtains a share of it by chance or by pleasing the gods; he identifies with his parents and receives direction from them; he considers planning a waste of time and does not defer gratification; he feels at the mercy of obscure environmental forces and is prone to mysticism; he sees interpersonal relations as an end, rarely as a means to an end, and does not believe that he can control his environment but rather sees himself under the influence of external, mystical powers. (Triandis, 1972, pp. 352–353)

Thus, various ideas have been nominated as the moving—or stabilizing—forces of cultures. In the terms of the model, the effectiveness of boundary conditions for generating cultural change would depend on whether they transform these particular ideas. For example, White (1969) theorized that "the functioning of culture as a whole . . . rests on and is determined by the amount of energy harnessed and by the way in which it is put to work" (pp. 367–368). According to this theory, cultures change primarily with the acquisition of knowledge about new sources of energy and ways to transform them into work. Cultural epochs can then be meaningfully characterized by their ideas about energy, so that cultural history in these terms has had "ages" of human muscle, animal muscle, water power, steam, electricity, the atom, and so on. Individuals would shape their culture most decisively if they would alter its ideas about the sources of energy, and the most profound cultural influence on individuals would be through what energy it makes available to them.

For his part, Sorokin (1947/1962) nominated the epistomology of a culture as the controlling idea, of which there are dimensions.

> [T]he problem of the ultimate nature of true reality and value is the ultimate and most general problem of thought. Being such, it serves as the major premise for building the vastest possible ideological supersystem, integrating into one consistent whole the greater part of the basic principles of science and philosophy, religion and ethics, law and politics, fine arts and economics. The character of an answer to this ultimate problem decisively determines most of the scientific, philosophical, religious, esthetic, and other ideological systems and congeries. Some ideological cultures answer that the *true reality and true value is sensory*, that beyond the reality and value perceived by our sense organs there is no other reality and no value . . . Such ideological supersystems can be called *sensate*.

Other highly integrated ideological cultures answer the problem by stating that *the true reality and the true value is the super-sensory, super-rational god* ("Tao," "World Soul," Brahman, etc.), *the sensory reality being either a mere illusion or the least important, least real, sometimes even negative, reality and value.* The vastest ideological supersystem built on this premise can be called *ideational.*

Still other highly integrated cultures assume that the *true reality and value is partly sensory, partly rational, partly supersensory and super-rational infinite manifold.* The ideological supersystem erected upon this major premise can be called *idealistic.* (p. 320)

In Sorokin's view, cultures are not necessarily ruled by a single idea—and certainly not by a materialistic idea like White's energic one; for they may vary along the dimension of integration. A "great" culture, however, must be single-minded about its epistemology.

Many of the substantive formulations of cultural dimensions are in terms of patterns of dimensions rather than a dominant one. One example is Parsons (1951), who proposed that five "pattern–variables" taken together adequately describe values–motives at the psychological level of analysis, norms–roles at the social organizational, and ideology at the cultural. In Parsons's terms, a culture may be *affective,* encouraging emotional expression and giving significant weight to feelings in determining courses of action, or affectively neutral; may be either specific or diffuse, valuing either concreteness or abstraction; may be relatively universal in its application of norms or quite particular or differentiated; ascribe statuses on the basis of ancestry or other characteristics beyond human control, or permit status to be achieved; and elevate the welfare of the individual or of the collective in its value system. The terms are polar descriptions on continuous dimensions. Parsons did not assert that the pattern–variables are interdependent, such that a culture's position on one dimension limits its probable range on another. Rather, it might be expected that the pattern–variables would emerge from an orthogonal factor analysis of cultural materials. Parsons did not assume that one dimension is controlling.

Note that Parsons's dimensions are exclusively ideological. Other non-hierarchical schemes of substantive cultural dimensions include both ideological and technological components. F. Kluckhohn and Strodtbeck (1962) proposed that the basic beliefs of a culture can be organized into a few categories of assertions: about innate human nature, which, in assertions of fact could vary from mutable to immutable, and, in assertions of value might be good, bad, or indifferent; about man's relation to nature, whether master of, subject to, or in harmony with; preoccupation with the past, the present, or the future; valuing activity for itself or as a vehicle for self-actualization; and regarding the proper relationship between people as hierarchical, collateral (egalitarian and cooperative), or individualistic.

Concerning current culturological thinking regarding dominant ideas, Kroeber and Kluckhohn's summary (1952/1963) seems still valid:

Various social theorists ... have tried to make particular forms the main dynamic in the historical process: ideas; religious beliefs and practice; forms of social organization; forms of technological control of the environment. One modern group would place forms of intra-family relationship in a central position ... a few ... have recently stressed the role of linguistic morphology. But if there be any single central tendency in the attempts to conceptualize culture over eighty years, it has been that of denying in principle a search for *"the"* factor. (pp. 355–356)

Research on Culture

I have elected to illustrate research at the cultural level of analysis with a case study of the introduction of the steel axe into a stone age culture. The nature of this particular research is exemplary of the research in the discipline of social anthropology–culturology, being a dense description of several facets of one technologically less developed culture. Unlike most anthropological reports, however, this one describes a culture observed while undergoing profound change.

Methodology

The focus is first on the method of Sharp's study "Steel Axes for Stone Age Australians" (1952) in order to anticipate a later discussion of how the model's conception of the social environment opens up the possibility of an efficient and ethical experimental culturology. Most culturological reports cover a fairly static, albeit often interesting, situation. Some, like Kardiner and Linton's (1939) report on the wet and dry rice technologies of the Tanala-Betsileo, compare two cultures that once were quite similar but then diverged as a result of some event. Culturologists commonly regard this method as the closest they can come to an experiment. Kaplan and Manners (1972) have explained that, "Not only does comparison provide a means of suggesting more general statements about cultural phenomena, but, more importantly, in the absence of the opportunity to experiment it is the only means we have of testing such general propositions" (p. 7).

Sharp's study, however, is in its design similar to the one-pigeon experiment on operant learning: A condition, in this case a new tool, is introduced into the environment of a single system, whose behavior is then observed without any explicit theoretical expectations or hypotheses. This N-of-one, atheoretical method is of course subject to the familiar criticisms, but it is more necessary to culturologists than to psychologists. A flock of pigeons is easily acquired and randomly allocated to controlled conditions; but it takes years to observe a single natural culture adequately and enormous effort to acquire comparative data on even a small flock.

Herein lies the tremendous value of anthropological databanks, like the Human Relations Area files at Yale (Murdock, 1954), a repository of descriptions of cultures from which selected variables can be abstracted and subjected to statistical analyses. Fishman, Ferguson, and Gupta (1968), for example, have contrasted peoples under a common government and having a common language with people commonly governed but linguistically heterogenous. In present terms, Fishman has ordered collectivities in the databank on a dimension of integration with respect to one important cultural component, their language, and then correlated this variable with other recorded cultural differences among them. He found that most of the effect of variation in linguistic integration can be accounted for by concomitant variation in the gross national product, an index of technological development.

Ordinarily, natural cultures are not amenable to experimentation. The closest approximation is the natural experiment, such as the one Sharp reported, in which, for reasons other than the search for culturological laws, the steel axe has been taken to a culture.

Even if social scientists could do such experiments on random cultures, our ethics prevent us. In this respect, a conceptualization of culture as a set of beliefs shared by as few as two people has huge methodological potential because it admits of an experimental culturology with small groups.

The literature includes reports of such work. Weick and Gilfillan (1971) have studied the intergenerational transmission of culture, introducing technologies into the knowledge of task-oriented laboratory groups and then successively replacing group members. Burnstein's studies of the polarization of group consensus (Burnstein & Vinokur, 1975, 1977; Burnstein, Vinokur, & Pichevin, 1974; Burnstein, Vinokur, & Trope, 1973) can be conceived as studies of the effects of the cultural environment on the decisions of a collectivity; for Burnstein has shown that the values and facts brought to the discussion by individuals and shared by them with the rest of the group are strong determinants of the consensus that the group reaches about the appropriate course of action.

Whether the culture of a short-lived small group deliberately subjected to experimental manipulation behaves differently from cultures as they are usually found in nature remains to be seen. One should not assume that the obvious differences actually make any effective difference. I return to how research on small groups provides an opportunity for experimental culturology in chapter 10.

Another methodological characteristic that sets Sharp's study apart from most anthropological research is that the account of the Yir Yoront covers more than 300 years, extending from a brief contact with Western civilization in 1623 to a concentrated field observation in the mid-1930s. This longitudinal feature documents stability of the culture up to the point of the introduction of the steel axe and thus lends credibility to a causal inference. This critical technological innovation was introduced toward the end of this period and preceded other changes. The inference is that the effects of technological innovation reverberated throughout the cultural system.

Theoretical Analysis

To deal with the case of the Yir Yoront within the cultural level of analysis, it is necessary to translate the steel axe into terms of beliefs. It is tempting to use Leslie White's (1969) hypothesis and reason that the effort-saving superiority in accomplishing traditional tasks was the cultural significance of steel axes. However, according to Sharp's account, that is not accurate. Actually, the steel axe was only marginally more efficient than the stone axe. Its impact stemmed, not from its capacity to mobilize energy more efficiently, but rather from its implications for Yir Yoront theory of causation. The steel axe challenged a fact of Yir Yoront life; it introduced a new technology in the wider sense of that term.

The governing belief that the steel axe challenged was that all significant contemporary events recapitulate sacred events in the distant past. The model for the present was laid down in time beyond living memory, not only for the ways things should have been but also for the way things were, as undesirable as these sometimes were. This belief stood at the apex of Yir Yoront cosmology. It explained why things happened as they did, including the presence of evil in the world.

The idea of axes was believed to have originated among the ancients of the Sunlit Cloud Iguana clan, and therefore all axes had belonged to members of that clan. Once upon a time, members of the clan gave some of their inventions to elderly male members of other clans. This clan continued to "give" axes to the elders of the tribe because the original inventors had made such gifts. The fact that men in other clans actually traded independently for the stone and made their own axes did not, in the ideology of the Yir Yoront culture, abrogate the property rights of the Sunlit Cloud Iguana clan to all axes. The others engaged in this manufacture under the franchise, so to speak, of the Sunlit Cloud Iguana clan.

There was no historical account that axes had ever been given to the women or to the young men in the tribe; thus, there was no myth to validate the women and young men possessing them. Although the women and young men customarily used axes, they always had to borrow them from their elders. Then they suddenly and unaccountably acquired axes of their own.

The technological significance of the steel axe lay then in the fact of its inexplicable ownership. It had not been anticipated in the past; it was something new under the sun. If the past did not model the present in this respect, then all else was thrown into question. Even if the past had been the sole cause up to a point, it clearly was no longer. Perhaps the Yir Yoront had been correct in relying on the myths, but the rules had now changed. What would be, from then on, the correct explanation—for suffering and for sin?

Apparently too many of the important beliefs constituting the Yir Yoront cultural system were incompatible with the fact that women and young men now owned axes. The ownership of an axe signified mature masculinity; it signified that one had a trading partner in some distant tribe; it testified to the inherent superiority of certain ascribed statuses.

The established web of ideas was complex and fundamental. The new reality undermined a regnant belief, one high in the hierarchy of Yir Yoront culture. Wanting reasons and losing faith in the existence of reasons, the Yir Yoront no longer shared beliefs. Their culture fell into chaos.

How was it that Yir Yoront women and young men could acquire axes? Why was that not prevented? In contrast, as Sharp related, Yir Yoront technology did not incorporate the bark canoe of their northern neighbors, although the fact of its usefulness and the means to acquire it were part of the Yir Yoront belief system. An explanation for why the culture of the Yir Yoront did not reject the steel axe requires an understanding of the dynamics of cultural change. Several general explanations are available.

Within the cultural level of analysis, one might adopt the developmental principle, holding that growth is an inherent property of the system. The principle of growth seems to cover a lot of the dynamics of organic systems, and indeed the capacity for growth characterizes what is called *organic*. These systems change or die. White (1969) conceptualized the cultural system in the same way: "Cultural systems like those of the biological level are capable of growth. That is, the power to capture any energy is also the ability to harness more and still more of it. Thus cultural systems, like biological organisms, develop, multiply, and extend themselves" (p. 391). Whereas the steel axe improved only marginally on the efficient use of human energy relative to the stone axe, perhaps that margin was enough to constitute growth and satisfy the condition for developmental change. It trumped the idea of eternal recapitulation of significant events. If so, then why did the Yir Yoront not adopt the bark canoe? Or would they?

White did not assert that progress is inevitable. An advanced culture can slip back; that is, in his terms, technologies may become less efficient. Retrogression could result, for example, from a source of efficient energy like oil running out. The theoretical problem is to state the conditions for developmental change—its sequence, its pace, and its aberrant reversals.

At the psychological level of analysis, Piaget's (1928) theory of cognitive development posits conditions for developmental change. Using the strategy of a metalanguage, one can invoke Piagetian concepts to explain the crisis of Yir Yoront culture following the introduction of the steel axe. Ownership of axes by women and young men upset an equilibrium in the belief system of the Yir Yoront. Two facts were in contradiction, an event had occurred which was inconsistent with an existing schema. According to Piaget, equilibrium can be restored by assimilation, accommodation, or by some combination of these two transformations. The new observation can be assimilated into the old schema, made out to be a specific case of what was known already. Or the schema itself can be changed to accommodate the cognition. Whether assimilation is used depends in part on the functionality of the old schema in the light of the new fact. In addition, schemas are more or less integrated with other schemas; the tighter the integration, the more resistant they are to change. If they prove to be dysfunctional, they tend to change to accommodate to the new idea. From this perspective, the chaotic state of Yir Yoront culture may be a temporary and, in the long run, a salutary condition that will eventuate in a more functional system of beliefs.

Sharp raised the possibility that some creative genius—perhaps someone with what Sorokin called "favorable heredity"—might invent an interpretation of the old schema that would assimilate all these new facts, resolving the contradictions and saving the old culture. It is also possible that that genius would prove to be a revolutionary who creates a radically new belief system, that is, an accommodation rather than an assimilation.

He or she might offer a new testament that legitimated new bases of ownership. The bark canoe may then follow. Until the new culture becomes widely accepted, the culture would remain in disequilibrium, in a state of chaos.

This is where Sharp's (1952) account left off. He did not record whether or how the crisis was resolved. Perhaps the missionaries who gave the women and young men of the Yir Yoront the steel axes also gave them the Book of Job. Meanwhile, the governing idea about the reason for things being as they were and should have been was challenged: "[The] horrid suspicion arises as to the authenticity of the origin myths . . . The steel axe . . . is hacking at the supports of the entire cultural system" (p. 88).

Sharp did not invoke principles of culture change to explain the effects of the steel axe on Yir Yoront culture or Yir Yoront rejection of the bark canoe. Nor did he use the Yir Yoront case to test hypotheses derived from a body of culturological theory. His account is a superior example of current work in contemporary social anthropology—a dense description of a system of ideas waiting for an explanation of how they got that way.

The science of culture has not yet developed to the point of integrated and elaborate theories. Kroeber and Kluckhohn (1952/1963) provided an apt summary for this discussion of culture as a conceptually independent level of analysis:

> as yet we have no full theory of culture. We have a fairly well-delineated concept, and it is possible to enumerate conceptual elements embraced within that master concept. But a concept, even an important one, does not constitute a theory . . . Concepts have a way of coming to a dead end unless they are bound together in a testable theory. In anthropology at present we have plenty of definitions but too little theory. (p. 357)

Perhaps social psychological attention to culture will spur development of theory at its own level of analysis.

This presentation of the cultural level completes the structural model of the social psychological domain. Now we turn to its dynamics.

Part III

Dynamics

Introduction

Having laid out a structural model of the social psychological domain, I turn now to the problems of dynamics. The focus shifts to events whose investigation defines social psychology, the reciprocal influence of the individual and the social environment. It is useful to think of this influence as exerted through a set of related but conceptually distinct processes. The dynamics of social psychology are tripartite, each influence process operating at a boundary between the individual and the environments of social organization, interpersonal relations, and culture, respectively.

The proposition that individuals stand in a different relationship to each social environment leads to the proposition that the respective processes of reciprocal influence are different. Their nature derives from the nature of the particular environment interacting with the person.

People participate in interpersonal relations as identities. Their participation is wholehearted, both in the sense of willing and in the sense of total involvement. Ideally, they feel no constraints to be other than themselves. The influence process that emerges under these conditions and that explains the psychological effects of interpersonal relations is *identification*.

Individuals' participation in social organization is quite different. They are aware that roles involve obligations as well as privileges and that they are under some constraint in them. The social organizational environment influences individuals through the process of socialization. Individuals may effect social change through institutionalization of their innovations in defining roles.

People stand under no constraint in their relationships to their cultural environment. Insofar as they are constrained to adopt certain values and beliefs, it is by nature of the roles they play in their social organizational environment, rather than in their relationship to culture. That is, people may hold the most peculiar beliefs, and even act on them, and they are considered merely eccentric so long as their peculiarity does not interfere seriously with role expectations. Moreover, in contrast to their interpersonal relations, individuals are not distinguishable from others in their participation in culture but are simply units in a dispersed, unrelated, and undifferentiated mass. Exposed under these conditions to a body of beliefs, individuals become enculturated by the process of persuasion. For their part, they may influence culture through the reciprocal process of invention.

Each of these dynamic processes draws primarily from one or another body of theory prominent in contemporary social psychology. Social learning theory accounts for socialization, encompassing how social roles are learned and how individuals are motivated and trained to conform to them. Ego analytic theory supplements social learning theory by explaining the more enduring effects of socialization. Psychoanalytic theory provides an explanation of the influence of interpersonal relations. Cognitive social psychology, with its insights into the attributions of causes, person perception, and attitude formation and change, covers persuasion, in the sense that "persuasion" is used here.

It is noteworthy that these major psychological theories each makes a distinctive contribution to social psychology. Many of the arguments about the superiority of one or another theory can be resolved by recognizing that each theory assumes a different set of conditions; that is, each assumes conditions of individuals' relationships with a different social environment. If their assumptions were made more explicit and specific, then the theories themselves could be strengthened at their foundations. Psychoanalytic theory, for example, in its explanations of social influence, always assumes emotional attachment between individuals. Social learning theory always assumes the power and will to manipulate contingencies, never that significant rewards like love are unconditional. Cognitive social psychology assumes an environment of communicable ideas, irrespective of interpersonal attachments and power. Each deals with a recognizable set of conditions, and each can build a set of coherent explanations of social influence under its particular conditions. Each, however, is partial in relation to the variety of social environments in which people live.

Few concrete social situations are pure instances of an encounter with but one social environment. Individuals' actual experiences usually include some combination of interpersonal interactions, role taking, and membership in a mass audience. Still, what happens in concrete instances can best be understood by analyzing the forces at work in terms of the three conceptually distinct processes. Hence, one initially invokes the strategy of idealization: One assesses the person's relationship to each of the three environments as though it were an independent and pure case and translates those forces into the terms of the appropriate levels of analysis. Synthesis follows as one then assesses the relative weights and the configuration of the various forces, toward an explanation of the concrete phenomenon.

This section on dynamics follows this strategy. It presents each of the three processes of influence in turn, as if each operated in the absence of the other two. Only then are they synthesized in trying to explain certain social psychological phenomena.

7

Socialization and Institutionalization

Socialization is the process whereby social organizations influence the actions and experience of individuals. Individuals influence social organizations through the process of *institutionalization,* meaning that they create or substantially alter the roles they and others are to take. The former is by far the more common experience, and this chapter is devoted largely to it. Institutionalization is not neglected, however. Later I discuss under what psychological and social conditions this is more likely to occur. I suggest that, for the most part, individuals effect major social organizational change indirectly, through their impact on culture.

The process of socialization has several components. Individuals are taught to recognize their own and the other roles that make up their social organizations. Small children are taught to recognize "boy," "girl," "letter carrier," "police officer," "doctor," and "nurse"; new employees are taken implicitly or explicitly through the organization chart. People are also taught the obligations and privileges that define each role. They are taught the skills and are shown how to marshall the other resources necessary to enact their roles. Moreover, they are motivated to conform.

DiRenzo (1977) regarded socialization as the process by which a Homo sapiens becomes human. People become human only by becoming human for their time and place. It is common for people to regard those who act radically different from what they believe is appropriate as less than human, as "savages." Behaviors that distinguish humans from nonhumans are also patterned for their particular society. So this process that fits individuals for their organizational environment is essential for their very humanity.

This chapter consists first of a discussion of two major sources of social psychology's understanding of socialization, the social learning and ego analytic theories, and how they complement one another. Then the usefulness of the concept of socialization as it is used in the model is explored by using it to explain two phenomena important to social psychology, the effects of roles on attitudes and the acquisition of language. Finally, I discuss conditions under which individuals may turn around their own socialization and reorganize their social institutions.

Social Learning Perspective

In the terms of the social psychological model, that a person learns a role means that a set of shared prescriptions for the behavior and experience of someone in a particular social position has been translated across the boundary between the social organizational and psychological levels of analysis. Social learning theory currently accounts for this process better than any other body of theory, albeit incompletely.

Social learning theory (Bandura, 1973, 1977) is a humanizing elaboration on general learning theory. It too is rooted in the law of effect, but it also takes into account that human learners do not depend as much as other animals do on trial and error in order to discover what is reinforcing. Humans are markedly more capable of learning from observation and explicit instruction. Furthermore, humans find con-species approval markedly more reinforcing than other species do. Social learning theory is "social" in the same sense that social psychology is "social": With few exceptions, it pertains exclusively to humans.

The assumptions of social learning theory match the conditions of the encounter between individuals and the social organizational environment. People have the capacity to acquire and store understanding through instruction and observation without any immediate reinforcement, our actions are shaped according to the law of effect, and we are motivated to attain certain goals, social approval decisively among them. Humankind encounters a social organizational environment that instructs, provides models, and manipulates reinforcements in order to induce conformity.

Observation and Instruction

People acquire a cognitive map of their social organizational environment partly through observation. Furthermore, they learn the norms governing their own roles by observing the behavior of others who are in the same socially defined categories as themselves and noting the reinforcement consequences of that behavior. Bandura, Ross, and Ross (1961, 1963) have shown that children more often imitate the behavior of someone whom they have seen rewarded for that behavior, especially if that someone is clearly similar in some way to themselves, than they do if the other is different or is not rewarded. Gewirtz (1969) has noted that such vicarious reinforcement is a way of teaching norms inasmuch as it is "a cue . . . indicating the 'permissibility' of reproducing the behavior" (p. 148). In this way, children discover that although the norms do not permit them to harm others, they do permit them to smack around a bobo doll if they feel like it.

Others' roles are learned by the same processes as people's own roles are, except that there may be no forces impelling learners to conform. This learning is usually a cognitive matter in the sense that Baldwin (1962) distinguished cognitive, as being affectively neutral. Still, some roles of others may generate motive forces. Learners may depend on certain actions of the incumbent of another role, as one depends on the police to enforce the law. Whereas people do not feel impelled to play a particular role themselves, their relationships to those roles are like their relationships to resources such as tools, and they are motivated to somehow control the incumbents of those roles.

People are not necessarily conscious of their cognitive organizational maps. Giddens (1979) distinguished between discursive consciousness, practical consciousness, and unconscious levels of awareness of the rules by which social systems are reproduced. The Navaho children studied by Carroll and Casagrande (1958) could not recite the grammatical rules for forming verbs to denote the handling of objects; nevertheless, the way they matched objects gave evidence that at some level of awareness, the children knew the rules. This is what Giddens seemed to have in mind by practical—working—consciousness. It is tempting to translate Giddens's distinctions into the psychoanalytic terminology of conscious, preconscious, and unconscious levels, but they do not quite fit. Practical consciousness is not preconscious in the sense that objects can be brought into consciousness merely by the act of attention. Practical consciousness, as Giddens's seemed to mean it, describes preverbal awareness, as psychoanalytic theory depicts the state of memories that are unavailable to consciousness because the events occurred prior to the acquisition of adequate language to describe them. Common parlance calls such things common sense, the kind of thing one takes for granted, the things that go without saying. To say that social movements aim to raise people's consciousness often means that awareness of certain role requirements should be shifted, in Giddens's terms, from practical to discursive—verbalizable—consciousness.

Most norms of language usage are in practical consciousness. Observations have been made, but little explicit instruction has been given. Other roles and aspects of roles are also apprehended at that level. Sex differences in talents, interests, and ways of walking are examples of role playing according to norms of which individuals are ordinarily only practically aware. For example, Jenni and Jenni (1976) documented developmental differences in the ways boys and girls carry their schoolbooks. There are familiar masculine and feminine patterns: Boys tend to grasp the long edge of their books in one hand, either over or under the books; girls tend to enfold their books in arms crossed across their bosoms or cradle them in one arm with the short edge supported by their hip. These patterns become increasingly differentiated with age, the differences accelerating at adolescence. Physical maturation might contribute to the acceleration at adolescence, when boys' arms typically become stronger than girls' and girls' hips typically widen. At the same time, the load of schoolbooks students must carry gets heavier. However, Jenni and Jenni found that boys and girls conformed substantially to their appropriate carrying style well before adolescence, when these physical differences had not yet developed. It is unlikely that the youngsters are consciously aware of sex role norms about styles for carrying their books to the point where they can verbalize them, although many may be able, if prompted, to describe the difference. Some few may have been teased for carrying their books like "sissies" or "tomboys." Usually, children learn how to carry their books and themselves by watching others who, they have learned, are like themselves, without a word being spoken and, consequently, without being able to articulate the norms.

Thus, much of the effect of the social environment on people is due to their observing role enactments, and the informativeness of such observation depends on properties of the social environment being observed. The theoretical strategy of levels of analysis prescribes that one consider, among other factors, how variations in the social environment affect the probability of valid observations. A plausible hypothesis is that individuals learn roles well to the degree that their norms are clear, which they are if the roles are enacted uniformly by people in the associated social positions. Observers may attribute the causes of behavior to various origins —personality, interpersonal relations, physical stimuli, and so on. If it is clear that all the actors in a particular position behave in the same way, then the behavior is more likely be attributed to the role. Properties of roles that increase uniform enactment are their rigidity, their coherence, and strong sanction potential. People tend to learn more accurate personal role definitions if they observe others taking roles with these properties.

Familiarity of the social setting is another factor that contributes to role learning by observation. If actors are behaving in bizarre situations, then it is difficult to know whether their behavior, however consistent it may be in that context, is appropriate to their roles or peculiar to the situation. Thus, realistic drama is more instructive than fantasy. Furthermore, a developmental dimension must be considered here. Because children are generally less able to distinguish fact from fancy or the abnormal from the normal, familiarity of setting is not so differentiated for children as adults and thus makes less difference in the instructiveness to them of role portrayals in the media and elsewhere.

Motivation

Social learning theory posits that, in addition to observation, direct reinforcement also contributes to role learning. Its primary critical function is to motivate individuals to enact their roles appropriately. Social approval and disapproval figure prominently in the social learning explanation.

The plausibility of a genetic basis to the reinforcing property of social approval is supported by the existence of certain more easily domesticated species of animals, dogs in particular, and the differential domesticability of breeds of dogs. Some animals respond eagerly to the sight, smell, sound, and touch of familiar humans. That humans are almost universally responsive to social approval, with all the individual differences among them, also supports the argument of innateness.

The universal human experience of survival being associated with human care might also be responsible for the ubiquitous potency of social approval. Along these lines, Eysenck (1967) suggested that individual differences in responsiveness stem from differences in the more general characteristic of conditionability, which in turn rest on genetic differences in the nervous system.

In any case, most people usually respond positively to social approval, present or imagined. Conformity to social norms depends heavily on this. People learn not only what is expected of them but also that they are rewarded when they act and feel as expected.

Because they are not directly observable, motives are not as efficiently reinforced as behaviors are, but socializers learn to infer them more or less accurately from facial expressions, postures, and gestures. Once individuals have gained the ability somehow to infer what is on others' minds, then they can socialize motives as well as overt behavior. Because accurate inference requires understanding cues that are often subtle and complex, it is a skill that takes some experience to acquire. Hence, children generally recognize behavioral conformity before commitment. This developmental trend is manifested in the changing bases of children's moral thought (Hoffman, 1977; Kohlberg, 1981). Early on, what is considered right or wrong is closely tied to overt behavior—what people do and what is done to them as a consequence. Older children tend more to consider what people think and feel about behavior in judging morality because they are now better able to tell how others think and feel and have learned more about what thoughts and feelings are appropriate.

There are other developmental changes in role learning. Social learning theory itself does not take these developmental changes adequately into account. For one, the potency of various reinforcements increases and decreases over the life span. McCandless (1970) has made social learning theory relevant to adolescent development by noting that the onset of the sex drive drastically enhances both the capacity for certain feelings and the environmental contingencies concerning them. McCandless posited that heightened libido, characteristic of adolescents, may disrupt customary patterns of behavior and present new opportunities for learning. Psychoanalytic theory (Spiegel, 1972) also recognizes this source of greater malleability of adolescent behavior and feelings. In cultures where sexual outlets are restricted, the sex drive can reach high levels indeed and thereby have pervasive effects on adolescents' role enactment. At the same time that levels of drive may be destabilizing, the reinforcement value of objects and activities changes. This changes who controls the more effective contingencies; in other words, the potency of role senders shifts. In some societies adolescents consequently come under greater peer control than they had been. However, in other societies where the norms severely limit legitimate peer control over the reinforcements that adolescents find increasingly satisfying, conformity to peers does not increase (Heilbrun & Norbert, 1970).

Social learning theory does not take development adequately into account, nor does it explain adequately why some people become deeply committed to the norms of a role whereas others merely conform. These theoretical weaknesses can be remedied without altering the application of social learning principles over the life span by noting developmental changes in motivation and consequently in potential reinforcements. Ego analytic theory has this feature and therefore is a useful supplement to the social learning explanation for socialization.

Ego Analytic Perspective

Superego

Sigmund Freud (1923/1962) conceived of the superego in order to bring the influence of the normative environment into the psychic structure of the individual. He intended the concept to be central to the translation of the social environment into psychological terms, and he proposed that the superego is created by identification. No doubt Freud observed that adults evaluate themselves in styles and with standards that their parents and other caregivers had used to evaluate them. Children believe that adults possess more or less imperious authority, an authority that maintains constant surveillance over their behavior and inner thoughts and feelings, a judge both part and not part of themselves—an "over I." Freud also observed small children imitating their caregivers and admonishing and warning themselves in their caregivers' manner especially in an effort, he thought, to gain control of their impulses. Faced with the task of explaining the internal conflicts between drives and social convention with closed theory at the psychological level, Freud postulated the formation of an abiding superego that battled the animal drives of the id for control of the ego agency.

Theorists have found the whole idea troublesome ever since. This is not the place to address all the theoretical problems concerning the superego. Controversies abound about the source of the superego's energy, its relationship to the ego and to the ego ideal, and other issues (cf. Hartmann, Kris, & Lowenstein, 1964; Rapaport, 1942). As important as these are, they need not be resolved to use the concept to address the social psychological problem of socialization.

Parsons (1964) rejected Freud's conception of the superego as internalized morals of the same-sexed parent. He preferred a broader conception of the substance of the superego, including in it the norms defining the role relations of the parent with all the members of the family. Accordingly, children internalize in the first instance the role of son or daughter in relation to mother and father. They also internalize the norms governing their relationships to their siblings and any others who may be part of the family group. Parsons proposed further that children internalize the incipient roles of husbands or wives and fathers or mothers by observing first how their parental models play these roles and learning how to be the husband–wife and the father–mother in their families of origin. Later they elaborate on the internalized norms in light of further experience to fashion for themselves the roles of husband–wife and father–mother in their families of procreation. These internalized familial roles are also the templates after which other extrafamilial roles are modeled, thus leaving the traces of early experience on all social relationships. This, for Parsons, described the nature and influence of the superego, not only constraining sexual and aggressive impulses but also governing social relationships in the broadest sense.

Perhaps no substantive conceptualization of the superego is very useful, whether the narrower Freudian one that consists of social constraints against direct expression of sexual and aggressive impulses, or the broader Parsonian one, with its inclusion of familial role relations. More helpful for social psychological theory is a relational concept of superego. What is internalized in early childhood and takes hold psychologically is not social norms but rather a sensitivity to social norms that varies interindividually in degree and kind, depending on early experiences of role learning.

From this perspective, theoretically useful dimensions of superego are its rigidity, scope, coherence, and other structural dimensions, which are also dimensions of roles. This parallel conceptualization facilitates translation between the social organizational and the psychological levels of analysis. Moreover, the terms of social learning theory provide a rich theoretical, methodological, and empirical source for understanding and investigating how this interpenetration occurs. This leaves the normative content of individuals' psyches open to change without necessarily altering individuals' predispositions for internal conflicts and anxieties and for ways of relating normatively to others.

For example, the pervasiveness of adults' guilt feelings may be explained by contemporary precipitates of the scope and potentiality for sanction in the role of son or daughter as they learned it when they were children. The hypothetically determining factor is not the behaviors but rather how many different behaviors caused how much withdrawal of loving care when children learned how rewards and punishments worked. To the degree that the son–daughter role had wide scope and high potential for negative sanction, then perhaps people learned early that their behavior is under constant surveillance and subject to unpleasant consequences. Because they have only an imperfect understanding of social norms and only tenuous self-control, it is natural that children frequently misbehave and may frequently experience severe sanctions. These are the sort of learning conditions that lead people in adulthood to anticipate social disapproval if they act on their wishes and thus to feel persistently guilty even when merely wishing for something socially disapproved. It is a situation in which aversive consequences are not risked even after severe consequences no longer really threaten, and therefore their expectations are not tested (Aronfreed, 1964).

Consistent with psychoanalytic theory, this sensitivity to social norms called *superego* is conceived to emerge and persist according to developmental principles. That is, the superego ordinarily develops during a particular stage in the life span and resists change once that formative stage is past. Its enduring character makes it, by definition, a component of personality. These ideas of development and personality are necessary to social psychological theory but cannot be supplied by social learning theory.

Identity

Social learning theory cannot account for individual differences in commitment to roles. Taking roles often includes not only displaying appropriate behaviors but also valuing the motives and resources appropriate to the performance of roles. Kelman (1958) distinguished three levels of commitment to attitudes, and his distinctions can be usefully applied to motives and resources as well. *Compliance*, as Kelman defined it, refers to action performed consistent with an attitude in the anticipation of social approval or some other reward; but compliant actors do not actually hold the attitude. Kelman proposed *identification* to mean that individuals hold the attitudes prescribed by a role in order to participate in the social organization of which the role is a part, but they change their minds if the prescribed attitudes change, because the role governs. If *internalization* has occurred, people hold attitudes because they seem intrinsically right; people would rather abandon a role than change their minds. In Kelman's model, internalization is the deepest level of personal commitment.

There is risk of a kind of alienation in compliance and identification, greater in the former but present in the latter as well. *Alienation* means many things in the social psychological literature (Gold, 1969; Seeman, 1972). The kind that is at risk here is estrangement from one's self, the belief that one's actions are not altogether willed. Compliant individuals sometimes recognize the disjunction, and sometimes they justify it with a broad cost–benefit analysis. Still, it can be an uncomfortable experience. If the role neglects or disallows important motives, persons feel self-abandon.

Erikson's (1969) concept of identity and the ego analytic theory of which it is a constituent provides another vocabulary by which social organizational events can be translated into psychological terms. It helps to account for both developmental factors and for differences in levels of commitment. The hope that Levinson (1964) placed in ego analytic theory for integrating sociology and psychology is a sound one, and the idea of identity is the principal reason.

The idea of identity is an important supplement to social learning theory for two reasons. First, it combines many of the developmental processes that lead to personal commitment to motives, whereas social learning theory by itself pertains only to behavioral conformity. Second, the idea of identity recognizes that individuals may enter roles with a more or less stable personality, depending on age and life history, whereas social learning theory neglects the more enduring personal characteristics with which individuals encounter models, instructions, and reinforcements.

Erikson (1969) implied that there is a universal human motive to construct an identity, that there is a basic need for personal continuity. He found role confusion at the root of much of the psychological disturbance of the college students who sought his clinical help, and he believed it causes the profound depression that he observed in many African American and Native American youth. It makes intuitive sense that people strive for personal continuity; after all, one would hesitate to marshal one's resources to attain one's goals if one believed that at any moment, those goals would no longer be one's goals or those resources would disappear. Confident action would be paralyzed without answers to the questions, "What do I want to make of myself, and what do I have to work with?" The need for an identity qualifies as an axiom in a closed theory at the psychological level of analysis. This need for an identity encourages people to commit themselves to roles, not merely to comply with role demands.

Any durable society arranges the conditions for most of its members to formulate identities. This is accomplished in complex societies by ensuring its members broad discretion in choosing and adopting roles; and in simple societies, by training its members from their earliest days to the psychological properties suitable to the limited role opportunities. It follows from this that members of a society whose rearing does not foster a confident self-awareness or training in psychological characteristics within the range of the requirements of available and respectable roles are unable to achieve an identity.

The need for an identity can be thwarted especially when, led to anticipate more opportunity, people find access to only a severely limited set of rigid roles. This is a condition of life prevalent among oppressed groups in a putatively open society. It was the condition of a Jim Crow childhood and youth for Richard Wright, who described it vividly in his autobiography, *Black Boy* (1966). Wright's response was to formulate what by definition must be classified as a negative identity, that is, an identity which, however much it constitutes a sense of personal continuity, is a dangerous and undesirable one to those who matter in one's life. Because of fortuitous failure in important aspects of his socialization, Wright became an incorrigible grandson, religious apostate, juvenile delinquent, and aspiring author, and he would not shuffle. This identity could have cost him his life, and he knew it. Ultimately, Wright escaped the Jim Crow South and searched out an environment in which the core of his identity was neither dangerous nor undesirable.

Not everyone has the talent and opportunity to achieve a positive identity by migration, but discussions of identity resolutions tend to overlook another way some people with limited choices nevertheless achieve satisfactory accommodations. This shortsightedness is due to the preoccupation in the literature on identity with work roles. It is not surprising that intellectuals whose occupation is to create this literature tend to overvalue occupation. It is typically at the core of our identities. For many (perhaps most) people, however, occupation is not the thread of their role continuity. Of course, occupation powerfully determines the availability of other roles and how one plays them, but it is not necessarily at the core of identity. Some work is simply not ego involving; some people make their living in the service of other more self-defining roles and relationships.

The tendency to regard occupation as secondary to one's identity is an example of the more general mechanism of ordering role subidentities. When individuals have few and relatively inflexible roles available to them and are consequently hard put to negotiate a satisfying merger of self and social organization, they may fulfill their need for an identity by committing themselves fully to one or a few roles that fit or can be made to fit the contours of their personalities. Everything else they do may be subordinated to their being husbands or wives, fathers or mothers. Some people run political campaigns, collect art, garden, or bowl in the service of formulating and maintaining their identities.

The formulation of an identity is a reciprocal process between individuals and their social organizational environments. The results in most instances are people who do not feel alienated while playing various roles. The roles contain elements of themselves, and their selves incorporate their roles. The socialization process has fostered their commitment to the motives and resources required and allowed by their roles.

Although forging the link between the psychological and social organizational levels of analysis requires paying attention primarily to the role aspect of identity, one must not ignore the life-historical or ego component. Personality is more than an integration of roles. It also includes the givens of temperament and the personal characteristics accrued over the life span as individuals encounter, define, and redefine roles they are expected to play. Whenever permitted by role flexibility, people enact their roles in their personal styles, as they have developed through the stages of their lives. Nevertheless, personality and roles are not independent, as Brim (1960) correctly pointed out. In Parsons's terminology, the two interpenetrate. Identity formation is a useful way to conceptualize their interpenetration and to understand socialization with commitment beyond compliance.

Two Applications

The utility of this social psychological model can be tested by exploring whether it provides any additional understanding of familiar phenomena or at least raises researchable questions that might lead to greater understanding. Although the three chapters in the Applications section of this book purport to demonstrate that the model does, two briefer discussions toward that same end in this chapter illustrate the model's use of socialization specifically.

Role Change and Attitude Change

Lieberman's (1956) findings (see chapter 4) revealed that changes in roles tend to be accompanied by obviously role-congruent changes in attitudes. Lieberman did not propose in any detail the social psychological processes responsible for the effect. Invoking the process of socialization suggests several ways in which change in their roles may have caused workers *cum* foremen to express more positive attitudes toward management and workers *cum* shop stewards to feel more positively about the union.

The social psychological model requires that role change be translated into attitude change through a change in motives or resources, a change that turns certain attitudes into resources. One may assume that salient goals of workers did not change, that higher wages and greater power and prestige were valued all along. That the attitudes of future foremen and shop stewards toward management and the union did not differ prior to their respective appointments can be attributed to workers giving little weight at the time to holding the appropriate attitudes as a resource for achieving their goals. This might be due to their belief that their chances at those positions were generally slim or that the display of appropriate attitudes would not increase their chances. In any case, after their appointments, the valence of the appropriate attitudes probably increased because holding certain attitudes was required for keeping their desirable new positions.

How did workers learn that certain attitudes were required of their new roles? Social learning processes are apparent. The change in roles probably sensitized foremen and stewards to observe potential models differently, because they became similar to different role takers in the factory than they had been. Thus, they might have imitated new models in their behavior and in their attitudes. Moreover, the foremen and shop stewards were then governed by a different set of contingencies: They were undoubtedly rewarded for expressing attitudes that would not have been rewarded had they expressed them as workers. Thus, a more complete understanding of the conditions responsible for attitude change in such studies might be gained by assessing the perceived benefits of the new roles and testing the hypothesis that these greater rewards induce greater conformity. One might also inquire about changes in who is taken as a model as a consequence of role change.

Analyzing the socialization of attitudes with the conceptual tools of social learning and ego analytic theories opens an interesting question: What conditions were conducive to some of the men internalizing their new attitudes as compared with merely complying or identifying? Apparently many of the men were not strongly committed to their attitudes toward management and the union; Lieberman found that attitudes reverted somewhat to what they had been when the foremen and stewards became workers again. For some, however, attitude change endured. Ego analytic theory proposes that the conditions for internalization–commitment are those that encourage formation of role identity. These include the consonance of an individual's personal organization with the obligations and privileges of a role and the approval and encouragement of others who matter. This approach suggests inquiring into workers' personal role definitions and the fit between these definitions and their relevant motives and resources.

Recognizing that dissonance reduction can be a mechanism for identity formation opens up other lines of inquiry about the socialization process that accounts for Lieberman's findings. Having been chosen for their respective roles, the factory workers were subject to contingencies that induced them to act appropriately in role. Among other things, the new foremen enforced the policies of management and the new shop stewards protected the perquisites of workers as union members. The theory of dissonance reduction posits that, if individuals are induced to act as if they possessed the motives and resources required of a role, then they may become committed to them. In the terms of ego analytic theory, they can avoid alienation by revising their identity.

As the psychological process of dissonance reduction is supposed to work, one condition for psychological change is that individuals cannot otherwise justify their behavior. If the foremen and stewards could justify their actions as consonant with an identity other than foreman or shop steward, then they should have been less prone to change. That is, motive forces impelling change are weakened if behavior can be assimilated to an established identity. Earning higher wages, for example, may have been sufficient justification for a man to act as a foreman should if being a good breadwinner was central to his identity. The privileges of shop steward-ship were much more sparse. Thus, shop stewards were more prone than foremen to internalize their new attitudes.

Approaching Lieberman's findings from the perspective of socialization generates additional specific research questions. Did the private expressions of attitudes toward management and union in response to Lieberman's questionnaire reflect compliance, identification, or internalization? Did foremen's and shop stewards' responses differ in this respect? Did the reversion to the role of worker increase the control of reinforcements of the other workers more for former foremen than for former stewards? The pattern of initially equal, then different degrees of attitude change suggests that foremen were complying or identifying with management and stewards were internalizing the values of the union, and that the commitment of former stewards to the value of the union was abetted by the reference group of workers, which also encouraged the later disaffection from management of the erstwhile foremen.

The model also draws attention to indirect ways in which role changes may have affected the workers' motives and resources, by exposing them to new subcultures and by encouraging the development of new interpersonal relations. Foremen presumably engaged in more casual communication with managers than they had, and shop stewards with officials of the union. By "casual," I mean the kind of communication that carries no obligation, either to engage in it or to believe the messages received. Persuasion ensues. It is also plausible that new foremen got to know their supervisors better and new shop stewards the officers and staff in the union, also because of the opportunities afforded for casual interaction. Friendships may have sprung up that, through the process of identification, effected psychological changes. Lieberman did not report about the friendships that may have developed between men as a consequence of their changed roles. There is reason to believe that the situation of the shop stewards made the influence of interpersonal relationships more effective in achieving their more enduring commitment than the situation of the foremen. The egalitarian ethos of the union culture probably provided more fertile ground for the cultivation of interpersonal relations across the organizational hierarchy than the subculture of management did. Management believed more in authority to ensure compliance to role demands than the union did, and this lessened the opportunity for friendships. It is likely therefore that shop stewards identified more with others who held these pro-union attitudes, so their attitudes did not change as much as the erstwhile foremen's did when they left their respective roles.

Language Acquisition

Although learning theory has been invoked to explain the acquisition and perfection of language (cf. Bohannon & Warren-Leubecker, 1989; Mowrer, 1960; Skinner, 1957), it is not ordinarily considered as an instance of role learning. Allusions to role learning appear, as in Lock's (1991) observation that "Vygotsky and Macmurray posited a new language development as rooted in the social process of communication, a vehicle whereby communication is structured into *conventional*, rather than idiosyncratic, forms" (p. 292; emphasis added). It is instructive to think of it this way. The use of language is after all permeated by moral imperatives. There is no more inherent reason to call a car a *car* than there is to drive a car on the right or left, or to eat with a fork rather than chopsticks, or to place verbs soon after nouns rather than at the tag end of a sentence; people do so by social agreement. It is functional to have such agreements, and it is critically important in the case of language. So the collective effort to teach the norms of language is great, and the social sanctions for nonconformity are strong. Those who do not conform in important respects to local speech patterns may find themselves ostracized, even shut away in mental institutions.

Its importance has attracted many disciplines to the study of language. Why languages differ from one culture to another is a problem for culturology. Sociology's interest in language concerns how usage differs from one role to another, including not only how individuals consistently use patterns peculiar to their social class, ethnic group, or age grade but also how individuals' usage changes as they occupy different roles, speaking differently, for example, to their spouses, to their small children, and to fellow workers. Translating brain structure into linguistic rules is a problem for neuropsychology. Chomsky (1972) asserted that the fundamental rules of usage are not social but rather are given in the structure of the brain. Nevertheless, if there is indeed such a "deep structure" to language, it supports a large variety of elaborate superstructures as the vocabularies and grammars of known languages make plain.

One problem concerning language for social psychology is to identify the social sources of similarities and differences in usage among individuals and their psychological consequences. Explanation for individual variation is largely to be found in differential socialization. Another problem is to explain the rare event of individuals affecting the language of their social environment. In the terms of the model, language resides in the cultural environment as a technology. Its development and initial dissemination follow the principles of psychocultural influence, invention, and persuasion. Actually, few people participate in this process under modern conditions of mass communication; rather, it is an activity of expert writers, their editors, and their chroniclers who compile dictionaries and grammars. Since the invention of the printing press, the institutionalization of language has broadened and the band of arbiters has narrowed. The vast majority of people are socialized into a language group; we are not inventors of this technology.

In the model, socialization is taken not in the broad sense of social training but more narrowly as induction into roles. Then into what role does the socialization of language induce an individual? Individuals are born into a language group, and when they become developmentally able, they are ascribed the role of user of a specific language. Although not explicitly identified as a role, the common definition of a role and its dimensions fit the role of specific language user as well as any other. There are shared norms about proper linguistic behavior applicable to people in a particular position in a social organization. The social organization is the specific language group. It is not very complex, being composed only of a few interdependent roles: users—a role which all members occupy, and essentially three other specialized roles: authors, arbiters, and trainers.

That language groups are distinctive social organizations with their own identifiable roles is apparent not only in their distinctive vocabularies, grammars, and inflections but also in the loyalties differentially required of members. The importance of loyalty that distinguishes some language groups is best exemplified nowadays by Francophones in France and Quebec and those in the U.S. who want to outlaw any language but English in official documents and public institutions.

The dimensions along which roles may be ordered apply to the role of user of a specific language as well. The role is very broad in its scope, covering a wide variety of situations in which role takers find themselves, with only a few notable exceptions; so broad indeed that the language group should therefore obey the general social psychological propositions about roles with broad scope, such as the high probability that they help shape individuals' personality. The rigidity of the role varies, being greater for example in the later stages of training in formal institutions of learning (high schools, colleges) and less in private conversation. Its sanctions are informal but severe, so that noncompliance is rare because the rewards are so great and the pressures inexorable. The role of specific language user is initially a relatively informal one and becomes progressively more formal.

The developmental course of the role of language user from informal to formal may resolve a puzzle about language acquisition. Is it possible that children under 4 years of age or thereabouts can acquire language so quickly through training by caregivers, or does some innate mechanism, triggered by conversation, quickly sort words and phrases into a functional syntax? Observers provide mixed reports of how assiduously caregivers socialize their wards as specific language users, some so little that it seems hardly possible that their training is responsible for the children's rapid progress (Bohannon & Warren-Leubecker, 1989). I suggest that the earliest language used by caregivers and their wards be cast in role terms as informal, that is, its norms are negotiated between them. The small child assigns a name to an object or event and the caregiver agrees to call it that, so for example the pair speak of gastrointestinal discomfort as an "ow-ey belly," and the phrase "long time" signifies past tense, as in the child's report about an outing on the preceding day, "I go long time to Granma's." It may seem then that caregivers are not socializing their wards, but actually the children are being taught a great deal about how to take the role of language user, albeit not a role recognizable to observers who do not know the norms that caregiver and ward have negotiated between them.

Soon enough, as caregivers come to believe that their wards have the capacity and with growing need for children to communicate with others not party to private negotiations, the role of specific language user becomes increasing formal, and children learn the widely accepted norms for signifying events in the past, and so on. In the process, learners may first simply model their behavior on other speakers, then perhaps they use their capacity to generalize and apply rules to new situations. Ervin (1964) has pointed out how small children initially learn to use irregular verbs in the correct tense—"I come," "I came"; "I run," "I ran"—but soon after begin to use them incorrectly— "I comed," "I runned"—as they apply a newly acquired general norm inappropriately until they are corrected.

Hence, language is acquired and maintained by substantially the same process as are other social norms. Individuals are socialized to a role in their language group. What is learned are rules and practices not merely stated but backed by moral imperatives. Social learning theory seems to be an adequate explanations for this process. It is significant, as Skinner (1957) pointed out, that a good deal of reinforcement for this learning must be social, because linguistic acts are almost never rewarded by direct commerce with other environments. ("Almost never" because domesticated animals respond as desired to a limited set of commands, and computers will make elaborate, often desired, responses to words—at this writing, just beginning to be available with the capacity to respond to spoken words.) People who want something to drink can of course learn how to obtain a drink without involving other people, but only other people can reward them with a drink when they ask for one.

Expectations regarding language usage are imposed differentially on members of a language group, depending on other circumstances. Children's spelling and grammatical errors are tolerated; adults assume that they are still learning proper usage and patiently correct their errors. Nor are foreigners expected to speak the native language so skillfully. However, one ordinarily becomes annoyed should natives speak in a foreign tongue because they ought to communicate in the agreed-upon way. If the natives have a low socioeconomic status or are Hispanic, their lower level of skills in standard English tends to be accepted as "good enough" for their purposes. Their errors are tolerated, but with prejudice. On the other hand, college students are actively socialized to standard usage, systematically rewarded and punished for their linguistic behavior because their present and future stations require it. Iconoclast G. B. Shaw played with this facet of the normativity of language in *Pygmalion*.

The necessity for social reinforcement and the basis of most if not all linguistic rules in the social consensus of a specific language group justify conceptualizing language acquisition and maintenance as role learning. Whereas the role of speaker of a particular language includes virtually all members of a language group, this does not vitiate its characterization as a role. A particular usage is not a fundamental value of a cultural sort; it is not an idea but a practice prescribed by social norms.

Nevertheless, one should not overlook the importance of language as technology, however much it also resides in social consensus. Some usages have more utility in some contexts than others do. Differences among languages reflect different cultural solutions to the problems facing subscribers to the culture. People must be clear with one another about certain matters as they interact in a common environment; thus, the familiar examples of the distinctive words for snow in the language of Native Americans in the Arctic Circle and the distinctive words for flying machines in the languages of modern cultures. Still, recognizing that language is adapted to its environments makes language no less normative. The same is true of every normative system. All social organizations are under the joint influence of the capacities of individuals that depend on such things as the structure of their brains and of the culture that in turn adapts to its environments. From this perspective, linguistic behavior is a matter of role obligations and privileges.

Socialization to a particular language has more profound effects on individuals than any other training. According to the Whorfian hypothesis (Fishman, 1960; Whorf, 1941), conformity to the norms of language means uniformity in experiences of the world. What one perceives and how one organizes the relationships among one's perceptions are shaped by the options available in one's vocabulary, grammar, and inflections. As the norms of language are shaped by the realities of the environment in which the language group lives, these norms in turn shape the reality in which the individual lives. Perceptions of the fundamentals of time, space, and causality are substantially determined by linguistic conventions. Carroll and Casagrande (1958) demonstrated how the grammar of a language calls the attention of its users to certain features of their environment and thereby affects how they organize it. The Navaho language requires different verb forms to connote the handling of objects, depending on their shape, flexibility, or other physical characteristics. English has no such grammatical rule. Carroll and Casagrande enlisted Navaho children, some of whom spoke Navaho exclusively or predominantly, and the rest, English. The children were presented pairs of objects and asked which one of each pair "went best" with which one of a third set of objects. Although none of the 3- to 10-year-old children could state the grammatical rule of Navaho usage, the Navaho-speaking ones significantly more frequently matched objects that are handled similarly, that is, on the bases of criteria implied by their grammar. The older children manifested the rule more than the younger. Obviously, the Navaho-speaking children were not consciously conforming to a moral dictate in the way they matched objects or, in a larger sense, organized their physical environment. Still, extensive experience acting as a Navaho speaker should have led them unwittingly into certain ways of perceiving and acting.

Role taking typically has such direct and indirect effects. People become more or less aware of role requirements and are motivated more or less to conform to them. Often their conformity then has psychological ramifications beyond the requirements of the role. Conformity in language usage above all has such ramifications.

Psychological Effects on Social Organization

Some individuals sometimes influence social organization. They make more or less enduring changes in their own and others' roles.

An informal organization, by definition, is shaped by those who people it. However, individuals have not had a substantial effect on their social organizational environment as long as the organization remains informal, dependent on the agreement only of the individuals who negotiated it. Substantial and enduring effects occur when innovations in roles are institutionalized, formalizing an organization to carry out some function in a significantly different way.

Invention is the most frequent way by which individuals affect their social organizational environment significantly. In the terms of the model, this is an indirect effect of individuals on social organization, through culture.

Henry Ford is a familiar example of an individual who effected significant changes in his social organizational environment by means of cultural change. Ford's major contribution was not the invention and development of the internal combustion engine, in which he actually played only a small part, but rather in the elaboration and perfection of mass production and distribution. With this innovation, Ford introduced an enduring radical change in the social organization of manufacture. The assembly line was widely adopted and required other social organizational changes.

Ford is a particularly interesting example because his invention is itself social organizational; the parts he fabricated and assembled were essentially roles, consisting of and held together by social norms. The assembly line represents a decisive shift from craftsmanship to mechanization; assembly line workers do not work with machinery, they are parts of the machinery. This difference has in turn profound effects on the individuals subject to it, and much has been written about the potentially alienating effects of the assembly line on the worker (e.g., Blauner, 1964). Other inventions of course are altogether material, like the contraceptive pill, and they too change the technological premises in the cultural environment on which social organizations like marriage are based.

Cultural change affecting social organization can be ideological rather than technological. Martin Luther indirectly reorganized the religious institutions of his time and place by altering beliefs about the actual and ethical relationship between individuals and their god. Like Ford's invention, Luther's directly affected social relationships by redefining the obligations and privileges of people in their religious roles. Luther's impact was especially broad and deep because the social organization immediately affected by him was a dominant one that at the time exercised the function of legitimizing virtually all the rest of the culture and society.

It is ordinarily more difficult to effect social organizational change by changing ideology rather than technology because ideological change is harder to validate. By definition, technology can be validated by empirical observation and ideology cannot. That Ford's assembly line was "right" could be seen in the profits. That Martin Luther was "right" about individuals needing no earthly mediator between themselves and their god had to be taken on faith; no one expected a proliferation of miracles to confirm this. Conditions at the time permitted Luther to abrogate the governing authority. (Social psychological conditions conducive to individuals affecting culture are discussed later in relation to the dynamics of persuasion.)

I think that understanding Martin Luther as an ideological inventor requires a consideration of interpersonal relations and the idea of negative identity. Individuals may alter role relations by demonstrating their own commitment to new roles. That means that they model the roles themselves. If these new roles radically challenge established social norms, then it is often necessary for innovators to adopt a negative identity. This identity status is particularly important to social psychologists because of its potential for effecting major social change, by the right person at the right time in the right social environments.

Erikson wrote of negative identity as the choice of roles that are "undesirable and dangerous" (1968, p. 174). The most familiar example of such a choice in adolescence is the role of juvenile delinquent. This example assumes that there are social norms governing the behavior of delinquents, defined with temporal and local variations by the young people who have chosen the role (with help from the mass media), enforced by them on those who want to belong, and widely disseminated by the mass media with accompanying condemnations and warnings. Central to the delinquent role is the norm of opposition to conventional rules, that is, subscription to a contraculture. Thus, delinquents are not supposed to obey their parents, go to school, participate in organized sports or social activities, attend church, and so on. Their commitment to their negative identity is conceived to be as firm and as functional as a commitment to a positive identity; the role is played as genuinely and provides as full a sense of continuity to the delinquent's life. The essential difference between it and a positive identity is that delinquents apprehend the disapproval and danger involved in their choice.

The juvenile delinquent is in many respects an apt but misleading example of a negative identity. Its ubiquity in descriptions of negative identity has distorted the meaning of the status. For one thing, the role of *juvenile* delinquent is by definition temporary, and that has led the nature of a negative identity to be construed as always more tenuous than a positive identity. It is true that the disapproval and danger inherent in a negative identity makes it more precarious, but it may nevertheless be felt as a long-term commitment. The example of a professional thief would express this better.

More important, claims that a person may make to the legitimacy of a negative identity are preempted in the example of the delinquent. It is within the conceptual scope of a negative identity that people who formulate one do so with moral conviction rooted in their own society, even while apprehending dangerous opposition. Erikson offered Martin Luther (1958) and Mohandas K. Gandhi (1969) as examples of such people.

Challenging the moral order can lead one into dangerous territory. Many of the people who matter in one's life do not follow; they instead try to enforce the prevailing norms. Individuals who strike out on new paths can find the going lonely. Their capacity to persist is strengthened by social support, particularly by the accepting and warm support found in interpersonal relations. Inherent to interpersonal relations is mutual recognition and acceptance of partners' identities. Thus, it is frequently critical that individuals who persist in trying to change their society and culture have at least one if not a circle of intimates. These intimates may, from the outside and from a historical perspective, appear to be disciples who identify with the leader in something a great deal less than a mutual interpersonal relation. Some of these discipleships may, however, be reciprocal relationships of genuine affection and unconditional acceptance. Erikson proposed that both Luther and Gandhi participated in such relationships and that their participation was crucial to their ideological persistence.

This seems also to have been true of Richard Wright. His impact on his culture has not been as strong as either Luther's or Gandhi's on theirs, but he played an important part in changing cultural stereotypes of African Americans. His account of his childhood and youth in *Black Boy* (1966) is in large part a portrayal of the development of a negative identity. Wright reports that most of his immediate family regarded him as an evil boy. Several uncles and an aunt whipped him or tried to even when he was already an adolescent, and his zealously religious maternal grandmother, the matriarch of the family, gave him up to the devil. Although he was a successful student, Wright was troublesome in school. His adolescent peers generally thought him strange because he was an avid reader and already a published author. Most dangerous, Wright would not shuffle before Whites.

In his youth, Wright had no chums and no trusting relationships with any adult, save one. Only his mother provided him with the support he needed. He recounted a revealing incident in which he defied his grandmother's edict that he could not work on the Seventh Day Adventist Sabbath:

> My clothing became so shabby that I was ashamed to go to school. Many of the boys in my class were wearing their first long-pants suits. I grew so bitter that I decided to have it out with Granny; I would tell her that if she did not let me work on Saturdays I would leave home.

> But when I opened the subject, she would not listen. I followed her
> about the house, demanding the right to work on Saturday. Her answer
> was no and no and no . . .
> "I'm going to get a job anyway."
> "Then you can't live here," she said.
> "Then I'll leave," I said, trembling violently.
> "You won't leave," she repeated.
> "You think I'm joking, don't you?" I asked, determined to make her
> know how I felt. "I'll leave this minute!" I ran to my room, got a battered
> suitcase, and began packing my ragged clothes. I did not have a penny,
> but I was going to leave. She came to the door.
> "You little fool! Put that suitcase down!"
> "I'm going where I can work!!"
> She snatched the suitcase out of my hands; she was trembling.
> "All right," she said. "If you want to go to hell, then go. But God'll know
> that it was not my fault. He'll forgive me, but He won't forgive you."
> Weeping, she rushed from the door. Her humanity had triumphed over
> her fear. I emptied the suitcase, feeling spent. I hated these emotional
> outbursts, these tempests of passion, for they always left me tense and
> weak. Now I was truly dead to Granny and Aunt Addie, but my mother
> smiled when I told her that I had defied them. She rose and hobbled to
> me on her paralytic legs and kissed me. (R. Wright, 1966, pp. 158–159)

A few years later, Wright left home and the Jim Crow South. Up north,
he found personal and organizational support to continue the training that
eventually equipped him to write his searing accounts of Black life in
America. Richard Wright's works (1940, 1953, 1966) helped to cultivate
the ground for social change that is still in progress.

Summary

This account of the interaction of the psychological and social organizational levels of analysis has been built largely with the conceptual tools of
social learning theory. The concepts of that theory cover pretty well the
components of socialization—discriminating among roles, learning the
norms that define roles, learning which roles one is supposed to play, acquiring the skills and other resources necessary to enact roles, and becoming motivated to conform. The concepts of social learning theory, including
observation, direct instructions, imitation, and reinforcement, are not,
however, wholly adequate. Other theories are needed to account for intraindividual differences in responsiveness over the life span and for inter-
individual differences in levels of commitment to roles.

Developmental theory is needed to understand why the processes and
results of socialization are in some ways markedly different from one point
in the life span to another. Cognitive growth is conceived in the model as
a change in resources that enables individuals to profit more from their
observations and their experiences of reinforcement. Physiological change
is both a resource that widens the individual's ability to imitate action and
a change in motives that affects the value of potential reinforcers. Social

development—the sequence of role changes associated with the life span—is located at the social organizational level of analysis, where it determines the incentives offered for developing particular motives and resources.

Ego analytic theory supplements social learning theory by accounting for deeper levels of commitment to roles than behavioral compliance. The concept of identity interpenetrates the psychological and social organizational levels by translating the organization of roles into the enduring organization of motives and resources that is personality.

Ego analytic theory also offers an explanation for how and under what conditions a personality makes marked and enduring changes in social organization through the process of institutionalization. Psychohistorical accounts, such as Erikson's biographies of Luther and Gandhi, reveal how the identity resolutions of certain critically placed individuals become the models for others. Much of the influence of personality on social organization is indirect, with individuals' talents generating cultural invention.

The social psychological model reveals various specific paths by which individuals and facets of the social organizational environment can exert reciprocal influence. Whereas the findings of studies such as Lieberman's on changing attitudes through changing roles demonstrate a social psychological effect, the model offers several plausible hypotheses about why the effect occurs. One is prompted, for example, to investigate further whether the effect Lieberman found was direct, by means of the model of socialization offered by social learning theory; to what extent interpersonal or cultural forces were operating; whether differences in the roles of foreman and shop steward mattered; whether there were individual differences in the effect, including differences in levels of commitment; and under what conditions the various levels of analysis more or less determined the effect.

Discussion of the social psychological dynamics at the interpersonal and cultural boundaries with the psychological level can now proceed from this base in the dynamics of the social organizational environment. In the next chapter, I suggest that socialization is inadequate to explain the influence of interpersonal relations as defined here. The conditions for socialization are present in role relationships and the conditions for identification, in interpersonal relations. Central to the former is contingent reinforcement, and to the latter, unconditional affection, that is, the absence of contingent reinforcement.

Anticipating discussion of cultural influence, I call attention here particularly to observational learning. The conditions for the ideal typical relationship of individuals to their culture is that they are observers over whom there is no power to manipulate their reinforcements. The absence of contingency makes the cultural relationship similar to the interpersonal one and different from the role relationship. Under this condition, models are only informative. Without power, and furthermore without interpersonal affect, what is left as a basis of cultural influence is an appeal to pragmatism: Individuals observe what might enable them to attain their goals, and what they observe is persuasive to the degree that it has utility.

In the following chapters, I take up interpersonal dynamics first and then cultural influence and change.

8

Interpersonal Dynamics: Identification

A common explanation of social influence is that the compliance of one individual to the wishes of another is an exchange for something, given contingent on that compliance (e.g., Kelley & Thibaut, 1978). As P. H. Wright (1978) has observed, exchange "does not do justice to the depth, the personal involvement, or the continuity of many interpersonal relationships" (p. 198). There are certain instances of social influence and certain characteristics of its effects that the exchange explanation does not cover. One instance is that in which an individual changes as a result of an encounter with another in ways that the other did not particularly press for or intend and did not make as a condition for exchange. Another is when influence follows after something is given rather than in hopes of its being given. Exchange theory also does not explain why sometimes similarity between individuals is an important condition to the development of an influential relationship between them, or why the psychological change that occurs goes beyond that necessary to guarantee an exchange, affecting genuinely held motives rather than merely overt compliance. It is possible, however, to subsume such phenomena under a theory that posits identification as the basic process of influence in certain social relationships, namely interpersonal relations.

These inadequacies of exchange theory are not due to inadequacies of the general principle of reinforcement from which exchange theory is derived. That individuals change their minds because it is gratifying for them to do so is a valid principle. This is essentially the basic assumption of human purposiveness that underlies the social psychological model presented here. There are, however, kinds of influential social relationships in which reinforcement is not intentionally contingent. In interpersonal relations, the individual gets something that the other gives unconditionally while retaining it undiminished. The rules of exchange do not apply.

French and Raven (1959) have recognized such a relationship as a basis for influence in what they call *referent power*.

> The referent power of O[ther]/P[erson] has ... its basis in the identification of P with O. By identification, we mean a feeling of oneness of P with O, or a desire for such an identity. If O is a person toward whom P is highly attracted, P will have a desire to become closely associated with O ... The basic criterion for distinguishing referent power from both coercive and reward power is the mediation of the punishment and the reward by O: to the extent that O mediates the sanctions (i.e.

has means control over P) we are dealing with coercive and reward power; but to the extent that P avoids discomfort or gains satisfaction by conformity based on identification, regardless of O's responses, we are dealing with referent power. (pp. 161–162)

An element of French and Raven's conceptualization of referent power needs some qualification. The authors make special mention in the case of the referent basis of power that the individual may be unaware of it, but the possibility of unconscious levels of responding is not explicit in their descriptions of the other bases. Nevertheless, there is in all cases the possibility of unconscious processes. People may unconsciously fear punishment from others, expect rewards from them, or depend on others' special competence, without being able to articulate these feelings. Nevertheless, French and Raven's special emphasis on unconscious aspects of identification is well-taken because none of the other bases of power reside so deeply in unconscious processes. There is more unconscious fantasy in referent power than in any of the other bases: Rewards and punishments may or may not actually be under the others' control, others may or may not be expert, and they may or may not occupy a position of legitimate authority over the individual; but the individual definitely cannot become the other, and the belief vanishes in the light of mature consciousness. When people identify with another, it means not merely that they wish to be like the other, but that they imagine unconsciously that they are the other. "If the other person benefits, the subject benefits, even in the absence of tangible or immediate personal gain. If the other person suffers, the subject suffers, even in the absence of immediate or tangible loss" (P. H. Wright, 1978, p. 199).

This is the psychoanalytic conceptualization of identification. One of its consequences is that identifiers come to believe that they not only know how the other feels and what the other wishes, but that they also share the other's motives and resources. Taking the concept of identification in its psychoanalytic meaning sharpens French and Raven's concept of referent power and illuminates its operation in interpersonal relations.

Motivation to Identify

Evidence is scattered throughout the social psychological literature that people who are engaged in an interpersonal relation tend to identify with one another. Before reviewing the evidence, I want to consider why people identify with a partner in an interpersonal relation. I suggest that the interpersonal relation offers an opportunity to satisfy an important motive.

What motive does it satisfy? The answer to this question prompts a second qualification of French and Raven's approach to referent power. French and Raven proposed that "If O is a person toward whom P is highly attracted . . . ," P grants O referent power. Whereas the partners' affection for one another is an essential component of their interpersonal relation and is always associated with true identification, the one's affection for the other is not the essential condition for identification with the other. Instead, if P is someone to whom O is highly attracted, then P identifies with O. That is, people tend to identify with those who are attracted to them.

Narcissism is an important component of identification. It is a common observation that individuals' self-esteem is enhanced by the love and admiration of others (Sternberg, 1986), which then tends to be returned (cf. Aronson & Worchel, 1966; Curry & Emerson, 1970; Kenny & Nasby, 1982; Mettee & Aronson, 1974). The esteem of another becomes self-esteem when individuals incorporate the other's affection by identification with the other. This is the initial reinforcement people gain by identification with someone who loves them.

The influence of identification is broad because, being unconscious and fantastic, it tends to be diffuse. Both the psychoanalytic theory of identification (S. Freud, 1923/1962) and Lewin's field theoretical concept of the fantasy "level of irreality" (K. Lewin, 1936) make this assumption. When individuals are motivated to interiorize the other's affection for themselves through identification, they also assume many of the other's psychological characteristics. The psychological fusion with the other is so encompassing that significant parts of the other's psyche become their own. Thus do interpersonal relations exercise their influence.

What follows first is the rationale for positing that identification is the dynamic of interpersonal social influence, arguing that interpersonal relations ideally satisfy the motive for one person to identify with another. Then I detect identification in seemingly unrelated social psychological experiments on social influence, including research on memory, conformity, and helping. Next, the concept of identification brings the social psychological model's perspective to the socialization of children and psychotherapy. Finally, I discuss the challenges to the idea of identification presented by the phenomena of identification with the aggressor and dominance in interpersonal relations.

Effects of Identification

The operation of identification has been detected in many situations that seem to have nothing in common except that the people are partners to an interpersonal relation. The effects on the people involved are various, but identification is a plausible explanation for all of them.

Recall "On Deck"

Malcolm Brenner's study (1977) of close relationships so nicely demonstrates the phenomenon of identification that it merits extended discussion. Brenner recruited heterosexual couples for an experiment using campus newspaper advertisements that announced a "psychology experiment on love"; another ad read simply, "a psychology experiment," and a third, "a psychology experiment—length of dating not important." Still other couples were "fillers" recruited from the corridors near the experimental room to fill in when not enough dating couples showed up. Brenner enlisted 69 dating couples to participate in a memorization task.

In a previous study, Brenner (1973) had replicated the phenomenon that under certain circumstances, memorization is hindered by an "on deck" effect. In the standard design that produces the effect, each person is given a unique list of words, which he or she recites out loud to the group in an assigned order that for further emphasis follows their seating arrangement. After each round of recitation, participants are instructed to write down as many of their own words and the others' as they can remember. The "on-deck" effect is that participants typically remember their own set of words best and remember least well the words recited by those immediately preceding or following them.

In Brenner's study of interpersonal relations, about 12 couples participated in each experimental session. Members of each pair were seated opposite one another in the circle and hence recited midway from one another in order. At the end of each round, participants were asked, as usual, to write down as many of the words as they could remember.

The patterns of remembered words not only demonstrated the "on deck" effect, they also indicated that each participant sat psychologically in two places around the table: his or her own and his or her partner's. That is, people tended to recall their own and their partner's words best, and the words of those on either side of themselves and of their partner least. This finding is plausible evidence that partners identified with one another.

Furthermore, the strength of the effect varied with the closeness of the couples' relationships. Couples recruited by the "love ad" remembered their partners' words best and this phenomenon declined successively through the other two ads and the "fillers." (However, the inhibition effect did not follow this order.) This suggests that the strength of identification varied with the interpersonality of the relationship.

It is also noteworthy that the "on deck" effect was more similar between partners whose relationship endured. Those partners who did not remember more nearly the same number of words read preceding and following the other's recitation were more likely still to be dating, and this was true to a lesser degree of partners remembering about the same number of each other's words. In other words, similarity in the strength of partners' identification determined the stability of the relationship. Unfortunately, Brenner did not report whether those couples who displayed a greater mutual identification during the experiment maintained or developed a more intimate relationship later.

Dion and Dion (1979) replicated Brenner's study and found that the women, but not the men, tended to remember more of the words read by a partner whom they liked more. This raises the questions of whether women tend to view their relationships as more interpersonal and whether they are more prone to identify.

Attribution

From studies of person perception comes the finding that under many conditions people tend to attribute their own behavior, especially negative behavior, to the exigencies of the situation they are in rather than to their own volition, and attribute the behavior of others to their personalities (e.g., E. E. Jones & Nisbett, 1972; Manson & Snyder, 1977; Nisbett & Ross, 1980; Watson, 1982). However, if one likes another and is engaged with the other in a long-term relationship—that is, has some degree of interpersonal relation with the other—then one attributes the causes of the other's behavior as one attributes the causes of one's own (Fielder, Semin, Finkenauer, & Berkel, 1995; Regan, 1978).

Equity

Findings of studies of differential concerns with equity in communal and exchange relationships (Clark, 1984; Mills & Clark, 1994) show that people working with a friend for rewards on experimental tasks do not make sure, as strangers do, that their own contributions to the work are distinguishable from the other's.

Menstrual Synchrony

Especially revealing of the more unconscious nature of identification among friends, McClintock (1971) has documented that the menstrual cycles of young women who are close friends tend to become synchronous. This was true only if the friends interacted frequently, but frequent interaction among nonfriends did not effect synchrony. Synchrony occurred even when the young women could not reliably report their friend's cycle.

Conformity

Identification in interpersonal relations may explain certain instances of dyadic influence observed in the literature on group dynamics. This assertion includes certain dyads that have been created by experimental manipulation, even though one might suppose that interpersonality cannot be induced reliably and quickly enough to satisfy the conditions of most experiments in group dynamics. It seems, however, that the degree of interpersonality that can be created under experimental conditions has observable effects for which identification is the most plausible explanation.

One of the earliest experiments on the effect of group cohesion on individual conformity provides evidence for the proposition that identification, essential to the reciprocal influence of the interpersonal relation, is conditioned, not on people's attraction for another, but rather, in the first instance, on people's belief that the other is attracted to them.

Kurt Back (1951) created what has become a standard technique for manipulating group cohesiveness through interpersonal attraction in an experimental design. Participants who meet their partners in the experiment for the first time are told that questionnaires that they had previously answered indicated whether they would get along well together. To create strong cohesiveness, participants are told:

> You remember the questions you answered in class about the people you would like to work with? Of course, we usually cannot match people the way they want, but for you, we have found almost exactly the person you described. As a matter of fact, the matching was as close as we had expected to happen once or twice in the study, if at all. You'll like him a lot. What's even more, he described a person very much like you. It's quite a lucky coincidence to find two people who are so congenial, and you should get along extremely well. (p. 12)

Note that participants are not told merely that they will like their partners, they are also informed that they are just the kind of person the other wants to work with. This feature is significantly absent in the instructions to create weak cohesiveness:

> You remember the questions you answered when you signed up in class? We tried to find a partner with whom you could work best. Of course, we couldn't find anybody who would fit the description exactly, but we found a fellow who corresponds to the main points, and you will probably like him. You should get along all right. (p. 12)

Here participants are led to believe that they will "probably like" the other, but they are given no indication about the other's feeling toward themselves. There are also instructions designed to create negative feelings:

> I am sorry, but the idea of putting people together who are congenial didn't work. Especially in your case we had some trouble because of scheduling. So the fellow you are going to work with may irritate you a little, but I hope it will work out all right. The trouble is that the whole thing is quite frustrating and the conversation somewhat strained, so we would have preferred to have you with a person you liked. But, anyway, do the best you can. (p. 13)

Kurt Back then set the stage for the pairs of participants to try to influence one another. Each participant was shown a set of three photographs and asked to write a story about the incident depicted. Then participants were instructed to discuss their stories with their partners with the aim of improving their stories in a second draft. Partners were led to believe that they had looked at identical sets of photographs, but their photographs were significantly different in some details. The major measure of partners' influence over one another was the degree to which their second story differed from their first in the direction of their partner's story. The researcher also observed the partners' story conference and recorded influence attempts and their effects.

The introductory comments about partners' compatibility did not seem to generate differences among the experimental groups in the degree to which participants liked one another. Whereas Back's article does not include an explicit test, the participants' ratings indicate that, on the average, those receiving high, low, and negatively cohesive inductions felt the same about their partners. Therefore, the greater amount of influence demonstrably effected by anticipating greater compatibility was not the result of individuals deferring to partners whom they liked more.

The greater influence seems based rather on participants' belief, induced by the introduction, that their partners liked them. Unfortunately, Back did not measure this variable. However, the data suggest that participants in the high cohesive groups were more confident of their partners' positive regard; they apparently felt freer to argue seriously with them about the events depicted in the photographs rather than carrying on a polite discussion. In other words, the norms regulating conversation with strangers seemed more readily abandoned when participants were led to believe that the other liked them. Furthermore, the participants who were influenced the most liked their partners less than their partners liked them.

An interpretation of Back's findings in terms of interpersonal relations seems plausible: Participants who were led to believe most strongly that their partners liked them tended to identify most strongly with their partners and therefore to adopt their stories as their own. It would be worthwhile to pick up this line of research now, after some years of neglect, to discover whether identification is actually involved in the influence process. This would call for measures of partners' perceptions of the others' feelings about them and of changes in interpersonal attraction over the course of the experiment. Direct measures of identification should also be introduced. (One might use the "on deck" effect.) Then one could test hypotheses about the effects of the various components of actual and perceived interpersonal attraction on the influence process.

The interpersonal relations that are created by experimental instructions seem pallid in comparison to the ideal type. The emotions invested and the freedom permitted in a friendship are, of course, much greater than those between strangers who are put at ease with one another before they participate together in a psychological experiment. It is some testimony to the potency of interpersonal relations that even in small measure they have significant influence, at least over the sorts of feelings and behaviors involved in such experiments. If one wants to observe the effects of deeper interpersonal relations, one usually must look elsewhere than in the experimental literature; for such commitments are not ordinarily amenable to experimental manipulation, for practical and ethical reasons. However, these phenomena have been observed scientifically and sometimes under conditions that approach the rigorous controls of experiments. One way to do this is to import established interpersonal relations, as Brenner (1973), Clark (1984), and Latané and Rodin (1969) have done.

Especially intriguing is that Stanley Milgram (1974) also imported friendship into his famous study of obedience to authority, but he never reported this investigation or its findings. Responses to being ordered to deliver powerful electrical shocks to a friend are strikingly different from those when the other is a stranger (see chapter 12).

Helping

Latané and Rodin (1969) were following a line of research that had been prompted by accounts of people in urban areas neglecting to aid others in some sort of distress. The most famous of these incidents was the murder of Kitty Genovese in Brooklyn, New York, while 38 people watched from their apartment windows and did not even call the police. A series of laboratory studies (Latané & Darley, 1970) had demonstrated that more individuals offered help more quickly when they were alone with the apparent victim of an accident in the laboratory than when they witnessed the emergency along with others.

Several explanations for this difference seem plausible. One is that individuals depend on social reality to determine whether an event is an "emergency" that demands action. Emergencies are often ambiguous, and if other bystanders ignore the event—as did Latané and Darley's confederates in some of their experimental conditions—then fewer individuals regard the situation as requiring their intervention. Another plausible explanation is couched in terms of responsibility: The more witnesses there are to an emergency, the less obligation any one of them feels to make the effort or take the risks of intervening. If nonintervention proves deleterious to the victim, then the blame is shared among the several witnesses.

This last hypothesis led Latané and Rodin to speculate that bystanders would act differently in the presence of friends than in the presence of strangers. Perhaps a person does not risk so much being embarrassed by overreacting before friends; perhaps responsibility diffuses less among friends than among strangers. So Latané and Rodin invited male students at Columbia University to participate in a "market research study" on preferences for puzzles and games. They imported interpersonal relations by instructing their recruits to "bring a friend."

I must pause here to consider this manipulation of the experimental condition. In the terms of the model, Latané and Rodin, realizing that interpersonal relations are not created easily, relied on the prior natural development of friendships to generate the condition they wanted to study. How surely were interpersonal relations imported? It is reasonable to suppose that friendship bonds varied among the participants: Some may have indeed been "best friends" or "close friends," men who liked each other a great deal and laid few if any norms on one another's behavior; others simply may have called on acquaintances to accompany them in what seemed like an interesting study and to pick up a couple of bucks. (Latané and Darley, 1970, reported that in a similar experiment, one "friend" was "captured . . . on the way to the experiment"; p. 107.) Therefore, it is hard to tell to what degree the friendship condition in Latané and Rodin's study constituted an interpersonal social environment, as that is defined here, compared with the stranger condition.

The "emergency," a contrivance of an audiotaped episode played in the next room, occurred while the participants were filling out the "market research" questionnaire. A random selection of the participants witnessed the emergency while their friends also filled out the questionnaire in the same room. Under the stranger condition, men were separated at random from their friends and witnessed the "emergency" in the company of someone else's friend, a stranger to themselves. Other participants in the experiment were the sole bystanders to the "emergency," and still others were in the company of a passive confederate of the researcher.

Latané and Rodin found that about 70% of the participants in the presence of their friends went to the aid of a female research assistant who seemed to be crying out in pain; in the presence of a stranger, 40% offered assistance; when in the presence of a passive confederate, 14% offered assistance; and when alone, 70%. Clearly more men in the more interpersonal environment of a friend than in the more social organizational environment of a stranger went to the aid of the apparent victim. Their proportion equaled the high proportion who witnessed the accident alone. Latané and Rodin reasoned, however, that the valid comparison with the "alone" condition should consider the likelihood of any one of two solitary people offering aid. They calculated that probability to be 91%. Following Latané and Rodin's reasoning that the appropriate comparison is with this hypothetical proportion, then somewhat fewer men offered help when a friend was present. Is that because not all of these men were with friends, in the interpersonal sense of that relationship, but were with strangers, actually in role relationships with the fellows they brought with them? If so, then some of these pairs actually should have been classified in the stranger condition, under which only 40% offered help; and hence, the proportion offering help under the friend condition would be between the proportion of the alone and stranger conditions, as found.

Latané and Rodin's results demonstrate the difference that the social environment makes, particularly the difference between interpersonal and social organizational environments. These concepts provide a useful framework for discussing their findings. First, the four experimental conditions may be located on a bipolar dimension representing degrees of social organizational or interpersonal environments; specifically, as normative to some degree and in some prescriptive direction. Second, the concepts prompt reconsideration, not only to the nature of the friend condition, but to the alone condition as well. Referring to those men sitting by themselves in an experimental setting as "alone" is not precise and obscures the nature of the prevailing social environment. The supposedly injured research assistant is in the adjacent room; still others, like the friends who accompanied the participants, are in the person's immediate vicinity, in both space and time, potentially about to find out what happened. Moreover, the men brought with them interiorized norms about behavior in emergencies, in psychological experiments, in university activities, and so on. The point is that the alone condition is very much a social environment, populated by present and imaginary others, one of them perhaps a friend, others bearing norms.

Latané and Darley (1970) discounted the influence of norms in bystander behavior for reasons compatible with the model. First, they pointed out that norms can be contradictory and vague, which the model recognizes as dimensions of roles that affect their influence. Second, they stress that an individual chooses among "various courses of action available to him as *he sees them*" (p. 28), which, so far as norms are involved at all, implies what the model treats as the "personal role definition" at the psychological level of analysis. Elsewhere, in introducing their discussion of this study of "a lady in distress," Latané and Darley suggested that "Friends should be less likely to feel *embarrassed* about acting in front of each other . . ." (p. 56; emphasis added), a hypothesis that could be derived from a normative premise.

One of the crucial differences among the various conditions may be the degree to which norms are operating, which raises consideration of the strength of the prescriptions regarding giving aid to victims. The condition of the presence of a friend is the least normative environment, depending on the depth of the friendship. It is not so easy to identify the most normative environment, but it is plausible that the presence of another student, one who is in the same role as oneself and is also a direct observer of one's behavior, presents the clearest norms, if not the most powerful. The most powerful norms, the ones backed by the greatest potential sanctions, are plausibly implied by the presence of the research assistant, representing the university institution.

Considering the Latané and Rodin experiment in these terms considerably complicates the interpretation of the findings and suggests some features of future research that might clarify the reasons for the different behaviors in the various conditions. Is it because the most powerful norms operating in the alone condition emanated from the "injured" woman, moaning in pain? That explanation implies that there are contradictory norms about such matters among Columbia University undergraduates, because the research assistant's predicament was not so compelling in the presence of another, strange undergraduate. Had the researchers imported not only friendship to their Columbia laboratory, but also the norm legendary to New Yorkers to "mind your own business"? Was this norm implied by the passivity of the researcher's confederate when the woman's "accident" was overheard from the next room; was that such a clear normative gesture that only 2 out of 14 bystanders moved to give assistance? One explanation for the relative responsiveness to the emergency of the people in the presence of a friend is that the presence of a friend released many of them from the norms governing them as research participants, as students, and as New Yorkers, and permitted them to answer the call of the stricken woman.

Another explanation that Latané and Rodin offered for their findings is that, when there are multiple bystanders, responsibility is diffused: The moral forces impelling each to make some effort, to brave some risks, to violate some norms, are distributed and weakened. Latané and Rodin speculated that "Friends may . . . be less likely to diffuse responsibility than strangers" (p. 201), but why should that be so? If friends identify with one another, then what happens to the one also happens psychologically to the other. In interpreting similar findings about people responding to a supposedly epileptic seizure, Latané and Darley (1970) wrote, "Instead of a situation where there is a 'me' and a stranger, there is simply 'we,' and 'we' may have 100 percent of the responsibility" (p. 107). F. E. Millar and Rogers (1975) suggested that *transferability* is an important characteristic of intimacy: The more that "ego's alter's ego is equivalent to ego's ego for both participants" (p. 94), the more intimate the relationship. There can be no laying off of responsibility under such conditions. Thus, the effect of whatever norms may have impelled the participants in the experiment to go to the victim's aid could not have been weakened by diffusion between friends, and there was therefore more helping in the presence of friends.

(An aside on continuities in social psychological research: A tape-recorded simulation of an epileptic seizure for the experimental purposes of Latané and Darley was created by Richard E. Nisbett, the same Nisbett who later, with Ross, initiated the series of studies on attribution of causes of behavior cited earlier in this chapter and who subsequently imported cultural values into the laboratory in a study of "Southernism"; Nisbett & Cohen, 1996.)

Approaching Latané and Rodin's study with the tools of the social psychological model in hand opens the results of the study to a far-ranging inquiry, raising questions that might otherwise not become apparent. Considering the interpersonal–social organizational dimension raises potentially fruitful questions about the relative strengths and directions of the social prescriptions operating on the individuals. The experiment is then seen in the context of the various social environments in which it was carried out: the social relationships among students; the institutional setting of the university; the culture of the city. Specifying the nature of friendship led first to a re-examination of the experimental manipulation, and second to consideration of just why it may be that friends did not seem so prone to "let George do it." Placing the experiment in the larger context of the social psychological model provides a systematic map to follow in tracing the reasons for the individuals acting as they did.

Identification and Socialization

Identification is a central element in psychoanalytic theory about the socialization of children. Delineating the interpersonal from the social organizational environments more sharply than occurs with psychoanalytic theory sheds additional light on the process of socialization and the function that identification plays in it.

The family occupies a pivotal position in the model of the social environment. Largely an informal social organization, it stands at a potentially powerful point of leverage, combining interpersonal and social organizational properties in various and shifting degrees. Identifications encourage actions that are then sorted out for selective reinforcement by familial and extrafamilial role senders. Acting out the socially desirable qualities of the other that have become one's own then may elicit social approval, thus advancing socialization and contributing as well to the child's self-esteem.

The limits on what one can learn about interpersonal influence from research on the socialization of children inhere in the nature both of socialization and of its targets. By definition, socialization is a matter of role regulation. Its function is to inculcate motives and resources appropriate to individuals in their social organizational environment. Achieving conformity to norms is the heart of the process, and it allows only a modest degree of the unconditional acceptance that characterizes interpersonal relations.

Moreover, children are ordinarily incapable of participating in relationships that closely approximate the ideal typical interpersonal relation. Not only have they not yet achieved a sense of their own identity sufficient to relate interpersonally with another, they also do not yet apprehend that the other has a kernel of selfhood that can be accepted and appreciated. Lickona (1974) pointed out that, "With increasing powers of inference and understanding of social causation would come higher levels of empathy, sympathy, communication and ability to solve interpersonal conflicts. These factors obviously play an important role in maintaining reciprocal positive feeling in any social relationship and in restoring positive relations after negative interaction occurs" (p. 53). In a cross-sectional study, Bigelow and LaGiapa (1975) showed that empathy and understanding rarely appear in children's descriptions of their relationships with their best friends until they are on the threshold of adolescence; even then, these qualities are less frequently mentioned than the balance of personal rewards over costs and the adherence to norms of reciprocity and conventional behavior. So the social relationships of children are typically minimally interpersonal, and with liberal and loving caregivers, heavily one-sided.

Nevertheless, within these limits drawn by the aims and targets of socialization, families can be interpersonal in varying degrees. Hess and Shipman (1965) distinguished two types of family control:

> One is oriented toward control by *status* appeal or ascribed role norms. The second is oriented toward *persons*. Families differ in the degree to which they utilize each of these types of regulatory appeal. In status- (position-) oriented families, behavior tends to be regulated in terms of role expectations. There is little opportunity for the unique characteristics of the child to influence the decision-making process or the interaction between parent and child. In these families, the internal or personal states of the children are not influential as a basis for decision . . . In the family, as in other social structures, control is exercised in part through status appeals. The feature that distinguishes among families is the extent to which the status-based control maneuvers are modified by orientation toward persons. In a person-oriented appeal system, the unique characteristics of the child modify status demands and are taken into account in interactions. The decisions in this type

of family are individualized and less frequently tied to status or role ascriptions. Behavior is justified in terms of feelings, preference, and unique reaction, and subjective states. (pp. 872–873)

Person-orientation may be indicative of the informal role relationships common in families (see chapter 4), rather than of interpersonal relations. However, Hess and Shipman seemed to suggest that the relationship of caregiver to child may approach an interpersonal one as it is defined here. Inasmuch as interpersonality communicates affection and acceptance of the child, it encourages the child to identify with his or her parents. It follows that the more interpersonal the caregivers, the more the child adopts the caregivers' motives and ways of achieving them.

Differences in interpersonality among families may have important consequences. Hess and Shipman have asserted that interpersonality is a key dimension in what is often referred to as *cultural deprivation*: "The meaning of deprivation is a deprivation of meaning—a cognitive environment in which behavior is controlled by status rules rather than by attention to the individual characteristics of a specific situation. . ." (p. 885). They measured the degree of interpersonality in families' socialization practices by having mothers describe what they would do if their child had some hypothetical school-related problems.

Hess (1967) has reported a positive relationship between maternal interpersonality and Stanford–Binet IQ scores. Because Hess and Shipman found that the responses of upper middle-class mothers more often reflected an interpersonal orientation (e.g., these mothers cited personal characteristics of the child about three times more often than welfare mothers did), it is not certain that the correlation is due to a direct association between children's cognitive growth and maternal behavior; it may be due to their common association with socioeconomic status. If the correlation is direct, its causal direction also is unclear: It is plausible that higher levels of cognitive function may contribute to children's ability to take the complexities of their caregivers' personality into account and thus enhance the interpersonality of their families. Nevertheless, these data are compatible with the conclusion that a lack of interpersonality in caregiving is a form of deprivation.

Identification and Psychotherapy

Studies of the effects of counseling (Rogers, 1957; Truax & Carcuff, 1967) may also be cast as systematic observations of effects of various degrees of interpersonal relations. In a published interview with Richard I. Evans, Carl Rogers described what he believed to be the essence of the therapeutic relationship (R. Evans, 1975):

> Let me talk about the conditions that I feel are necessary to therapy . . . We've gradually built up a fairly solid theory, and backed it up with some pretty satisfactory research which shows that if these con-

ditions are not the ultimate or best statement of what fosters personal growth, they are at least an approximation of it. The existence of these three conditions is very important to the relationship. First, and most important, is therapist congruence or genuineness—his ability to be a real person with the client. Second is the therapist's ability to accept the client as a separate person without judging him or evaluating him. It is rather an unconditional acceptance—that I'm able to accept you as you are. The third condition is a real empathic understanding. That's where the term *reflection* was used. If it is simply reflection, that's no good. That's just a technique. It must be a desire to understand empathically, to really stand "in the client's shoes and to see the world from this vantage point." (p. 29)

In the terms of the model, Rogers is describing a counselor's ability to establish an interpersonal relationship with the client. The requisite *genuineness* is a stipulation that counselors not restrict themselves to a narrow professional role but should bring their identity into the interaction. *Unconditional acceptance* connotes a suspension of norms in the counselors' reactions to the other's experiences and behavior. Acceptance is not necessarily affection, however. Still, a consequence of this therapeutic strategy is that clients come to believe that their counselor likes them. Rogers did not mention the affective temperature of the therapeutic relationship as a condition of its effectiveness. However, it has been shown elsewhere that therapists who appear more genuine and empathic to independent observers of their interactions with clients also appear warmer, and that warmth is related to effectiveness (Truax & Carcuff, 1967, p. 86). In some of the Rogerian literature, *unconditional positive regard* and *nonpossessive warmth* are used synonymously with *unconditional acceptance* (Truax & Carcuff, 1967, pp. 34–38).

Truax (Truax & Carcuff, 1967) found that the more a leader of a therapeutic group demonstrated accurate empathy, genuineness, and warmth, the greater the clients' "engagement in the process of therapy, self-revelation, and self-exploration" (p. 83). This suggests that the more the therapist encouraged interpersonal relations, the more trusting clients became and thus the more they disclosed about themselves.

The Rogerian school considers a favorable self-concept as central to mental health and has therefore investigated whether the differential qualities of the therapeutic interaction are related to changes in clients' self-esteem. It has been found that clients who are engaged in more interpersonal relations show greater positive changes in the self-concepts they describe by means of Q-sorts. This change in self-esteem is just that personal satisfaction posited to derive from interpersonal relations and to encourage partners' identification with one another.

Research on the effects of counseling has focused on the therapists' capacity for and skill in creating more interpersonal relations with their clients. However, an interpersonal relation is, by definition, mutual and hence the capacities and skills of both partners determine how fully their relationships realize interpersonality. This point raises a question about counseling: How much do clients determine the quality of the therapeutic relationship? It is conceivable that clients' readiness for the intimacy of interpersonal relations draws out interpersonal behavior from the counselor; at the same time, their readiness may itself be a positive prognostic sign. Thus, counselors' interpersonal behavior may not be the only determining factor. Clients' capacity for intimacy may account at least partly for differential effects of Rogerian counseling.

Mortality

Research by Lowenthal and Haven (1968) demonstrated, in another context and by still another research method, benign, even life-sustaining effects of participating in an interpersonal environment. One of Lowenthal and Haven's concerns was the impact of potentially traumatic changes in the social environments of elderly people. Their data were gathered by interviews with 280 men and women aged 60 or older residing in San Francisco. The mental health of the respondents was rated by psychiatrists who read the interview protocols.

Many of the elderly in this study had recently been widowed, had retired from their jobs, or had undergone other changes in their social relationships. As might be expected, such events lowered their morale, as the participants reported it, and disturbed their mental health. However, some of the respondents reported that they had a confidant, a particular someone with whom they talked about themselves and their problems. Most instances seem to have constituted fairly high levels of interpersonality. Their presence in the respondents' lives made a significant difference, because they often acted as buffers against the social losses of the elderly: Whereas 73% of those who had been widowed within 7 years prior to the study and had no confidant reported themselves depressed, only 45% of those with confidants said that they were depressed; 64% of those who had retired and had no confidant felt depressed, compared with half of those who had confidants. Lowenthal and Haven concluded that "the impact of adjustment of a decrease in social interaction, or a loss of social roles, is considerably softened if the individual has a close personal relationship" (p. 29).

The affective component of the interpersonal relation was plausibly the important determinant of the different reactions of the elderly. It seems likely that the buffering effects of having a confidant resides in the warmth and support characteristic of interpersonal relations. When an elderly person has a close friend, when widowhood does not mean that he or she is altogether alone or, at best, engaged only in impersonal relationships, there remains a warm reflection of oneself in the attentions of the other. Retirement does not betoken severe withdrawal from social interactions and a loss of social status; one remains engaged and valued.

Lowenthal and Haven noted the difficulty of unraveling the direct causal from the conditioning links among their variables. They pointed out that the capacity for intimacy has been considered by Erikson and other developmental theorists as an achievement toward optimal personal adjustment and maturity. This suggests a hypothesis alternative to the benign effect of a confidant: The presence of a confidant in a person's social environment may indicate a higher degree of ego strength that also reveals itself in better coping with potential trauma; the elderly's psychological resources rather than the presence of a confidant may be the significant agent. However, many of the respondents who had but recently lost a confidant were not able to cope effectively: 70% reported that they were depressed. Apparently, the mere capacity for intimacy is often inadequate as a buffer against potential trauma; an ongoing interpersonal relation helps.

Duck (1983) has noted that the loss of interpersonal relations can be fatal: People die sooner after the death of their spouse than would be predicted by average life expectancies.

Identification With the Aggressor

The phenomenon of identification with the aggressor (Bettelheim, 1960; A. Freud, 1937) seems to contradict the proposition that identification is motivated by ego enhancement. Internalizing aggression against one's self is inherently threatening and potentially suicidal. On the other hand, identification with the aggressor may be due to the same ego-aggrandizing dynamics as positive identification. The fantasy that one is powerful imbues the person with power. The problem, of course, is that, identification being diffuse, a person also incorporates the hostility that the aggressor feels toward himself or herself.

How then do people act when they become the instrument of someone else's aggression against a friend with whom they may identify? This is the situation in which Milgram placed some of the participants in his experiments on obedience to authority (see Rochat & Modigliani, chapter 12 of this book). Some of their behavior might be interpreted as identification with the aggressor, or on the other hand, it might have been compliance with the norms governing Subjects in an experiment.

Bandura (1969) suggested that identification may be selective. He pointed out that modeling nurturant others is a less general phenomenon than a theory of identification would suppose. That is, nurturance does not lead to imitation of all of a model's performance. He cited the finding that "a prior nurturant interaction with the model enhanced children's spontaneous reproduction of the model's socially neutral behaviors, but it did not increase their willingness to perform matching responses that possessed aversive qualities" (p. 227). Perhaps these unmatched behaviors are just those that run counter to the functions of identification, those whose internalization would be inimical to positive self-regard.

At this time, I can only acknowledge that identification with the aggressor, if it occurs, challenges the hypothesis of the ego-enhancing function of identification. It is one instance of a more general theoretical problem, the existence, varieties, and consequences of what might be called a *counterpersonal relation*, one in which the affect is negative. These are relationships in which interacting individuals dislike each other intensely and very personally. I am aware of no systematic research on the problem. A program of research on the influence of interpersonal relations should test whether identification has the primary purpose of enhancing self-esteem and should address the problem of identification with the aggressor.

Dominance and Identification

This discussion of the social psychological dynamics of interpersonal relations would be incomplete without at least brief reference to two related matters. The first concerns expertise as a secondary basis of influence, and the second has to do with the effects of individuals on interpersonal relations. Both of these have already been discussed in the chapter on the structure of interpersonal relations and are recalled here to consider their contribution to understanding dynamics.

Even while partners to an interpersonal relation are not necessarily equal in their influence on one another, they may identify equally with one another. This case is an instructive one because it suggests some limits on partners' identification with one another. If identification included the belief that one had the expertise of the other, unequal influence could not occur, at least not for long. However unconscious and fantastic identification may be, it is not unaffected by reality. Knowledge, intelligence, prowess, and the other resources that constitute expertise are defined pragmatically: They work. Normally, the fantasy of identification stops short of psychosis, and people realize whether they have certain resources. In comparison, motives are not so subject to tests of reality because they are usually more ambiguous than resources. Furthermore, people can actually change their motives more readily than their skills and other resources. Therefore, motives are more subject to influence through identification than resources are. It would be interesting to research the conditions under which an interpersonal relation motivates an individual to acquire his partner's resources.

A change in the relative expertise of partners changes the hierarchical character of their interpersonal relationship. This is an example of how changes in interpersonal relations may originate in their psychological environment. In general, interpersonal relations are especially responsive to any change at the psychological level because this relationship shelters its participants from social organizational and cultural influence.

This is not to say that interpersonal relations are unaffected by other social environments. Whereas the nature of a relationship—its hierarchy, its insularity, what partners do together, and so on—depends primarily on the personalities of the partners, its possibility depends more on the social environment. Social conditions breed more or less interpersonal trust, bureaucracies require impersonality, and total institutions claim absolute primacy.

Therefore, individuals may affect not only their own interpersonal relations but the possibility of interpersonal relations in their society by altering the cultural and social organizational environments. Changing marital roles in contemporary Western society is a case in point. Technological and ideological changes affecting, among other things, work at home and for wages, conception and child rearing, and public responsibility for private welfare have made it more possible for marriages to be friendships, too.

Summary

Interpersonal relations influence individuals because partners identify with each other. The motive for identification is the enhancement of the person's self-esteem; partners thereby internalize the other's affection for themselves that characterizes the relationship. Because identification tends to be diffuse, interpersonal partners exert broad influence on one another. This influence extends to the core of the individual's personality. Personality resists change, so individuals who are similar to one another in important ways are more likely to join in an interpersonal relation. They then become even more similar. The proposition that identification in the service of ego enhancement is the process by which interpersonal relations exerts influence over individuals provides explanations for otherwise seemingly diverse phenomena. For examples, it brings together under one rubric the therapeutic benefits of friendships and certain kinds of therapeutic interventions, the effects of the presence of friends on helping behavior and memory, the influence of cohesive groups, and the effects of different styles of parenting. The idea covers phenomena that theories based on contingent reinforcement do not cover.

9

Cultural Dynamics: Persuasion

On the one hand, culture is defined here as an organization of shared beliefs; on the other hand, the psychological individual has been conceptualized as an organization of motives and resources. This chapter considers the processes by which these two systems influence one another, emphasizing the influence of culture on the individual. The social psychological questions are: How do shared belief systems maintain and change individuals' goals and determine their perceptions of their resources? How do individuals maintain and change the beliefs shared by others? In the model, *persuasion* and *invention* are identified as the processes by which such influence is exerted.

The direct influence of culture on the individual—epitomized through encounters with the mass media—occupies the first part of the following discussion. Here again I use the strategy of idealization, as though individuals might engage in pure cultural relations without the mediation of other social relationships. That strategy narrows the focus to the joint characteristics of message and target that determine the message's persuasiveness. Then the focus widens to take into account characteristics of the source of a message, including the role and interpersonal relations that the source may have with its target. The discussion widens further still to consider other conditions affecting persuasion—medium and context. This chapter closes by using this approach to persuasion to suggest the conditions under which a person might influence culture through the process of invention.

Persons in Masses

Granting that social organizational and interpersonal relations contribute to the process of acculturation, it is useful to consider the direct encounter between individuals and shared systems of beliefs. To deal with this situation, one must suppose that people encounter beliefs unencumbered by any obligation to accept or reject them and with no anticipation of entitlements if they do either. In other words, individuals encounter the culture free of any immediate role obligations or privileges. Furthermore, one must suppose that the individuals have no interpersonal relation with those who hold and assert the belief. Stipulating this to be the ideal typical cultural relation means that whatever happens between people and culture depends wholly on the joint characteristics of the individual and the belief system.

The epitome of this unalloyed encounter with culture is the situation of the person as a member of an atomized mass audience. One sits alone before one's television, watching the news, being entertained, or being urged to buy something. One has no obligations to the media; one does not even have to watch or listen. The viewer does not know the people being watched, has no strong feelings about them, and realizes that they are even more oblivious to the viewer. It is in this sense that the viewer is a member of a mass audience. The number of people in the audience is irrelevant to its mass characteristic; what is essential is that none of the parties has any other social relationship to the others.

It might be argued that even the person alone before the television is engaged at the same time in other social relationships. It is true that the ideology and technology of a culture are woven into the fabric of the social organizations and interpersonal relations of the people who share it. In a 1969 review of the literature on attitude change, McGuire concluded, "It is clear that any impact that the mass media have on opinion change is less than that produced by informal face-to-face communication of the person with his primary groups, his family, friends, coworkers, and neighbors" (p. 231).

The presence of other social relationships can easily be overlooked in situations that seem to represent pure mass communication. The person may be in relevant role relationships with other members of the audience. Mass communicators who intend to influence may deliberately enlist social relationships in their behalf, appealing to members of the audience in their various roles or capitalizing on whatever interpersonal attachments they may have or can create with their audience. In the absence of any intention on the part of communicators, recipients of messages may inject role or interpersonal relationships into the encounter. To fully understand the influence of particular instances of mass communication, one must be alert to the sometimes subtle elements of all the social relationships that are operating. The mediation of these other social relationships is discussed later.

Thus, it may be that one cannot capture much of the actuality of persuasion and cultural change in the unalloyed cultural encounter. This is quite true for less technologically developed cultures, but this kind of encounter may not be unusual in contemporary advanced industrial society. McGuire more recently (1985) observed that, "In the past quarter century the mass media, primarily television, may be replacing home and school as society's primary institutions for inculcating social values" (p. 256).

To the degree that the cultural relation predominates, then the belief system itself bears the burden of influence. Viewers watch the late evening news or a situation comedy; the communicators do not seem to be trying to influence them about anything, and almost always they are not. Still, assertions of fact and value beam from the tube and, depending on the conditions, viewers are more or less affected by them. When they are, even in the absence of any attempt on the part of the communicators to do so, individuals have been persuaded. The social psychological task is to discover the joint conditions of the person and culture under which persuasion occurs.

The Persuasion Paradigm

There is a vast literature on persuasion, much of it created directly by or under the influence of Carl Hovland and his colleagues at Yale University (Hovland, 1954; Hovland, Janis, & Kelley, 1953). I do not attempt to summarize that literature here but, rather, to integrate it with the rest of social psychology by invoking that part of the model that addresses the reciprocal influence of individuals and culture. That literature commonly distinguishes among the factors that determine persuasion in ways that can be mapped into the model: the message, the target of the persuasion, the source of the message, the medium of communication, the context in which the communication occurs, and the interactions and relationships among these elements.

The social psychological model's conceptualization of the cultural relation focuses on the boundary between the culture and the person. In the terms of the literature on persuasion, the focus is on the target and the message, which is the expression of the culture.

To say that a message expresses a culture means that it is a set of assertions about what is, what should be, or both. These assertions, if they are elements of culture, must be shared with others beyond its source and its target. The limiting case is the assertion of beliefs to which only the source subscribes. In this case, the message, by the definition of *culture*, does not express a culture but only the source's ideas. It may create a small "culture" if the target is persuaded by it. Ordinarily, the source is a messenger of culture.

A message is persuasive if it asserts effectively that people should commit themselves even more strongly or change their goals, or convinces them that certain resources are necessary to reach certain goals (Roseman, 1994). Consistent with the social psychological model's conceptualization of the person, people's beliefs are conceived to consist of the motives and the resources that they believe are useful for satisfying those motives. Similarly, M. G. Millar and Tesser (1986) recognized that attitudes may be based on "consummatory" beliefs about appropriate goals or on "instrumental" beliefs about resources, and they assert that the processes of attitude change may depend on either of these.

Petty and Cacioppo (1986) called the link between target and message the "central route" of persuasion, in contrast to the "peripheral route," which relies on other factors such as the source. Inasmuch as other social sources of influence are put aside at least temporarily for the purpose of diagnosing the contemporary cultural situation, the properties of the message itself and the interactions of those properties with the characteristics of the individual—the "central route"—must suffice for explanation of effects in the idealized cultural relationship.

The Central Route: Message and Target

Discussion of message and target in the framework of the model requires some alignment of terms. Research on persuasion has identified two critical relationships between messages and targets, familiarity and involvement. In the terms of the model, a message is familiar to the degree that people already have in their minds a structure of goals and resources relevant to the topic of the message. For example, a person may or may not be aware of inventions in male contraception. The persuasiveness of a message about the costs and benefits of their use depends on different variables depending on the idea's familiarity, that is, on whether one has existing structures that may be scanned to assess the credibility of the message and its personal implications. Involvement refers to whether the person is motivated to attend to a message and to engage in scanning extant relevant structures, if they exist; this is a matter of the valences of the goals to which the message pertains (Johnson & Eagly, 1989).

Familiarity and involvement are positively related, though not perfectly. Whereas familiarity is motivated and may itself motivate, people may be deeply involved with a belief about which they have little information or know a lot about something and could hardly care less. Whether a message is persuasive depends on both variables.

If the topic of a message is familiar, then whether the central route proves persuasive depends on how the message addresses the target person's motives or resources. Thus, the message itself matters more to people's perceptions of resources than to the nature and strength of their motives, especially if they are already highly involved (Johnson & Eagly, 1989). Assertions themselves have little power to create values unless they associate themselves successfully with established values. Consummatory beliefs develop rather from direct experience or the urging of a compelling source. Thus, whether a message changes people's goals depends mostly on the peripheral route of persuasion. Most important in this case, the peripheral route includes the source, who may have normative or interpersonal influence. Assertions themselves may, however, effectively restructure people's perception of their resources (paths for attaining goals). Taking the central route, a persuasive message may assert that a hitherto unrecognized path exists, thus identifying a new resource; it may assert that a perceived path is illusory; or it may point out that a path to one goal also leads inevitably away from another, more desirable goal and therefore should be avoided.

Messages vary in ways that affect how persuasive they are in restructuring people's beliefs in the relationships between resources and goals. These variables contribute to the credibility of the message to recipients. A message is credible when people accept it as a true assertion of what is (or, when they address goals, what should be).

Involved people who are familiar with the topic are more likely to believe the message if it is consistent with their established patterns of belief. One tends to stick to what has worked unless one is powerfully persuaded that a new idea will work better. So a strong argument for a new way of attaining a valenced goal is more persuasive to informed and involved people (Johnson & Eagly, 1989, 1990; Perloff & Brock, 1980; Petty & Cacioppo, 1986, 1990).

Complexity. The complexity of a message makes the task of assimilating it to the current belief system more difficult. The more conditional an assertion, the harder it is for recipients to relate it to their motive–resource structures. A complex message under some circumstances may define a path to goals, and under other circumstances it may challenge the efficacy of an accustomed path. Thus, a complex message is less readily accepted as credible. This obstacle to the credibility of a complex message is ameliorated, however, when recipients can consider the relationships of its assertions to their current beliefs carefully and especially if they are helped to find its consonant conditions. Presenting a complex message through the medium of durable writing rather than as ephemeral sound facilitates thoughtful scanning (Petty & Cacioppo, 1986). Somewhere in its complexity, the message is likely to seem consonant with current beliefs under some conditions and be accepted.

Need for cognition. Even so, people differ in their motivations to consider a message in the context of their extant belief systems. Some people seem to have a greater "need for cognition" than others. That is, having elaborate motive–resource structures is a highly valenced goal for them, so they value the belief structures that have developed, protect them, and seek to elaborate them even more. These people tend to engage in scanning even when a message is complex. People who are not so motivated tend instead to look for other bases for determining the credibility of a message, such as a trustworthy source (Priester & Petty, 1995). People also differ in the degree to which they can tolerate uncertainty, and more tolerant people are not so put off by complex messages. Particularly when targets are involved and familiar with the topic, a message that presents both sides of an argument tends not to deter them from scanning (Sorrentino, Bobocel, Gitta, & Olson, 1988).

Mood. The mood of targets also affects whether they actively scan their motive-resource structure to relate it to the message (Bohner, Crow, Erb, & Schwarz, 1992). When targets are in a bad mood, they tend to scan more actively, as though they are more involved with the topic. The researchers attributed this to a bad mood informing targets that something is wrong and motivating them to examine the message more closely. In the terms of the model, a bad mood casts suspicion on the compatibility of the message with the extant structure and thus calls forth efforts to reconcile them.

It appears then that messages themselves are more persuasive under certain conditions, conditions that encourage targets to attend to them and to consider how the belief fits into their extant structure of relevant beliefs. These conditions are joint characteristics of the message and of the target. In any case, messages themselves are more likely to influence beliefs about resources than beliefs about goals.

When recipients are unfamiliar with the topic of an assertion, then of course they cannot judge the credibility of the assertion by comparison with their extant beliefs. Under this condition, memory for the assertion is a major determinant of its persuasiveness (Petty & Cacioppo, 1981). That is, any characteristic of the message that establishes it among the person's beliefs adds to the message's credibility. Furthermore, in the absence of extant beliefs, other factors beside the message itself take on added weight in determining credibility. Under this condition, the peripheral route is more consequential (Zaller, 1992).

The Peripheral Route: Sources

Taking the peripheral route to consider such factors as the source of a message leads this discussion into sectors of the social environment other than the cultural. Social relationships between the source and the target also shape the target's judgment of the source's credibility and thus the credibility of the assertions that the source makes. Among the characteristics of sources of messages are their trustworthiness, intentions, and social relationships to the target. Research on persuasiveness has studied all of these.

Trustworthiness. Researchers on persuasion have frequently investigated the effects of one- versus two-sided messages. Under certain conditions, this difference in the way a belief is asserted makes a difference because of its implications for the trustworthiness of the source.

Two-sided messages on familiar topics may be more likely to persuade an undecided target than one-sided messages do (Petty & Cacioppo, 1981) because the former demonstrate the trustworthiness of the source. It should be recognized that, in this context, a two-sided message is not an even-handed presentation of the pros and cons; it argues for one side while also laying out some of the counterarguments. Sources that do this seem more credible by seeming more expert—in more complete command of the topic—and more reasonable.

One-sided messages are more persuasive if targets are unfamiliar with the topic, but their persuasiveness depends on the trustworthiness of their source. Hence, R. A. Jones and Brehm (1970) found that informing targets that there was another side to the argument that the source had not presented substantially minimized the persuasiveness of the message, suggesting that the information cast doubt on the trustworthiness of the source. One-sided messages bolster the trustworthiness of a source when their thrust runs counter to what their target might expect of someone like the source, as when a cigarette manufacturer asserts that nicotine is addictive (Perloff, 1993; Priester & Petty, 1995).

Thus, certain characteristics of the message may lead its target to believe that its source is credible. The reverse is also true: Characteristics of the source lend credibility to the message. Demonstrated expertise is one of these and apparent motivation is another. Both of these have been shown to operate in the Asch-type experiment.

In terms of the social psychological model, the Asch-type experiment on "conformity" is not, in the terms of the model, about conformity but rather about the effects of culture through the process of persuasion. The conditions of the experiment do not include communication with moral force but rather information about what is real. Reputed strangers are gathered and asked to judge which of several lines is the same length as a standard line and to announce their choices publicly. No social norm is at issue; the participants are under no role obligations to agree with one another (and most do not). If consensus is reached, it is because the one naive participant in the group is persuaded by the pseudo-"participants" who are in fact confederates of the experimenter. The confederates establish their trustworthiness in their first several choices by exhibiting normal consensus about the lengths of lines; then they apparently grow at odds with the participant about that reality, making choices that contradict the evidence of the participant's own eyes. The confederates' announced choices are their message, and the participant is in a cultural relation with it.

It has been shown that if but one confederate agrees with the lone participant, the other confederate's message is substantially less persuasive and many fewer believe it (Asch, 1955, 1956). This, however, depends on the expertise of that one confederate. If at that time the competence of the one continually honest confederate is undermined, then his agreement with the participant does not diminish the persuasiveness of the others. Allen and Levine (1971) undermined the credibility of the honest confederate by having him stumble in to the laboratory and announce that he does not see very well.

Source's intentions. The credibility and hence the persuasiveness of the confederates' message is also diminished if the confederates seem to be motivated to make mistakes. Ross, Brierbrauer, and Hoffman (1976) reasoned that if participants could attribute to the others some motive to misperceive, then the others' judgment would not be so persuasive. So the experimenters stipulated that some lines in the Asch-type experiment would earn bonus points if correctly identified, thereby encouraging biased judgments. When the participants in the experiment could attribute to the others this reason to be mistaken, they almost never were dissuaded from the evidence of their own perceptions. In this case, a perceived property of the source, their motives, made their message less credible.

Most of the research on persuasion is conducted under the condition that the source intends to persuade. As the term is used here, however, persuasion does not necessarily imply any intent to persuade. The source of a message may have intended that it persuade, but persuasion may be unintentional as well. Persuasion is a potential effect of a message, regardless of the intent of its source.

However, a good deal of culture is transmitted without any intent to convince people of what is true or proper. Viewers usually settle in front of their television sets and readers open their books just to be entertained or informed, and communicators aim only to satisfy those desires. Sometimes, people are not the active targets of persuasion, but they are nevertheless exposed to versions of reality and implications of value. The characteristics that determine the credibility of the message and the source—the consonance of the message with targets' extant beliefs, the expertise of the source, and so on—are present potentially to affect whether the unintentional assertions are believed. Thus, theories and findings on intentional persuasion are relevant to unintentional persuasion as well.

However, unintentional persuasion may create a critically different condition, one that interacts with characteristics of message and source to change their effects. When they believe, rightly or wrongly, that communicators do not intend to persuade them, people are not so motivated to respond. Under this condition, targets ordinarily do not have to express their agreement or disagreement with the messages they've received. Not needing to respond, targets are not prompted to compare their extant beliefs with the beliefs implied by the communication. Because this active integrating of incoming messages with extant beliefs is important to the process of persuasion, the tendency for it to be absent when persuasion is unintentional makes this an important qualifying condition.

It is sometimes the case that, when persuasion is unintentional, targets are nevertheless motivated to respond. For example, some viewers of a television sitcom may be especially alert to social issues raised by the program, noting a racial stereotype or value carried subtly in the plot. Thus involved, perhaps occupying a role that obligates them to respond, they may engage in a mental debate with the message and respond as if persuasion were intended. Furthermore, how motivated people are to respond to unintentional persuasion depends not only on their involvement but also on their expectations of the effectiveness of their response. Simply turning off the television is a minimal response, requiring little marshalling of arguments; writing a letter to the editor or complaining to the broadcaster requires more scanning of extant beliefs. Whether the viewer engages that much in the persuasion process depends on whether the viewer's role or other resources promise to make the response effective.

Social relationships. Acculturation and culture change are often accomplished with the mediation of the roles people play and the attachments they have to others. The interchange between culture and individuals is filtered through these other sectors of the social environment. Those individuals who have marked effects on their cultures may owe their influence in part to the roles they play as well as to the compelling character of the ideas they advance.

At this point, the discussion enters that fuzzy interpenetrating area between the cultural and the social organizational sectors of the social environment to consider another means by which messages that are not intended to persuade seem to affect people's behavior. Research has shown, for example, that exposure to violence on television makes people more prone to commit aggression (Berkowitz & Rogers, 1986; Eron, Gentry, & Schlegel, 1994). The conditions of this exposure are not ordinarily conducive to active processing of ideas: Viewers are not encouraged to respond to the mayhem but merely to enjoy watching it. If people are not engaging in the persuasion process, what explains this effect? Socialization rather than persuasion may be operating. That is, the message sent is probably not received as an assertion of a value or a fact; the violence may be taken instead as a license for action. Its implications for underlying values and the nature of reality remain unexamined. Berkowitz and Rogers (1986) suggested that the effect of exposure to violence "might be due to an increased acceptance of aggressive behavior . . . [The observers are more apt to think (at least for a short time) that aggression is proper or worthwhile" (p. 76). The appropriate explanatory concepts may be those of social learning theory, such as role models and social approval, rather than the concepts of persuasion, such as message and source.

Whether a message serves to socialize or persuade depends on several characteristics of the message and its source. If sources invoke their role relationship to targets, then the situation is social organizational and the process by which the message may influence the target is socialization. This is especially true if the role relationship grants the source some authority over the target. The message is likely to invoke the socialization rather than the persuasion process to the degree that its assertions are qualified by the target's role. Thus, in Bandura's (1973) research on the effects of children observing aggression, it proved to be important that the aggressive model was also a child rather than an adult. The subsequent behavioral effects of such role-specific messages are more likely to be seen in situations in which the target acts in the role to which the message referred. A message depends on persuasion rather than socialization for its influence to the degree that it is delivered in a cultural rather than a social organizational relation, (i.e., a relation in which the source has no role relationship to the target) and to the degree that the message asserts values and facts that transcend roles people play.

If the source's role requires a certain expertise and objectivity, then it lends credibility to the message. For example, individuals in a mass audience are not obliged to believe the pronouncements of an expert from a prestigious university. Nevertheless, I suspect that they are more likely to be persuaded by messages from this source than from most others. Orson Welles's Mercury Theater (Koch, 1970) was able to panic thousands of listeners one Halloween with their radio dramatization of H. G. Wells's "War of the Worlds" (1898/1930) partly because they created a Princeton University professor to interpret the fictional events occurring on the farm at Grovers Mills (Cantril, 1940).

Sources may encourage the inference of expertise and trustworthiness implied by their roles by the way they assert their beliefs. For example, using the "objective" passive voice and mentioning their credentials increases their appearance of credibility (Hurwitz, Miron, & Johnson, 1992).

Sources may also deliberately enlist social relationships in their behalf, appealing to members of the audience in their various roles. Thus, a belief that "every *patriot* should adopt . . . ," that "every good *parent* will take as his guide . . . ," or that "every *man* needs. . . ." invokes role obligations and privileges on behalf of the message.

Certain role relationships preclude sources' attempts at persuasion and arouse negative reactions when they do. Wright, Wadley, Danner, and Phillips (1992) had the person in the role of Experimenter tell the Subjects what choices they should make and thereby got opposite choices.

(My colleague, Carol Slater, pointed out to me one interesting and personally familiar instance in which a role relationship actually creates the conditions for a cultural encounter. This is the strictly intellectual dialogue, as may sometimes ensue between scientists or theologians. There is a critical social norm governing such discussions—that neither any personal relationship nor any role relationship that the parties may have with one another or with others should affect the discussion. It is this norm that makes the encounter a cultural one, because it prescribes that elements of the message itself are to be wholly determinative of its credibility.)

Interpersonal relations may also be important vehicles of influence in both directions. As the partners identify with one another, they sustain each other in the beliefs that they already share, and they tend to recruit each other to the beliefs that they do not yet share. This recruitment need not be deliberate and in most cases probably will not be.

Partners may defer to each other's expertise and change their minds accordingly. Here is ground covered earlier: the possibility that one party to an interpersonal relation is dominant, at least in certain matters, on account of his or her relative expertise.

Interpersonal relations imbue partners' messages with some credibility also because the relationship implies trust in the other's well-meaning. People would not knowingly try to convince friends of a false belief. They might be forgivably biased or lacking in judgment on the matter, and for these reasons, be unpersuasive. They might also perpetrate a benevolent deception, but they generally would not commit a hurtful fraud. Thus, partners' persuasiveness is a function of the credibility with which an interpersonal relationship lends their messages. When trust prevails, expertise is especially convincing.

Sources who intend to influence may capitalize on whatever personal attachments the auditors may have. An earlier discussion of interpersonal relations described a facsimile that sometimes develops between communicators and their mass audiences. For example, Lazarsfeld (1946) attributed the effectiveness of singer Kate Smith's marathon radio campaign to sell U.S. war bonds to the friendship many felt toward her and a personal desire to please her. Tannenbaum and Gaer (1965) produced evidence that members of mass audiences may identify with communicators: People who rate themselves as more similar to the protagonists in a film are more likely to experience the stress presumably felt by the protagonist.

Lazarsfeld and his colleagues (E. Katz & Lazarsfeld, 1955; Lazarsfeld, Berelson, & Gaudet, 1944) seemed to invoke both social organizational and interpersonal relationships when they proposed a two-step process by which mass media typically affect public opinion. According to the two-step hypothesis, the media attract the close attention of those opinion leaders who are for various reasons particularly interested in the issues and persuade them to a point of view. Through the roles they play in their communities and in the friendships they have, opinion leaders in turn shape the beliefs of others. In support of the two-step hypothesis, Lazarsfeld and his colleagues have presented data from community surveys of public opinion, showing that only a relatively small proportion of the population follows political campaigns very closely and is aware of the issues and where the candidates stand. Most people report that they make up their minds on such matters only after hearing directly from one of these opinion leaders. On the other hand, Cerha (1967) asserted that survey data do not in fact support the two-step hypothesis, citing the finding that direct exposure to the media is actually widely reported.

In sum, greater understanding of how the source of a message affects the acceptance of the message may be gained by placing the source in the social environment of the target. The source should be characterized in terms of its relationship to the target as well as to the message. The conditions that make persuasion more or less effective differ depending on this characterization of the source.

Medium and Context: Broadcast Messages

Recall that I have presented the image of a person alone before a television screen as the epitome of the cultural relationship. This image permits one to more nearly idealize the social situation as such. It is useful to note that a mass of people are in the same situation, simultaneously receiving the same message. This is an important feature of the context in which a message is received, a feature that mass media create. In this way, the cultural environment becomes more integrated, the body of beliefs becomes more uniform among people who exchange ideas and coordinate their actions.

In the past, ideas were conveyed through myriad channels, through competing newspapers, by traveling lecturers, and by word of mouth. Each source could slant or embellish the idea according to its own understanding and values. Today, broadcasting technology simultaneously exposes mass audiences to a limited set of sources that are virtually interchangeable. Masses of individuals, many of them alone, all witness the same events and receive the same interpretation of their meaning. A very small number of news wire services feed a similarly small number of newspapers and broadcast networks. The creators of popular entertainment present a

fairly homogeneous set of images and values as they ape the current leaders in the ratings and box offices.

Ruesch and Bateson (1951) observed:

> When participating in a cultural network, people are in many cases
> unaware of being the receivers or senders of messages. Rather, the
> message seems to be an unstated description of their way of living.
> They attribute to it no human origin, but they themselves convey the
> message to others by being in accordance with its content, which they
> may regard as "human nature." (p. 282)

When individuals turn to another to discuss the news, they might as well
be talking to themselves, because they have all been exposed to exactly
the same ideas.

Thus, when listeners to Mercury Theatre's "War of the Worlds" phoned
relatives or friends to check out the reality of an invasion by Martians, or
when they looked out their windows to see if others were behaving as if
there were indeed an invasion, they were merely listening to echoes and
looking into mirrors. They might as well have consulted themselves, for
the others had been listening to the same broadcast at the same time
(Cantril, 1940).

The mass media also have dis-integrating effects on the cultural environment that may be persuasive. The technology of modern communication exposes people to messages that contradict their beliefs, showing
them people whose ways of living testify to quite different beliefs from
theirs. The sounds and images of alien ways of life, implying disparate
views of reality and different values, are now broadcast to mass audiences.
People look down distant streets and peer into distant homes. For many,
the previously unimagined now becomes real. When people become aware
that others have attained goals that they themselves believed unattainable, some may attend more searchingly to their own resources, their expectations may rise, and they may be spurred to strive. When others, who
seem to be otherwise quite respectable and credible sources, appear to be
living by values very different from their own, some people may begin to
question their own and alter their valences. The cameras and microphones
of modern communication gather up far-flung sights and sounds and lay
them before a multitude of individuals; insofar as they imply ideas not
already believed by those individuals, these sights and sounds may initiate
processes of persuasion.

In general, however, mass media seem to be unpersuasive. Their effects are ordinarily small (McGuire, 1985). If it is true that scanning enhances the persuasiveness of messages, then this may be a reason that
broadcast messages are not ordinarily very persuasive. That the mass media broadcast their messages may not encourage targets to scan their own
belief systems and find associations between new messages and their extant motives and resources. Their ineffectiveness may be because broadcasting does not motivate targets to respond.

Inherent in broadcasting is that the source usually does not know if a specific target has been reached or, if reached, whether or how the target responds. This is true whether the messages are intended to persuade, like television commercials, or are only to entertain. Under this condition, targets are not usually prompted to respond, and if prompted to respond, do not need to articulate arguments in support of their position. They can easily ignore the message unless they feel otherwise involved, and they can accept or reject the message without having to support their beliefs. The more the broadcast message pertains to targets' goals, the more they compare it with their current beliefs. If the message is consonant with their beliefs, it is accepted and strengthens their beliefs even more. If the message opposes their interests—and they do not need to respond at all to it—targets comfortably ignore it.

This feature of broadcasting is not limited to the mass media. It has been manipulated in laboratory experiments on "overheard" conversations (Brock & Becker, 1965; Walster & Festinger, 1962). When a person (it is not appropriate under these conditions to refer to the person as a "target") merely overhears a message, he or she need not respond.

Walster and Festinger (1962) arranged for individuals to hear someone present information under one of two conditions: the source either knew or did not know that specific targets were listening. (That is, this is what targets were led to believe. In fact, the source was a confederate of the experimenter and knew the research design.) Findings demonstrated that targets were more persuaded by broadcast messages when they had a motivated interest in an acceptable message. Smokers were more convinced than nonsmokers that smoking does not cause cancer when they believed that that assertion had been made by someone who did not know they were listening; the assertion was no more persuasive to smokers than nonsmokers when the targets believed their presence was known. Similarly, those college women who thought they had overheard a conversation favorable to permitting women to live off-campus were themselves more favorable to the idea a week later than women who heard the same conversation from people who knew they were listening; however, overhearing a conversation about compulsory military training for the men on the campus, an issue in which the women were presumably less interested, was no more persuasive than listening with the knowledge of the conversants. Whether or not the conversation was overheard did not make a difference in students' opinions about tripling their tuition, a message presumably contrary to their interests.

Broadcast media effects are ordinarily small or nonexistent. Research on overheard messages, which are in an important respect essentially the same as being broadcast, supports the findings on media effects. Broadcast messages tend to confirm interested people's beliefs if they have any effect at all.

Invention

Rare individuals change cultures substantially. In our time, I believe only four giants are generally granted this distinction: Darwin, Marx, Einstein, and Freud. They made assertions of fact that had profound implications for values, and they have been enormously persuasive. More common, but still infrequent, are individuals who have caused only small changes in culture, "small" in the sense that only a few beliefs in a culture are changed.

The process by which individuals change cultures is here called *invention*. Inventions may be ideological as well as technological; that is, they may consist of new values or of new facts. Although inventions may give rise to material things such as machinery or chemicals or to innovative processing of materials, these materials are not themselves the stuff of culture, but reflect it. In the model, *invention* refers to beliefs, which are the stuff of culture.

This chapter closes with a brief discussion of the conditions under which individuals might influence culture through the process of invention. Consistent with the social psychological model's conceptualization of culture and the individual, this discussion focuses on the functions of messages, which express beliefs, and individuals as sources.

Cultures are collective ways that people solve common problems. If a person offers a better way for people to achieve their goals, and his or her message is widely recognized as a good idea, then the invention is likely to be incorporated into the culture. If a person occupies an authoritative social relationship with a mass of others, his or her values may change.

Messages with potential for radical culture change are those that not only increase the resources of a culture but also directly or indirectly challenge the regnant values in the belief system. For example, the invention of more efficient means for contraception broke the link between copulation and reproduction. That people can consequently copulate with little risk of reproduction raises the question of whether people should, touching on fundamental values of some cultures. Galileo's assertions about the shape of the solar system and Darwin's about the nature of biological evolution are well-known examples of technology challenging ideology at its base. Such assertions of fact reverberate throughout the belief system. The ideological problems they raise are weighed along with the problems they solve in determining their acceptance.

An ideological invention, an assertion of a new value, is neither intrinsically more or less problematic than a technological one. However much it may challenge established values, it may solve more problems than it creates. For example, M. K. Gandhi's advocacy of nonviolence in India's struggle for independence from Britain was not merely strategic. Elevating the value of nonviolence resolved ideological and practical problems of Indian culture, making the struggle acceptable to a wider set of Indians as well as more likely to succeed.

Thus, a person's influence on a culture depends on the utility of his or her message. Its utility is not only a matter of its truth, although that is one criterion for the utility of a fact. Conversely, a criterion for the truth of a message is its utility, and this is particularly true of assertions of value.

In the terms of the process of persuasion, potential culture-changers are sources. As sources, they may lend credibility to their assertions. This depends on the reputation of the source as trustworthy and expert, and the role that the source plays may contribute to the source's reputation. It might seem then that the same conditions for the persuasiveness of sources hold for the process of invention. This is helpful, but it does not take sufficiently into account the differences between cultures and individuals as targets of change. Effective changers of cultures must not only persuade individuals, they must change their collective "mind," the beliefs that they knowingly share.

If the culture involved is shared, in the limiting case, by only the source and the target, then the situation is identical to the situation of persuasion. This analysis suggests that theory and research on persuasion is relevant to the process of invention and the effect of individuals on culture. The limiting case falls far short, however, of one's interest in culture change. When the targets of persuasion are multiple, then another condition must be considered, namely, that the targets may influence one another in the process. It follows from the definition of *culture* that culture change is more than persuading isolated individuals; they must know that they share their convictions. This implies that they communicate directly or indirectly, and therein lies their potential to influence one another. The persuasive characteristics of the source of an invention must be considered under this condition.

Thus, people's reputation for trustworthiness and expertise, important source characteristics for individual targets of a persuasive message, enhances the influence of inventors to the degree that their reputation is widely known. Although the reputation of a source can be built on a useful invention, its previous widespread establishment may add considerably to the acceptance of a new idea. For examples, Sigmund Freud, M. K. Gandhi, and Martin Luther were already respected for their contributions to medicine, advocacy, and theology, respectively, before they asserted revolutionary ideas. The solid reputation of a source may not be known by as wide an audience as his or her ideas ultimately affect; it may be limited to people in the source's field. It can, however, marshall the support of those people, who in turn can vouch for the source to the wider audience if the source's message proves controversial.

Besides a personal reputation, the social role of an inventor may affect his or her reputation, just as the role of the source does in the process of persuasion. In the case of culture change, the role enhances the source's reputation to the degree that his or her credentials are widely respected. At present, the reputations of previously respected roles seem to be at their nadir: Lawyers, physicians, and clergy have become widely suspect. It might be argued that this decline creates conditions ripe for culture change because it signals disaffection from traditional beliefs. On the other hand, the decline might also deter culture change because potential inventors cannot so well rely on their roles to establish their credentials.

The capacity of individuals to change their culture may also depend on their interpersonal relations. Challenging the accepted dogma can be a threatening enterprise, and those who attempt it can use all the social support they can get. Support may be especially crucial when the new ideas are radically different from the conventional ideology. An innovative technology that facilitates the achievement of cultural values would not meet opposition, but ideas that contradict the central values of a culture will surely be resisted, and their advocates may be attacked. It is hard to imagine, for example, that Sigmund Freud could have advanced his theories publicly and persistently without his circle of friends and colleagues not only to assist him in the work of elaborating, testing, and promulgating psychoanalysis, but also to give him personal support. The social support inherent in interpersonal relations is a crucial element in the discipleship that gathers around effective shapers of culture.

Summary

This discussion of the dynamics of social influence between the person and culture derives mainly from the social psychological model's conceptualizations of each of its components (see chapters 3 and 6). Analyzing the cultural encounter has been facilitated by a certain parallel between them—the psychological individual as an organization of motives and resources and the culture as an organization of ideological and technological beliefs. Both conceptions describe systems of goals and means to reach them. This parallelism has suggested ways to translate the conditions at the one level of analysis into the conditions at the other, which is the social psychological strategy for trying to explain how individuals and culture affect one another.

Delineation of the idealized cultural relation sets the terms of its dynamics, here called the processes of persuasion and invention. These dynamics describe the interchange in terms of messages as the embodiment of beliefs, psychological and cultural, and in terms of persons, individually and collectively, as targets or sources of messages. This framework is then a tool with which one can sort through social psychological theory and findings to locate and organize those that meet the conditions of the cultural relation. This approach brings to bear on the problems of acculturation and culture change not only the obvious material on persuasion and mass communication but also some less obviously relevant theory and findings about conformity in small groups, the influence of overheard conversations, and social support in interpersonal relations.

Explanation of acculturation as a joint function of messages and their targets leans heavily on whether this encounter prompts targets to compare their extant beliefs with those expressed in the messages, and how carefully, with what intentions, and with what background targets make this comparison. The individuals' contribution to the encounter is their life space, particularly the extant organization of their motives and resources. The culture's contributions are the symbols with which messages are expressed and the ideas that are asserted. The consequences of persuasion are determined by how variations in life spaces and messages affect individuals' attempts to integrate the two.

Explanation of the effects of a person on culture through the process of invention point to the problem-solving utility of the person's idea for the collective carriers of the culture. The acceptance of the inventor's assertions about values or means to attain them depends on whether on balance they solve or create problems. The acceptability of a cultural invention also depends on the inventor as a source, particularly in the case of large-scale culture change, on his or her credibility to a wide collectivity of culture bearers.

Explanations of the process of persuasion and invention and their consequences are necessarily probabilistic. Because these processes involve entities defined in terms of different levels of analysis, the principles governing them cannot be derived from a single theoretical base and thereby claim universality. These explanations are assertions about the relative likelihood that characteristics of persons and cultures jointly affect one another, and they are complete explanations to the degree that they take into account the effective characteristics and their interaction.

The approach taken here reveals that experimental research on persuasion is germane to the social psychology of the effects of culture on the individual. The relevance of experiments on persuasion resides in the source as a bearer of culture. That is, the source is the proximal condition of the cultural environment. It follows that experiments with culture are feasible, although culture as commonly conceived is not considered amenable to controlled experimentation. The social psychological model suggests that experiments can be conducted on the processes of persuasion and invention in which a culture itself is the proximal condition or the immediate target.

This possibility is created by the conceptualization of culture as something that might be carried by a small group. The Asch-type experiment was cited as an example of an experiment on persuasion; and the consensus of the group about reality—that is, the group's culture—is critical to its experimental design rather than the credibility of an individual source. The persuasiveness of the message asserting which is the "correct line," resides in its collective source. An experimental design in which expressed group consensus is systematically varied can be exploited to investigate the process of persuasion by a culture. Researchers can vary characteristics of the collective source such as the degree of consensus and the goals of the group as they affect the group's credibility. They can also vary the substance of the group's message in relation to the beliefs that recipients already hold and the medium by which the message reaches the target. Experiments can also investigate the process of invention by systematically varying the characteristics of sources and their message and observing effects on a group's culture.

Experimentation on the culture of small groups limits inquiry to a narrow range of the size of the collectivity that bears the culture. Generalization to cultures larger in this sense must be tentative. It is not obvious, however, that important conditions relating to the size of the collective are beyond manipulation in small groups. The feasibility of this should be tested, and experimental findings should be compared with findings about cultural relations obtained by other research methods.

Small groups provide opportunities for an experimental social psychology as social psychology is defined in this model. They can actualize not only culture but any of the social environments, and they can engage in any of the dynamic processes posited by the model. The next chapter discusses small groups as an enormously useful tool for an experimental social psychology that is truly social as well as experimental.

Part IV

Applications

Introduction

The three chapters in this section illustrate how the social psychological model illuminates theory and findings in specific areas of research. Chapter 10 deals with group dynamics, at this writing an old and faltering field. Its main points are that groups have actually continued to be studied by social psychologists, but in disguise, and that the abiding contribution of the study of small groups is methodological, enabling an experimental social psychology, indeed experimentation in social sciences generally.

Chapter 11, "Sex and Gender in Social Psychology," applies the model to a relatively new and vital line of inquiry. The chapter was written by Elizabeth Douvan, who has been my partner in this conceptual enterprise from its earliest days. She uses the model to sharpen our understanding of the bases of contemporary sex role differentiation. To do this, she takes the social organizational rather than the psychological level of analysis as her focus, incidentally demonstrating how the model might be used by social sciences other than social psychology.

François Rochat and Andre Modigliani of the University of Michigan contribute chapter 12, wherein they use the model to organize and interpret the theory, methods, and findings of a classic series of experiments in social psychology, Stanley Milgram's (1974) studies of obedience. Rochat and Modigliani present some hitherto unpublished data from these studies, data collected in the interpersonal environment of friends.

10

Group Dynamics

Group dynamics, or the study of small groups, flourished, then seemed to decline in the 50 years since social scientists began to give it systematic attention. In 1927, Thrasher, a sociologist of the Chicago school, published rich descriptions of boys' groups. Twelve years later, K. Lewin, Lippitt, and White (1939) initiated experimental research on groups with their study of the effects of styles of adult leadership on recreational boys' groups. Several compendia, like the three editions of Cartwright and Zanders's *Group Dynamics* (1953, 1960, 1968) and others (Hare, Borgatta, & Bales, 1955; McGrath & Altman, 1966; Shaw, 1971), document the high interest that groups attracted among social psychologists over the next 25 years. By 1974, however, Steiner was asking, "Whatever happened to the group in social psychology?" Interest had faded. In the first edition of *Handbook of Social Psychology* (Lindzey, 1954), one section of its volume on "special fields" was titled "Group Psychology and the Study of Interaction"; there was no such section in the third edition (Lindzey & Aronson, 1985). Research on small groups continues to be reviewed in contemporary texts in social psychology, but groups are no longer at or even near the center of the attention of social psychology.

In a very important sense, there only appears to be a decline in social psychology's interest. In fact, social psychology has had to continue to attend to groups insofar as it remains social. The nature of these groups has changed: Instead of being composed of boys or students in introductory psychology classes or workers in a shop, groups now more often consist of social psychologists and their laboratory participants. Groups appear regularly in social psychological research in this disguise.

In the earlier discussion of Thibaut and Kelley's work on interpersonal relations (see chapter 2), I argued that the experimenters were very much a part of the social organization that also included two identified participants. The experimenters were there, I pointed out, prescribing the social norms by which the other two participants were supposed to act. Similarly, I maintained that the participants described as being "alone" in Latané and Rodin's experiment on bystander intervention (see chapter 8) were actually in the company of a "lady in distress," the experimenters' collaborator, who might also be supposed to have brought social norms to bear in the situation. When researchers on persuasion send messages to the individuals, they join them in a group.

Thus, it may be said that groups remain ubiquitous in social psychology; indeed, they are methodologically invaluable to social psychology. The model of social psychology that I present here reveals how and why this is so, even though no level of analysis has been designated as "group." Almost from the first moment of group dynamics research, there was drawn directly from the philosophy of science of its founder, Kurt Lewin, a powerful experimental method that is now so ubiquitous that it is taken for granted. The model's conceptualization of "group" points to uses of the method that have hardly been realized.

This discussion of groups should go no further without a definition that distinguishes groups as a particular sort of collectivity. Then I distinguish among groups with the proposition that even groups as small as dyads are either one or another or some combination of the three social environments posited in the model. That groups may be small and still represent all of the social environment leads into a discussion of the significance of the small group method in experimental social psychology. This point is illustrated with small group experiments on close relationships, social organization, and culture. The chapter closes with some cautions about the limitations of the small group method but nevertheless with a call to exploit its potential even more, not only for social psychology but for the social sciences generally.

Collectivities and Groups

In its simplest definition, a group is two or more of anything. However, this definition does not facilitate finding answers to the questions that prompt social scientists to investigate groups. Two general questions require a concept like "group": (a) What are the conditions for the regular patterns of behavior that collectivities of people seem to exhibit, regardless of who composes them? and (b) What are the conditions for the kinds and degrees of influence that collectivities have on individuals and individuals on them?

In noting that regularities in behavior across groups appear despite differences in their membership, the first question suggests that the answer to it cannot be stated in terms of the behavior of the individuals. There are certain behaviors that only two or more people can perform—inter-individual behaviors such as establishing norms, agreeing on facts, sharing resources, cooperating on tasks, and mutual love. These behaviors may change as a consequence of changes in inter-individual conditions. An example is that altering norms about who may communicate directly with whom may change group productivity, although individuals' behavior does not change at all (Bavelas, 1950; Leavitt, 1951). The group is the entity that behaves in these ways, exhibiting the property that Shaw calls *entitivity*.

The second question also assumes that two or more individuals may constitute an emergent entity. It implies that one person's influence over another, or the influence of several people over someone, or the influence of one person over several others is at least sometimes determined by characteristics of the collectivity, such as their consensus, rather than by the characteristics of the individuals taken one at a time.

The answers to these questions require a distinction between two or more individuals considered together, which I call a *collectivity*, and a collectivity that has the character of an entity, which (when it is small) I call a *group*.

In the first two editions of *Group Dynamics*, Cartwright and Zander (1953, 1960) did not attempt to define *group*. They proposed only that group behavior and influence varied according to properties such as group size, interdependence, cohesion, and so on. In the third edition, however, Cartwright and Zander's (1968) thinking about groups had evolved to the point where they advanced the criterion of interdependence as definitive: "A group is a collection of individuals who have relations to one another that make them interdependent to some significant degree" (p. 46). In his text, Shaw (1971) concurred: "In our view, definitions in terms of interdependency or interaction more directly delineate the basic elements of the concept 'group'" (p. 9). Interdependence is the useful criterion by which to distinguish groups from collectivities. It is the essential property of collectivities from which lawful patterns of collective behavior and collective influence may be derived.

Interdependence can be defined in terms of the goals of the individuals who compose the social group. When the attainment of one person's goals depends on whether others attain their goals, the people are interdependent, they constitute a social group. This definition is better framed relatively: The more one person's goal-attainment depends on others', the more they compose a social group. Furthermore, interdependence may be, in Morton Deutsch's (1973) terms, promotive or contrient; for some to attain their goals, others must also; or conversely, for some to attain their goals, others must not. There are degrees and mixtures of promotive and contrient interdependence. Thus, left-handed people constitute a collectivity in the sense that there is more than one of them, and they constitute a category by virtue of their common characteristic; but they do not necessarily constitute a group because they may not depend on one another to attain any of their goals. Left-handed people would become a group if they were to band together to make life easier for left-handed people in a right-handed world. Two left-handed people could become a contrient group if they compete for the only left-handed desk chair in a classroom or a promotively interdependent group if they organize to petition for more left-handed chairs.

Groups as Social Environments

It seems worthwhile to distinguish groups from other collectivities according to the criterion of goal interdependence—but this is not sufficient. Interdependence itself suffices to generate some patterns of group behavior and some influence potential between the group and its individual members, but the nature of group behavior and influence cannot be adequately specified without further delineation of the nature of the interdependence that defines the group. The kind of interdependence can be specified by invoking the three kinds of social relationship that constitute the social environment. That is, groups may be interpersonal relations, social organizations, or culture, or some mixture of these.

Others have characterized groups along roughly these same lines. Jennings (1947), for example, has distinguished between *psyche-groups* and *socio-groups*, the former "based on a *private criterion* which is totally *personal* in nature," the latter, "on a criterion which is collective in nature" such as "working in a common work unit . . . a *largely impersonalized* base" (p. 78). Kurth (1970) distinguished between *friendship* and *friendly relations*, the former more intimate and particularistic than the latter. Hagstrom and Selvin (1965) factored out from questionnaire data two dimensions to the cohesiveness of small groups, interpersonal attraction and task interdependence. Siegel and Siegel (1957) distinguished between membership groups, which have a component of interpersonal interaction, and reference groups, whose members may not interact at all. All of these distinctions, and others, touch one way or another on the tripartite division of the social environment into interpersonal relations, social organization, and culture.

When the relevant goals of the members flow from their mutual attraction, the group is of course an interpersonal relation. The group's existence, manifested in members' expressions of their unity and in their frequent interaction, is the primary goal. What the members say to one another and what they do together are important only to the degree that they enhance their interpersonal relation. When on the other hand the group's activities are paramount, when the accomplishment of its task is the reason for its existence, then the group is a social organization, manifested by division of labor and, most critically by definition, by a set of rules that regulate the behavior of the members. Alternatively, groups may be cultures, or more precisely, repositories of culture. There are groups whose members depend on one another for their definitions of reality. When direct experience is not adequate for them to achieve sufficient certainty about an important element of the world they live in, individuals may look to one another for advice and consensus. When individuals for some personal reason require confirmation of a doubtful belief, they may unite with others to establish the necessary reality (Cohen, 1955).

Identifying a collectivity whose members are interdependent in one or more of those three ways establishes a critical premise from which to derive the behavior of the group and the process of reciprocal influence between the group and its members. This goes far beyond recognizing merely that the particular collectivity is in general a group.

The Small Group Method

The field of group dynamics is also known as the study of *small* groups. Does the size of the collectivity make a qualitative difference in its behavior and in its influence process?

Is being small a significant condition? Simmel (1950b) reasoned that there is a qualitative difference between collectivities of two and of three or more, primarily because the latter permits the formation of coalitions. It seems that whether coalitions may form and the effects of their formation depend not only on the size of the collectivity but also on the nature of its social relationship. Coalitions do not form in interpersonal relations, not because they are typically dyadic, but because the nature of interpersonal relations does not admit of coalitions of some against others. In groups that are depositories of culture, the effect of the numbers in the group as a source seems to depend on conditions of the message and the target. Under some conditions, one ally is sufficient to sustain a dissenter's belief in an obvious fact, no matter how large the opposition (Allen & Levine, 1968); under other conditions, a coalition of three members is necessary, and it is as effective in persuading a dissenter as a larger number. For establishing consensus on a matter of opinion, on the other hand, majorities seem to be more effective the larger they are, up to a point (Asch, 1956; M. Deutsch & Gerard, 1955). The significance of size for collectivities that are formal social organizations depends on the norms for decision making. Influence in the setting of norms and their enforcement lies more in the definitions of the relationships among roles than in coalitions. For example, whether the number of workers who press for a change in working conditions against a single employer is decisive depends on the workers' organization and other conditions of production.

Thus, from the perspective of the model, the size of a collectivity—that is, whether it is a "group"—is important only because size helps to determine what kind of social relationship the collectivity is. This is particularly true of collectivities that are, to begin with, informal social organizations. Group size may significantly qualify the dynamics of social organizations, particularly informal ones.

Few if any groups are purely one kind of social relationship or another, and small groups are particularly prone to hybridization. This observation grows out of a conceptualization of group size that does not count members, but rather captures a peculiar dynamic of interaction. Bales (1950) proposed that *small* be defined in terms of the likelihood that each member of the collectivity forms a personal impression of every other member. This number varies according to conditions such as the physical availability of channels of communication, norms regarding communication, and the flexibility of the roles members play. From Bales's conceptualization of group size, one may hypothesize that the smaller they are, the stronger the tendency for social organizations to take on interpersonal characteristics, and conversely, that interpersonal relations give way to role regulation the larger the group. Small groups then occupy this special niche in the panoply of social relationships: They tend to be hybrids straining from social organization to interpersonal relations. At the very least, informal organization, in the sense that this was defined earlier, tends to replace formal role regulation when membership is small.

The hybrid character of collectivities presents important theoretical, methodological, and practical problems. Almost all concrete instances of social influence occur between individuals and a hybrid social environment, whether that social environment is a small group or a larger entity. This requires that, in order to apply the general principles of the social psychological model to concrete situations, one must follow analysis with synthesis. Social psychology must investigate the way different mixtures of social environments and the different processes of influence of each interact in their relations to individuals. To the degree that small groups are especially prone to hybridization, synthesis is particularly important to understanding them.

If it is true that concrete instances of the social environment rarely represent themselves as idealized interpersonal relations, social organizations, or cultures, this presents a critical methodological problem: How is social psychology to do its empirical investigations of analysis and synthesis? Because pure social environments rarely present themselves for analysis naturally, one must create them as best one can, and one must systematically combine them to study their synthesis. Paradoxically, small groups, which are arguably most prone to impurity, provide the best opportunity. The field of group dynamics has developed a method well-suited to this need.

The small group method has been used in social psychology almost since the beginning of the discipline. It was developed rather rapidly to its present form, and its utility has assured its regular and frequent use. Smallness has several methodological advantages. It is efficient, reducing the time and cost of research, and enables closer observation of process. For example, Weick and Gilfillan (1971) miniaturized culture and accelerated culture change with three people in one room. Sometimes, even more efficiently, the existence of "other group members" may be illusory, created by deceiving a solitary individual.

Smallness also facilitates experimental control. Independent and qualifying variables can be carefully manipulated. For example, under natural conditions one would usually have to observe boys' groups for months in order to observe many clear expressions of hostility and aggression. However, an experimenter can arrange for the carefully timed appearance of a reputed custodian who instigates hostility, in order to assess how prone to aggression boys become under certain conditions (K. Lewin et al., 1939). Similarly, one must observe groups for some time to observe instances when the group decides to throw out one of its members, but can set up a member for rejection and give groups the opportunity to do so (Schacter, 1951). Ordinarily, one has little or no opportunity to observe people seriously, perhaps fatally, injuring others, and one would be ethically required to limit that observation to at most the first instance per person if one could. Still, it is possible—but not without its own ethical problems—to encourage people to administer high voltage shocks that are real only where it counts psychologically, in the minds of the individuals who deliver them (Milgram, 1974). The potentially qualifying effects of personality differences are commonly neutralized by random assignment of individuals to the various experimental conditions. Independent variables are varied systematically, typically by the experimenter's instructions to the participants. Carefully controlled manipulation of experimental conditions has so often been done through deception that deception has become almost a hallmark of the study of small groups, but of course it is no more inherent to the method than is the use of students in introductory psychology and sociology classes as experiment participants, another common practice. The rigorous experimental character of the small group method makes any site where it is used a "laboratory," because a laboratory may be thought of as any place where experiments are conducted. Ingenious researchers have turned waiting rooms and city streets and boys' clubrooms into laboratories.

Finally, the small group method is intended to produce findings that can be validly generalized to conditions beyond those specific to its experiments and often not amenable to experimental control. Critics have disparaged group dynamics as the study of college sophomores playing games in campus laboratories, lacking external validity. Although many of its experiments have involved college sophomores playing games in campus laboratories, many of its findings have and are intended to have much wider import. It is clear from most of the reports of group dynamics research that there is some broad principle of behavior under investigation or some serious social problem to be solved. Milgram's research (1974) into people's compliance with commands to be cruel was prompted by the Nazis' attempts to exterminate the Jews. Latané and Darley's (1970) interest in helping behavior was sparked by the murder of Kitty Genovese. The long sequence of studies of group polarization began as an analogue to corporate decision making (Burnstein et al., 1973; Stoner, 1968). Back (1951) was certainly not interested in how two people could jointly create a short story; he was attempting to understand how group cohesiveness affects members' influence over one another. Neither Kelley nor Thibaut (1978) were particularly fascinated with the prisoners' dilemma; they were trying to state the principles that govern the outcomes of bargaining.

For its findings to be generalizable, the method stipulates that the hypothetically essential conditions be incorporated into the experiments. The specific trick of doing this is unimportant. If the research aims to further understanding about the conditions under which people help in emergencies, then the experiment must create what at least seems to be a real emergency, regardless of its nature; it need not be a murder in a dark parking lot. If the theoretical proposition to be tested involves interpersonal attraction, then genuine liking between participants has to be created or imported somehow, and the various instructions or selection techniques should make no difference. So the small group method does not assume that a verisimilitude of experimental conditions to the "real world" is required but tries rather to create hypothetical essentials.

Of course, the underlying premise here is that small groups may manifest all the essential variations of culture, social organization, and interpersonal relations. It assumes that the number of participants is not one of the critical conditions of the collective behavior and influence of any of these kinds of groups. The small group is assumed to be not merely an approximation or analog of these larger collectivities, but literally one or more of these collectivities in all important respects. This characterization of the small group method, together with the conceptualization of small groups as hardly different from any other interdependent collectivity in the social environment, permits experiments in interpersonal relations, social anthropology, sociology, and social psychology. A discussion of selected studies in the literature of group dynamics show how this is done.

Small Group Experiments on Interpersonal Relations

The model classifies as studies of interpersonal relations those studies of small groups whose cohesiveness is based on members' mutual liking. That each person in a small group may form an impression of all the others makes it possible to study interpersonal relations with the method, and it also permits the creation and control of interpersonal relations. Interpersonal relations can be created by providing participants with information that encourages them to like one another (Back, 1951). One can also import interpersonal relations into the experiment, with appropriate controls on the selection of the kind of people who engage in interpersonal relations (Brenner, 1977; Latané & Rodin, 1969).

Importation presumably is the stronger manipulation, on the assumption that genuine affection develops only after frequent and extended interaction. This reduces the pool of appropriate individuals to those who are currently engaged in close friendships, and the strategy relies on their assessments of their relationships.

The creation of interpersonal relations by manipulation is more efficient and potentially more tightly controlled, but the intensity of mutual affection is probably quite low. Nevertheless, these synthetic attractions have proved to have marked effects in countless studies. It remains to be seen whether interpersonal relations that are created for the experiment are of the kind and degree that seem to have generated the identification demonstrated in Brenner's and Dion and Dion's (1979) studies or would have the strength to withstand other influences in the kind of emergency created by Latané and Rodin. One benefit of applying the social psychological model to small groups is that it reveals that these three seemingly different kinds of studies have to do with identical principles of social influence, and it suggests for further research particular transpositions of their methods that are not merely arbitrary variations "to see what happens."

The model locates studies of balance at the interpersonal level of analysis, insofar as they involve objective groups rather than simply cognitive processes. Recall that Newcomb's (1956) AtoBreX theory posits an affective relationship between A and B but no role regulation; it therefore assumes interpersonal relations. Almost all the studies under the rubric of this theory aim to test the conditions of attitude formation and change, given an interpersonal relation, and conversely, the effects of established attitudes on the formation of interpersonal relations. Whereas theories of cognitive balance have generated numerous fruitful studies, research on balance in group processes has not been pursued. Nevertheless, balance theory may be illuminating if one recognizes it as a component of a more general theory of interpersonal relations. In this context, balance theory may illuminate such phenomena as cohesiveness and conformity, phases in the life span of families, marital conflict, and leadership.

Another line of theoretically significant research should have developed out of Festinger and colleagues' (1950) finding that friendship among members reduced the unity of otherwise cohesive groups. The researchers corrected the cohesiveness scores of groups of residents in student housing units in order to take friendships into account. They noted that friends supported one another if they cared to dissent from the normative pressures of the larger group. In the light of the model, one can see that the researchers were statistically purifying the social organizational characteristic of the groups by discounting their interpersonal components. Revealing studies can be done of the forces created in social organizations that include members who have interpersonal bonds by systematically placing or creating pairs of friends in small groups that are as a whole created to accomplish specific tasks under certain conditions.

Small Group Experiments on Social Organization

Most studies of group dynamics have been studies of social organization and its influence on individuals. Experimental groups typically have been assigned some task to perform and have been instructed in the rules by which they should work together. The different conditions within a study have often been variations in organizational norms, set by the authority of the experimenter, who regulates who may communicate with whom, how rewards are allocated, the division of labor, and so on. When it has purposely been left to the participants to negotiate further arrangements among themselves, the experiments have been, in the terms of the model, on the development of informal organization.

Although the independent variables in these studies have often been internal to the experimental organization—that is, variations in norms— variations in their external environments have also been created, such as the personal characteristics of their members and the technology available to them. When Schacter, Ellertson, McBride, and Gregory (1951) assigned group members to be cutters or pasters or painters of cardboard houses, the researchers were creating a formal social organization into which they experimentally introduced variations in members' attitudes toward productivity, for the purpose of studying informal modification of role relations and its effects on group members. Sakurai (1975) systematically varied interpersonal relations within groups as well as the effectiveness of their technology in order to test whether interpersonal cohesiveness would obstruct an organization's attempts to enhance its productivity through technological innovation.

Small Group Experiments on Culture

No research in group dynamics is more obviously experimental social anthropology than Weick and Gilfillan's (1971) study of intergenerational transmission of technology. Imagining culture from the perspective of traditional cultural anthropology has distracted social scientists from the cultures of small groups. Lawson and McCauley (1990) have expressed the common belief that "socio-cultural entities are neither the sorts of things that scientists can isolate in labs nor manipulate experimentally" (p. 64). Actually, however, there have been several active lines of research on small groups as repositories of culture. Some of these were cited in the earlier discussion of culture. Identifying these studies as experimental social anthrology, or culturology, rests on the definition of culture as systems of shared beliefs.

The early experiments of Asch (1956) and of Sherif (1936) are, in terms of the model, experiments on cultural processes. The nature of the interdependence among the participants of these studies was to achieve some certainty about reality. The participants had no affective relationship that would qualify as an interpersonal relation. Neither was there any common task that required social organization (although it is true that participants played the roles of subject, stranger, male, etc.). There was no requirement even that they arrive at a consensus. However, the nature of their individual tasks was such that previous experience led them to expect agreement about such obvious facts as the relative lengths of lines or the distance traveled by a spot of light, and so they depended on one another. Sherif's study of stability and change in judgments of the movement of light as members of the group are successively replaced is from this perspective of a piece with Weick and Gilfillan's experiment. The variations introduced by Weick and Gilfillan were in the utility of technologies and the necessity for consensus, which incorporated in their experiment more of the determinants of cultural formation under natural circumstances. On the other hand, the Asch and Sherif experiments, because they lacked these features, more closely reproduced the conditions under which mass media influence members of an audience.

The line of research begun by Asch and Sherif has given rise to other experiments using the small group method. For example, Ross et al. (1976) varied the credibility of other group members by giving them an apparent motivation to distort their judgments, and they found that this diminished the others' persuasiveness. Allen and Levine (1971) reduced the credibility of one other group member by demonstrating that his eyesight was too impaired to be reliable. M. Deutsch and Gerard (1955) showed that the size and degree of unanimity that makes a majority persuasive depends on whether technological or ideological beliefs are at issue.

The research prompted by Stoner (1968) on what was initially called "the risky shift" is also research on groups as repositories of culture, using the small group method. Again, the situation created by the experiment involves neutrally affective strangers making public judgments, sometimes under the requirement of arriving at a consensus and sometimes not. Participants were given the opportunity to persuade one another about how much risk is justified in certain hypothetical situations. Research has shown that how much individuals' judgments shift toward or away from risk depends on the factual and evaluative arguments advanced in the course of group discussion (Meyers & Lamm, 1976; Vinokur & Burnstein, 1978). The literature on the "risky shift" grew voluminous, and as the dynamics of changing judgments were revealed, the phenomenon was renamed "group polarization"; for the facts and opinions presented in discussion could persuade individual members to adopt either more or less risky decisions, and the average risk advocated by members was either greater or less than it had been prior to discussion. Having achieved this level of understanding, research on the phenomenon has come virtually to a halt—prematurely. The nature of the situation, the research designs that have been created, and the measures developed present a promising opportunity to study cultural processes. One might easily arrange systematic variations in the arguments presented, thereby experimenting with the internal dynamics of belief systems. Researchers could investigate the regnance of facts or values under varying conditions; observe the interplay of Rokeach's (1968) ultimate and instrumental values as they may be invoked to justify risks; or vary the certainty of facts as a condition of their influence. One might also inject various environmental conditions in the cultural process: pairs of friends, individuals in some kind of authority relationship, personalities that differ in the need for closure, and so on. Such research is bound eventually to lead back to the practical issues that prompted Stoner's initial study of the risky shift, that is, the formation, maintenance, change, and effects of corporate cultures.

Moscovici and his associates (e.g., Moscovici & Lage, 1976; Moscovici, Lage, & Naffrechoux, 1969; Moscovici & Personnaz, 1980) have also used small groups to study phenomena of larger cultural significance. Moscovici's experiments with small groups were intended to test the general conditions whereby minorities without formal political power may nevertheless be influential, namely by changing attitudes and perceptions. Moscovici and Personnaz concluded that a persistent minority is more persuasive than a majority: "Our results support the notion that majority and minority influence are different processes, the former producing mostly public submissiveness without private acceptance, and the latter producing primarily changes in private responses. These processes, called compliance and conversion, are mutually exclusive and to a certain extent, opposite" (p. 280). In the terms of the model, Moscovici and Personnaz asserted that majorities are mainly social organizations that enforce norms, whereas persistent minorities are persuasive advocates of beliefs. The persistence of the minority in the face of normative pressures is persuasive because this enhances the minority's credibility. There is at this writing some controversy over whether majorities merely exact superficial compliance and over whether credibility, suspicion, or attention is critical to the influence of persistent minorities (Doms & Van Avermaet, 1980; Sorrentino, King, & Leo, 1980). In any case, the substantive ideas and the research designs created for this line of inquiry have potential for the experimental study of cultural change and persuasion. More specific attention should be given to the possible differences in the effects of persistent minorities on individuals' beliefs in objective facts—like the color of a perceptual afterimage that has been the stimulus in some of these studies—as compared with political opinions. The relative influences of normative pressures and persuasion under various conditions might be determined by assessing participants' reactance (Brehm & Mann, 1975) or by varying the directness with which the majority and minority attempt to get their agreement. These would be studies of social organizational and cultural influence on individuals, as previous studies of the influence of persistent minorities have been.

Cultural change could be studied using the small group method involving persistent minorities if certain conditions were established. Perceptions or opinions would be made instrumental for goals important to individual group members, and the members would be given the opportunity to communicate with one another during their deliberations. What would be the effect of a persistent minority on the shared beliefs of individuals, each of whom would receive a reward for his or her own correct answer: Would their stake in the outcome inhibit individuals' desertion of a safe majority, or would the stakes enhance the persuasiveness of the minority's persistence? Suppose the nature of the reality—the fact or opinion at issue—were critical to some interdependent effort whose success would be rewarded, then what influence would a persistent minority have in determining the culture of the group? Experimental variations such as these, which encourage or require that salient beliefs be shared, would create the conditions for observing the formation of culture and the influence of minorities in that process.

Summary

An observation by Homans (1974) would serve this chapter well as an epigram: "small groups are not so much what we study as where we study it" (p. 4). Because they may take any form found in the social environment, and because their size facilitates manipulating them in experimental designs, small groups are enormously useful for social research. They are to social scientists what mice and guinea pigs and rabbits are to biological science. The major contribution of group dynamics has been its method, which despite its enormous literature and its present state of decline, has hardly been exploited. Its potential for an experimental social anthropology especially has been neglected.

To say that small groups should be studied as representatives of broader collectivities is not to deny that they should be studied also for their own sake. In his statement quoted above, Homans is careful to leave room for small groups themselves: They "are not *so much* what we study" (emphasis added). A substantial share of social events occur in small groups, which fight battles, produce goods, make love and decisions. The point is that these events are covered by the same principles as are all social events, their locus in small groups notwithstanding. Constructive theory and research on small groups requires the same kinds of analysis and synthesis of them as of any entity in the social environment.

Inasmuch as small groups are not qualitatively special phenomena in the social environment, they are methodologically useful. Nevertheless, enthusiasm for the small group method should not obscure some of its limitations. As perhaps with any experiment, small group experiments are not as clean and rigorous as they may appear. Take research on cohesiveness and conformity, for example. Systematic variations in the degree to which randomized strangers are task interdependent does not necessarily completely wash out the influence of interpersonal attraction. If mere exposure to others is enough to generate a detectable amount of affection for them, then a few minutes or an hour of discussion may taint a small social organization with at least a modicum of interpersonal relations. The small group may permit as close an approximation to the pure social organization as physical research approximates a vacuum, which is close enough. However, generalizing from small group research to large social organizations in which most individuals never develop any personal impression of most of the other functionaries should be done with cognizance of the inherent strains of small groups toward interpersonal relations. If the purity of role relationships is crucial to the experiment, then special steps need to be taken to minimize this natural tendency of small groups.

The life span of small groups created for experiments is usually brief. This means that members do not expect to interact again in some uncertain future. This condition may reduce the validity of generalizations to social relationships that have a future. This seems particularly problematic in experiments that require people to violate important social norms. People may simply act differently in the brief relationship than they do in ongoing relationships. Milgram's experiment on obedience (1974) illustrates this point nicely: His inclusion of pairs of friends as Teacher and Learner may be seen as addressing the question, do individuals respond as readily to the experimenter's commands to deliver severe shocks if they believe that they will be interacting with their victims for some time afterward? (See chapter 12.) If generalizations are to be made to the natural world and the likelihood of further interaction seems critical, then the future must be brought into the experiment if possible, or the generalizations should be made with reservation.

One wonders also whether the results of some experiments with small groups would have been different had they been done in a different cultural context. Would Milgram's participants have acted differently in a small town, where people are likely to run into each other afterward on Main Street or to have mutual acquaintances, than they did in New Haven and Bridgeport? Would Asch's participants have resisted a majority more often at Yale University than they did at Swarthmore College?

These inherent limitations of the small group method should not discourage its use. Every research method has its limitations. No other method gives us a better opportunity to experiment in the social sciences.

11

Sex and Gender in Social Psychology

Elizabeth Douvan

The area of sex and gender roles, which has revived and burgeoned under the influence of the political women's movement, has made contributions to and critiques of psychology's methods as well as its substance. Substantively the study of sex and gender roles can fruitfully be positioned in relation to the levels of analysis established in chapter 2—indicating how particular concepts and research are integrated in the model's three distinct arenas of social influence. Beyond this relationship to the model, critical feminist analysis has encompassed the methods of social psychology as well. Both of these lines of association are discussed at least briefly in this chapter.

When examining the position of sex and gender role substantive research in relation to the model, the best place to start is at the social organizational level, because the study of sex differences and gendered behavior places the construct of "sex role" or "gender role" prominently among its concerns.[1]

Just as in the previous chapter Gold begins by deconstructing the concept of "group"—pointing to the fact that social psychology has neither need nor place for it in the model he proposes—here I note a peculiarity of the concept of gender role. The social category of gender comprises a role—that is, a set of shared behavior expectations that carry moral force in a social collectivity—only in a limited sense. In contemporary Western culture virtually all norms other than asymmetry in power and prestige have been detached from gender categories. That is, women have lower status and prestige than men. Deference is the only widely held expectation of women; authority, power, and dominance is expected of men.

This is, of course, a critically important norm. It accounts for many if not most of the behavior differences (outside of the purely biological spheres of sex and reproduction) traditionally found between men and women (Kanter, 1976), and it accounts for the astounding appeal and power of the feminist movement as well as the fear and backlash it has

---

[1]The concepts of sex role and gender role have been differentiated in much social psychological literature: *Sex role* refers to aspects of behavior associated closely with biological sex, whereas behavior elaborated on biological differences by socialization defines gender. This chapter deals largely with the latter concept.

stimulated on the religious right and to some extent in the broader population (Faludi, 1991).

The fact that 30 years into the resurgent feminist movement there is still a significant wage gap between men and women performing the same functions in the labor market (Tavris, 1992) is powerful testimony to the sex asymmetry that continues to mark our society and affect market forces. The biological fact that women bear children is still used as a basis for wage discrimination (BacaZinn & Eitzen, 1993; Tavris, 1992) ("After all, we'll train you and then you'll leave the company to have children"). On the other hand, barriers to women's entry into virtually all areas of the labor market have been lowered through the efforts of women, their political activities, and the courts.

Nevertheless, gender asymmetry is still a dominant fact in our society, as it is in all known societies, so that girls and women must be socialized to see themselves serving men and to think of themselves as somehow less valuable than men. This socialization process has been studied extensively and in some cases in microscopic detail (Clark-Stewart, 1973; Stiver, 1995). It has been demonstrated in adults' responses to infants, responses that vary depending on the gender label assigned to the infant (Clark-Stewart, 1973; Moss, 1967). Parents have been observed to behave in distinctly different ways toward their boy and girl babies. They are more likely to play roughly with baby boys and to talk more to baby girls (Kagan, 1971). Schools and teachers treat boys and girls differently in ways that are related specifically to the dominant stereotypes and to the high value placed by the culture on males (Eccles, 1984).

Gender asymmetry has been attributed to all levels of the social environment by social scientists trying to account for its universality. It has been attributed to the mother–infant interaction—the interpersonal level (Chodorow, 1978)—and to bifurcation of the social organization under market conditions—bifurcation into production for use and production for profit or private and public realms (Rosaldo, 1974). Because the female bears and rears children, she has been geographically tied and less mobile than the male. This has meant that in the social organization she performs a different and less public role than the male (social organizational level). Cultural forces are also adduced as the driving force in gender asymmetry (Ortner, 1974, e.g., whether the dominant cultural concept of the female is affinal or kin-based affects the status and power of women).

Finally, nonsocial factors are held to be critical determinants of the relative position of males and females. Sociobiologists and evolutionary theorists as well as many psychologists and social theorists who do not claim these titles point to biological differences in muscle mass and hormones as providing the basis for male dominance. Their claims are based on a relatively simple proposition: Males are, on average, larger and stronger than females. If, then, there is any contest and if we assume that the desire to dominate is always prominent in the motivational makeup of humans, clearly males will dominate. Their strength and larger size is also posited as the basis for their assignment of the functions of hunting and defense, whereas females' relative immobility is construed as barring her from these activities.

These extra- or nonsocial factors do not lie within the purview of social psychology. Although we can hold that such variables only gain their meaning as they are interpreted by particular cultures (e.g., hunting for game and intergroup conflict and defense must be considered of greater value than bearing and nurturing babies in the examples described in the previous paragraph), the physical variables in themselves are not of critical concern to us in this discussion. It is those more clearly social aspects of the environment that focus and preoccupy the interest of social psychology. How these factors translate into the lives of individuals and groups is more fully discussed in the next section.

Social Organization: Sex and Gender Roles

As indicated above, gender is a role only in a limited sense. The concept of role carries the clear connotation of shared expectations. There was a time in the not-so-distant past when middle class women lived lives defined by normative expectations. They were to be chaste until marriage, uninterested in sex, dependent on men, restricted in their activities to homemaking and the gentle arts, vessels for the maintenance of the species, and instillers of moral values in the next generation (Cott, 1977). The corresponding male role, in the United States and England, was exemplified by the rugged individualist who could wrest a living from the jungle of the city and its enterprises (Sennett, 1974). He was to be strong and tough, never given to emotional expression or even much emotional experience. He was the protector of the hearth and kept his gentle wife on a pedestal. If she was sexually unresponsive (which was almost guaranteed by the myth imposed on her), he could find alternative sources of sexual satisfaction in the underside of puritan Victorian life and society. That many individuals did not live up to society's expectations does not mean that the norms were not clear or forceful (Barker-Benfield, 1976). We have evidence from Freud's theories (S. Freud, 1909, 1923/1966; Masson, 1984) and practice that those who broke the rules paid a heavy price in guilt and hypocrisy.

Today with the sexual revolution and the mass entrance of women into virtually all areas of the labor force, there are few prescriptions for women except that they defer to men. Men too have been freed (at least theoretically) from the very constraining norms that previously governed their lives. Surely some men and women still adhere to old patterns, but normative expectations of male and female behavior have been reduced to the point where it no longer makes sense to speak of "the male role" or "the female role." Except for a few roles as gender related as nun and priest, it is hard to think of roles that cannot accommodate either men or women. Moreover, when one looks at roles in our society that do carry such clear and specific gender associations, they are often contradictory in the view of maleness or femaleness they connote. So, for example, priest and hitman imply different characteristics of maleness; nun and whore both allude to females (though even here, whore is not exclusively female) but to contradictory behavioral expectations.

A crucial fact about gender in contemporary industrial society is the dramatic change it has undergone in the recent past. This is certainly one of the things that must be understood and related to concepts and changes in the social environment that have affected gender roles. Before the cultural and interpersonal factors are discussed, consider briefly the nonsocial factors that have been adduced as critical sources of gender differentiation.

Nonsocial Factors

At least since Margaret Mead's critical work (1949), it has been known that culture defines the meaning of male and female. Biology provides only the most general backdrop (the rationale, as it were) for defining what it means to be male or female. The biological givens—the presence of an X chromosome and particular genital organs—define positions and contributions to specific sexual–reproductive acts, particularly the heterosexual coital act of copulation. Aside from this very restricted, limited sex act, biology may also contribute to a larger measure of aggressiveness in the human male (Money, 1972; Tavris, 1984, 1989).

Men's larger frames, more muscular development (on average), and their more active initiating aggressivity may have had some influence on the origins of sex roles and gender differences, although these characteristics are heavily overlaid with cultural definitions and may come to be associated with differences in power, because a culture defines power as dominance and construes physical force as the default position for all authority. Individual characteristics that are often thought to underpin differences in resources—like spatial relations, verbal ability, or interpersonal skill—cannot be disentangled from differences in socialization of boys and girls and must, therefore, be treated as ambiguous cases with strong social components. We can treat them as resources that differentiate among individuals and consider social variables at the various levels of the social environment that may affect them. In any case there is a large overlap in the distributions of male and female individuals on these and most behavioral variables.

Feminist biologists have even challenged the validity of the conception of sex as a binary opposition: male and female. They have argued for a more complex construction that recognizes the various forms of sex—bisexuality, homosexuality, and others—that present themselves in behavioral and biological expression (Fausto-Sterling, 1985; Keller, 1990; Tavris, 1992). Though these are often considered "anomalies" by Western medicine and are treated ("corrected") with surgery and other medical interventions, the fact is that they occur in nature and are capable of expression. It is Western medicalized culture with its narrow definition of normality that designates all but a few forms pathological.

In any case, biological sex definition (however ambiguous this may be in particular cases) is outside the realm of social psychology. It is among those nonsocial factors that influence the person and is therefore not part of our theoretical concern as social psychologists except as it acquires symbolic significance through the imputation of cultural or social meaning.

Culture

In the scheme presented in this book, culture is in some sense the most encompassing conceptual sector of the social environment. It consists of belief systems extant in a group: beliefs about and beliefs in or, another way of putting it, technology and ideology. Norms are part of the belief system of any group—and these include norms about behavior in roles. Thus, the norms that we have discussed earlier under social organization are part of culture. However, culture includes beliefs in addition to those beliefs that define roles: beliefs in and about the supernatural as well as the natural world.

The two types of belief included in culture mark the difference between those things a society (or some part of it) understands and can control and those things that remain mysteries. When science moves in to an area and clarifies events and their causes, ideology or faith in its various forms tends to diminish in that area. As we gain understanding of the workings of nature, for example, superstition, myth, and religion withdraw as dominant explanations of natural events. The same rough distinction can be made when considering the cultural elements in sex and gender.

Technology

The most obvious example of technology's influence on sex and gender roles is modern birth control technology. Biological science has come to a refined understanding of the biology of reproduction and with this knowledge has developed hormonal and mechanical birth control that is essentially 100% effective in preventing conception. By decisively separating heterosexual sex from reproduction, this innovation allows women to control their reproductive lives and thereby restrict both the number of children they bear and the number of years they devote to reproduction. This frees women to take an active role in the productive life of their society of a kind and to an extent that has not been possible in any society previously. This, in turn, has led to a serious and thoroughgoing analysis and revision of gender roles and the ideology that supports them. The intense questioning, experimenting, and conflict around sex roles that has developed in industrialized societies over the last 50 years is a direct result of modern birth control technology (S. Evans, 1981; Tavris, 1984; Thorne & Yalom, 1982).

Language is an area that has come under critical analysis by women scholars (Lakoff, 1975; Henley, 1975). One of the early thrusts of feminist criticism aimed at language and usage: Why should women be referred to as Miss or Mrs., thus associating or identifying women immediately and exclusively with marital status, whereas the male form (Mr.) carries no such designation? Why was the generic for humans or for an undesignated human always masculine (e.g., *mankind*; "The participant came and *he* responded")? Though newly invented substitute forms are resisted and parodied by critics, it is remarkable how effective the linguistic critique has been in stripping at least formal language of hierarchical and other gender associations (cf. American Psychological Association, 1977).

Ideology

Stimulated by theorists who took the universality of male dominance to mean that it is somehow wired into the human brain, feminists offered an interpretation to counter this biological attribution. The alternative feminist view held that male dominance was a historical development that occurred in prehistory when males overthrew what had been matriarchal, birth-centered societies and religion (Judd, 1979; Spretnak, 1982; Stone, 1978, 1991). The claim is supported by archeological evidence: the broadly distributed female fertility figures excavated throughout Mediterranean Europe. Patriarchy, according to this hypothesis, gradually displaced a matriarchal system, moving from the Middle East where it began to other parts of the Mediterranean and northward until it lost force in the extreme northwest of Europe. In the Nordic countries, where creation myths are centered on the brother–sister dyad, patriarchy never took hold (Judd, 1979).

This construction attracted enthusiastic adherents among feminists but has been widely rejected by mainstream anthropology. The argument of anthropologists against this alternative is that the fertility figures in no way contradict the presence of male dominance and that the theory of a matriarchy overthrown is just the kind of tale that would be constructed by females under a system of male dominance—an example of wish-fulfilling fantasy (S. B. Ortner, personal communication, September 13, 1994).

To understand the source from which male dominance arose, anthropologists who theorize about the origins of the state have developed detailed, painstaking theoretical explanations for the universality of male dominance, based in biology and culture (Cucchiari, 1981). A good deal of this discourse, on both sides, seems ideological, one's position bearing the stamp of faith rather than clearly supported belief.

It is quite easy to point to cases where discussion of sex and gender seem overlaid with ideology. Again, feminists have deconstructed much of Freud's work—both his conduct of clinical cases and some of the central hypotheses in his theory—and have revealed the patriarchal bias on which they rest. The Oedipus complex and the case of Dora both carry patriarchal assumptions and limit the value of the theory and raise ethical questions in the case of the treatment of the young woman (Lakoff, 1993; Mitchell, 1975).

Contemporary evolutionary behavior theory also makes assumptions that do not square with empirical work in primatology. The assumptions that survival of the fittest always implies competition and dominance and that in the last analysis all competition is a race for reproductive advantage are certainly not universally true for all species and are specifically at odds with recent work with rhesus monkeys. B. Smuts (personal communication, September 20, 1996) and Wallen (1996) and her colleagues at the Yerkes laboratory have reported that alpha males do not necessarily use their dominance to increase their reproductive advantage, that in many cases it is the males two or three steps down the hierarchy of power who most actively reproduce. Alpha males often use their position for other purposes, such as alliances with other males who may be helpful in the future.

Closer to social psychology, the theories of Talcott Parsons (1942), a patriarch of the field, held sway for decades before feminists questioned his unconditional assignment of life roles according to gender, what appeared to be an assignment handed down from god without the slightest nod to historical or cultural variations. Cultural assumptions and patriarchal bias reigned without question or objection until a political movement raised them two decades later.

Thus far, this discussion has focussed on instances in which scientific positions and advances in the area of gender role theory are determined or obstructed by cultural forces, by the unwitting impact of cultural assumptions on the course of science purporting to clarify sex roles and their effects. In a sense this is a case of technology being invaded by unacknowledged ideology. Disentangling such effects and correcting the lenses through which we look at various aspects of social reality takes painstaking analysis, research, and time.

A striking example of this corrective work on the fundamental myths of a culture is the work of feminist theologians who have returned to the original ancient texts and demonstrated that errors and biases were introduced into their reading long after the originals were written. The brilliant analyses of Phyllis Trible (1978) and other scholars have reconnected us with the nonsexual or bisexual nature of the construct of God—the inclusion of a feminine principle (along with the masculine) in the original Judeo–Christian conception of a supreme being. This and many other revelations chip away at the dominant patriarchal myth. Elaine Pagels (1988) put it sharply when she asked what could be more powerful in the lives and unconscious assumptions of people than the creation myths and other aspects of the biblical heritage with which they grew up.

Dominant images in our media have been shown to emphasize sex and gender differences that reinforce stereotypes of male and female and the relative power and prestige of males. Perhaps the very clearest demonstration of the cultural impact on sex and gender roles comes from cross-cultural studies: the clear preference in China for male offspring that has led to the abandonment of large groups of female infants; the hierarchical structure of the family in Islam, most strikingly symbolized in the chador and the other customs designed to make women invisible and isolated in the private sphere of the household. These signs, the universally lower wages women earn, and other discriminatory and exploitive patterns emphasize the ways in which culture maintains power relations in sexual exchange.

Interpersonal Relations

The field of close interpersonal relationships has had a patchy history in social psychology. In a certain sense, the field itself can be seen as stemming from the work and thought of Charles Horton Cooley (1922) and George Herbert Mead (1982), for whom close interpersonal interaction defined the source of humanity, the social medium from which human nature arose. It was only in the 1950s, however, that academic psychology began systematic study of small group and face-to-face behavior. Another lull occurred during the 1970s in empirical work, although important theoretical work in social interactionism and other areas of close relationships continued (Goffman, 1963). Beginning in the 1980s and continuing to the present, there has been increasing interest in expanding our theoretical and empirical knowledge of close relationships. It is among the most active areas of the discipline of social psychology at the present time (Duck, 1990; Perlman, 1987).

Interpersonal skill has been considered a "feminine" trait and has been attributed at various times in various theories to the female's closer association with childbirth (Douvan, 1977; Gutmann, 1970; Ruddick, 1982). The thought is that because women are in constant contact with preverbal infants and oversee the welfare of the next generation, it is critical that they develop heightened sensitivity to interpersonal nuance. Because they have to read subtle signals of hunger or discomfort in babies, they are thought to become attuned to aspects of the interpersonal. Thus, their socialization is designed to develop these skills in girls and women (Gutmann, 1970; Ruddick, 1982).

This association with the "natural" sphere of reproduction has been used to justify women's less powerful and privileged position in many cultures. In early periods of human history the female needed to remain relatively close to the hearth and, thus encumbered, could not hunt or travel long distances (Cucchiari, 1981). Because the hunt was critical to survival (or so the theories held) in producing the major source of protein for the tribe, prestige accrued to those who hunted. The same condition barred women from those activities that defended the tribe against enemy marauders. Women were again excluded by their "natural" condition from a critical survival (i.e., prestigious) arena.

It is now known that most of the dietary protein of hunter–gatherer tribes came from the grains, insects, and other small life forms that women provided for themselves and their dependent infants. The causal relationship between men's prestige and hunting and warfare runs in the reverse direction: that is, whatever men do in a culture is more highly valued, accorded more prestige than activities that women perform and control.

Whereas women's more restricted mobility may originally have played in to the set of circumstances that led to male advantage, the connection to foodstuffs was not the mediator for it (B. Smuts, personal communication, September 20, 1996).

At the same time that feminist scholars have critiqued the line of thought that associates female with nature and male with culture (Ortner, 1974), a good deal of thought and research has explored the idea that women are the socio-emotional experts (J. Bernard, 1981; Ruddick, 1982), that women's identity is developed *in relation* (Jordan, Surrey, & Kaplan, 1995; Surrey, 1995; Jordan, Kaplan, Miller, Stiver, & Surrey, 1995), and that their moral development is a morality of caring in contrast to male morality as described by Kohlberg (1981), which evolves toward an abstract concept of justice (Gilligan, 1982; Jordan et al., 1995; Stiver, 1995).

Robert May (1980), anticipating aspects of Gilligan's (1982) work and theory, demonstrated that in response to story pictures, males expressed anxiety in response to stimuli that cued intimacy, whereas females expressed anxiety about separation.

David Gutmann (1970) and other theorists have suggested that the birth of a baby requires a bifurcation and crystallization of roles along gender lines. The female, charged with protecting the infant and insuring its survival, must give up aggressive behavior and aggressive motives. The male's role is to support the mother and infant by providing income or the grounds for survival, to win a living in the competitive world of the market. In this formulation, the adult male (the husband–father) can use all the aggression he can muster, and he in turn must give up his soft and tender motives. Each adult partner, then, yields one side of her–his motivational system to the other partner for the duration of the child raising phase of their lives (Gutmann, 1970; Ruddick, 1982). At midlife the partners can retrieve what they have temporarily yielded, reclaiming their nurturant or aggressive impulses. This theoretical formulation received some empirical support for the description of women's motives and behaviors at various stages (Veroff, Douvan, & Kulka, 1981) but not for men's developmental stages.

The bifurcation of roles and women's expertise in the interpersonal realm is assumed by Rosabeth Kanter in an early brilliant analysis of the design and effectiveness of executive training for males and for the newly developing pool of women executives (Kanter, 1977). Whatever one may think of these theories and the research they have stimulated, one certainly must credit the fact of changes in the sex–gender system in developed nations over the last 50 years.

In discussing technology I pointed to the forceful impact of modern birth control methods on the gender system: When women gain greater control over their reproductive lives—over how long and how often they actively bear and rear children—they are freer to take up other occupations, including roles in the paid labor force. However, technology alone does not effect such dramatic role changes; other factors also contribute by influencing women to *want* to take on new roles and limit their traditional ones.

In this process of conversion, interpersonal relations and identification —the dynamic through which interpersonal relations have their influence—play a critical role. In American culture and in most industrialized countries, a very rapid shift occurred from an ideal that held out the two-parent, one-worker family with two or more children as the perfect life-organization at least for middle class women (in the 1950s) to one in which most women work in the labor force continually except for short maternity leaves (in the 1980s and 1990s). This was one of the most dramatic shifts in norms ever witnessed in so short a time period.

Many factors facilitated the change, factors at each of the levels of the social environment. The political movement that influenced many women to change—to insist on equal rights and a place in the world beyond the private space of their roles as wife and mother—recognized the particular power of interpersonal relations in women's lives. The invention of "consciousness raising" groups both permitted women to discover that their private problems and unhappiness were not really private but were shared with other women and made use of processes of identification to broaden the effects of the movement. When one woman in the group (or neighborhood or Parent Teacher Association) hired a baby-sitter and went to work, other women identified both with her dissatisfaction with a life narrowly constrained and with her yearning for self-expression. Many women responded with "If Mary Lou can do it, so can I." There are hints in the literature that identification may be more available as a mechanism to women than it is to men—at least in Western culture. It may be more accurate to say that women use an earlier and more generalized form of identification than do men (J. B. Miller, 1976).

In psychoanalytic theory, the little boy identifies with the father out of a specific fear that the father is jealous of him and wants to kill or castrate him. To experience these fears assumes a certain antecedent level of differentiation of the self. That is, the little boy distinguishes himself and his interests from those of his father. Afraid of dying, being killed by the jealous father, the little boy *becomes* the father through identification (S. Freud, 1917/1966).

What of the little girl? In psychoanalytic theory and in more social-development theory, it seems that the little girl does not have such a clear, differentiated sense of self. Little girls are not asked to give up being dependent or to become "a little (wo)man," as boys are. Her erotic focus is not so clearly limited to the father. Her boundaries are not as clear, thus making identification easy and somehow less decisive than the little boy's. This fluidity of boundaries has been used to explain women's interpersonal sensitivity and empathy, and it is central to much recent work on female personality development (Caplan, 1981; Chodorow, 1978; Jordan et al., 1995; A. Kaplan, 1982; J. B. Miller, 1995; Ruddick, 1982).

Socialization and persuasion, social learning and identity all were involved in the dramatic changes that occurred in the social roles of women and men over the last generation. They added force to the mechanism of identification, but it seems clear that identification was a key point of interpenetration: Many women in the middle and working classes identified with those women who defined a new identity that included both home and paid employment. Women's friendship groups and consciousness raising groups and book clubs all became settings in which women could encounter new definitions and possibilities for women's role—and women explored and identified with these new constructions.[2] Identification with women who were expanding the possibilities allowed women to see other possibilities for their own lives.

Person: Individual Influence on Sex–Gender Roles

In his goals for this model of social psychology, Gold includes an understanding or clarification of the ways in which the social environment (at each level of analysis) influences the person (the individual). He also hopes to clarify the reciprocal effect—the way in which the person influences each of the levels of the social environment. Clearly the effects are stronger from the environment to the person, but effects in the other direction, that is, person to environment interpenetration, should at least be recognized.

The big story in the area of gender roles is the huge changes that have occurred in the last 40 years. Can it reasonably be asserted that one or more individuals had a major impact on this history of change? I think that it can. The model holds that *invention* is the principal mechanism by which the person affects the social organization. This represents an indirect path: The person influences social organization by influencing *culture*, which in turn requires changes in roles.

It can reasonably be held that a signal event initiating the snowball that eventuated in radical changes in the dominant construction of the sex–gender system and gender roles in industrialized societies was the publication of Betty Friedan's book, *The Feminine Mystique* (1960). Here Friedan presented her critical analysis of our society's definition of gender roles and the ephemeral, illogical grounds on which those definitions stood. Sara Evans (1981), a major archivist of the political women's movement, represents the rapid, radical nature of the change in the introductory section of her history:

> In the mid-1950s Betty Friedan wrote and edited articles entitled "Millionaire's Wife," "I Was Afraid to Have a Baby," and "Two Are an Island." . . . How shall we explain that by the early 1960s Betty Friedan had issued her famous denunciation of "the Feminine Mystique"—her definition of the identification of womanhood with the roles of wife and mother? (p. 3)

It is certainly true, as Evans (1981) acknowledged, that many forces were at play in this conversion: perfected birth control, increased education of women, increasing economic pressures that had already led many

---

[2]Davis (1975) has explored the role of cultural symbols (represented in the youth courts of misrule and carnival celebrations) in expanding women's conceptions of possible roles and relationships in early modern times.

middle class and working class women to enter the paid labor market—not necessarily for careers but to supplement family income and assure their children's education. However, Friedan's book created a new frame for looking at domesticity and work as expressions of identity. Her sophistication and experience provided her the insight that the women's magazines were systematically used to convince women that their highest goal in life was creating a happy family and that they had no need for or interest in other identity anchors or sources of satisfaction and personal meaning. She described in detail the magazines' part in urging women out of the labor force at the end of World War II so that men returning from the war would find a welcoming labor market.

The book was an instant and astounding success. Middle class, educated women read it and had the experience (rare in their lives) of someone having read their minds. The impact was enormous. Consciousness raising groups, study groups, and dialogue groups spread Friedan's ideas and stimulated the development of a literature that has established itself in the last 30 years among the most active, innovative, and imaginative areas of research and theory. The personal had become public and continues to influence our public life today. Polls taken during these years reveal a shift in public view on all aspects of women's lives—from equal pay to couples' sharing household and child care work, from day care to whether a working mother can raise healthy children (Veroff et al., 1981).

Following Friedan's initiating call, the National Organization of Women and the National Women's Political Caucus developed. Backlash and second thoughts, counter movements and increased political visibility —all these contributed to the prominence of the issue in our public life. However, few would dispute the central, signal role that Friedan's book played in setting off the resurgence of the movement for women's rights.

Methodological Critique

One strand of contemporary criticism, in part sparked by the political woman's movement, has placed the scientific study of sex differences in the context of patriarchy and male dominance. This critique maintains that in nearly all behavioral features, the overlap between males and females is much greater than the differences between them. The emphasis on difference, according to these critics, is another way of reinforcing male privilege, of establishing male as the standard from which the "other" (that is, female, child, people with various sexual orientations) deviates. In a classic study, researchers (Broverman, Broverman, Clarkson, Rosenkrantz, & Vogel, 1970) established the fact that clinical psychologists operate with this patriarchal model in assessing and labeling clients.

The feminist critique of science is more broadscale than this: The whole enterprise of science with its reliance on reductionism and analysis, its reliance on quantification and comparisons of people on quantified variables—the emphasis on individual differences and rankings—all of this has been questioned and challenged. At the moment, however, many feminist researchers have concluded that for the forseeable future some combination of qualitative and quantitative methods, some system that recognizes and legitimates "women's ways of knowing" (Belenky, Clinchy, Goldberger, & Tarule, 1986) while simultaneously taking the best from the positivist tradition, represents our best hope for advancing knowledge.

Conclusion

Clearly there is no longer the least survival justification for male dominance and privilege in industrialized societies. As Jessie Bernard (1981) has asserted: "Men *can* tend babies and women can just as easily push the button that releases all kinds of energy." Strength no longer qualifies one for much of anything but the Mr. Universe contest. This is not to say that cultural forms regarding power that have been in place for centuries, albeit grounded entirely in social construction, are easy to displace. Gender roles carry few expectations and are relatively slim constructs, of limited use in social psychological theory, but the privilege associated with male gender will not disappear any time soon.

Philip Slater (1977) has said that if the feminist movement ever achieves its goals—that is, true equality between the sexes—it will be the first time in the history of humanity that authority is not ultimately based on the threat of physical violence. Surely this is a goal worth aspiration and effort.

12

Authority: Obedience, Defiance, and Identification in Experimental and Historical Contexts

François Rochat and Andre Modigliani

In the spring of 1962 Stanley Milgram was conducting his final two experiments on obedience to authority. One of these, which he called the Bridgeport condition, was designed to test the effects of institutional context on people's obedience to the commands of an authority figure. Milgram chose the industrial city of Bridgeport, Connecticut, to replicate some research he had conducted earlier in the academic setting of Yale University. Participants were recruited through a newspaper ad and asked to come to the offices of (the fictitious) "Research Associates of Bridgeport" to participate in an experiment on memory and learning.

Milgram conducted a second experiment that spring, which he called the "bring a friend" condition. Here, participants were asked to come to the same office, for the same purposes, and to bring a friend with them. All the participants in both conditions were men.

Although Milgram reported the results of the Bridgeport condition in his book *Obedience to Authority* (1974), he did not report his findings from the second condition, either in the book or in any of his articles. In this chapter we use the data from both conditions to examine how personal relationships influence obedience and defiance toward authority. We begin with a description of the two experimental conditions.

Experimental Conditions: An Overview

Bridgeport Condition

On entering the offices of the "Research Associates of Bridgeport," participants were introduced to the "Memory and Learning Project" by the experimenter. Two participants were present at each session. The other "participant" was actually an accomplice of the experimenter, a 47-year-old accountant of Irish American descent who, according to Milgram, was seen by most observers as "mild-mannered and likable" (Milgram, 1974, p. 16). The experimenter began the session by explaining to both participants that the purpose of the research was to better understand the effects of punishment on learning and that the experiment in which they were about to participate involved the administration of a test. One participant would be the "teacher," who would administer the test, and the other would be the "learner," who would attempt to master the test items as quickly as possible. Which person played what role was, ostensibly, determined randomly by drawing slips of paper. Actually, however, the drawing was rigged so that the accomplice–participant always became the learner and the real participant always became the teacher. The experimenter then explained that each time the learner gave a wrong answer on the test, the teacher would be expected to punish him with an electric shock. To make this possible, the teacher was seated in front of a very large shock generator displaying 30 switches, each corresponding to a voltage level ranging from 15 to 450 volts, whereas the learner was placed in an adjacent room and wired to leads ostensibly coming from the same shock generator. He was also strapped down in his chair so that he could not leave. (In reality, the learner was not wired to the shock generator, and he never received any shocks.) Next, the experimenter informed the teacher that, each time the learner made an error on the test that was about to be administered, he (the teacher) should move up one switch on the shock generator, thus increasing the shock level by 15 volts.

As the administration of the test and the shocks got under way, the accomplice–learner began making a good many errors according to a prearranged plan. As a consequence, the teacher soon found himself delivering what he believed to be higher and higher intensity shocks to which the learner reacted with grunts and then groans. After administering the 10th level (150 volts), he heard the learner cry out in pain and ask to be released from the experiment. However, the experimenter coolly insisted that the procedure continue. After delivering each higher shock, he heard the learner escalate his expressions of pain until they became agonized screams, and he heard the learner's pleas to be released grow increasingly desperate. Yet, if the teacher sought reassurances from the experimenter or otherwise sought to delay or halt the procedure, the experimenter simply prodded him to continue by saying "Please go on," or "The experiment requires that you continue." If the teacher expressed concern about the victim's health or suffering, the experimenter further prodded them by such off-handed replies as "No, although the shocks may be painful, they're not dangerous. Continue, please," or "Whether the learner likes it or not, we must go on until he's learned all the items correctly. Go on, please." It was only after using four such prods in succession, with the participant refusing to resume his task each time, that the experimenter stopped making further requests and officially acknowledged that the participant had become fully defiant. If the participant did not refuse to continue, the procedure was halted after the delivery of 450 volts, and he was considered fully obedient. Whichever way the procedure ended, the experimenter then began a process of debriefing.

Bring-a-Friend Condition

The bring-a-friend condition was identical to the condition just described except that the "other participant" among the 20 pairs was the friend who had accompanied the participant to the laboratory. The friendship between these two persons was generally close, having lasted for at least 2 years. For examples, in two cases the friend was a neighbor, in one case a colleague from work, and in three cases a relative: son, brother-in-law, and nephew. In this condition there was no rigged drawing to determine who would play which role. Instead, the participant was always assigned the role of teacher, and the friend whom he had brought with him was always assigned the role of learner. Because the learner was not a confederate of the experimenter in this condition, steps had to be taken to insure that he behaved in approximately the same way as the trained accomplice in the previously described condition. To accomplish this, the friend–learner was coached throughout the course of the procedure. After being taken into the adjacent room and ostensibly hooked up to the shock generator and strapped down to his chair, the friend–learner was joined by an employee of the project who instructed him on how to respond to the test, as well as on how to react to each new shock that was ostensibly being delivered.

In sum, within the limits imposed by having to train a series of naive persons to role-play the part of learner, the Bridgeport and the bring-a-friend experiments were very similar. Both were conducted in the same place, under the same circumstances, by the same experimenter, following the same procedures. The only difference was that, in the first condition, participants did not know the other man who was assigned to the role of learner, whereas in the second condition, the learner was their friend. What difference did it make for individuals to be ordered to administer electric shocks to a stranger each time he made an error, as opposed to being ordered to administer such shocks to a friend?

Levels of Resistance in the Two Experimental Conditions

As it turned out, having to give painful electric shocks to a stranger, as opposed to a friend, made a very substantial difference. In the stranger condition, 19 out of 40 participants (48%) were fully obedient, whereas in the friend condition only 3 out of 20 (15%) were fully obedient—a difference of 33%. We were able to observe several other interesting behavior differences by listening to audiotapes of the sessions—tapes that Milgram faithfully recorded and that now have been deposited with The Milgram Papers in the Yale University Library Archives. To study these differences carefully, we coded participants' verbal behavior during the experiment using a system designed to describe the extent of their resistance to the experimenter's repeated instructions to inflict further pain on the learner. (The system used to code utterances is described in Modigliani & Rochat, 1995.)

A comparison of participants' behavior in the two conditions shows not only that they resisted much more resolutely when the learner was a friend rather than a stranger, but also that they broke off the experiment much earlier. In other words, when participants were ordered to administer electric shocks to a friend, they showed clear signs of resistance to the experimenter's orders much earlier in the experiment and also took less time to go from these early protests to flat refusal to continue with the task. As a result, they also delivered lower levels of punishment (shock intensity) to the learner: When the learner was a stranger, the mean maximum shock level administered was 310 volts; when he was a friend, it was only 210 volts. In addition, participants did not hesitate or vacillate for as long a period when their friend asked them to stop; either they promptly acceded to his request (85%) or else they did not honor it at all (15%). This is an interesting finding, especially when compared with the way they behaved toward a stranger. With strangers, even though all participants were quite agitated about having to carry out the task, only 52% refused to follow the experimenter's orders. Moreover, those who resisted successfully did so in a more gradual, step-by-step manner which, initially, consisted in trying to get the experimenter to do something about the learner's pain and only later shifted to more personal and direct forms of defiance.

In short, by analyzing the unfolding sequence of the interaction between the experimenter and the participant, we found that when the learner was a stranger, most participants had a difficult time finding a way out of the experiment. In contrast, when the learner was a friend, it seemed self-evident to most of them that they simply had to break off when their friend called for them to stop. Why was it so self-evident?

Evolution of Relationships

To pursue this question, we must re-examine how the social relationships among the experimenter, the teacher, and the learner evolved over the course of the experiment in the two different conditions. In the Bridgeport condition individuals met both the experimenter and the learner at the same time—just after their arrival at the offices of "Bridgeport Research Associates." At that time they did not know what the experimental task would entail, nor did they know what they and the other apparent participant would be expected to do. Thus, the experiment began with two similar strangers both being instructed by an experimenter whom they did not know. On the other hand, in the bring-a-friend condition participants arrived at the office with their friend—someone they had known for at least 2 years—and then met the experimenter for the first time. Here, then, the experiment began with two close friends who were being instructed by an experimenter, whom they did not know.

In examining the audiotapes with a view to comparing how individuals in the two conditions behaved during the first few minutes of these encounters, we found that when the other participant was a stranger, participants tended to be polite but not talkative, listening to the experimenter's introductory remarks rather quietly. In contrast, when they came to the office with their friend, there was much more talking and even some joking during the early portions of the encounter. Furthermore, in this condition they tended to ask questions about the task as the experimenter gave them their instructions, something that happened very rarely when the other "participant" was a stranger. Thus, the presence of a friend created more space for talking and, hence, for showing curiosity about the experimental procedure, as well as for their expressing personal views. This played a role not only at the beginning of the experiment but also later on when it came time to question the experimenter's resolve to complete the experiment despite the learner's protests.

As the experimental session proceeded, and as the learner began protesting and yelling out in pain, it became increasingly difficult for participants to go on with their task. Here again, participants in the two conditions responded in contrasting ways to the experimenter's prods. In both conditions participants were surprised both by the learner's protests and by the experimenter's apparent indifference to the learner's suffering. When the learner was a stranger, almost half the participants left it up to the experimenter to decide whether the learner should continue being punished. In contrast, when the learner was a friend, they often responded to the experimenter's pressure to continue by insisting that the task they were being told to complete was an impossible one: How could they go on inflicting pain on a friend? For example, one said curtly, "Sir, I'm not a sadist," then refused to continue. What seemed patently obvious to them, namely that they could not continue to make their friend suffer, was apparently not registering with the experimenter. It was this seeming obtuseness that led participants to hold the experimenter responsible for their having to break off the experiment.

There was, in fact, a very interesting reversal in participants' attributions of responsibility from the Bridgeport condition to the bring-a-friend condition. In the first case the experimenter was seen as responsible for making the participant continue, whereas in the second case he was seen as responsible for making it impossible for him to continue. The latter perspective could be seen most clearly in exchanges that occurred toward the end of the session. In pressing reluctant participants to continue, the experimenter's last prod was, "You have no other choice, you must go on," to which defiant participants often replied by saying, in effect, "Why?" To this the experimenter would answer, "Otherwise we'll have to discontinue the whole experiment." Defiant participants were in no way troubled by this response. Indeed, they treated the experimenter as if he had finally come to his senses by replying, in effect, "Yes, you'll have to. We certainly can't go on like this."

Identification With Authorities and Victims

In this book, Gold advances the hypothesis that identification is the critical mediator of social influence under interpersonal conditions (see chapter

8). Applied to the data collected by Milgram in these two experiments on obedience to authority, this hypothesis suggests that when participants were ordered to punish the learner who was a friend, they tended in some way to identify with the learner (the victim), whereas when the learner was a stranger, they tended in some fashion to comply with the experimenter (the authority figure) or possibly to identify with him (as the aggressor). To determine whether friendship had affected participants' patterns of identification during the experiment, we compared their interactions with the experimenter across the two conditions and examined how they related to the learner when he was a stranger as opposed to a friend. We found two salient differences between the conditions.

First, in the Bridgeport (stranger) condition, when the experimenter ignored the learner's protests to the point of talking directly over these protests, most of the participants who ended up fully obedient did exactly the same thing: Sooner or later they stopped listening to what the learner was saying and began talking over him—either by reading the next test item or by conversing with the experimenter, while the learner was still protesting. This act of "talking over the learner" occurred only after the experimenter had done so and appeared to be a superficial form of identification with the experimenter, or more precisely, a distinctive *imitation* of his demeanor. This pattern of behavior occurred only once in the bring-a-friend condition; a single obedient participant "talked over" a friend who was calling out for him to stop.

Second, when the learner was a friend, half of all participants talked to him during the course of the experiment, whereas this form of conduct occurred only once when the learner was a stranger. At 150 volts, when the learner made his first serious protest and asked to be released from the experiment, nearly half of the participants talked to him when he was a friend, whereas none talked to him when he was a stranger, tending instead to turn questioningly to the experimenter. This propensity for participants to talk to the learner when he began seriously protesting was a salient feature of the bring-a-friend condition. For instance, at 150 volts, one person said to his friend, "Okay, its over, Doug," even though the experimenter was still prodding him to continue. Two (of the three) who obeyed the experimenter's orders fully talked to their friend in response to his protests. For example, one of these obedient participants, after saying, "sorry" several times to the friend who was crying out in pain, went on to say, "All right, there's not too many left here." The other fully obedient one who talked to his friend said, at 285 volts, "Only a few more, guy." Just after saying this he indicated to the experimenter that, "This guy is a good friend of mine." These few quotes illustrate a typical feature of participants' behavior when the learner was a friend—namely, they tended to identify with him when he was in pain. This kind of empathic or emotional *identification* is much deeper than the imitation of the experimenter described earlier. Its quality is well conveyed by one participant who, after twice exclaiming, "Ho! this is mean," in response to his friend's yells, said at 105 volts, "Oh boy! I got a feeling I'm going to be in there next."

The important finding here is that, when both the experimenter and the learner were strangers, participants tended to imitate the experimenter (half of them did so), and if they did imitate him, they also tended to obey his orders fully (all but one did so), thereby leaving the learner all by himself. In contrast, when the experimenter was a stranger and the learner a friend, participants tended to identify with their friend, talk to him, and resist the experimenter's orders, thus, allying themselves with the learner.

In their analysis of different types of social influence, Kelman and Hamilton (1989) make a useful distinction between *compliance* and *identification*. Following their distinction, a compliant participant is one who adopts the behavior induced by the experimenter in order to gain positive, or avoid negative, social consequences. In Milgram's experiments, adopting the behavior induced by the male experimenter could mean not only cooperating with him to complete the task, but actually imitating the authority's demeanor—in particular, the tendency to "talk over" the learner's protests. As already noted, this form of behavior was common when the learner was a stranger but was observed only once when the learner was a friend. According to Kelman and Hamilton (1989), "In identification, in contrast to compliance, the person is not primarily concerned with pleasing others, with giving them what they want, but is instead concerned with meeting the others' expectations for his own role performance" in order to actualize a desired self-identity (p. 106). When the learner was a friend, talking to him was one means that participants could use to actualize their role as a friend; another was to stop when their friend protested. As noted earlier, when the learner was a stranger, only one participant talked to him, and only about half stopped.

We consider it somewhat of an open, and very interesting, question as to whether participants' tendency to imitate the experimenter represented pure compliance or, instead, a mixture of compliance and identification. Did "talking over" the learner reflect their adherence to norms set forth by the experimenter, or did it reflect their efforts to experience the situation from the perspective of the experimenter—to model themselves after him in order to better carry out the enormously stressful task being demanded of them? There is no question that those who obeyed the experimenter were complying with his social expectations. It is less clear whether their tendency also to imitate him was merely an extension of this compliance or whether, instead, it entailed a broader effort to actualize the self-identity of a "good" participant, in a manner that went well beyond what was strictly required to complete the task.

In any event, the distinction between these two processes of social influence helps us to account for the difference in proportion of obedient participants in the two conditions. In the Bridgeport condition, they tended to comply and possibly to identify with the experimenter (in the superficial sense of *imitate*), but not to identify with him in the full emotional sense of the concept. Although the experimenter was an authority figure, he remained a stranger whom they had known for only a short time. In the bring-a-friend condition, participants tended to identify much more fully with the learner because they had a personal and often very close relationship with him that went well beyond the experiment. As one participant said to the experimenter when pressed to continue administering shocks, "Look, I have to face this guy. He's my neighbor. I can't go on with this." Thus, it certainly appears that obeying the experimenter's orders was related to the differing social conditions associated with each experimental condition, as Gold's hypothesis suggests.

Considering that all but one of the obedient participants in the Bridgeport (stranger) condition talked over the learner, and that only one of the obedient participants in the other condition did so, it is possible to go a step further and suggest that they tended to imitate and comply with the experimenter *only* when they did not identify with the learner. Can one then conclude that identification with the learner is a critical factor in inducing defiance of authority? If so, by what process does it have this effect?

To address these questions, we begin by noting that an earlier analysis of the unfolding interaction between experimenter and participant showed that the sooner in the course of the experiment a participant began to show notable resistance, the more likely he was to end up defiant (Modigliani & Rochat, 1995). When the learner was a friend, participants identified with him and, as we saw above, tended to begin resisting much earlier than when he was a stranger. Not only did they tend to respond more quickly to a friend's protests than to a stranger's, but they also tended to take these protests more seriously. As a consequence, they were prone to continue maintaining their reluctance to going on despite the experimenter's pressures to continue. What appeared to happen over the course of these confrontations was that the experimenter's authority was rather quickly eroded so that participants soon became less certain about the legitimacy of his commands.

Initially, participants trusted the experimenter because they perceived him as a competent authority who was formally in charge of the ongoing procedure. Consequently, they were quite willing to suspend their own personal judgment concerning the dangers of the task, allowing their behavior to be determined by the authority's instructions (Simon, 1966, pp. 125–128). The following quote from one of the very few obedient participants in the bring-a-friend condition conveys the essence of this mental set:

> I have learned that my training in the Army has also helped me in civilian life. I am still able to take orders and to do things, whether I like or dislike the job I am told to do.

However, the vast majority of participants in the bring-a-friend condition were not able to maintain this attitude. When the task called for them to continue administering electric shocks to a good friend who was yelling in pain, they understood that such a request was not legitimate and, therefore, that they did not have to obey. As one participant shouted at the experimenter just before breaking off, "That's my boy in there!" Evidently, this father could not imagine that it might be appropriate for him to go on with the task when his son was in pain—the experimenter's insistence that he continue seemed outrageous. The validity of the whole experiment became questionable, and most participants had little difficulty in breaking off. Because they identified with their friend's suffering, they could not leave it to the experimenter to decide their course of action. One participant who was told by the experimenter that "You must continue, you have no other choice," responded defiantly, "Why? What can you do to me?" Such a response makes it clear that, for him, the experimenter was no longer an authority figure, and that henceforth he intended to choose his course of action in accord with his own personal judgment.

On the other hand, when the learner was a stranger, participants experienced the situation as being much more difficult. They were being asked to treat the learner as a mere object of scientific research whose fate should be left to the professional judgment of the scientific investigator who was in charge of the ongoing procedure. One way to manage this highly stressful situation was to force themselves to follow the experimenter's instructions by imitating his attitude and behavior toward the learner—including "talking over" the learner's protests.

Forming Coalitions

Another way to appreciate the role that identification plays is to view the experimental situation as providing opportunities to form coalitions. As the procedure unfolded, participants in both conditions discovered that the desires of the learner and the intentions of the experimenter were inexorably in conflict and that they, themselves, would have to ally themselves with one or the other. Although virtually all of them found the required task highly distasteful, those who were in the condition that paired them with a stranger were far more prone to ally themselves with the authority figure. In a laboratory setting such an alliance may well have seemed appropriate, but in view of the stressful nature of the task, it may also have seemed a safer way to get through the situation. By holding aside their own judgment and allowing the experimenter to decide whether the learner's pain was sufficient to call a halt to the experiment, these participants were able to discharge their obligation to the authority (Simon, 1966, pp. 125–128). By imitating the experimenter when he "talked over" the learner, they adopted a model who could help them get through the difficult task facing them. As noted earlier, this form of imitation was a superficial form of identification—one that was very close to compliance. It was a direct consequence of having sided with the experimenter in response to the contradictory demands of the experimenter and the learner.

Participants in the condition that paired them with a friend tended overwhelmingly to resolve the conflict by allying themselves with the learner rather than with the experimenter. This, in turn, led them to see the experimenter's demands as illegitimate and to refuse to go on with the task. Because these participants identified with their friend and empathized with his pain, they were (predictably) upset by the experimenter's apparent lack of concern for him and, hence, equally unconcerned about spoiling the experimenter's research. Their identification with their friend was a far deeper phenomenon than mere imitation. It was anchored in a strong friendship: a long-term, reciprocal, sharing relationship which, for most of them, had lasted many years. Not surprisingly, the experimenter was unable to destroy such a relationship, or even to threaten it seriously, over the course of a single experimental session. Possible exceptions might be the three participants in this condition who were fully obedient. The experimenter's success in these cases may have been due to his ability to show these participants another way to minimize the learner's pain—a way that came close to dehumanization, namely, to view their friend as a mere object of the experimenter's ongoing scientific inquiry. (On the concept of dehumanization, see Kelman & Hamilton, 1989.) In the large majority of cases, however, the learner was protected from being dehumanized by the participants' strong identification with him, which served to insulate him against the cold and impersonal attitude being advocated by the experimenter.

Identification in Historical Contexts

In considering the overall social structure of these authority situations, it appears that imitating the experimenter and identifying with the learner are mutually exclusive. Because imitating someone is much less personal than emotionally identifying with them, this finding should come as no surprise; indeed, it helps to account for the fact that once Milgram imported personal relationships into the office of the "Research Associates of Bridgeport," the proportion of obedient participants dropped by a factor of three. It is helpful to take into account this finding when considering the question of how ordinary people responded to the persecutions launched by the Nazis during the Holocaust. Although we cannot undertake an analysis of the historical data, we would like to address this question briefly, because one of Milgram's primary purposes in designing his series of experiments on obedience was to contribute to an understanding of how the Holocaust happened.

If the findings presented above hold true beyond Milgram's laboratory, they might indeed help explain how ordinary people came to participate in the persecution of minorities during the Holocaust. As Helen Fein (1979) put it, "The life and liberties of minorities depend primarily upon whether the dominant group includes them within its universe of obligation" (p. 92). For a dominant community to include any minority within its universe of obligation means having some form of identification with that minority. Such an identification is difficult to establish or maintain when authority figures within the dominant community behave as if the minority were not entitled to be fully respected and actually encourage people to treat them negatively. Research on rescuers of Jews during the Holocaust (Fogelman, 1994; Rochat & Modigliani, 1995) seems to support the hypothesis that identification with the victims of the Nazis played a key role in moving rescuers to resist the authorities and protect the Jews from arrest and deportation. Here, as in the experiments, it seems that because of their identification with the victims, rescuers resisted the persecution process early and could quickly see through the authorities' propaganda. They understood, for example, that talk of "resettling the Jews in Poland" really amounted to sending them to their deaths.

The question of how ordinary people can do horrendous things to their fellow human beings was raised anew by Daniel Goldhagen (1996), who argued that the real cause of the Holocaust was the extensive and virulent nature of German anti-Semitism. He explained that 19th-century German anti-Semitism was exactly what the Nazis needed and used to achieve their goals. Without it, they would not have been able to induce so many Germans to take part, one way or another, in the persecution of the Jews. So, according to Goldhagen, obedience to authority was not a key factor in explaining ordinary Germans' propensity to go along with Nazi policies, including the wholesale murder of Jews. Rather, these ordinary people were the willing executioners of the Holocaust.

The findings presented earlier are not so much a refutation of Goldhagen's thesis as an illustration of how social psychology can contribute to the analysis of perpetrators in the Holocaust by showing, for instance, that a lack of identification with the victims can explain how large numbers of ordinary Germans began to imitate their authorities and gradually came to take part in the persecutions initiated and organized by the Third Reich. Given the hardships of the 1930s in Germany, many ordinary people followed their authorities as a way of getting through the difficult times and in the hope that it would lead to better times. In this context, anti-Semitism was a contributing factor to the Holocaust in that people were unable or unwilling to identify with the Jews when the Nazis began to persecute them, but it is highly unlikely that anti-Semitism was their main motive for cooperating with the persecutory program of the Nazis.

Conclusion

Identification may come in a variety of forms and strengths ranging from surface patterns of imitation that can help people find their way through a temporary stressful situation, to deep emotional bonds that link a parent and child throughout their lives. When identification is sufficiently strong, it can serve as a powerful barrier against the inhumane commands of malevolent authorities. We live in a world where recurrent episodes of genocide are all too common—where the authority figures of a dominant group can give the order to round up and exterminate members of minority groups. As long as majority group members do not identify with these minorities, such orders are all too likely to be carried out with impunity. The minorities will simply be dehumanized. Helen Fein's (1977) central concept of a "universe of obligation" refers precisely to those who cannot be dehumanized—those with whom we identify sufficiently to treat as equals. They are the people who "must be taken into account, to whom obligations are due, by whom we can be held responsible for our actions" (p. 7). Not all such persons can be called *friends* in the same close sense that applied to the pairs of individuals who visited Milgram's laboratory in Bridgeport, but such bonds of obligation can certainly be strong enough to undercut the smooth, impersonal functioning of authority hierarchies bent on destruction. A day may come when the universe of obligation of dominant groups includes all of humankind.

13

Conclusion

In this last chapter, I return to my starting point. I review the model of the discipline that I have offered to see how it helps to integrate social psychology and locate it among the social sciences. I suggest what, from the standpoint of the model, seems to me to be some of the most important and interesting theoretical and empirical cutting edges in contemporary social psychology.

The Scope and Function of Social Psychology

No one can impose a consensus on social psychology, of course. However, I hope I have persuaded readers that the model of the discipline is useful and indeed encompasses most of what social psychology has been about since its beginnings some 80 years ago.

My definition of *social psychology* is brief and simple, but it has required this whole book to flesh it out. I have proposed that social psychology is the study of the reciprocal influence of the person and the social environment. I have tried to be precise about the psychological nature of the "person," the meaning of "social," and the forms of the social as environment, precise enough, that is, even to reveal the fuzziness of some of the distinctions.

In defining the social environment, I have made three important stipulations: (a) that the social environment is distinctively human; (b) that it is useful to conceive of it both as a construct that exists independent of the individuals that jointly construct and inhabit it and as a construal of each individual; and (c) that it is usefully analyzed into three components which, although they are commonly social, are qualitatively different from one another and have different relationships to individuals.

What makes the social environment particularly human, in this view, is that it is composed of relationships that require the capacity to communicate with symbols. This capacity is so much greater in humans than in other beings that humans must be considered qualitatively different. This approach to the social environment does not demarcate it absolutely from the physical and internal milieux. From an objective perspective, even humans are social and physical at the same time; and when we stand in someone's way, it is hard to tell which is our most determinative characteristic. From a subjective perspective, people sometimes confuse their social with their physical and internal environments, when for example they plead to a balky car motor or attribute a willful malevolence to an ailing stomach. There is nevertheless enough clarity in this delineation of the social to distinguish social psychology from other branches of psychology, and by its focus on the person to distinguish social psychology from other social sciences. The model takes the discipline significantly further than the point at which Roger Brown (see p. 43) found the discipline in 1965.

This conception of social psychology sharpens its theory and makes its findings less ambiguous. If one takes it seriously, then one is prompted first to consider whether a substantive problem is a social psychological one or not.

This is important because it has direct implications for the utility of open or closed theory and for how variables are conceptualized and measured. To test whether a problem is social psychological, I suggest that one try to analyze it in terms of the model by sorting its variables into the model's levels of analysis. I have tried to document that applying this strategy to what purports to be the social psychological literature reveals that some of it is not social psychological at all, as social psychology is conceived here. Frequently the hypothesized determinants of psychological effects include no social conditions but are, rather, physical stimuli or, even more often, exclusively other psychological conditions. Many supposedly social psychological investigations of social change consider no psychological variables at all but only social conditions. Of course, these works should not be abandoned, but it should be recognized that they are not social psychological, and social psychological theory and methods are not useful to them.

The model of social psychology includes a great deal of what self-identified social psychologists have been thinking and doing. I take this to be an advantage. It indicates that the model is not eccentric. I have drawn abundantly on the social psychological literature to illustrate, clarify, and argue for the model.

It is particularly notable that three major psychological theories find their place in the model. Social learning theory is invoked to describe the process of socialization, the psychoanalytic concept of identification is posited to mediate the influence of interpersonal relations, and a purposive cognitive psychology elucidates the persuasiveness of culture. In this respect, the model rests on established foundations. However, it is not haphazardly eclectic. The model recognizes that each of these theories covers a differentiated kind of social relationship and represents each kind as the boundary condition between the person and the particular sector of his or her social environment that satisfies the theory's conditions.

A Basic Social Psychological Vocabulary

According to the model of social psychology, its content is drawn from psychology, social anthropology, sociology, and interpersonal relations. The model identifies a limited set of prismatic concepts, or units of analysis, at each level of analysis. These concepts serve theoretically to marshall all the relevant aspects of their respective levels to the point of interaction with the other levels. They constitute the basic vocabulary of social psychology.

The psychological content of social psychology—at the personal level of analysis—consists of individuals' motives and resources. The literature on each of these is rich in structural and substantive dimensions, as is the literature on their organization. These are conceptualized in terms of Lewinian field theory: life space, forces, valences, regions, and paths.

The unit of analysis of interpersonal relations is identity, the organization of each of the partner's more enduring motives and resources that is recognized by each of them. Partners' identities are conceptualized in terms of their relationships, being in various ways similar and complementary. The scientific literature on interpersonal relations has a sparse common vocabulary at this time, but the scientific discipline is growing and its culture is forming. Its potential invites social psychological investigation, and I discuss some of its problems at the cutting edge of social psychology later.

At the social organizational level, social role is the fundamental concept. The substance of roles—normative obligations and privileges —is rendered more useful for social psychological purposes when it is conceived in terms of the motives and resources that the roles prescribe. A rich vocabulary has developed to conceptualize social organization, with concepts such as *functional interdependence*, *hierarchy*, and *power*; the structural relationships among roles are described, for example, as formal and informal.

Beliefs, roughly classified into ideology and technology, constitute the stuff of culture. Here, too, social psychological work is facilitated by conceiving of the substance of beliefs in terms of motives and resources: The values that individuals hold are their governing goals, and they are derived from and may alter the ideology of their culture. Technology consists of the reputed facts about the means, or resources, necessary to realize the values from which individuals derive their notions of reality.

The model also specifies certain dynamic processes by which individuals and their social environments exert reciprocal influence. The boundary between individuals and their interpersonal relations is bridged by *identification* of one partner with another. The influence of individuals and social organizations over one another is exerted through reciprocal processes of socialization and institutionalization. The interaction of individuals and culture is through persuasion and invention. The vocabulary for these dynamics are provided by three bodies of broad theory that are useful here: psychoanalytic theory, particularly pertaining to interpersonal relations and identification; social learning theory for socialization and institutionalization; and cognitive social psychology for persuasion and invention.

These concepts compose a basic vocabulary of social psychology. Introductory textbooks might be organized around them, and the concepts would appear prominently in the tables of contents. They might be used to organize broad scholarly reviews of social psychological theory and research on specific topics. They can also fill out and organize the variables of empirical research. For all kinds of social psychological work, the model maps the domain, integrates its parts, and generates hypotheses. It even facilitates the consideration of salient factors outside of social psychology, at the boundaries to environments physical and internal, foreign to the social psychological domain.

Theoretical Strategy in Social Psychology

Its focus on the translation of events between the psychological and social levels of analysis makes social psychology a boundary science. It is not therefore altogether phenomenological. It is social as well as psychological, which means that it takes into account the pre-perceptual, objective social environment as well as the post-perceptual situation of the person. By thus maintaining the independent status of social reality, this social psychology rises above the moment just prior to action and experience to get a broader view of the probabilities in the immediate and more distant future.

When addressing problems that span several levels within its domain, the discipline often contributes more by addressing the problem a piece at a time. Analysis often must precede synthesis. Understanding the causal conditions at each of the relevant social psychological boundaries must often precede understanding and doing something about their complex interaction.

That social psychology is a boundary science has specific implications for its theoretical and methodological strategies. The levels of analysis approach, supplemented by ideal typical, reductionist, and metalanguage strategies, suggests a particular sequence to the analysis of a social psychological problem. Take the usual case of the effects of the social environment on the person. The analysis calls first for the precise assignment of variables to their appropriate levels. (It is at this point that one may discover that the problem is not a social psychological one at all, that the variables are not both social and psychological.) Once having conceptualized the problem in its psychological terms, the causal factors are sorted into levels of the social environment. This often requires disentangling a knot of social circumstances, in order to isolate hypothetically critical conditions and make them more manageable in theory and research. Here the idealization strategy is useful. One ignores for the moment the fact that real social situations ordinarily are a social fabric woven from the threads of interpersonal, social organizational, and cultural relationships. The various conditions are compared with the ideal social relationships defined in the model and placed at their most appropriate levels with the reservation of "as if . . .": Whatever personal attachments are believed to be operating are treated as if they were ideal interpersonal relations; obligations and privileges are organized into discriminable roles as if they exerted influence insulated from relationships outside their social organization; and beliefs are treated as a self-contained culture which, if influential at all, must be persuasive in its own right.

Then one synthesizes the various elements. The influence of each of the various social relationships needs to be weighted, both their direct influence on the person and their indirect influence on one another. For this purpose, one considers such variables as the strengths of the interpersonal relations, the flexibility permitted by the roles, and the centrality of the pertinent beliefs to the wider culture. Translation and reductionism are necessary at this point; although an objective assessment of the social environment is necessary, it is critical to determine how all this appears to the individual. Objective conditions, if properly assessed, indicate what will probably be the subjective condition at some time hence. Assessment of the subjective conditions—most usefully, I think, in terms of life space—produces the adequate contemporary diagnosis that explains the individual's action and experience at a point in time.

Social psychological work proceeds then with the strategy of integration through metalanguage to find the most likely points of interpenetration of the psychological and social systems. The effective bridging concepts are usually just those whose status as either psychological or social is most fuzzy.

The theoretical strategy just described is of course an idealized outline. Actually, one must usually cycle through defining and conceptualizing, sorting variables into their social psychology levels, and analyzing and synthesizing the dynamic influence processes.

Cutting Edges

This model of social psychology has the advantage of trading general methodological problems that have beset contemporary social psychology for more constructive specific and substantive ones. The model identifies interesting and largely unexamined questions about the reciprocal effects of the psychological and social. Here are some of the problems that I believe merit immediate attention.

The interpersonal level of the social environment is the one now least well recognized. Only recently in the brief history of social psychology have theory and research attempted to delineate it, describe and explain its dynamics, and relate it to the psychological level (Canary, Cupach, & Messman, 1995; Duck, 1992; Shulman, 1995). The dynamic process of identification, which I hypothesize links the interpersonal with the psychological, has been neglected in social psychology, particularly in comparison to the attention given to the dynamics of socialization and persuasion. This, it seems to me, is one of the most promising cutting edges for social psychological theory and research.

It is understandable that interpersonal relations has received so little attention, because its study presents considerable methodological problems. Relatively pure interpersonal relationships are rarely found in nature, and it is difficult to control interpersonality experimentally. However, the model's conceptualization of the interpersonal suggests how some of these problems may be surmounted. It has identified extant social psychological studies that point the way (see chapters 5 and 8). Established strong-enough interpersonal relations can be imported into experimental designs. Moreover, because it appears that even a small degree of ephemeral interpersonality has detectable psychological effects, strong-enough interpersonality can be created experimentally.

With the methods available, social psychology can test the hypothesis, up to now only sparsely supported, that interpersonal conditions give rise to the process of identification. To begin with, the studies into which established interpersonal relations have been imported should be brought under tighter control by replication with experimentally created interpersonality; and experiments that have created interpersonality should be replicated by importing stronger interpersonal relations that are already established. In the course of this research, measures of identification should be taken to determine whether it occurs more frequently and strongly under interpersonal conditions, and to test whether identification is the critical mediator of social influence under interpersonal conditions.

A critical question of personality comes into focus at the social psychological interface. "Personality" is not one of the basic terms in the social psychology of the model. It is defined rather as that subset of motives and resources that endure. The critical question is, What are the conditions under which organizations of motives and resources endure? It amazes me that personality psychology has focused so little on this question.

There is general consensus that the social, however variously defined, affects personality formation, maintenance, and change. (Indeed, this consensus has been institutionalized in professional journals devoted jointly to both personality and social psychology.) It is likely that social conditions contribute to the enduring quality of individual characteristics, that is, to the establishment of personality. Longitudinal studies (e.g., Kagan & Moss, 1962) point to stable roles in the social organizational environment as one such social condition.

Social conditions probably affect enduringness, and it is likely that they do so in combination with developmental factors, which may be biological or cognitive. There probably are critical periods in the life span when specific social conditions contribute more heavily to the crystallization of personality than at other periods. Hypothetical specifications of these social conditions and of the developmental status of the person in the terms of the model would have to be tested with longitudinal research.

The expense and patience required for longitudinal research have discouraged investigations into enduringness, even though this is the core question for personality psychology. The potential of the model of social psychology to generate interesting and plausible hypotheses might enhance the probability of payoffs enough to make longitudinal studies more attractive. These studies might profitably follow Levinson's suggestion (1964) to use ego analytic theory, in order to specify the conditions that create personality. Erikson's bipolar psychosocial crises—trust versus basic mistrust, autonomy versus shame and doubt, and so on—might be considered basic psychological traits, described in the terms of the model as certain patterns of motives and resources. Which patterns endure might be attributed hypothetically to the resolution of each crisis at its critical moment in the life span, the adequacy and nature of the resolution shaped by the social conditions of interpersonal relations, social organization, and culture in the proximal environment of the individual at that time. For example, the relevant culture of an infant's caregivers consists of the ideology about children and their nurturance to which caregivers subscribe and the technology at their command that provide the level and kind of care that more or less fixes the infant as more or less trusting. The infant's interpersonal and social organizational environments and their combinations would also be assessed.

Another set of potentially fruitful questions for social psychology has to do with combinations of social conditions across levels of analysis. These are questions that have to be addressed in the synthetic stage of adequate contemporary diagnosis of the situation. Individuals rarely encounter a social environment in its ideal state; certainly culture and social organization are almost omnipresent, and effective if weak interpersonal relations may also exist. It is likely that conditions in any one of these environments have different effects on the individual, depending on the conditions in the others.

The combination of interpersonal relations and social organization is an interesting and familiar case in point. The model indicates that these relations are in important respects mutually exclusive. Their combination in a concrete social situation therefore creates social and psychological tensions that demand resolution. How great the tension and the nature of possible resolutions are hypothetically determined by conditions at the psychological, interpersonal, and social organization levels. For example: How much interpersonal egalitarianism is permitted by the social organization? How much exclusive loyalty does the social organization prescribe? Are the personalities that the interpersonal relation permits its partners to actualize consistent also with the requirements of the roles they play?

One more cutting edge issue for social psychological attention: Under what conditions do individuals significantly shape culture? Put in the terms of the model, what are the conditions for effective invention? The model indicates that this question should be approached with a contemporary diagnosis of the psychological, interpersonal, social organizational, and cultural levels of analysis. The way the question is put—as the extraordinary phenomenon of a person affecting his or her culture—locates the person in the unusual position of an environmental condition of cultural change, the phenomenon to be explained. The question asks: What motives and resources of the person, in combination with his or her interpersonal relations, roles in the prevailing social organization, and the state of the culture will more or less probably alter the culture?

A few plausible hypotheses may be derived from the extant literature. Moscovici and Lage (1976) and Moscovici et al. (1969) suggested that the persistence of a minority (in this case, a minority of one) is an important source of its credibility. Erikson (1958, 1969) proposed that the persistence of radical inventors, in the face of powerful, perhaps dangerous opposition, is facilitated by the support of their interpersonal relations. Mutual commitment with at least one other person enables a potential mover and shaker to persist. Insofar as discipleships approach interpersonality (they are not close friendships), they may provide a degree of such support. Thus, it may be hypothesized that individuals are more likely to affect their cultures significantly to the degree that they participate in interpersonal relations. Corollaries to this hypothesis are hypotheses having to do with the personal capacity of individuals to establish interpersonal relations, social organizational factors affecting the availability of such relationships, and so on.

Another set of hypotheses about the effects of individuals on culture involves the social organizational location of the individuals. If, as the model hypothesizes, persuasion is the model for the dynamic process of invention, then the credibility of the individual's beliefs is a key factor in their acceptance. Credibility can be established by the role occupied by the inventor. If the role he or she occupies testifies to his or her expertise, then his or her invention is more likely to be adopted.

There seem to be major obstacles to testing hypotheses about the conditions under which individuals significantly affect culture. The phenomenon is rare; the sufficient combinations of personal and social conditions seldom occur in nature. Social science has perhaps to content itself with nonexperimental analyses of extremely small samples. The methods of history seem most useful but not altogether satisfactory.

However, the model offers a way to investigate invention experimentally. One must grant the contention that a small group can have a culture governed by principles similar enough to those governing the cultures of peoples to stand in for the wider cultures. If this is true, then small group cultures can be imported and created, and the groups can be populated with members with systematically controlled personal properties, interpersonal relations, social roles, and inventions to offer.

The Nature of Social Psychological Science

The characteristic of a social psychological analysis, that it must in its distinctively social psychological phase use probabilistic statements, seems to be the basis of the challenge to the status of social psychology as science. If one grants that science is at least in part defined by the aim to discover the universal principles that govern reality, then an open theoretical social psychology is indeed in that respect unscientific. Where it makes an assertion in the form of the clause "if [social conditions] . . . then [psychological consequences]" or vice versa, the social psychological clause may be an adequate contemporary diagnosis, but it does not nevertheless lead logically to universal principles governing social psychological relationships. Social psychological principles are rather statements about the likelihood of relationships between events that have no definitional or axiomatic connection.

Thoughtful theoretical and empirical efforts in social psychology should generate valid statements about relationships between social and psychological events, in the sense that they should explain unambiguously and predict consistently. Nevertheless, however clear and reliable they are, social psychological statements cannot be claimed universal in a theoretical sense. Social psychology's status as a science must rest mainly then on its theoretical insights and its empirical methods rather than on its theoretical elegance.

This is a consequence of social psychology being a boundary science, insisting on independent constructs of both the psychological person and the social environment. If this separation is useful and its points of interpenetration consequential, then it merits scientific inquiry. This calling is appealing to me, even though it limits the construction of elegant theory, with its primitive definitions, axioms, and logical chains.

Because the discipline recognizes the reality of the social environment, where efforts at social change must ultimately be made, it has the potential to contribute to the solution of the many social problems that have important psychological components. Practical social problems even more often than theoretical ones span the boundaries of the several levels of analysis. Although an important function of social psychology is to try to find solutions to social problems, it is not equally useful for all social problems. The domain of social psychology is limited to those problems and those facets of problems that involve the psychological as well as the social levels of analysis. Social psychology has, at most, psychological insights to offer to problems within and between other levels, such as the effects of technological change on the institution of the family.

Perhaps someday a masterful philosopher of science will invent a way to construct closed theory at the boundaries. Meanwhile, I remain enthusiastic about social psychology. The discipline encompasses social science. This book merely samples its domain. It serves up puzzles of apparently distant but somehow related phenomena whose links we are challenged to discover. In addition to the opportunity for the pleasures of discovery, social psychology also may enable us to do something about the social and the psychological when their encounters seem to us to be not coming out right.

References

Abelson, R. P. (1981). The psychological status of the script concept. *American Psychologist,* *36,* 715–729.

Adelson, J., Green, B., & O'Neil, R. (1969). Growth of the idea of law in adolescence. *Developmental Psychology, 1,* 327–332.

Ajzen, I. (1987). Attitudes, traits, and actions: Dispositional prediction of behavior in personality and social psychology. In L. Berkowitz (Ed.), *Advances in experimental social psychology* (Vol. 20, pp. 1–63). New York: Academic Press.

Alexander, C. N., & Knight, G. (1971). Situated identities and social psychological experimentation. *Sociometry, 34,* 65–82.

Allen, V. L., & Levine, J. M. (1968). Social support, dissent, and conformity. *Sociometry, 31,* 138–149.

Allen, V. L., & Levine, J. M. (1971). Social support and conformity: The role of independent assessment of reality. *Journal of Experimental Social Psychology, 7,* 48–50.

Allport, F. H. (1924). *Social psychology.* Boston: Houghton Mifflin.

Allport, G. W. (1935). Attitudes. In C. Murchison (Ed.), *The handbook of social psychology* (pp. 798–844). Worcester, MA: Clark University Press.

Allport, G. W. (1954). The historical background of modern social psychology. In G. Lindzey (Ed.), *Handbook of social psychology* (Vol. 1, pp. 3–56). Cambridge, MA: Addison-Wesley.

American Psychological Association. (1977, June). *Guidelines for nonsexist language in APA journals.* Washington, DC: Author. (Available from the American Psychological Association, Publications Office, 750 First Street, NE, Washington, DC 20002-4242)

Aronfreed, J. (1964). The origin of self-criticism. *Psychological Review, 71,* 193–218.

Aronson, E., & Cope, V. (1968). My enemy's enemy is my friend. *Journal of Personality and Social Psychology, 8,* 8–12.

Aronson, E., & Worchel, P. (1966). Similarity vs. liking as determinants of interpersonal attractiveness. *Psychonomic Science, 5,* 157–158.

Asch, S. E. (1955). Opinions and social pressure. *Scientific American, 193,* 31–35.

Asch, S. E. (1956). Studies of independence and conformity: A minority of one against a unanimous majority. *Psychological Monographs, 70*(9, Whole No. 416).

Atkinson, J. W. (1957). Motivational determinants of risk-taking behavior. *Psychological Review, 64,* 359–372.

Atkinson, J. W., & Birch, D. (1970). *The dynamics of action.* New York: Wiley.

Atkinson, J. W., & Birch, D. (1978). *Introduction to motivation* (2nd ed.). New York: Van Nostrand Reinhold.

BacaZinn, M., & Eitzen, S. (1993). *Diversity in families* (3rd ed.). New York: Harper Collins.

Back, K. W. (1951). Influences through social communication. *Journal of Abnormal and Social Psychology, 46,* 9–23.

Back, K. W. (1992). This business of topology. *Journal of Social Issues, 48,* 51–66.

Backman, C. W., & Secord, P. F. (1959). The effect of perceived liking on interpersonal attraction. *Human Relations, 12,* 379–384.

Baldwin, A. L. (1962). *Behavior and development in childhood.* New York: Holt, Rinehart & Winston.

Bales, R. F. (1950). *Interaction process analysis.* Reading, MA: Addison-Wesley.

Bales, R. F., & Slater, P. (1955). Role differentiation in small decision-making groups. In T. Parsons & R. F. Bales (Eds.), *Family, socialization, and interaction process* (pp. 259–306). New York: Free Press.

Bandura, A. (1969). Social-learning theory of identificatory processes. In D. A. Goslin (Ed.), *Handbook of socialization theory and research* (pp. 213–262). Chicago: Rand McNally.

Bandura, A. (1973). *Aggression: A social learning analysis.* Englewood Cliffs, NJ: Prentice-Hall.

Bandura, A. (1977). *Social learning theory.* Englewood Cliffs, NJ: Prentice-Hall.

Bandura, A., Ross, D., & Ross, S. A. (1961). Transmission of aggression through imitation of aggressive models. *Journal of Abnormal and Social Psychology, 63,* 575–582.

Bandura, A., Ross, D., & Ross, S. A. (1963). Imitation of film-mediated aggressive models. *Journal of Abnormal and Social Psychology, 63,* 3–11.

Barker, R. G., & Wright, H. F. (1949). Psychological ecology and the problem of psychosocial development. *Child Development, 20*, 131–144.

Barker-Benfield, T. (1976). *The horrors of the half known life: Male attitudes toward women and sexuality in nineteenth century America.* New York: Harper & Row.

Bates, A. P., & Babchuk, N. (1961). The primary group: A reappraisal. *Sociological Quarterly, 2*, 181–191.

Baumgardner, S. R. (1976). Critical history and social psychology's "crisis." *Personality and Social Psychology Bulletin, 2*, 460–465.

Bavelas, A. (1950). Communication patterns in task-oriented groups. *Journal of the Acoustical Society of America, 22*, 725–730.

Belenky, M., Clinchy, B. M., Goldberger, N. R., & Tarule, J. M. (1986). *Women's ways of knowing: Development of self, voice, and mind.* New York: Basic Books.

Bem, D. J., & Allen, A. (1974). Predicting some of the people some of the time: The search for cross-situational consistencies in behavior. *Psychological Review, 81*, 506–520.

Berkowitz, L., & Rogers, K. H. (1986). A priming effect analysis of media influences. In J. Bryant & D. Zillman (Eds.), *Perspectives on media effects* (pp. 57–81). Hillsdale, NJ: Erlbaum.

Bernard, C. (1927). *An introduction to the study of experimental medicine* (H. C. Greene, Trans.). New York: Macmillan. (Original work published 1865)

Bernard, J. (1981, November). *Women and work.* Presentation to the Wingspread Conference on women and work, Racine, WI.

Bettelheim, B. (1960). *The informed heart.* Glencoe, IL: Free Press.

Bigelow, B. J., & LaGaipa, J. J. (1975). Children's written descriptions of friendship: A multidimensional analysis. *Developmental Psychology, 11*, 857–858.

Blau, P. M. (1970). Comment [on Homans, 1970a]. In R. Borger & F. Cioffi (Eds.), *Explanation in the behavioral sciences* (pp. 329–339). Cambridge, England: Cambridge University Press.

Blau, P. M., & Scott, W. R. (1962). *Formal organizations.* San Francisco, CA: Chandler.

Blauner, R. (1964). *Alienation and freedom: The factory worker and his industry.* Chicago: University of Chicago Press.

Block, J. (1977). Advancing the psychology of personality: Paradigmatic shift or improving the quality of research? In D. Magnusson & N. S. Elder (Eds.), *Personality at the crossroads: Current issues in international psychology* (pp. 37–63). New York: Wiley.

Bohannon, J. H., III, & Warren-Leubecker, A. (1989). Theoretical approaches to language acquisition. In J. Beroko Gleason (Ed.), *The development of language* (pp. 167–223). Columbus, OH: Merrill.

Bohner, G., Crow, K., Erb, H.-P., & Schwarz, N. (1992). Affect and persuasion: Mood effects on the processing of message content and context cues and on subsequent behavior. *European Journal of Social Psychology, 22*, 511–530.

Bordin, E. S., Nachman, B., & Segal, S. J. (1963). An articulated framework for vocational development. *Journal of Counseling Psychology, 10*, 107–116.

Brehm, J. W. (1966). *A theory of psychological reactance.* New York: Academic Press.

Brehm, J. W., & Mann, M. (1975). Effect of importance of freedom and attraction to group members on influence produced by group pressure. *Journal of Personality and Social Psychology, 31*, 816–824.

Brenner, M. W. (1973). The next-in-line effect. *Journal of Verbal Learning and Verbal Behavior, 12*, 320–323.

Brenner, M. W. (1977). Memory and interpersonal relations. *Dissertation Abstracts International, 37*(10-B), 5430.

Brim, O. G., Jr. (1960). Personality development as role learning. In I. Iscoe & H. W. Stevenson (Eds.), *Personality development in children* (pp. 127–159). Austin: University of Texas Press.

Brock, T. C., & Becker, L. A. (1965). Ineffectiveness of "overheard counterpropaganda." *Journal of Personality and Social Psychology, 2*, 654–660.

Broverman, I. K. M., Broverman, D. M., Clarkson, F. E., Rosenkrantz, P. S., & Vogel, S. R. (1970). Sex role stereotypes and clinical judgments of mental health. *Journal of Clinical and Consulting Psychology, 34*(1), 1–7.

Brown, R. (1965). *Social psychology.* New York: Free Press.

Buber, M. (1957). *Pointing the way: Collected essays.* London: Routledge & Kegan Paul.

Burgess, A. (1963). *A clockwork orange*. New York: Norton.

Burnstein, E., & Vinokur, A. (1975). What a person thinks upon learning he has chosen differently from others. *Journal of Experimental Social Psychology, 11*, 412–426.

Burnstein, E., & Vinokur, A. (1977). Persuasive argumentation and social comparison as determinants of attitude polarization. *Journal of Experimental Social Psychology, 13*, 315–332.

Burnstein, E., Vinokur, A., & Pichevin, M. F. (1974). What do differences between own, admired, and attributed choices have to do with group-induced shift in choices? *Journal of Experimental Social Psychology, 10*, 428–443.

Burnstein, E., Vinokur, A., & Trope, Y. (1973). Interpersonal comparison versus persuasive argumentation: A more direct test of alternative explanations for the group induced shifts in individual choice. *Journal of Experimental Social Psychology, 9*, 236–245.

Buss, D. M. (1990). Evolutionary social psychology: Prospects and pitfalls. *Motivation and Emotion, 14*, 265–286.

Campbell, D. T. (1975). On the conflicts between biological and social evolution and between psychology and moral tradition. *American Psychologist, 30*, 1103–1126.

Canary, D. J., Cupach, W. R., & Messman, S. S. (1955). *Relationship conflict: Conflict in parent–child, friendship, and romantic relationships*. Thousand Oaks, CA: Sage Publications.

Cantril, H. (1940). *The invasion from Mars*. Princeton, NJ: Princeton University Press.

Caplan, P. (1981). *Barriers between women*. New York: SP Medical and Scientific Books.

Carkhuff, R. R. (1969). *Helping and human relations: A primer for lay and professional helpers*. New York: Holt, Rinehart & Winston.

Carroll, J. B., & Casagrande, J. B. (1958). The function of language classifications in behavior. In E. Maccoby, T. M. Newcomb, & E. L. Hartley (Eds.), *Readings in social psychology* (3rd ed., pp. 18–31). New York: Holt.

Cartwright, D., & Zander, A. (Eds.). (1953). *Group dynamics: Research and theory* (1st ed.). Evanston, IL: Row, Peterson.

Cartwright, D., & Zander, A. (Eds.). (1960). *Group dynamics: Research and theory* (2nd ed.). Evanston, IL: Row, Peterson.

Cartwright, D., & Zander, A. (Eds.). (1968). *Group dynamics: Research and theory* (3rd ed.). New York: Harper & Row.

Cary, E. L. (1899). *Browning: Poet and man*. New York: G. P. Putnam.

Cerha, J. (1967). *Selective mass communication*. Stockholm: P A Norstadt & Sons.

Chodorow, N. T. (1978). *Reproduction of mothering: Psychoanalysis and the sociology of gender*. Berkeley: University of California Press.

Chomsky, N. (1972). *Language and mind*. New York: Harcourt Brace Jovanovich.

Cialdini, R., Petty, R. E., & Cacioppo, J. T. (1981). Attitude and attitude change. *Annual Review of Psychology, 32*, 357–404.

Clark, M. S. (1984). Record keeping in two types of relationships. *Journal of Personality and Social Psychology, 47*, 549–557.

Clark-Stewart, K. A. (1973). Interactions between mothers and their young children: Characteristics and consequences. *Monographs of the Society for Research in Child Development, 38*(6–7, Serial No. 153).

Cohen, A. K. (1955). *Delinquent boys: The culture of the gang*. Glencoe, IL: Free Press.

Collins, N. L., & Miller, L. C. (1995). Self-disclosure and liking: A meta-analytic review. *Psychological Bulletin, 116*, 457–475.

Cooley, C. H. (1909). *Social organization: A study of the larger mind*. New York: Scribner.

Cooley, C. H. (1922). *Human nature and the social order*. New York: Scribner.

Cooley, C. H., Angell, R. C., & Carr, L. J. (1933). *Introductory sociology*. New York: Scribner.

Coser, L. A. (1974). *Greedy institutions: Patterns of undivided commitment*. New York: Free Press.

Cott, N. F. (1977). *Bonds of womanhood: "Woman's sphere" in New England, 1780–1835*. New Haven: Yale University Press.

Craik, K. J. W. (1952). *The nature of explanation*. Cambridge, England: Cambridge University Press.

Crano, W. D. (1989). Whatever became of Kurt Lewin? Reactions to Nuttin's quasi-social analysis of social behavior. *European Journal of Social Psychology, 19*, 385–388.

Cucchiari, S. (1981). The gender revolution and the transition from bisexual horde to pat-rilocal band: The origins of gender hierarchy. In S. B. Ortner & H. Whitehead (Eds.), *Sexual meanings: The cultural construction of gender and sexuality* (pp. 31–79). New York: Cambridge University Press.

Curry, T. J., & Emerson, R. M. (1970). Balance theory: A theory of interpersonal attraction? *Sociometry, 33,* 216–238.

Curtis, R. C., & Miller, K. (1986). Believing another likes or dislikes you: Behaviors making the beliefs come true. *Journal of Personality and Social Psychology, 51,* 284–290.

Cushman, D. P., & Craig, R. T. (1976). Communication systems: Interpersonal implications. In G. R. Miller (Ed.), *Explorations in interpersonal communication* (pp. 37–58). Beverly Hills, CA: Sage.

Czander, W. M. (1993). *The psychodynamics of work and organizations.* New York: Guilford Press.

Danner, F. W., & Day, M. C. (1977). Eliciting formal operations. *Child Development, 48,* 1600–1606.

Darwin, C. (1958). *The origin of species.* New York: Dutton. (Original work published 1859)

Davis, N. Z. (1975). *Society and culture in early modern France.* Palo Alto, CA: Stanford University Press.

Derlega, V. J. (Ed.). (1984). *Communication, intimacy, and close relationships.* Orlando, FL: Academic Press.

Derlega, V. J., & Winstead, B. A. (1986). *Friendship and social interaction.* New York: Springer-Verlag.

Destutt de Tracy, A. C. L. (1801). *Projet d'elements d'ideologie: A l'usage des ecoles centrales de la Republique Francaise* (Toward principles of ideology: On the function of the central schools of the French republic). Paris: P. Dodot.

Deutsch, K. (1963). *The nerves of government: Models of political communication and control.* London: Free Press of Glencoe.

Deutsch, M. (1973). *The resolution of conflict: Constructive and destructive processes.* New Haven, CT: Yale University Press.

Deutsch, M., & Gerard, H. B. (1955). A study of normative and informational social influences upon individual judgement. *Journal of Abnormal and Social Psychology, 51,* 629–636.

Dindia, K., & Allen, M. (1992). Sex differences in self-disclosure: A meta-analysis. *Psychological Bulletin, 112,* 106–124.

Dion, K. L., & Dion, K. K. (1979). Personality and behavioral correlates of romantic love. In M. Cook & G. Wilson (Eds.), *Love and attraction* (pp. 213–220). New York: Pergamon Press.

DiRenzo, G. J. (1977). Socialization, personality, and social systems. *Annual Review of Sociology, 3,* 261–295.

Doise, W. (1986). *Levels of explanation in social psychology* (E. Mapstone, Trans.). Cambridge, England: Cambridge University Press. (Original work published 1982)

Doms, M., & Van Avermaet, E. (1980). Majority influence, minority influence and conversation behavior: A replication. *Journal of Experimental Social Psychology, 16,* 283–292.

Douglas, J. D., & Wong, A. C. (1977). Formal operations: Age and sex differences in Chinese and American children. *Child Development, 48,* 689–692.

Douvan, E. (1974). Commitment and social contract in adolescence. *Psychiatry, 37,* 22–36.

Douvan, E. (1977). Interpersonal relationships: Some questions and observations. In G. Levinger & H. L. Raush (Eds.), *Close relationships* (pp. 17–32). Amherst: University of Massachusetts Press.

Dubin, R. (1969). *Theory building.* New York: Free Press.

Duck, S. W. (1979). *Theory and practice in interpersonal attraction.* New York: Academic Press.

Duck, S. W. (1983). *Friends for life: The psychology of close relationships.* New York: St. Martin's Press.

Duck, S. W. (1990). *Personal relationships and social support.* London: Sage.

Duck, S. W. (1992). *Human relationships* (2nd ed.). Newbury Park, CA: Sage.

Durkheim, E. (1950). *The rules of sociological method* (S. A. Salovey & J. H. Mueller, Trans.). Glencoe, IL: Free Press. (Original work published 1894)

Durkheim, E. (1951). *Suicide: A study in sociology* (J. A. Spaulding & G. Simpson, Trans.). Glencoe, IL: Free Press. (Original work published 1897)

Durkheim, E. (1972). *Selected writings* (A. Giddens, Ed. & Trans.). Cambridge, England: Cambridge University Press. (Original work published 1924)

Durkheim, E. (1982). *The rules of sociological method* (2nd ed.) (S. Lukes, Ed., & W. D. Hall, Trans.). London: Macmillan. (Original work published 1901)

Duveen, G., & Lloyd, B. (1990). Introduction. In G. Duveen & B. Lloyd (Eds.), *Social representations and the development of knowledge* (pp. 1–10). Cambridge, England: Cambridge University Press.

Eccles, J. (Parsons). (1984). Sex differences in mathematics participation. In M. Steinkamp & M. Maeher (Eds.), *Advances in motivation and achievement* (Vol. 2, pp. 93–137). Greenwich, CT: JAI.

Elkins, W. F. (1976). *Black power in the Caribbean: The beginnings of the modern national movement.* New York: Revisionist Press.

Elms, A. C. (1975). The crisis of confidence in social psychology. *American Psychologist, 30,* 967–976.

Erikson, E. H. (1943). *Observations of the Yurok: Childhood and world image.* Berkeley: University of California Press.

Erikson, E. H. (1950). *Childhood and society.* New York: Norton.

Erikson, E. H. (1958). *Young man Luther.* New York: Norton.

Erikson, E. H. (1959). *Identity and the life cycle: Selected papers.* New York: International Universities Press.

Erikson, E. H. (1963a). *Childhood and society* (Rev. ed.). New York: Norton.

Erikson, E. H. (Ed.). (1963b). *Youth: Change and challenge.* New York: Basic Books.

Erikson, E. H. (1968). *Identity, youth, and crisis.* New York: Norton.

Erikson, E. H. (1969). *Gandhi's truth: On the origins of militant nonviolence.* New York: Norton.

Eron, L. D., Gentry, J. H., & Schlegel, P. (Eds.). (1994). *Reason to hope: A psychological perspective on violence.* Washington, DC: Americal Psychological Association.

Ervin, S. M. (1964). Imitation and structural change in children's language. In E. H. Lenneberg (Ed.), *New directions in the study of language* (pp. 163–189). Cambridge, MA: MIT Press.

Etzioni, A. (1961). *A comparative analysis of complex organizations.* New York: Free Press of Glencoe.

Evans, R. I. (1975). *Carl Rogers: The man and his ideas.* New York: Dutton.

Evans, S. (1981). *Personal politics.* New York: Vintage.

Eysenck, H. J. (1967). *The biological basis of personality.* Springfield, IL: Charles C Thomas.

Faludi, S. (1991). *Backlash: The undeclared war on American women.* New York: Crown.

Fancher, H., & Peoples, D. (1982). "The blade runner." Burbank, CA: Warner Brothers.

Fausto-Sterling, A. (1985). *Myths of gender: Biological theories about women and men.* New York: Basic Books.

Fein, H. (1977). *Imperial crime and punishment: The massacre at Jallianwalla Bagh and British judgment, 1919–1920.* Honolulu: University of Hawaii Press.

Fein, H. (1979). *Accounting for genocide: National responses and Jewish victimization during the Holocaust.* Chicago: University of Chicago Press.

Festinger, L. (1954). A theory of social comparison processes. *Human Relations, 7,* 117–140.

Festinger, L., Schachter, S., & Back, K. (1950). *Social pressures in informal groups.* New York: Harper.

Fielder, K., Semin, G. R., Finkenauer, C., & Berkel, I. (1995). Actor–observer bias in close relationships: The role of self-knowledge and self-related language. *Personality and Social Psychology Bulletin, 21,* 525–538.

Fishman, J. A. (1960). A systematization of the Whorfian hypothesis. *Behavioral Science, 8,* 323–339.

Fishman, J. A., Ferguson, C. A., & Gupta, J. D. (1968). *Language problems of developing nations.* New York: Wiley.

Fiske, A. P. (1992). The four elementary forms of sociality: Framework for a unified theory of social relations. *Psychological Review, 99,* 687–723.

Fogelman, E. (1994). *Conscience and courage: Rescuers of Jews during the Holocaust.* New York: Anchor Books.

Forster, E. M. (1939). *What I believe*. London: Hogarth Press.

French, J. R. P., Jr., & Raven, B. (1959). The bases of social power. In D. Cartwright (Ed.), *Studies in social power* (pp. 150–167). Ann Arbor, MI: Institute for Social Research.

Freud, A. (1937). *The ego and the mechanisms of defense*. London: Hogarth Press.

Freud, S. (1909). *Selected papers on hysteria*. New York: Nervous and Mental Disease Publishing Company.

Freud, S. (1962). *The ego and the id*. New York: Norton. (Original work published 1923)

Freud, S. (1966). *Introductory lectures on psychoanalysis* (J. Strachey, Trans.). New York: Norton. (Original work published 1917)

Friedan, B. (1960). *The feminine mystique*. New York: Dell.

Friedman, E., Katcher, A. H., Lynch, J., & Thomas, S. A. (1979). *Pet ownership and survival after coronary heart disease*. Paper presented to the Second Canadian Symposium on Pets and Society, Vancouver, British Columbia, Canada.

Gallatin, J., & Adelson, J. (1971). Legal guarantees of individual freedom: A cross-national study of the development of political thought. *Journal of Social Issues, 27*, 93–108.

Gaskell, G., & Fraser, C. (1990). *The social psychological study of widespread beliefs*. Oxford, England: Clarendon Press.

Geertz, C. (1973). *The interpretation of cultures: Selected essays*. New York: Basic Books.

Gergen, K. J. (1973). Social psychology as history. *Journal of Personality and Social Psychology, 26*, 309–320.

Gergen, K. J. (1989). Social psychology and the wrong revolution. *European Journal of Social Psychology, 19*, 463–484.

Gergen, K. J., & Davis, K. E. (Eds.). (1985). *The social construction of the person*. New York: Springer-Verlag.

Gergen, M. (1989). Induction and construction: Teetering between two worlds. *European Journal of Social Psychology, 19*, 431–437.

Gewirtz, J. L. (1969). Mechanisms of social learning: Some roles of stimulation and behavior in early human development. In D. A. Goslin (Ed.), *Handbook of socialization theory and research* (pp. 57–212). Chicago: Rand McNally.

Giddens, A. (1979). *Central problems in social theory: Action, structure, and contradiction in social analysis*. Berkeley: University of California Press.

Gilligan, C. (1982). *In a different voice: Theory and women's development*. Cambridge, MA: Harvard University Press.

Godow, R. A. (1976). Social psychology as both science and history. *Personality and Social Psychology Bulletin, 2*, 421–427.

Goffman, E. (1961). *Asylums: Essays on the social situation of mental patients and other inmates*. Chicago: Aldine.

Goffman, E. (1963). *Behavior in public places: Notes on the social organization of gatherings*. New York: Free Press.

Gold, M. (1969). Juvenile delinquency as a symptom of alienation. *Journal of Social Issues, 25*, 121–135.

Gold, M. (1994). Changing the delinquent self. In T. M. Brinthaupt & R. P. Lipka (Eds.), *Changing the self: Philosophies, techniques, and experiences* (pp. 89–108). Albany, NY: SUNY Press.

Goldhagen, D. J. (1996). *Hitler's willing executioners: Ordinary Germans and the Holocaust*. New York: Knopf.

Gottlieb, A. (1977). Social psychology as history or science: An addendum. *Personality and Social Psychology Bulletin, 3*, 207–210.

Gottman, J. M., & Parker, J. G. (Eds.). (1986). *Conversations of friends: Speculations on affective development*. Cambridge, England: Cambridge University Press.

Greenwald, A. G. (1976). Transhistorical lawfulness of behavior: A comment on two papers. *Personality and Social Psychology Bulletin, 2*, 391.

Gutmann, D. (1970). Female ego styles and generational conflict. In J. Bardwick, E. Douvan, M. Horner, & D. Gutmann (Eds.), *Feminine personality and conflict* (pp. 77–96). Belmont, CA: Wadsworth.

Hagstrom, W. O., & Selvin, H. C. (1965). The dimensions of cohesiveness in small groups. *Sociometry, 29,* 30–43.

Hamilton, E. (1949). *The Greek way.* New York: Norton.

Haney, C., Banks, C., & Zimbardo, P. (1973). Interpersonal dynamics in a simulated prison. *International Journal of Criminology and Personology, 1,* 69–97.

Harary, F., Norman, R. Z., & Cartwright, D. (1965). *Structural models: An introduction to the theory of directed graphs.* New York: Wiley.

Hare, A. P., Borgatta, E. F., & Bales, R. F. (Eds.). (1955). *Small groups: Studies in social interaction.* New York: Knopf.

Harris, R. J. (1976). The factors contributing to the perception of the theoretical intractability of social psychology. *Personality and Social Psychology Bulletin, 2,* 411–417.

Hartmann, H., Kris, E., & Lowenstein, R. M. (1964). Papers on psychoanalytic psychology [Monograph]. *Psychological Issues, 4*(No. 14).

Hebb, D. O. (1949). *The organization of behavior.* New York: Wiley.

Heider, F. (1958). *The psychology of interpersonal relations.* New York: Wiley.

Heilbrun, A. B., Jr., & Norbert, N. (1970). Maternal child-rearing experience and self-reinforcement effectiveness. *Developmental Psychology, 3,* 81–87.

Henley, N. (1975). *Language and sex: Difference and dominance.* Rowley, MA: Newbury House.

Heron, A., & Simonsson, M. (1969). Weight conservation in Zambian children: A nonverbal approach. *International Journal of Psychology, 4,* 281–292.

Hess, R. D. (1967). *The development of political attitudes in children.* Chicago: Aldine.

Hess, R. D., & Shipman, V. (1965). Early experience and the socialization of cognitive modes in children. *Child Development, 36,* 869–886.

Himmelweit, H. T., & Gaskell, G. (Eds.). (1990). *Societal psychology.* Newbury Park, CA: Sage.

Hoffman, M. L. (1977). Personality and social development. *Annual Review of Psychology, 28,* 5–321.

Holmes, J. G., & Rempel, J. K. (1989). Trust in close relationships. In E. Hendrick (Ed.), *Review of personality and social psychology: Vol. 10. Close relationships* (pp. 187–220). Newbury Park, CA: Sage Publications.

Homans, G. C. (1961). *Social behavior: Its elementary forms.* New York: Harcourt, Brace & World.

Homans, G. C. (1970a). The relevance of psychology to explanation of social phenomena. In R. Borger & F. Cioffi (Eds.), *Explanation in the behavioral sciences* (pp. 313–328). Cambridge, England: Cambridge University Press.

Homans, G. C. (1970b). Reply [to Blau, 1970]. In R. Borger & F. Cioffi (Eds.), *Explanation in the behavioral sciences* (pp. 340–343). Cambridge, England: Cambridge University Press.

Homans, G. C. (1974). *Social behavior: Its elementary forms* (Rev. ed.). New York: Harcourt Brace Javanovich.

Hovland, C. I. (1954). Effects of the mass media on communication. In G. Lindzey (Ed.), *Handbook of social psychology* (Vol. 2, 2nd ed., pp. 1062–1103). Reading, MA: Addison-Wesley.

Hovland, C. I., Janis, I. L., & Kelley, H. H. (1953). *Communication and persuasion.* New Haven, CT: Yale University Press.

Hurwitz, S. D., Miron, S. D., & Johnson, B. T. (1992). Source credibility and the language of expert testimony. *Journal of Applied Social Psychology, 22,* 1909–1939.

Ickes, W. (1983). A basic paradigm for the study of unstructured dyadic interaction. *New Directions for Methodology of Social and Behavioral Science,* No. 15, 5–21.

Jackson, J. M. (1960). Structural characteristics of nouns. *The fifty-ninth yearbook of the National Society for the Study of Education* (Part 3, pp. 136–163). Chicago: The National Society for the Study of Education.

Jenni, D. A., & Jenni, M. A. (1976). Carrying behavior in humans: Analysis of sex differences. *Science, 194*(4267), 859–860.

Jennings, H. H. (1947). Sociometric differentiation of the psychegroup and the sociogroup. *Sociometry, 10,* 71–79.

Johnson, B. T., & Eagly, A. H. (1989). Effects of involvement on persuasion: A meta-analysis. *Psychological Bulletin, 106,* 290–314.

Johnson, B. T., & Eagly, A. H. (1990). Involvement and persuasion: Types, traditions, and the evidence. *Psychological Bulletin, 107,* 375–384.

Jones, E. E., & Nisbett, R. E. (1972). The actor and the observer: Divergent perceptions of causality. In E. E. Jones, D. E. Kanouse, H. H. Kelley, R. E. Nisbett, S. Valing, & B. Weiner (Eds.), *Attribution: Perceiving the causes of behavior* (pp. 79–94). Morristown, NJ: General Learning Press.

Jones, R. A., & Brehm, J. W. (1970). Persuasiveness of one- and two-sided communications as a function of the awareness there are two sides. *Journal of Experimental Social Psychology, 6,* 47–56.

Jordan, J., Kaplan, A., Miller, J. B., Stiver I., & Surrey, E. (Eds.). (1995). *Women's growth in connection.* New York: Guilford Press.

Jordan, J., Surrey, J. L., & Kaplan, A. (1995). Women and empathy: Implications for women's development and psychotherapy. In J. Jordan, A. Kaplan, J. B. Miller, I. Stiver, and E. Surrey (Eds.), *Women's growth in connection* (pp. 27–50). New York: Guilford Press.

Jourard, S. M. (1971). *Self-disclosure: An experimental analysis of the transparent self.* New York: Wiley.

Judd, E. (1979). *Matriarchal origins of courtly love.* Unpublished doctoral dissertation, University of Michigan at Ann Arbor.

Kagan, J. (1971). *Change and continuity in infancy.* New York: Wiley.

Kagan, J., & Moss, H. A. (1962). *Birth to maturity: A study in psychological development.* New York: Wiley.

Kant, I. (1965). *Critique of pure reason* (N. K. Smith, Trans.). New York: St. Martin's Press. (Original work published 1781)

Kanter, R. M. (1976). Women in organizations: Sex roles, group dynamics, and change strategies. In A. Sargent (Ed.), *Beyond sex roles* (pp. 371–386). New York: West Publishing.

Kanter, R. M. (1977). *Men and women of the corp.* New York: Basic Books.

Kapek, K. (1923). *R.U.R.: A fantastic melodrama.* New York: S. French.

Kaplan, A. (1982). *Women and empathy.* Wellesley, MA: Stone Center Working Papers.

Kaplan, D., & Manners, R. A. (1972). *Culture theory.* Englewood Cliffs, NJ: Prentice-Hall.

Kardiner, A., & Linton, R. (1939). *The individual and his society: The psychodynamic of primitive social organization.* New York: Columbia University Press.

Katz, D., & Kahn, R. L. (1978). *The social psychology of organizations* (2nd ed.). New York: Wiley.

Katz, E., & Lazarsfeld, P. F. (1955). *Personal influence: The part played by people in the flow of mass communication.* Glencoe, IL: Free Press.

Keller, E. F. (1990). *Body politics: Women and the discourses of science.* New York: Routledge.

Kelley, H. H. (1983). The situational origins of human tendencies: A further reason for the formal analysis of structures. *Personality and Social Psychology Bulletin, 9,* 8–36.

Kelley, H. H., Berscheid, E., Christensen, A., Harvey, J. H., Huston, T., Levinger, G., McClintock, E., Peplau, L. A., & Peterson, D. (Eds.). (1983). *Close relationships.* New York: Freeman.

Kelley, H. H., & Thibaut, J. W. (1978). *Interpersonal relations: A theory of interdependence.* New York: Wiley.

Kelman, H. C. (1958). Compliance, identification, and internalization: Three processes of attitude change. *Journal of Conflict Resolution, 2,* 21–60.

Kelman, H. C., & Hamilton, V. L. (1989). *Crimes of obedience: Toward a social psychology of authority and responsibility.* New Haven, CT: Yale University Press.

Kenny, D. A., & Nasby, W. (1982). Splitting the reciprocity correlation. *Journal of Personality and Social Psychology, 38,* 249–256.

Kinter, E. (Ed.). (1969). *The letters of Robert Browning and Elizabeth Barrett Browning.* Cambridge, MA: Harvard University Press.

Kluckhohn, F. R., & Strodtbeck, F. L. (1962). *Variations in value orientations.* New York: Harper & Row.

Koch, H. (1970). *The panic broadcast.* Boston: Little, Brown.

Kohlberg, L. (1981). *Essays on moral development: The philosophy of moral development* (Vol. 1). New York: Harper & Row.

Kohlberg, L. (1984). *Essays on moral development: The nature and validity of moral stages* (Vol. 2). New York: Harper & Row.

Kraus, S. (1995). Attitudes and the prediction of behavior: A meta-analysis of the empirical literature. *Personality and Social Psychology Bulletin, 21,* 58–75.

Krebs, D., & Miller, D. T. (1985). Altruism and aggression. In G. Lindzey & E. Aronson (Eds.), *Handbook of social psychology* (Vol. 2, 3rd ed., pp. 1–71). New York: Random House.

Kroeber, A. L., & Kluckhohn, C. (1963). *Culture: A critical review of concepts and definitions.* New York: Vintage Books. (Original work published 1952)

Kroeber, A. L., & Parsons, T. (1958). The concepts of culture and social system. *American Sociological Review, Oct.,* 39–56.

Kubrick, S., & Clarke, A. C. (1968). *2001: A space odyssey* [screenplay]. New York: New American Library.

Kuhn, T. S. (1970). *The structure of scientific revolutions* (2nd ed.). Chicago: University of Chicago Press.

Kurth, S. B. (1970). Friendship and friendly relations. In G. J. McCall, M. M. McCall, N. K. Denzin, G. D. Suttles, & S. B. Kurth (Eds.), *Social relationships* (pp. 136–170). Chicago: Aldine.

Lakoff, R. (1975). *Language and woman's place.* New York: Harper & Row.

Lakoff, R. (1993). *Father knows best: The use and abuse of power in Freud's case of Dora.* New York: Teachers' College Press.

Langer, S. K. (1960). *Philosophy in a new key: A study in the symbolism of reason, rite, and art* (4th ed.). Cambridge, MA: Harvard University Press.

Latané, B., & Darley, J. M. (1970). *The unresponsive bystander: Why doesn't he help?* New York: Appleton-Century-Crofts.

Latané, B., & Rodin, J. (1969). Lady in distress: Inhibitory effects of friends and strangers on bystander intervention. *Journal of Experimental Social Psychology, 5*(2), 189–202.

Lawson, E. T., & McCauley, R. N. (1990). *Rethinking religion: Connecting cognition and culture.* Cambridge, England: Cambridge University Press.

Lazarsfeld, P. F. (1946). *The people look at radio: Report on a survey conducted by the National Opinion Research Center.* Chapel Hill: University of North Carolina Press.

Lazarsfeld, P. F., Berelson, B. R., & Gaudet, H. (1944). *The people's choice: How the voter makes up his mind in a presidential campaign.* New York: Duell, Sloan, & Pearce.

Leavitt, H. J. (1951). Some effects of certain communication patterns on group performance. *Journal of Abnormal and Social Psychology, 46,* 38–50.

Lee, S. C. (1964). The primary group as Cooley defines it. *Sociological Quarterly, 2,* 23–24.

LeVine, R. A. (1973). *Culture, behavior, and personality: An introduction to the comparative study of psychosocial adaptation.* Chicago: Aldine.

LeVine, R. A. (1984). Properties of culture: An ethnographic view. In R. Schweder & R. A. LeVine (Eds.), *Culture theory: Essays in mind, theory, and emotion* (pp. 67–87). Cambridge, England: Cambridge University Press.

Levinson, D. J. (1964). Toward a new social psychology: The convergence of sociology and psychology. *Merrill-Palmer Quarterly of Behavior and Development, 10,* 77–88.

Lewin, K. (1936). *Principles of topological psychology.* New York: McGraw-Hill.

Lewin, K. (1947). Group decision and social change. In T. M. Newcomb & E. L. Hartley (Eds.), *Readings in social psychology* (pp. 330–344). New York: Holt.

Lewin, K. (1951). Psychological ecology. In D. Cartwright (Ed.), *Field theory in social science* (pp. 170–187). New York: Harper & Row.

Lewin, K., Lippitt, R., & White, R. (1939). Patterns of aggressive behavior in experimentally created "social climates." *Journal of Social Psychology, 10,* 271–299.

Lewin, M. A. (1977). Kurt Lewin's view of social psychology: The crisis of 1977 and the crisis of 1927. *Personality and Social Psychology Bulletin, 3,* 159–172.

Liang, D. W., Moreland, R., & Argote, L. (1995). Group versus individual training and group performance: The mediating role of transactive memory. *Personality and Social Psychology Bulletin, 21,* 384–393.

Lickona, T. (1974). A cognitive–developmental approach to interpersonal attraction. In T. L. Huston (Ed.), *Foundations of interpersonal attraction* (pp. 31–59). New York: Academic Press.

Lieberman, S. (1956). The effects of changes in roles on the attitudes of role occupants. *Human Relations, 9,* 385–402.

Lindzey, G. (Ed.). (1954). *Handbook of social psychology.* Cambridge, MA: Addison-Wesley.

Lindzey, G., & Aronson, E. (Eds.). (1985). *Handbook of social psychology* (3rd ed.). New York: Random House.

Linton, R. (1936). *The study of man: An introduction.* New York: Appleton-Century-Crofts.

Lock, A. (1991). The role of social interaction in early language development. In N. A. Krasnegor, D. M. Rumbaugh, R. L. Schiefelbusch, & M. Studdert-Kennedy (Eds.), *Biological and behavioral determinants of language development* (pp. 287–300). Hillsdale, NJ: Erlbaum.

Logan, F. A., Olmsted, D. L., Rosner, B. S., Schwartz, R. D., & Stevens, C. M. (1955). *Behavior theory and social science.* New Haven, CT: Yale University Press.

Lopreato, J., & Alston, L. (1970). Ideal types and the idealization strategy. *American Sociological Review, 35,* 88–96.

Lott, A. J., & Lott, B. E. (1965). Group cohesiveness as interpersonal attraction: A review of relationships with antecedent and consequent variables. *Psychological Bulletin, 64,* 259–309.

Lowenthal, M. F., & Haven, C. (1968). Interaction and adaptation: Intimacy as a critical variable. *American Sociological Review, 33,* 20–30.

Maas, H. S. (1968). Preadolescent peer relations and adult intimacy. *Psychiatry, 31,* 161–172.

Magnusson, D., & Endler, N. S. (Eds.). (1977). *Personality at the crossroads: Current issues in interactional psychology.* Hillsdale, NJ: Erlbaum.

Maines, D. R. (1977). Social organization and social structure in symbolic interactionist thought. *Annual Review of Sociology, 3,* 235–259.

Manis, M. (1975). Comment on Gergen's "Social psychology as history." *Personality and Social Psychology Bulletin, 1,* 450–455.

Manis, M. (1976). Is social psychology really different? *Personality and Social Psychology Bulletin, 2,* 428–437.

Manson, T. C., & Snyder, M. (1977). Actors, observers, and the attribution process: Toward a reconceptualization. *Journal of Experimental Social Psychology, 13,* 89–111.

Masson, J. M. (1984). *Assault on the truth: Freud's suppression of the seduction theory.* New York: Farrar Straus & Giroux.

May, R. (1967). *The art of counseling.* New York: Abingdon Press.

May, R. (1975). *The courage to create.* New York: Norton.

May, R. (1980). *Sex and fantasy patterns of male and female development.* New York: Norton.

McCandless, B. R. (1970). *Adolescents: Behavior and development.* Hinsdale, IL: Dryden.

McClelland, D. C. (1951). *Personality.* New York: William Sloane.

McClelland, D. C. (1965). Toward a theory of motive acquisition. *American Psychologist, 20,* 321–333.

McClintock, M. K. (1971). Menstrual synchrony and suppression. *Nature, 229,* 244–245.

McEwen, C. A. (1980). Continuities in the study of total and nontotal institutions. *Annual Review of Sociology, 6,* 143–185.

McGrath, J. E., & Altman, I. (1966). *Small group research: A synthesis and critique of the field.* New York: Holt, Rinehart & Winston.

McGuire, W. J. (1969). The nature of attitudes and attitude change. In G. Lindzey & E. Aronson (Eds.), *Handbook of social psychology* (Vol. 2, pp. 138–364). Reading, MA: Addison-Wesley.

McGuire, W. J. (1985). Attitudes and attitude change. In G. Lindzey & E. Aronson (Eds.), *Handbook of social psychology* (Vol. 2, 3rd ed., pp. 233–346). New York: Random House.

Mead, G. H. (1982). *The individual and the social self.* Chicago: University of Chicago Press.

Mead, M. (1933). *Coming of age in Samoa: A psychological study of primitive youth for western civilization.* New York: Blue Ribbon Books. (Original work published 1928)

Mead, M. (1949). *Male and female: A study of the sexes in a changing world.* New York: W. Morrow.

Mead, M. (1970). *Culture and commitment: A study of the generation gap.* Garden City, NY: Natural History Press.

Merrill, B. (1964). People. In *Funny girl.* New York: Chappell & Wonderful Music Co.

Mettee, D. R., & Aronson, E. (1974). Affective reactions to appraisal from others. In T. L. Huston (Ed.), *Foundations of interpersonal attraction* (pp. 235–283). New York: Academic Press.

Meyers, D. G., & Lamm, H. (1976). The group polarization phenomenon. *Psychological Bulletin, 83,* 602–627.

Milgram, S. (1974). *Obedience to authority: An experimental view.* New York: Harper & Row.

Millar, F. E., & Rogers, L. E. (1975). A relational approach to interpersonal communication. In G. R. Miller (Ed.), *Explorations in interpersonal communications* (pp. 87–103). Beverly Hills, CA: Sage.

Millar, M. G., & Tesser, A. (1986). Effects of affective and cognitive focus on the attitude–behavior relation. *Journal of Personality and Social Psychology, 51,* 270–276.

Miller, J. B. (1976). *Toward a new psychology of women.* Boston: Beacon Press.

Miller, J. B. (1995). Development of the sense of self. In J. Jordan, A. Kaplan, J. B. Miller, I. Stiver, & E. Surrey (Eds.), *Women's growth in connection* (pp. 11–26). New York: Guilford Press.

Miller, J. G. (1978). *Living systems.* New York: McGraw-Hill.

Mills, J., & Clark, M. S. (1994). Communal and exchange relationships: Controversies in research. In R. Erber & R. Gilmour (Eds.), *Theoretical frameworks for personal relationships* (pp. 29–42). Hillsdale, NJ: Erlbaum.

Mischel, W. (1968). *Personality assessment.* New York: Wiley

Mitchell, J. (1975). *Psychoanalysis and feminism.* New York: Vintage.

Modigliani, A., & Rochat, F. (1995). The role of interaction sequences and the timing of resistance in shaping obedience and defiance to authority. *Journal of Social Issues, 51*(3), 107–123.

Money, J. (1972). *Man and woman, boy and girl: The differentiation and dimorphism of gender identity from conception to maturity.* Baltimore: Johns Hopkins University Press.

Moscovici, S., & Lage, E. (1976). Studies in social influence: III. Majority versus minority influence in a group. *European Journal of Social Psychology, 6,* 149–174.

Moscovici, S., Lage, E., & Naffrechoux, M. (1969). Influence of a consistent minority on the responses of a majority in a color perception task. *Sociometry, 32,* 365–380.

Moscovici, S., & Personnaz, B. (1980). Studies in social influence: IV. Minority influence and conversation behavior in a perceptual task. *Journal of Experimental Social Psychology, 16,* 270–282.

Moss, H. (1967). Sex, age, and state as determinants of mother–infant interaction. *Merrill-Palmer Quarterly, 13*(1), 19–36.

Mowrer, O. H. (1960). *Learning theory and the symbolic process.* New York: Wiley.

Murdock, G. P. (1954). Sociology and anthropology. In J. Gillan (Ed.), *For a science of social man* (pp. 14–31). New York: Macmillan.

Murray, S. L., & Holmes, J. G. (1994). Storytelling in close relationships: The construction of confidence. *Personality and Social Psychology Bulletin, 20,* 650–663.

Newcomb, T. M. (1950). *Social psychology.* New York: Holt, Rinehart & Winston.

Newcomb, T. M. (1953). An approach to the study of communicative acts. *Psychological Review, 60,* 393–404.

Newcomb, T. M. (1956). The prediction of interpersonal attraction. *American Psychologist, 11,* 575–586.

Newcomb, T. M. (1961). *The acquaintance process.* New York: Holt, Rinehart & Winston.

Nicotera, A. M., and Associates. (1993). *Interpersonal communication in friend and mate relationships.* Albany: State University of New York Press.

Nisbett, R. E., & Cohen, D. (1996). *Culture of honor: The psychology of violence in the south.* Boulder, CO: Westview Press.

Nisbett, R. E., & Ross, L. (1980). *Human inference: Strategies and shortcomings of social judgements.* Englewood Cliffs, NJ: Prentice-Hall.

Nuttin, J. J. (1989). Proposal for a heuristic quasi-social analysis of social behavior. *European Journal of Social Psychology, 19,* 371–383.

Ogburn, W. F. (1950). *Social change with respect to culture and original nature* (2nd ed.). New York: Viking Press.

Ortner, S. B. (1974). Is female to male as nature is to culture? In M. Z. Rosaldo & L. Lamphere (Eds.), *Woman, culture, and society* (pp. 67–87). Stanford, CA: Stanford University Press.

Pagels, E. (1988). *Adam, Eve and the serpent*. New York: Random House.

Parsons, T. (1942). Age and sex in the social structure of the United States. *American Sociological Review, 7*, 604–606.

Parsons, T. (1951). *The social system*. Glencoe, IL: Free Press.

Parsons, T. (Ed.). (1961). *Theories of society: Foundations of modern sociological thought*. New York: Free Press of Glencoe.

Parsons, T. (1964). *Social structure and personality*. New York: Free Press of Glencoe.

Parsons, T. (1969). *Politics and social structure*. New York: Free Press.

Parsons, T., & Platt, G. M. (1973). *The American university*. Cambridge, MA: Harvard University Press.

Perlman, D. (1987). *Intimate relations*. Beverly Hills, CA: Sage.

Perloff, R. M. (1993). *The dynamics of persuasion*. Hillsdale, NJ: Erlbaum.

Perloff, R., & Brock, T. (1980). . . . And thinking makes it so: Cognitive responses to persuasion. In M. Roloff & G. Millar (Eds.), *Persuasion: New directions in theory and research* (pp. 67–100). Beverly Hills, CA: Sage.

Petty, R. E., & Cacioppo, J. T. (1981). *Attitudes and persuasion: Classic and contemporary approaches*. Dubuque, IA: Brown.

Petty, R. E., & Cacioppo, J. T. (1986). *Communication and persuasion: Central and peripheral routes to attitude change*. New York: Springer-Verlag.

Petty, R. E., & Cacioppo, J. T. (1990). Involvement and persuasion: Tradition versus integration. *Psychological Bulletin, 107*, 367–374.

Piaget, J. (1928). *Judgement and reasoning in the child*. London: K. Paul, Trench, Trubner.

Porter, P. W. (1978). Geography as human ecology. *American Behavioral Scientist, 22*, 15–39.

Priester, J. R., & Petty, R. E. (1995). Source attributions and persuasion: Perceived honesty as a determinant of message scrutiny. *Personality and Social Psychology Bulletin, 21*, 637–654.

Rapaport, D. (1942). *Emotions and memory*. Baltimore: Williams & Wilkins.

Rapoport, A. (1976). General systems theory: A bridge between two cultures. *Behavioral Science, 21*, 228–239.

Regan, D. T. (1978). Attributional aspects of interpersonal attraction. In J. H. Harvey, W. J. Ickes, & R. F. Kidd (Eds.), *New directions in attribution research* (Vol. 2, pp. 207–233). Hillsdale, NJ: Erlbaum.

Rijsman, J., & Stroebe, W. (Eds.). (1989). Controversies in the social explanation of psychological behavior. *European Journal of Social Psychology, 19*(5, Whole).

Ring, K. (1967). Experimental social psychology: Some somber questions about some frivolous values. *Journal of Experimental Social Psychology, 3*, 113–123.

Rochat, F., & Modigliani, A. (1995). The ordinary quality of resistance: From Milgram's laboratory to the village of Le Chambon. *Journal of Social Issues, 51*(3), 195–210.

Rodin, J. (1976). Density, perceived choice, and response to controllable and uncontrollable outcomes. *Journal of Experimental Social Psychology, 12*, 564–578.

Rodin, J., Solomon, S. K., & Metcalf, J. (1978). Role of control in mediating perceptions of density. *Journal of Personality and Social Psychology, 36*, 988–999.

Rogers, C. R. (1957). The necessary and sufficient conditions of therapeutic personality change. *Journal of Consulting Psychology, 21*, 95–103.

Rogers, C. R. (1961). *On becoming a person: A therapist's view of psychotherapy*. Boston: Houghton Mifflin.

Rokeach, M. (1968). *Beliefs, attitudes, and values*. San Francisco: Jossey-Bass.

Rosaldo, M. Z. (1974). Woman, culture and society: A theoretical overview. In M. Z. Rosaldo & L. Lamphere (Eds.), *Woman, culture, and society* (pp. 17–42). Stanford, CA: Stanford University Press.

Roseman, I. J. (1994). The psychology of strongly held beliefs: Theories of ideological structure and individual attachment. In R. C. Shank & E. Langer (Eds.), *Beliefs, reasoning, and decision making: Psycho–logic in honor of Bob Abelson* (pp. 175–208). Hillsdale, NJ: Erlbaum.

Ross, L., Bierbrauer, G., & Hoffman, S. (1976). The role of attribution processes in conformity and dissent: Revisiting the Asch situation. *American Psychologist, 31,* 148–157.

Rubin, Z. (1973). *Liking and loving: An invitation to social psychology.* New York: Holt, Rinehart & Winston.

Ruddick, S. (1982). Maternal thinking. In B. Thorne & M. Yalom (Eds.), *Rethinking the family* (pp. 76–94). New York: Longman.

Ruesch, J., & Bateson, G. (1951). *Communication: The social matrix of psychiatry.* New York: Norton.

Sakurai, M. M. (1975). Small group cohesiveness and detrimental conformity. *Sociometry, 38,* 341–357.

Salinger, J. D. (1951). *The catcher in the rye.* London: Hamish.

Sarbin, T. R., & Allen, V. L. (1968). Increasing participation in a national group setting: A preliminary report. *Psychological Record, 18,* 1–7.

Schachter, S. (1951). Deviation, rejection, and communication. *Journal of Abnormal and Social Psychology, 46,* 190–207.

Schachter, S. (1959). *The psychology of affiliation.* Stanford, CA: Stanford University Press.

Schachter, S. (1964). The interaction of cognitive and physiological determinants of emotional state. In L. Berkowitz (Ed.), *Advances in experimental psychology* (Vol. 1, pp. 49–80). New York: Academic Press.

Schachter, S., Ellertson, N., McBride, D., & Gregory, D. (1951). An experimental study of cohesiveness and productivity. *Human Relations, 4,* 229–238.

Schlenker, B. R. (1974). Social psychology and science. *Journal of Personality and Social Psychology, 29,* 1–15.

Schlenker, B. R. (1976). Social psychology and science: Another look. *Personality and Social Psychology Bulletin, 2,* 384–390.

Schmalenbach, H. (1977). *Herman Schmalenbach on society and experience: Selected papers* (G. Luschen & G. P. Stone, Eds. & Trans.). Chicago: University of Chicago Press.

Schwartz, S. H. (1994). Are there universal aspects in the structure and contexts of human values? *Journal of Social Issues, 50*(4), 19–45.

Secord, P. F. (1976). Transhistorical and transcultural theory. *Personality and Social Psychology Bulletin, 2,* 418–420.

Seeman, M. A. (1972). Alienation and knowledge-seeking: A note on attitude and action. *Social Problems, 20,* 3–17.

Sennet, R. (1974). *Families against the city: Middle class homes of industrial Chicago, 1872–1890.* New York: Vintage Press.

Sharp, L. (1952). Steel axes for stone age Australians. In E. H. Spicer (Ed.), *Human problems in technical change* (pp. 69–90). New York: Sage.

Shaw, M. E. (1971). *Group dynamics: The psychology of small group behavior.* New York: McGraw-Hill.

Sherif, M. (1936). *The psychology of social norms.* New York: Harper.

Shipley, T. E., & Veroff, J. (1952). A projective measure of need for affiliation. *Journal of Experimental Psychology, 43,* 349–356.

Shulman, S. (Ed.). (1995). *Close relationships and socioemotional development.* Norwood, NJ: Ablex.

Siegel, A. E., & Siegel, S. (1957). Reference groups, memberships groups, and attitude change. *Journal of Abnormal and Social Psychology, 55,* 360–364.

Simmel, G. (1949). The sociology of sociability. *The American Journal of Sociology, 55*(3), 254–261. (Original work published 1910)

Simmel, G. (1950a). Faithfulness and gratitude. In K. H. Wolff (Ed. & Trans.), *The sociology of Georg Simmel* (pp. 379–395). Glencoe, IL: Free Press. (Original work published 1908)

Simmel, G. (1950b). *The sociology of Georg Simmel* (K. H. Wolff, Ed. & Trans.). Glencoe, IL: Free Press. (Original work published 1908)

Simon, H. A. (1966). *Administrative behavior: A study of decision-making processes in administrative organizations.* New York: Free Press.

Skinner, B. F. (1957). *Verbal behavior*. New York: Appleton-Century-Crofts.

Skinner, B. F. (1961). The design of cultures. *Daedalus, 90,* 534–546.

Slater, P. (1977). *Footholds*. New York: Dutton.

Smith, M. B. (1976). Social psychology, science, and history: So what? *Personality and Social Psychology Bulletin, 2,* 438–444.

Sorokin, P. A. (1957). *Social and cultural dynamics: A study of change in major systems of art, truth, ethics, law, and social relationships* (Rev. ed.). Boston: P. Sargent.

Sorokin, P. A. (1962). *Society, culture, and personality: Their structure and dynamics*. New York: Cooper Square Publishers. (Original work published 1947)

Sorrentino, R. M., Bobocel, D. R., Gitta, M. Z., & Olson, J. M. (1988). Uncertainty orientation and persuasion: Individual differences in the effects of personal relevance on social judgments. *Journal of Personality and Social Psychology, 55,* 357–371.

Sorrentino, R. M., King, G., & Leo, G. (1980). The influence of the minority on perception: A note on a possible alternative explanation. *Journal of Experimental Social Psychology, 16,* 293–301.

Spiegel, J. (1972). *Transactions: The interplay between individual, family, and society*. New York: Science House.

Spretnak, C. (1982). *The politics of women's spirituality*. Garden City, NY: Anchor Books.

Steiner, I. (1974). Whatever happened to the group in social psychology? *Journal of Experimental Social Psychology, 10,* 94–108.

Stephan, C. W., Stephan, W. C., & Pettigrew, T. F. (Eds.). (1991). *The future of social psychology*. New York: Springer-Verlag.

Sternberg, R. J. (1986). A triangular theory of love. *Psychological Review, 93,* 119–135.

Stiver, I. P. (1995). Beyond the Oedipus complex: Mothers and daughters. In J. Jordan, A. Kaplan, J. B. Miller, I. Stiver, & E. Surrey (Eds.), *Women's growth in connection* (pp. 97–121). New York: Guilford Press.

Stone, M. (1978). *When God was a woman*. New York: Harcourt Brace Jovanovich.

Stone, M. (1991). *Ancient mirrors of womanhood: A treasury of goddess and heroine lore from around the world*. Boston: Beacon Press.

Stoner, J. A. (1968). Risky and cautious shifts in group decisions: The influence of widely held values. *Journal of Experimental Social Psychology, 41,* 442–452.

Sullivan, A. (1991). Washington diarist: Taken seriously. *The New Republic, 204,* 42.

Sullivan, H. S. (1953). *The interpersonal theory of psychiatry*. New York: Norton.

Sundstrom, E., & Altman, I. (1976). Interpersonal relationships and personal space: Research review and theoretical model. *Human Ecology, 4,* 47–67.

Surrey, J. L. (1995). The self in relation: A theory of women's development. In J. Jordan, A. Kaplan, J. B. Miller, I. Stiver, & E. Surrey (Eds.), *Women's growth in connection* (pp. 51–66). New York: Guilford Press.

Swanson, G. E. (1965). The routinization of love: Structure and process in primary relations. In S. Z. Klausner (Ed.), *The quest for self-control: Classical philosophies and scientific research* (pp. 160–209). New York: Free Press.

Tajfel, H. (1974). *Intergroup behavior, social comparison, and social change*. Katz-Newcomb Lecture, University of Michigan.

Tannenbaum, P. H., & Gaer, E. P. (1965). Mood change as a function of stress of protagonist and degree of identification in a film viewing situation. *Journal of Personality and Social Psychology, 2,* 612–616.

Tavris, C. (1984). The longest war: Sex differences in perspective. San Diego, CA: Harcourt Brace Jovanovich.

Tavris, C. (1989). *Anger, the misunderstood emotion*. New York: Simon & Schuster.

Tavris, C. (1992). *The mismeasure of women*. New York: Simon & Schuster.

Thibaut, J. W., & Kelley, H. H. (1959). *The social psychology of groups*. New York: Wiley.

Thorne, B., & Yalom, M. (1982). *Rethinking the family: Some feminist questions*. New York: Longman Press.

Thorngate, W. (1975). Process variance: Another red herring. *Personality and Social Psychology Bulletin, 1,* 485–488.

Thorngate, W. (1976a). "In general" vs. "it depends": Some comments on the Gergen–Schlenker debate. *Personality and Social Psychology Bulletin, 2,* 404–410.

Thorngate, W. (1976b). Must we always think before we act? *Personality and Social Psychology Bulletin, 2*, 31–35.

Thrasher, F. M. (1927). *The gang.* Chicago: University of Chicago Press.

Tonnies, F. (1957). *Community and society* (C. Loomis, Ed. & Trans.). East Lansing: Michigan State University Press. (Original work published 1887)

Tooby, J., & Cosmides, L. (1992). The psychological foundations of culture. In J. Barkow, L. Cosmides, & J. Tooby (Eds.), *The adapted mind: Evolutionary psychology and the generation of culture* (pp. 19–35). New York: Oxford University Press.

Touhey, J. C. (1974). Situated identities, attitude similarity, and interpersonal attraction. *Sociometry, 37*, 363–374.

Toynbee, A. J. (1934). *A study of history.* London: Oxford University Press.

Trahair, R. C. (1975). Structural role theory and the total institution. *Australian Journal of Psychology, 27*, 31–40.

Triandis, H. C. (1972). *The analysis of subjective culture.* New York: Wiley-Interscience.

Trible, P. (1978). *God and the rhetoric of sexuality.* Philadelphia: Fortress Press.

Trist, E. L. (1981). *The evolution of socio-technical systems: A conceptual framework and an action research program.* Toronto: Ontario Ministry of Labour, Ontario Quality of Working Life Centre.

Trist, E. L., & Bamforth, K. W. (1951). Some social and psychological consequences of the long-wall method of coal-getting. *Human Relations, 4*, 3–38.

Truax, C. B., & Carcuff, R. R. (1967). *Toward effective counseling and psychotherapy: Training and practice.* Chicago: Aldine.

Tuan, Y. F. (1977). *Space and place: The perspective of experience.* Minneapolis: University of Minnesota Press.

Vallacher, R. R., & Nowak, A. (Eds.). (1994). *Dynamical systems in social psychology.* San Diego, CA: Academic Press.

Veroff, J., Douvan, E., & Kulka, R. (1981). *The inner American.* New York: Basic Books.

Veroff, J., & Feld, S. (1970). *Marriage and work in America.* New York: Van Nostrand Reinhold.

Vinokur, A., & Burnstein, E. (1978). Depolarization of attitudes in groups. *Journal of Personality and Social Psychology, 36*, 872–885.

Wallen, J. (1996, April 18). Interview. *New York Times,* p. B8.

Walster, E., & Festinger, L. (1962). The effectiveness of "overheard" persuasive communications. *Journal of Abnormal and Social Psychology, 65*, 395–402.

Ward, L. F. (1919). *Pure sociology: A treatise on the origin and spontaneous development of society* (2nd ed.). New York: Macmillan.

Watson, D. (1982). The actor and the observer: How are their perceptions of causality different? *Psychological Bulletin, 92*, 682–700.

Weber, M. (1949). *The methodology of the social sciences* (E. A. Shils & H. A. Finch, Trans.). Glencoe, IL: Free Press. (Original work published 1904)

Weick, K. E., & Gilfillan, D. P. (1971). Fate of arbitrary traditions in a laboratory microculture. *Journal of Personality and Social Psychology, 17*, 179–191.

Wells, H. G. (1930). *The war of the worlds.* London: W. Heinemann. (Original work published 1898)

White, L. A. (1969). *The science of culture: A study of man and civilization* (2nd ed.). New York: Farrar, Straus & Giroux.

White, L. A. (1973). *The concept of culture.* Minneapolis, MN: Burgess Publishing Co.

Whorf, B. L. (1941). The relation of habitual thought to behavior and to language. In L. Speier (Ed.), *Language, culture, and personality* (pp. 75–93). Menasha, WI: Sapir Memorial Publication Fund.

Whyte, W. F. (1961). *Men at work.* Homewood, IL: Dorsey Press.

Wilson, E. O. (1975). *Sociobiology: The new synthesis.* Cambridge, MA: Harvard University Press.

Winch, R. F. (1958). *Mate selection: A study of complementary needs.* New York: Harper.

Winer, B. J. (1955). A measure of interrelationship for overlapping groups. *Psychometrika, 20*, 63–68.

Wolff, M. (1977). Social psychology as history: Advancing the problem. *Personality and Social Psychology Bulletin, 3*, 211–212.

Wright, P. H. (1978). Toward a theory of friendship based on a conception of self. *Human Communication Research, 4*, 196–207.

Wright, R. (1940). *Native son*. New York: Harper & Brothers Publishers.

Wright, R. (1953). *The outsider*. New York: Harper & Brothers Publishers.

Wright, R. (1966). *Black boy: A record of childhood and youth*. New York: Harper & Row.

Wright, R. A., Wadley, V. G., Danner, M., & Phillips, P. N. (1992). Persuasion, reactance, and judgments of interpersonal appeal. *European Journal of Social Psychology, 22*, 83–91.

Yinger, J. M. (1965). *Toward a field theory of behavior: Personality and social structure*. New York: McGraw-Hill.

Zajonc, R. B., & Rajecki, D. W. (1969). Exposure and affect: A field experiment. *Psychonomic Science, 17*, 216–217.

Zaller, J. (1992). *The nature and origins of mass opinion*. Cambridge, England: Cambridge University Press.

Author Index

Subject Index

About the Author

Martin Gold, PhD, is a research scientist at the Institute for Social Research and Professor Emeritus of Psychology at the University of Michigan. His research includes national surveys and field experiments on juvenile delinquency (his most recent book, with D. Wayne Osgood, is *Personality and Peer Influence in Juvenile Corrections*) and studies of suicide, mother–daughter–friend relationships, sociometric structure of classroom groups, and effects of social status on family functioning. He has also published articles on social psychological theory, particularly on the field theory of Kurt Lewin. He is currently assembling a selective anthology of the works of Kurt Lewin, with commentary, to be published by the American Psychological Association.

Elizabeth Douvan, PhD, who collaborated with Martin Gold on this text, is Catharine Neaffie Kellogg Professor Emerita of Psychology and of Women's Studies at the University of Michigan. A social psychologist, she has written widely on adolescent development and on adult socialization through the acquisition and loss of roles in partnering, parenting, and retirement. Her most recent book (co-authored with Joseph Veroff and Shirley Hatchett) is *Marital Instability: A Study of the Early Years*. She also co-authored *The Inner American* and *Mental Health in America*, which reported changes in the attitudes and life satisfaction of American adults from 1957 to 1976.